A NATION DIVIDING?

The Electoral Map of Great Britain 1979–1987

A NATION DIVIDING?
The Electoral Map of Great Britain 1979–1987

This important new book is concerned with issues that affect the whole of society. Students and lecturers, politicians and journalists – indeed everyone interested in the present and future – will find it absorbing reading. Changes in society are vast and diverse, and this book is concentrating on particular aspects. Therefore Longman will be publishing a range of titles that cover other important aspects of British society in the late twentieth century. Future titles will include:

Dockland Decline and Redevelopment. *Andrew Church*

Urban Crises: The Geography of Social Distress in the Modern City. *Christopher J. Smith*

Gender and Housing: New Perspectives on the Urban Scene. *Susan J. Smith*

A NATION DIVIDING?

The Electoral Map of Great Britain
1979–1987

R.J. Johnston, C.J. Pattie and J.G. Allsopp

LONGMAN : LONDON

Copublished in the United States with
John Wiley & Sons, Inc., New York

Longman Group UK Limited,
Longman House, Burnt Mill, Harlow,
Essex CM20 2JE, England
and Associated Companies throughout the world.

Copublished in the United States with
John Wiley & Sons, Inc., 605 Third Avenue, New York, NY 10158

© Longman Group UK Limited 1988

First published 1988

British Library Cataloguing in Publication Data
Johnston, R.J. (Ronald John),
    A nation dividing?: the electoral map of Great Britain, 1979–1987. – (Insights on
    contemporary issues).
    1. Great Britain. Electorate. Voting behaviour, 1979–1987. Spatial analysis
    I. Title II. Pattie, C.J. III. Allsopp, J. G. IV. Series
    324.941'0858

    ISBN 0-582-02432-3

Library of Congress Cataloging-in-Publication Data

    ISBN 0-470-21133-4 (Wiley, USA only).

Set in 10/12 Baskerville Roman II Compugraphic

Printed in Great Britain by
The Bath Press, Avon

—— CONTENTS ——

PREFACE

This book is the latest output of a concern for studying aspects of electoral geography that has engaged one of the authors for nearly two decades. During the 1980s this concern has focused increasingly on voting patterns in Britain, because they were apparently growing in importance as influences on the crucial aspect of a general election result – which party wins power? The need for a geographical perspective in the study of voting was growing in importance.

The proximate causes for the present book were several. In 1985, one of us (RJJ) published a major study of the 1983 general election in England, establishing beyond any reasonable doubt, and with the deployment of a novel and powerful technical arsenal, the importance of the geographical perspective to the study of voting there. That book indicated the need to investigate the geography of voting, but provided only very tentative reasons for why that geography was important, and increasingly so. Thus research was necessary on why people vote the way they do, where they do. A study conducted in 1985–1986 suggested that the amount spent on local campaigns was of some importance, but clearly there was much more to it than that.

To begin the explorations, a pilot research project was designed to re-analyse some of the data sets derived from surveys of the British electorate in recent years. This was financed by a pump-priming grant from the University of Sheffield Academic Development Fund, on which CJP was employed as research assistant. That work took place over a six-month period in late 1986/early 1987, and was the basis of an application to the Economic and Social Research Council (ESRC) for a larger project developing the ideas that we developed as we explored the data. (The application was lodged in March 1987, under a scheme that promised a decision within 12 weeks; a positive decision was received in February 1988.)

During the research project funded by the University of Sheffield it became clear that a general election would probably be called in 1987, which would provide further data against which our ideas about the geography of voting could be tested. Consequently we created a data system that could rapidly accommodate the next election results, so that once our ESRC application was funded we would be in a position to incorporate a study of 1987 to our overall programme. The funding didn't come through. Fortunately, however, CJP obtained employment in Sheffield and could devote much of his spare time to an analysis of the 1987 data; during the summer of 1987 we were able to employ Lucy Johnston as a temporary research assistant on the remnants of the earlier grant, enabling much of the detailed data preparation to be done.

When the 1987 election was called we had no plan to produce a book on its results. It was immediately apparent as the results came in, however, that geography was a very important component of the pattern of voting, and that there had been major shifts in that pattern since the Conservative Party led by Margaret Thatcher first won office in 1979. Paul White suggested to us that we should produce a book on those shifts, their extent, causes and implications, and he and Vanessa Lawrence made its publication possible.

It was at this stage that the third member (JGA) joined the team. Displaying the geography of voting in all its complexity would require a great deal of cartographic exploration, linking a large data set to mapping procedures. He identified this challenge, and, while the election results were still coming in, was producing coloured maps (cartograms really) to illustrate the growing north:south divide. As the idea for the book developed, so the need for auto-mated cartography to illustrate its themes, initially to the authors and then to the readers, became imperative. This has been JGA's contribution to the project; without it, this product would not have been possible, for displaying the changing geography requires a large amount of cartography, giving the book in part the appearance of an Atlas.

Two imperatives have dominated the production of this book. First, it was necessary to complete it quickly, as a piece of 'contemporary history', provid-ing a substantial analysis of a major sequence of events while it was still fresh in people's minds and salient to the future. It is in the nature of many academic analyses of such events that by the time they appear their impact is less than it might have been. Thus we sought to produce a book within six months of the 1987 election – and just about succeeded; the publishers recip-rocated by agreeing to a rapid publication process. This is not to criticise the more measured, fuller academic studies in any way: indeed, there is little doubt that we will want to reflect on the work presented here and expand it in contributions to those studies in the future. Nor does it mean that we have cut corners in order to achieve rapid publication; we were fortunate that we were able to be ready and that others, notably Ivor Crewe, were prepared to meet our requests for data so soon after the 1987 election. It does mean that we have not been able to explore all avenues fully, in part because much more data than were available to us would be needed for that. But as we did our analyses over the summer of 1987 it became clear that we had an important story to tell, one that it was desirable to place before the audience sooner rather than later.

The nature of that audience provided the second imperative. The analyses reported here are based on relatively sophisticated statistical manipulations of data. But we have not presented them in a way that restricts the readership to people who are trained in interpreting the outputs of such analyses. While not compromising the academic standards of the work we have sought to make the findings accessible to a wider audience than the relatively small number of academic psephologists and their students. The results of our explorations are of interest to and importance for many people, outside academia as well as widely within it, and our presentation seeks to place those results before such people in an accessible format. The statistical details are all covered in other publications, to which we refer, and we expect to produce more technical pieces in the future.

In producing this book in the time period we are deeply indebted to many people. Our debt to the University of Sheffield Academic Development Fund is clear and fully acknowledged by us. Similarly, we could not have done the work without the preparedness of Ivor Crewe to make the results of the BBC/Gallup 1987 survey available to us within weeks of the election; the willingness of the BBC and Gallup to place their data files in the ESRC Data Archive is also acknowledged. Many people have encouraged and tolerated our preoccupation with this book over the second half of 1987. We are grateful to Stan Gregory and Alan Hay for allowing us full access to all facilities in the Department of Geography at the University of Sheffield; to the staff of the ESRC Data Archive at the University of Essex for their assistance and advice; to the staff at the University of Sheffield Computing Services Department (especially Stan Wardle, Verity Brack, and Ian Duckenfield) for much assistance and tolerance of the output we generated; to Lucy Johnston for her help; to Paul White and the Longman Scientific & Technical staff for their encouragement; to Joan Dunn for her willingness to translate a scrawl into a manuscript so excellently and efficiently; and above all to Rita Johnston, Eilidh Garrett and Paul Coles for putting up, in their different ways, with our obsession with the task.

This book, and the work that it embodies, has been a joint effort. Each of us has had particular responsibilities – JGA in producing the illustrations, CJP in managing the data, and RJJ in creating the text. But each needed the skills and dedication of the other two.

ACKNOWLEDGEMENTS

We are indebted to the following for permission to reproduce copyright material:

Longman Group (U.K.) Ltd. for fig. 3.4 (Keeble); Urban Studies for fig. 3.7 (Dunn, Forrest & Murie).

We are unable to trace the copyright owner of fig. 3.8 (Winn & McAuley) from p. 55 of *Contemporary Issues in Geography and Education* and would appreciate any information which would enable us to do so.

INTRODUCTION

Seldom can an election have been fought around two such discrepant accounts of economic and social reality. One was of a country in the grip of pestilence, writhing under the scourge of Thatcherism, its industry laid waste, its social fabric torn asunder, its people suffering. "Britain is crying out for Labour", was Labour's slogan. The other vision was of a country saved from socialism, pulled back from the abyss of its decline, resurgent, confident and prosperous. "It's great to be great again", was the Tory slogan . . .
Perceptions differed sharply along party lines. Only one in five Labour voters thought their standard of living had improved. The world could look very different as seen from, say, Swindon and Scunthorpe. "North-South" was to become during the campaign a metaphor for the "two nations", a shorthand for "them and us"

Peter Jenkins, *The Independent,* 11 Nov. 1987, p. 19.

This quotation, by one of Britain's most eminent political journalists, is typical of the immediate reactions of observers to the results of the 1987 general election in Great Britain. Suddenly, the north:south divide had become a major issue, not only in terms of 'who votes what, where?' but also, and ultimately much more importantly, in terms of the development of party policies and the long-term future of, in particular, the Labour and Alliance parties. From being an irrelevant issue to most observers, both lay and academic, insider and outsider, geography had come to the centre of the electoral stage.

For some, the importance of incorporating a geographical perspective with the study of voting patterns in Britain has long been recognised; indeed, a leading political scientist castigated the authors of a major study of elections in the 1970s for virtually ignoring the perspective (Berrington, 1983). And for those who had recognised the poverty of studies that ignored the geographical perspective, notably John Curtice, William Miller, and Michael Steed, the sudden discovery of the importance of mapped results and the simple dichotomy implied by a north:south divide was a much belated recognition of a trend that they had already clearly identified and analysed. Their work had shown that the geographical factor had become increasingly important over a period of at least three decades (Curtice and Steed, 1982, see 1955 as the watershed year). The north:south divide didn't suddenly appear in 1987; it had been opening-up for a long time, along with other spatial divisions that were perhaps not as easily recognised either in the journalistic analysis of maps of 'who won, where?' or the detailed examinations of national surveys of samples of voters.

Has the north:south divide widened over recent years, therefore, and if so, why? That question is the focus of the present book, which brings a geographical perspective to the study of the 1979, 1983 and 1987 general elections in Great Britain. Because of the nature of that question and the disciplinary origins of the authors, the book is therefore not a comprehensive study of voting over that period. It is addressed to a particular topic within the wider concerns of psephology and brings to the study of voting in Britain the particular perspective of geographers. Debates within that discipline mean that the nature of that perspective varies between practitioners and over time. The study of elections is very much a minority interest among geographers, even among the small group of political geographers, and those who have worked in the area have been very much influenced by major trends within the wider discipline at the time. Thus, for example, studies in the late 1970s and early 1980s, as reviewed in Johnston (1979), Taylor (1978) and Taylor and Johnston (1979), were set in the spatial science paradigm of the subject, which emphasised the role of space as an influence on individual behaviour, including voting. The validity of that approach (for which Cox, 1969, provides the best programmatic statement) was questioned by critics, and increasingly by the geographers involved who realised that their studies were at best partial and at worst misguided. Thus Taylor wrote (1985b, p. 142)

> It is not at all clear where electoral geography is leading . . . on the whole quality has lagged behind quantity of production.

and he sought to resituate the geographical study of elections in a wider, interdisciplinary framework that emphasised the interactions among voters and political parties, in places, and the constraints on those interactions set by the world economic system and the role of states within it. Concurrently, Johnston (1986c, 1986d) sought to reorient the geographical focus to place it within the mainstream of voting studies, while at the same time developing technical procedures (as exemplified in his detailed analysis of the 1983 general election in England: Johnston, 1985a) which allow much more detailed depiction of geographical variations in voting behaviour.

This reorientation of electoral geography has occurred at exactly the right moment for illustrating the value of its perspective, because of the apparent trends in British voting behaviour during the first seven years of the 1980s. The present book is therefore very timely, since it addresses a major issue raised by the 1979, 1983 and 1987 election results and focused on in the question identified above as central to our work. 'Has the north:south divide widened over recent years, and if so, why?'. We address this in the following way. The first chapter sets out the basic descriptive material on which the question is founded; the data presented there suggest, very clearly, that the question is a valid one, that there is a *prima facie* case for examining the changing geography of voting. We then turn, in the next two chapters, to a review of the literature on British voting and British society which can throw light on why the divide might have widened: Chapter 2 looks at the psephological literature, identifying its major strands and highlighting the growing argument regarding spatial variations in, and therefore influences on, voting behaviour; Chapter 3 follows it by examining recent trends in British economic and social geography that can be linked to those trends in voting behaviour.

The next three chapters form the core of the analyses reported here. Chapter 4 returns to the descriptive material presented in Chapter 1, in the context of the literature reviewed in Chapters 2 and 3, and asks whether the geographical patterns are statistical artefacts. Are there indeed spatial variations in voting behaviour, or are they just a by-product of other influences to which the geographical perspective is largely irrelevant? The answer to that question is a resounding 'yes' to the first part, and an equally resounding 'no' to the second. Thus we then turn, in Chapter 5, to exploring what those spatial variations are: what changes have taken place in voting behaviour, by region, over the period 1979–1987? Our analyses show a complex pattern of shifts; a growing north:south divide is clearly central to that pattern, but there are many other shifts within it that add up to an intriguing and substantial set of changes to Britain's electoral geography over such a short period.

Having established the contours of the shifts in Chapters 4 and 5, we turn in Chapter 6 to an analysis of the reasons for that changing topography. This is based on a reworking of survey and other data which, for the first time, tests models of voting behaviour which have locational influences built in to them. Initial analyses suggest that voters' perceptions of the country's economic performance in the period leading up to an election, their perception of their own changing circumstances during that time, and their expectations (both personal and for the country as a whole) for the year after the election are both spatially variable and probably the major influence on the changing geography of voting. Further analyses, that are limited by the nature of the available data but nevertheless are sufficient for a substantive evaluation of our thesis, show that indeed spatial variations in voter economic satisfaction and optimism are linked to the changing geography of voting.

What are the implications of these findings? In themselves, of course, they represent a major contribution to the understanding of this important component of contemporary Britain. But they have much more than an academic value because they provide pointers to the immediate future and the tasks of the political parties in the period prior to the next election(s). Those pointers are the subject matter of Chapter 7.

The literature on voting behaviour is both large and expanding rapidly. A major reason for the growth of interest in the topic is the development over recent decades, in most Western liberal democracies and not just in Britain, of major changes in the nature of voting habits – of how people are politically socialised and how they evaluate the partisan offerings presented to them.

There are major debates among psephologists over the causes of those changes. In reviewing those debates, Harrop and Miller (1987, p. 162) have recently summarised two of the major approaches in the following way:

> both models portray a voter who pays relatively little attention to politics, who develops a standing commitment to a particular party but is also susceptible to influence by major government successes or failure.

Our findings fit well into that general framework but they stress one aspect that Harrop and Miller ignore. They argue that 'How people vote depends on how people around them vote' (p. 207), a process 'due primarily to social interaction within a spatial context' (p. 211), but they pay no attention to the material aspects, as opposed to the inter-personal interaction aspects, of that context. Our analyses show major changes in the geography of voting which may be linked to major changes in the nature of inter-personal interaction in local milieux. We doubt that. Undoubtedly local milieux are crucial in the long-term processes of political socialisation, but in the short-term processes of political evaluation, of 'major government successes or failures', social inter-action is not a necessary preliminary to changing one's mind about who to vote for. People are reacting, within their socialised context, to their perceptions of material economic and social conditions. Those conditions have become spatially more variable in Britain in recent years and have provoked, we believe, the major shift in voting patterns that so many observers have identified. Thus geography matters in the study of those shifts, because it is both part of the cause and part of the effect.

BRITAIN'S CHANGING ELECTORAL GEOGRAPHY: A REGIONAL ISSUE?

This book focuses on the changing electoral geography of Great Britain over the period 1979–1987, enquiring into the extent of and reasons for a spatial polarisation of the country's electorate across the three successive elections won by the Conservative party under Margaret Thatcher. The present chapter provides the basic material for that inquiry, outlining the pattern of votes and of seats won at each of the three elections and indicating the spatial variations in changes to that pattern. That material is the context for the analyses reported in the rest of the book.

In 1983 and 1987 there were 633 constituencies in Great Britain (i.e. in England, Scotland and Wales). In 1979 there were 623, but all of the analyses here look not at that set but at the pattern of votes cast in 1979 as if they were recorded in the 1983/1987 constituencies. This provides for consistency of analysis: it is made possible by the work of a team of researchers employed by the BBC and ITN to compute the probable result in 1979 in each of the new constituencies introduced in 1983 (BBC/ITN, 1983). Thus all of the analyses to be reported here refer to the same set of 633 constituencies.

Two problems arise with this data set, and the solutions that we have adopted are introduced at the outset. They refer to the visual portrayal of the data and the ways in which the large numbers of observations may be summarised. Following that introductory material, the chapter turns to a description of the country's electoral geography over the three dates, focusing on: the seats won by the parties; the percentage of the votes won by the parties; and the changes in the percentage of the votes won.

PRESENTING THE ELECTORAL GEOGRAPHY

Our basic data set for this study comprises 633 observations. Each of these is a Parliamentary constituency, which is a bounded space. To illustrate certain features of those constituencies, in their spatial context, we need to present them in map form. This raises a major problem, however, because the constituencies vary greatly in their area, from 954,680 ha for the largest (Ross,

Cromarty and Skye) to 572 ha for the smallest (Chelsea). If we were to portray them in a conventional map form, so that each constituency occupied its correct portion of the land area of Great Britain, two difficulties would emerge: first, the smallest constituencies would hardly be visible; and second, the largest would dominate the map, and make it difficult to discern the overall pattern. The former problem is usually solved (as in the maps produced by the newspapers at election time and in atlases such as Kinnear's, 1981) by providing insets for the high population density, small constituency area parts of the country, although this produces a rather disjointed impression. (Kinnear has up to seventeen insets around his maps, for example.) Alternatively, the country could be divided into regions, with the scale for each regional map varying (as in Waller, 1985), but this means that the overall pattern cannot be displayed. The second problem – the dominance of the impression given to the map by the large-area constituencies – cannot readily be solved, however, without recourse to cartographic transformations. That is the approach adopted here, and described below.

Whereas maps, or cartograms, provide a general visual impression of a geographical pattern, it is difficult to get any precise description because of the large number of separate items of information that they contain. Some way of simplifying the map is needed. For geographers, that simplification involves the definition of regions, and this forms the foundation of most of our analysis. Thus the second part of this section describes the regionalisations that we have adopted.

Transforming the Map

Although British Parliamentary constituencies vary greatly in terms of their land area they are very similar in size on another criterion, number of registered electors. Indeed, it is one of the main requirements of British electoral law (under the House of Commons, Redistribution of Seats Act) that

> The electorate of any constituency shall be as near the electoral quota as is practicable . . . a Boundary Commission may depart from the strict application of [a previous] . . . rule if it appears to them that a departure is desirable to avoid an excessive disparity between the electorate of any constituency and the electoral quota, or between the electorate thereof and that of neighbouring constituencies . . .

although a 1983 court case, brought by four prominent members of the Labour party, failed to obtain a judicial ruling that equality of electorates was the major criterion on which redistricting should be based (Johnston, 1983c, 1986f).

The 1983 general election was fought on a new set of constituencies, promulgated earlier that year. The constituencies were defined using data several years old, however. For England, the electoral rolls for 1976 were used, producing an electoral quota (the total electorate in the country divided by the 516 seats then in existence) of 65,753. Of the 523 new constituencies, 393 were within ten per cent of that quota (between 59,178 and 72,328) and only 17 were either 20 per cent above or below it. But by 1982, only 366 were within

10 per cent of the new quota of 68,534 and, because of demographic changes, 24 now lay outside the 20 per cent limit. Thus, despite the long time gap, some 95 per cent of all constituencies in England had electorates between 54,827 and 82,241 (Boundary Commission for England, 1983) In Wales, the electoral quota was set at 58,753 in 1981, and 33 of the 38 constituencies were within 15 per cent of this figure then (Boundary Commission for Wales, 1983, p. 53). Finally, the Scottish quota was set in 1978 at 53,649; by 1982 it was 55,118, and 66 of the 72 constituencies were within 20 per cent of that figure (Boundary Commission for Scotland, 1983, p. 98). In Scotland, as in Wales, the constituencies that deviated substantially from the electoral quota were all in rural areas where the problems of representing a widely-scattered electorate are allowed for in the rules under which the Boundary Commissions operate; all were well below the quota.

It seems reasonable, therefore, that instead of representing constituencies by their different areas they should be treated as if they were all of the same size – i.e. had the same number of resident electors. (On another criterion, they were all of exactly the same size, since they each returned one MP to the House of Commons.) On such a map, the constituencies small in area would not be dwarfed, and those large in area would not dominate. Thus, all of our illustrations in this book treat all of the 633 constituencies as the same size.

Transforming the map of Great Britain into a *cartogram* comprising 633 equal-sized units, and yet as far as possible retaining the familiar shape of the island, was not a straightforward task. In the end, it was only achieved (Figure 1.1) by excluding Greater London from the general shape and thereby having one inset. The cartogram used is based on that employed in an earlier analysis of the 1983 general election in England (Johnston, 1985a). This was constructed on the principle that, so far as possible, the counties of England should be in their correct relative positions, and that has been retained here. Although the cartogram is in general faithful to that principle and to the shape of Great Britain, however, certain 'deviations' were necessary. As Figure 1.1 shows, one of the most salient of these was separating North from South Wales: each is portrayed as a separate 'peninsula' extending westwards from north and south of the West Midlands respectively. The other major problem was with the English/Scottish borders, where the Tyne and Wear conurbation extends from the east to the west coast.

Despite these problems, it was clear that the cartogram provided a much better illustrative device for the patterns to be displayed here than did a conventional map, because the latter is dominated by the large rural constituencies of central Wales, northern England, and all but the lowlands of Scotland. Thus all of our 'maps' of Parliamentary constituencies in this book are cartograms. The Appendix provides a full listing of the constituencies plus key cartograms identifying the counties and the major towns.

Regionalizing the Country

Maps and cartograms provide general illustrations of spatial distributions,

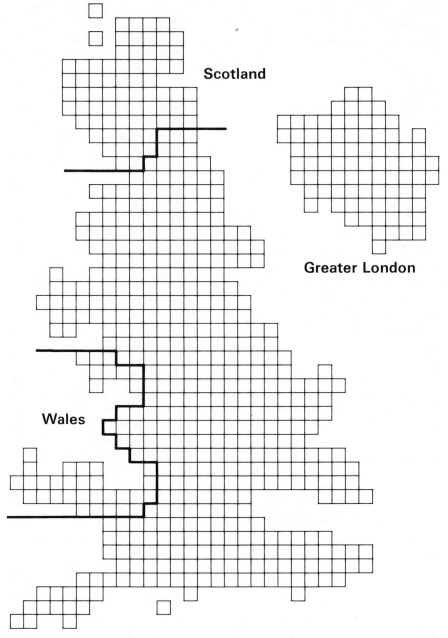

Figure 1.1 The cartogram of the 633 constituencies, showing the borders between England and Scotland and between England and Wales.

from which certain conclusions can be drawn, but for more precise quantitative statements of those distributions complementary statistical devices are needed. Since cartograms contain, yet simplify, a great deal of information – those to be used here have 633 separate units and usually only five or six shading categories – some method of compressing the data is needed. (Virtually all of the cartograms simplify since they reduce continuous data – the percentage of the votes cast won by a particular party, for example – into a small number of categories. Only the cartograms of seats won reproduce all of the data.)

In most geographical work, detailed spatial data are summarised by using regions as collective units. Regions are groupings of individual units (in this case constituencies) which are internally relatively homogeneous. They may be defined on a single criterion, such as relative location, or they may be identified via a sophisticated quantitative analysis involving numerous criteria. Two types of region are generally employed. In the first, a single criterion dominates – relative location – and the goal is to produce groups of units that comprise contiguous territorial units; other criteria may then be used to decide the boundaries of those units. We term such groupings *geographical regions*. In the second, relative location is irrelevant, and the goal is to define groups of units with similar characteristics (coal-mining communities, say) irrespective of location. We term these *functional regions*.

Much analysis of the regional pattern of Great Britain employs the ten *Standard Regions* that are widely used by the Government's Office of Population Censuses and Surveys and many other official bodies. These present a very coarse division of the country, however, and several of the regions are internally very heterogeneous on a variety of salient criteria: both Scotland and Wales clearly illustrate this criticism, since each contains densely-peopled industrial areas at one extreme and remote, almost empty areas at the other, but most of the other regions similarly contain marked contrasts. Thus we decided to use a finer division of the three countries, with a larger number of internally more homogeneous regions, separating out the major urban regions. The final selection was based on one used in *The Economist* for several decades to summarise British election results. It has 22 regions, and these are defined so as to separate the major conurbations from their surrounding 'rural' areas. (The term rural is undoubtedly a misnomer with regard to the occupations and homes of most of the residents of those areas, but it indicates that the majority of the land surface is not built over.) Not all of the major cities are separated from their hinterlands, however; the three major free-standing urban areas of Bristol, Leicester and Nottingham are incorporated with their environs, for example. Nevertheless, these 22 provide a sensible set of *geographical regions* which is used throughout the book.

The 22 regions are shown in Figure 1.2 (see also the Appendix for a conventional map) and the names that will be used to identify them throughout the book are identified in Table 1.1. Full details of regional membership are given in the Appendix.

Some functional regionalisations are based on a single criterion, selected for its salience to the task in hand. Others employ a large number of criteria, with

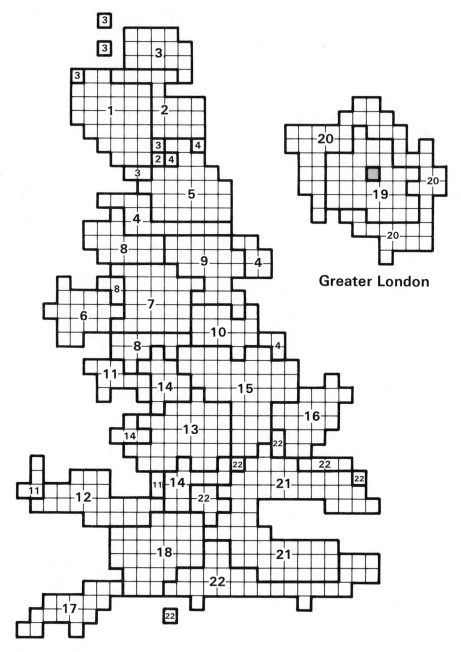

Figure 1.2 The geographical regions employed in the analyses in this book.

the goal of categorising places on as many characteristics as possible so as to obtain a general picture of their major features. The latter approach has been adopted here, since the constituencies with which we are dealing differ in a

Table 1.1 The Geographical Regions used in the analyses here (and the abbreviations used in the tables)

Strathclyde	East Central Scotland (E Scotland)
Rural Scotland	Rural North
Industrial Northeast	Merseyside
Greater Manchester	Rest of Northwest
West Yorkshire (West Yorks)	South Yorkshire (South Yorks)
Rural Wales	Industrial South Wales
West Midlands Conurbation	Rest of West Midlands
East Midlands	East Anglia
Devon and Cornwall	Wessex
Inner London	Outer London
Outer Metropolitan	Outer Southeast

Full membership of the regions is given in the Appendix

great variety of ways. The purpose of the search for a set of functional regions was to identify groups of constituencies with common socio-demographic characteristics which should lead them to have common political interests.

Censuses are almost always the main source of data for such classifications, since they cover a wide range of population and housing characteristics. The British Census of 1981 has provided such a data set, and the present analyses use a regionalisation of it produced by the market research organisation CACI Inc. and published by Crewe and Fox (1984) in their very useful compendium on *British Parliamentary Constituencies*. The data used comprised 41 variables, covering demographic characteristics (age structure, household structure, ethnic structure), occupational structure, and housing characteristics (size, tenure, amenities etc.). Using all 41 as the criteria, the constituencies were classified into 31 groups, and these form the functional regions for our analyses. For each of those regions, a brief title is given in Table 1.2; full descriptions are given by Crewe and Fox (1984, pp. 10–31) and lists of constituencies in each are given in the Appendix. Figure 1.3 shows where the constituencies in the various regions are. In general, the groupings correspond with one's appreciation of differences between places in Great Britain, and their emergence from the classification procedure indicates how places with certain economic functions (the textile towns of Lancashire and Yorkshire, for example) have populations which are identifiable in other ways (age structure; proportion of immigrants; relative importance of council housing; etc.)

These two sets of regions form the structure within which most of our analysis is set. As indicated in the Introduction, our major concern is to explore in depth the contention of many analysts that Great Britain has become increasingly spatially polarised electorally over recent years. The geographical and functional regions that we have defined here provide the route for that exploration. If we can demonstrate increased polarisation across one or both of those sets of regions, then the basic contention will have been confirmed.

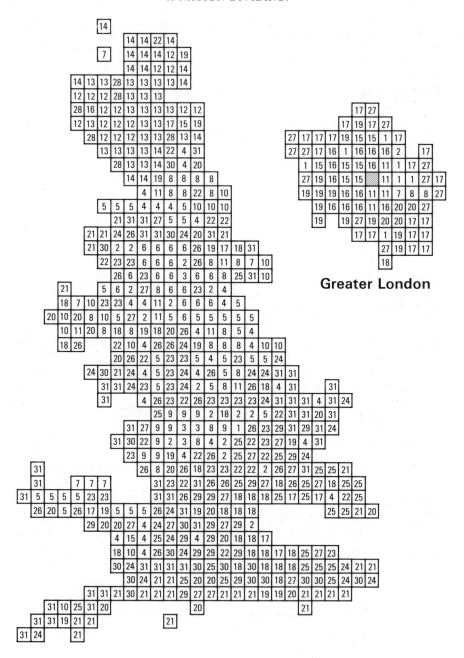

Figure 1.3 The functional regions employed in the analyses in this book.

Table 1.2   The Functional Regions used in the analyses here (and the abbreviations used in the tables)

Metropolitan Inner City with Immigrants	(IC/Immig.)
Industrial Areas with Immigrants	(Ind/Immig.)
Poorest Immigrant Areas	(Poorest Immig.)
Intermediate Industrial Areas	(Intermed. Ind.)
Old Industrial and Mining Towns	(Old Indust./Mining)
Textile Areas	(Textile)
Poorest Domestic Conditions	(Poorest Domestic)
Conurbation Local Authority Housing	(Conurb. L.A.)
Black Country	(Black Co.)
Maritime Industrial Areas	(Maritime Ind.)
Poor Inner-City Council Housing	(Poor I.C.)
Clydeside	
Scottish Industrial	(Scott. Ind.)
Scottish Rural	(Scott. Rural)
High-Status Inner Metropolitan	(High Status I.M.)
Inner Metropolitan	(I.M.)
Outer London Suburbia	(Outer London)
Very High-Status	
Conurbation White-Collar	(Conurb. W. Collar)
City Constituencies with Service Employment	(City Service)
Resort and Retirement	(Resort/Retirement)
Recent Growth and Modern Housing	(Recent Growth)
Stable Industrial Towns	(Stable Ind.)
Small Manufacturing Towns with Rural	(Small Towns)
Hinterlands	
Southern Urban	
Manufacturing Towns with Commuter Hinterlands	(Modest Aff.)
Metropolitan Industrial	(Met. Ind.)
Modestely Affluent Urban Scotland	(Modest Aff. Scot.)
Areas of Rapid Growth	(Rapid Growth)
Prosperous Towns with Little Industry	(Prosperous/No Ind.)
Agricultural	

Full descriptions of the regions are given in the Appendix

THE GEOGRAPHY OF THE ELECTION RESULTS

To many observers, the most important map recording aspects of a general election is the geography of seats won, and this indeed has been the case with most of those who wrote about the result of the 1987 contest as indicating a widening north:south divide within Great Britain. Thus our initial discussion here is of the geography of the results – the pattern of seats won at the contests of 1979, 1983, and 1987. Figures 1.4, 1.5 and 1.6 are the relevant cartograms.

The north:south divide is not a new element in British politics, a consequence of electoral developments in the 1980s. It was clearly present in the 1930s, for example, as Kinnear's (1981) maps make very apparent. But at the 1945 election Labour won a large number of seats in the south and east of England for the first time, including all but one of the Norfolk constituencies,

Labour   Nationalist

Conservative   Alliance

Figure 1.4 The geography of seats won, 1979.

Labour   Nationalist

Conservative   Alliance

Figure 1.5 The geography of seats won, 1983.

Nationalist   Labour

Alliance   Conservative

Figure 1.6 The geography of seats won, 1987.

and it came a respectable second to Conservative candidates in a substantial number of others there. By 1970, however, it had lost most of those seats, and its support in many other constituencies in the south of the country had been eroded very substantially. Thus by the start of the period studied here the country was already divided.

Figure 1.4, which portrays the result of the 1979 election, shows the north:south divide that was present at the start of our analysis very clearly. There is a readily identifiable distinction between the south and east of the country, which was predominantly represented by Conservatives, and the north and west, where the majority of constituencies returned Labour members. Nevertheless, there are several notable exceptions to this division. The first refers to Greater London which is clearly part of the south and east (as a geographical region, if not as a functional region), and yet 36 of its 84 constituencies returned Labour MPs. (Throughout this book, we are of course dealing with the 'invented' results of the 1979 election in the constituencies that were used in 1983 and 1987. For our purposes, that 'invented' election was 'real', which indicates great confidence in the reworking of the 1979 data undertaken by the BBC/ITN team. Crewe and Fox, 1984, p. 15 – both of whom were members of that team – suggest that non-trivial errors were introduced in only four constituencies.) Most of Labour's seats there were won in central and east London, and were ringed by Conservative-held suburbs which clearly indicates the need for functional as well as geographical regions. (Note that in their simple dichotomy of Britain into north and south, Sarlvik and Crewe, 1983, included London in the north!)

Outside Greater London, some fifteen seats were won by Labour in 1979 within the general area of Conservative dominance in the south and east. These included three in the Bristol urban area, and one in Plymouth, but also constituencies in the smaller towns of Swindon, Oxford, Slough, Basildon, Stevenage, Ipswich, and Norwich, as well as West Hertfordshire.

To the north and west of England, and in Scotland and Wales, although Labour was clearly the major party, there were substantial pockets of constituencies returning Conservative MPs. Most of these were in the more rural areas of, for example, the Welsh Marches, the Cheshire Plain, the East Riding, and the Vale of York. Others – such as Sheffield Hallam – were the more affluent suburbs of the large industrial cities; a further group included the resort and retirement centres of Blackpool and Harrogate. But there were also constituencies in the north of England that returned Conservative MPs when general expectations would suggest a Labour representative; the towns of Bolton and Bury on the northern edge of the Greater Manchester conurbation are the clearest examples of this. Further north, Labour dominated the Industrial Northeast and much of Scotland, with Conservative successes largely confined to the rural areas; the same was the case in Wales.

By 1983, when the general election produced a House of Commons with a Conservative majority over all other parties of 144, the general pattern outlined in 1979 had become much starker (Figure 1.5). Virtually all of the seats that Labour won in 1979 in the south and east outside London had been yielded to the Conservative candidates: only Ipswich, Thurrock, and Bristol South were retained, while Plymouth Devonport was lost to the Alliance (whose candidate, David Owen, won the seat for Labour in 1979) and the Liberal party won Yeovil from the Conservatives. The south and east of England was almost entirely Conservative in its elected representatives; in London, too, Labour's representation was reduced, with eight seats lost to Conservative candidates and two to the Alliance.

Further north, in the East and West Midlands, the Labour hold on seats was eroded also. North Warwickshire and Nuneaton were lost, for example, as were two of the three seats in Leicester and the two Nottingham constituencies that Labour notionally held in 1979. The Conservatives lost seats in Liverpool, on the other hand, but gained them in the textile towns, notably in Yorkshire where, for example, both Batley and Spen and Dewsbury were gained from Labour. This produced a solid block of Conservative seats across the country from east to west, with Blackburn and Preston an island of Labour support. Further north, the Conservatives lost ground, to the Alliance in Scotland as well as to Labour.

By 1983, therefore, the division between north (really north and west) and south (south and east) was clearly etched into the British electoral map, though each party had some representation in the other part. If anything, the 1987 result hardened that division (Figure 1.6). In the south and east, little changed. Labour lost two of its seats outside London (Ipswich and Thurrock) but re-gained two others (Norwich South and Oxford East); within London it lost a further constituency to the Alliance and two more to the Conservative party. In the East Midlands it regained seats in Leicester, and the number of Conservative MPs for Scotland and Wales was further reduced. But the Conservatives retained that solid block of seats across the country from Blackpool in the west to Scarborough in the east.

The overwhelming picture to be derived from these three maps is one of Conservative dominance in the south and east of Great Britain, therefore, matched by majority support for Labour in the north and west. This is confirmed by two further cartograms, that show the constituencies won by each party at all three elections. Figure 1.7 shows the Conservatives' southern power base, plus its not insubstantial support in certain parts of northern England; Figure 1.8 shows that outside inner London the Labour party's control has been confined entirely to the north and west of England, plus Scotland and Wales, with but one exception (Bristol South). And if we look at the seats which changed hands, we see that the Conservative victories over Labour in 1983 were largely in the south and east (Figure 1.9), and that very few of those were won back by Labour in 1987 (Figure 1.10). By 1987, it seemed, the Conservative hold over the south and east outside London was almost total, and it was gaining in London too (as later analyses of vote percentages make clear). In the north and west of England, in Scotland, and in Wales, Labour was firmly entrenched in most areas, though the rural districts and some of the textile towns continued to return Tory MPs. There can be little doubt, then, that the country was electorally divided, and increasingly so.

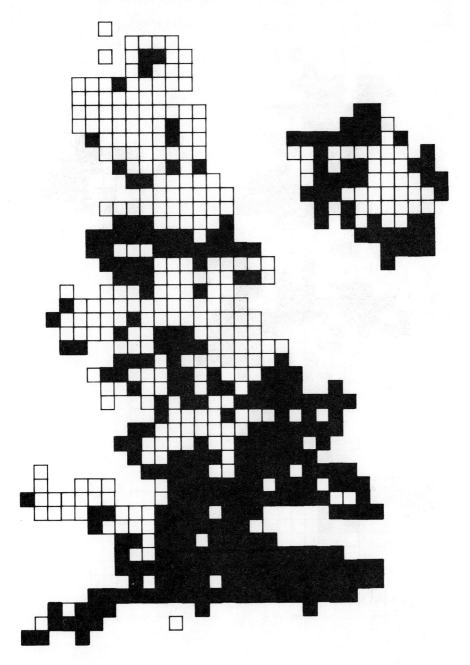

Figure 1.7 The constituencies won by the Conservative party at all three elections, 1979, 1983 and 1987.

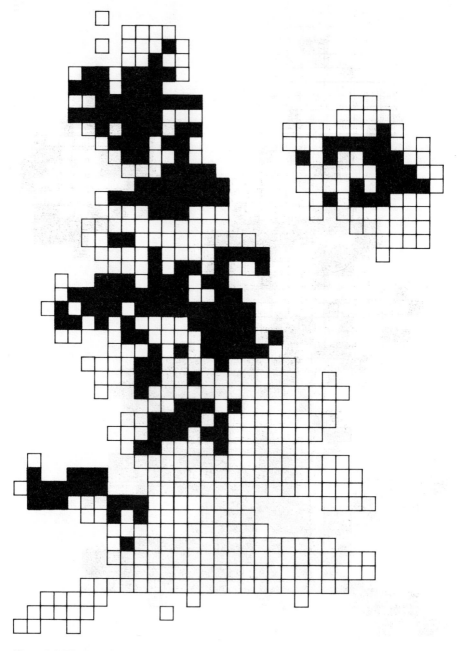

Figure 1.8 The constituencies won by the Labour party at all three elections, 1979, 1983 and 1987.

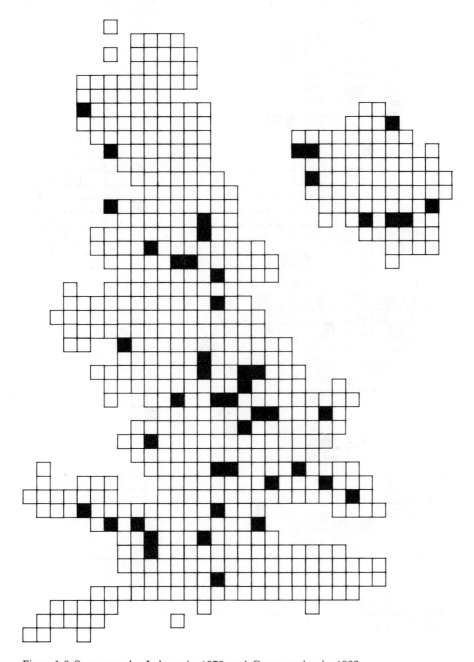

Figure 1.9 Seats won by Labour in 1979 and Conservative in 1983.

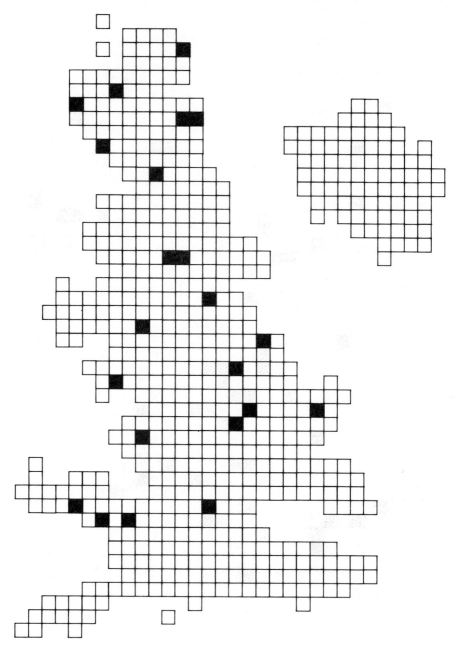

Figure 1.10 Seats won by Conservative in 1983 and Labour in 1987.

The Pattern of Seats Won: A Regional Analysis

To complement this impressionistic analysis of the cartograms, we present a brief tabular inquiry into the regional geography of representation at the three elections, using the geographical and functional regionalisations introduced above.

Table 1.3 shows the number of seats won by each party (excluding PC and SNP), at each election, by *geographical region*. The general pattern of spatial polarisation is immediately apparent, because the regions are roughly in north-south order; thus the lower a region is in the table, the greater the proportion of constituencies won by the Conservative party. The extremes are South Yorkshire, where Labour won 14 seats and Conservative one at each of the three contests, and the Outer Metropolitan zone, where in 1987 the Conservative party was successful in all 61 constituencies.

Table 1.3   Seats won by the Conservative, Labour, and Alliance (Liberal in 1979) Parties, 1979–1987, by geographical region

	Conservative			Labour			Alliance		
	1979	1983	1987	1979	1983	1987	1979	1983	1987
Strathclyde	4	5	2	28	26	30	0	1	0
E. Scotland	6	5	3	13	13	15	0	1	1
Rural Scotland	13	11	5	3	2	5	3	6	8
Rural North	15	17	16	10	8	9	1	1	1
Industrial Northeast	3	4	4	24	22	23	0	1	0
Merseyside	7	5	4	10	11	11	0	1	2
Greater Manchester	11	11	10	15	15	16	1	1	1
Rest of Northwest	19	20	20	10	9	9	0	0	0
West Yorks	7	11	9	16	10	14	0	2	0
South Yorks	1	1	1	14	14	14	0	0	0
Rural Wales	8	7	4	4	4	5	1	2	3
Industrial South Wales	4	7	4	19	16	19	0	0	0
West Midlands Conurbation	14	14	15	18	18	17	0	0	0
Rest of West Midlands	19	22	21	7	4	5	0	0	0
East Midlands	23	33	30	18	8	11	0	0	0
East Anglia	17	18	19	2	1	1	1	1	0
Devon and Cornwall	14	14	14	1	0	0	1	2	2
Wessex	28	30	30	4	1	1	0	1	1
Inner London	10	12	13	22	18	16	0	2	3
Outer London	38	44	45	14	8	7	0	0	0
Outer Metropolitan	55	60	61	6	1	0	0	0	0
Outer Southeast	44	46	46	2	0	1	1	1	0

Despite the general south:north differential, however, the table also illustrates further some of the 'deviant' groupings identified above in the cartographic analysis. In the northwest of England, for example, over one-third of the constituencies in Greater Manchester were won by the Conservative party at each election, and that party won a majority of the seats in the Rest of the Northwest region. Further south, too, the parties were fairly evenly balanced in the West Midlands conurbation, a situation very different from that in Strathclyde (whose main city, Glasgow, challenges Birmingham for the status of 'Britain's second city') and in South Yorkshire.

When the results of the three elections are compared, the regional contrasts become even more marked. Thus in the three Scottish regions, to take one 'extreme' example, the number of Conservative-held seats was halved; Labour was the main beneficiary in Strathclyde and E. Scotland, but the Alliance picked up most of the seats that the Tories lost in Rural Scotland. In the London area, on the other hand, the shift was towards the Tories, where the number of Labour constituencies was almost halved; even in Inner London, which according to some analyses (e.g. Harrison, 1983) has some of the worst urban deprivation in the country, Labour lost six seats, three of them to the Alliance. Elsewhere,the pattern changed little between 1979 and 1987, though 1983 saw some Conservative gains (notably in South Wales) that were reversed four years later. There was one exceptional region, however. In the East Midlands, the Conservatives won ten seats from Labour in 1983; three returned to the Labour fold in 1987, but the net gain to the Tories was still very substantial.

Turning to the *functional regions* (Table 1.4), again the organisation is such that the groupings that are likely to be pro-Labour are at the top and those likely to be pro-Conservative are lower down. With 31 rather than 22 regions, a greater degree of polarisation might be expected, and this is indeed the case, although there were few regions which lacked any representation for one of the parties. The Conservative concentration is clearly in the affluent areas, and the

Table 1.4 Seats won by the Conservative, Labour and Alliance (Liberal in 1979) Parties, 1979–1987, by functional region

	Conservative			Labour			Alliance		
	1979	1983	1987	1979	1983	1987	1979	1983	1987
I.C./Immig.	1	2	1	7	6	7	0	0	0
Ind./Immig.	1	4	3	16	13	14	0	0	0
Poorest Immig.	0	0	0	4	4	4	0	0	0
Intermed. Ind.	4	9	11	26	21	19	0	0	0
Old Indust./Mining	1	4	4	33	30	30	0	0	0
Textile	4	8	7	13	8	10	1	2	1
Poorest Domestic	0	0	0	6	6	7	0	0	0
Conurb. L.A.	5	5	4	21	20	22	0	1	0
Black Co.	0	0	1	9	9	8	0	0	0
Maritime Ind.	1	1	0	14	13	14	0	1	1
Poor I.C.	0	1	1	12	10	10	0	1	1
Clydeside	1	0	0	15	16	17	0	0	0
Scott. Ind.	0	1	0	25	24	25	0	0	0
Scott. Rural	12	10	5	2	1	1	3	6	8
High Status I.M.	9	9	8	0	0	1	0	0	0
I.M.	2	2	3	12	11	11	0	1	0
Outer London	24	24	24	0	0	0	0	0	0
Very High Status	31	31	31	0	0	0	0	0	0
Conurb. W. Collar	24	24	20	0	0	4	0	0	0
City Service	13	18	15	11	4	6	0	2	3
Resort/Retirement	28	28	28	0	0	0	1	1	1
Recent Growth	13	15	15	6	2	3	0	2	1
Stable Ind.	14	19	19	12	7	7	0	0	0
Small Towns	26	25	24	1	1	1	0	1	1
Southern Urban	24	24	24	0	0	0	0	0	0
Modest Aff.	24	25	24	2	1	2	0	0	0
Met. Ind.	18	29	27	12	1	3	0	0	0
Modest Aff. Scot.	5	5	4	0	0	1	0	0	0
Rapid Growth	16	16	16	0	0	0	0	0	0
Prosperous/No Ind.	19	19	19	0	0	0	0	0	0
Agricultural	40	39	38	1	1	2	4	5	5

Labour dominance is in the old industrial regions and the inner cities. Again, certain 'anomalies' stand out, however, such as the Textile Towns.

Over the period from 1979 to 1987 the polarisation between functional regions altered mainly because of Conservative success in certain types of constituency. No functional region showed an increase of more than two Labour seats over the period; the Alliance was successful in the Scottish Rural areas and in the City Service grouping (where the three constituencies won in 1987 were Greenwich, Woolwich, and Liverpool Mossley Hill). It was in the relatively prosperous industrial groupings that the Conservative successes of 1983 and 1987 were based. It nearly tripled its seats in the Intermediate Industrial region where, as Crewe and Fox (1984, p. 12) described it, these are 'areas of relative economic stability, in so far as unemployment is little worse than average'; the group includes both conurban constituencies and free-standing towns, and it was in the latter (places such as Derby North, Darlington, Ipswich, Swindon and Thurrock) that Labour lost control. Several of the Stable Industrial Towns, such as Nuneaton, similarly swung to the Tories, but the major switch (relatively and absolutely) was in the Metropolitan Industrial region, where Labour lost 11 of the 12 seats it held in 1979 by 1983, regaining only two of them four years later. Crewe and Fox's (1984, p. 14) description of these as 'areas of low unemployment, with fewer unskilled workers and less domestic deprivation' provides a pointer to the nature of the Conservative success, as does their pen-picture of the Stable Industrial Towns: 'Relatively low unemployment and an above-average presence of younger families all point to the buoyancy of the economy of such constituencies'. Labour was losing seats where the economy was apparently thriving under Conservative rule, it seems, an hypothesis that we follow further throughout this book.

THE PATTERN OF VOTES

Although the geography of representation is an important element of the country's electoral pattern, it presents only part of a relatively complex picture. Under the British electoral system, the winner in each constituency is the candidate with the largest number of votes, irrespective of whether they are a majority of those cast. With only two parties, or at least with only two parties winning substantial numbers of votes, most MPs returned to Parliament will have over 40 per cent of the votes cast in their favour. But with three or more parties winning substantial support, not only can MPs be elected on a minority of the votes cast (as little as 26 per cent if there are four candidates) but relatively small shifts in support between pairs of parties can produce substantial shifts in representation. The period being analysed here was clearly one where the two-party dominance of the 1950s and early 1960s was rapidly disappearing, as Table 1.5 indicates. Thus analyses of seats won cannot illuminate the full details of shifts in voter allegiance. For that we need an analysis of the changing pattern of voting.

In this analysis, and throughout the book, we deal not with votes won by

Table 1.5 The Inter-Party Distribution of Votes and Seats in the United Kingdom since 1955

A. Votes (%)

	Conservative	Labour	Alliance	Nationalist	Other	Turnout
1955	49.7	46.4	2.9	0.2	0.9	82.5
1959	49.4	43.8	5.9	0.4	0.6	78.7
1964	43.4	44.1	11.2	0.5	0.8	77.1
1966	41.9	47.9	8.5	0.7	0.9	75.8
1970	46.4	43.0	7.5	1.3	1.8	72.0
1974(F)	37.8	37.1	19.3	2.6	3.2	78.1
1974(O)	35.8	39.2	18.3	3.5	3.2	72.8
1979	43.9	37.0	13.8	2.0	3.3	76.0
1983	42.4	27.6	25.4	1.5	3.1	72.7
1987	42.3	30.8	22.6	1.7	2.6	75.4

B. Seats

	Conservative	Labour	Alliance	Nationalist	Other
1955	345	277	6	0	2
1959	365	258	6	0	1
1964	304	317	9	0	0
1966	253	363	12	0	2
1970	330	288	6	1	5
1974(F)	297	301	14	9	14
1974(0)	277	319	13	14	12
1979	339	269	11	4	12
1983	397	209	23	4	17
1987	376	229	22	6	17

each party as a percentage of all votes cast but with votes won as a percentage of the registered electorate. The reason for this is that, as Table 1.5 shows, a substantial, and increasing, percentage of the registered British electorate chooses not to vote. Further, analyses of the 1983 general election (Johnston, 1985a) showed that there are important social and spatial variations in that percentage. To some extent, such variations reflect on the accuracy of the electoral roll, which is compiled each October. Greater spatial mobility in some areas means that more people there are no longer resident where they are eligible to vote than is the case elsewhere; variations in death rates can produce the same outcome. Nevertheless, the geography of non-voting is an important element of the exercise of democratic choice in the UK, since voting is not compulsory, and our analyses recognise this.

The distributions of votes cast for the Conservative and Labour parties at each of the three elections are, of course, closely correlated with the patterns of seats won already displayed, so those cartograms are not presented here. The geography of seats won tells us little of the support for the Alliance, however, because its vote-winning (especially at the 1983 and 1987 elections) was not matched by success at obtaining MPs. Thus Figures 1.11, 1.12 and 1.13 are included here to illustrate where the Alliance won most of its votes. (Throughout we refer to the Alliance at all three elections; the SDP was not formed until

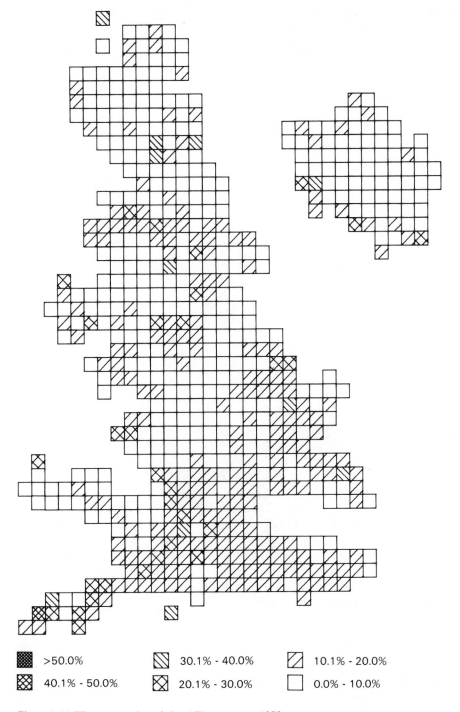

Figure 1.11 The geography of the Alliance vote, 1979.

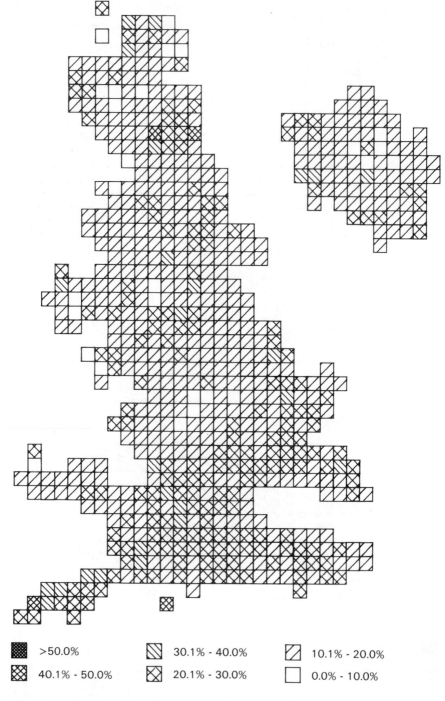

Legend		
▨ >50.0%	◩ 30.1% - 40.0%	▱ 10.1% - 20.0%
▩ 40.1% - 50.0%	⊠ 20.1% - 30.0%	☐ 0.0% - 10.0%

Figure 1.12 The geography of the Alliance vote, 1983.

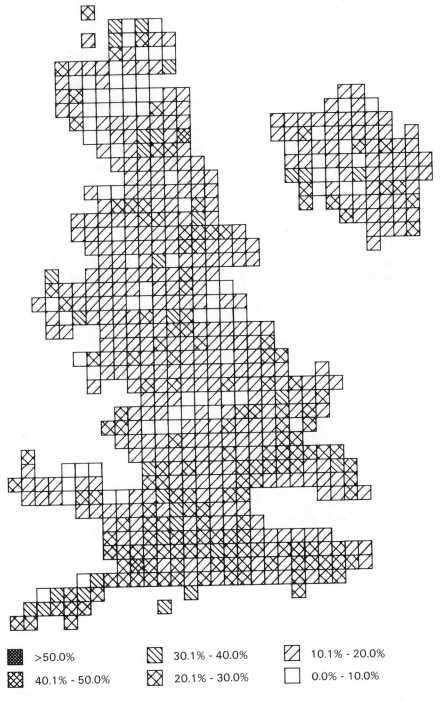

▨	>50.0%	◩	30.1% - 40.0%	▨	10.1% - 20.0%
▨	40.1% - 50.0%	⊠	20.1% - 30.0%	☐	0.0% - 10.0%

Figure 1.13 The geography of the Alliance vote, 1987.

1981, of course, so that for 1979 the Alliance is being used as a synonym for
the Liberal party.) Clearly in 1979 the Liberal party's support was predominantly in southern England, with only a few pockets where it won more than
10 per cent of the electorate (interestingly, including that band of seats from
Blackpool to Scarborough: see above). By 1983 the southern base had been
hardened and support was gained in most areas further north. In 1987, there
was some apparent major loss in the northern areas, especially Scotland.

Turning to the geography of changes in voting support, the first three
cartograms (Figures 1.14, 1.15, 1.16) refer to the Labour party. Between the
1979 and 1983 elections it lost support in nearly every constituency, with only
eleven of the 633 going counter to that trend. (Six of the eleven were in
Scotland, and none of those was in the main urban areas.) The greatest
concentrations of constituencies in which Labour lost 10 percentage points or
more of its support were in the south and east of England (notably in the
southeastern suburbs of London), but it also lost votes substantially in South
Wales, where it has traditionally been very strong (Figure 1.14) and there was
a not inconsiderable number of seats recording losses of ten points or more in
the northern regions of England. (In the south, its only gain was in Cornwall
North, where the increase was from 3.8 per cent of the votes cast to 3.9!)

The general election of 1983 saw the nadir in Labour's postwar electoral
fortunes, and its share of the poll increased over the next four years (Table
1.5). As Figure 1.15 shows, the recovery was experienced in most constituencies; the Labour percentage of the votes cast fell in only 44 of the 633
between 1983 and 1987. But the recovery was also spatially very uneven, and
in general Labour's increase was greatest where it was already strong. Scotland
(especially Strathclyde), South Wales, Merseyside and South Yorkshire stand
out as having the main concentrations of Labour growth (increases of 10
percentage points or more); the recovery was generally less in the southern
constituencies (including Greater London, which had 10 of the 44 constituencies recording declines in the Labour percentage), and also in that block of
constituencies stretching across the country from Blackpool to Scarborough.

Over the full eight-year period, Labour's vote fell substantially across the
whole country, but especially in the south and east, and then recovered somewhat, particularly in Scotland, Wales and parts of northern England. The net
result (as shown in Figure 1.16) was a growing spatial polarisation of support
for Labour between 1979 and 1987. Compared to the former date, voting for
Labour increased significantly (by five percentage points or more) in much of
Scotland and South Wales, in Merseyside and, somewhat surprisingly, in
Devon and Cornwall outside Plymouth. (In the last of these four areas, the
Labour vote in 1979 was very low; in the other three it was very high.)
Elsewhere, the general trend was one of slight decline in the north of England
(less than five percentage points) and more substantial decline in the south and
east of that country, including much of Greater London.

For the Conservative vote, we focus here only on the net pattern between
1979 and 1987, which again is characterised by a growing spatial polarisation
of support (Figure 1.17). Only two constituencies (Amber Valley and Stafford-

■	>10.0%	⊠	0.0% – 5.0%	▨	-10.0% – -5.1%
▨	5.1% – 10.0%	▱	-5.0% – 0.0%	▨	> -10.0%

Figure 1.14 The changing geography of the Labour vote, 1979–1983.

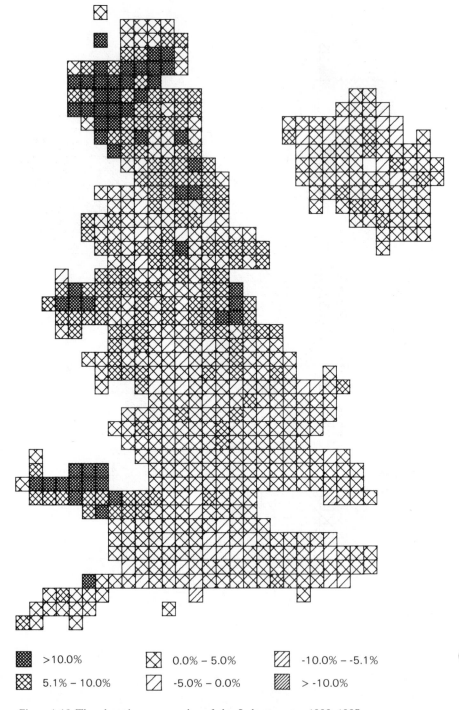

Figure 1.15 The changing geography of the Labour vote, 1983–1987.

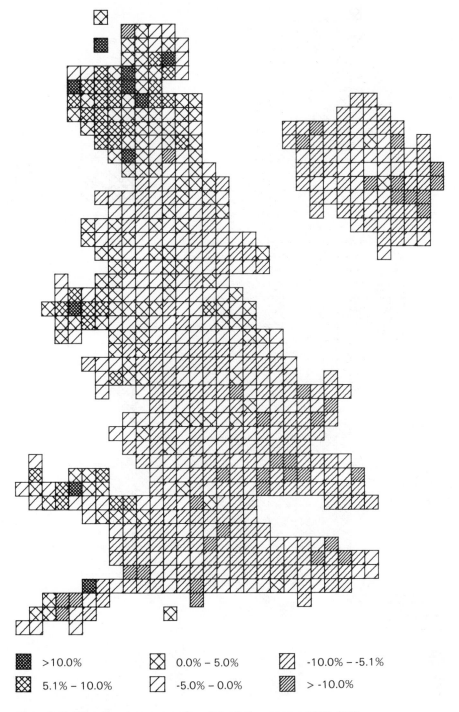

▨	>10.0%	⊠ 0.0% – 5.0%	◪ -10.0% – -5.1%
⊠	5.1% – 10.0%	◩ -5.0% – 0.0%	▨ > -10.0%

Figure 1.16 The changing geography of the Labour vote, 1979–1987.

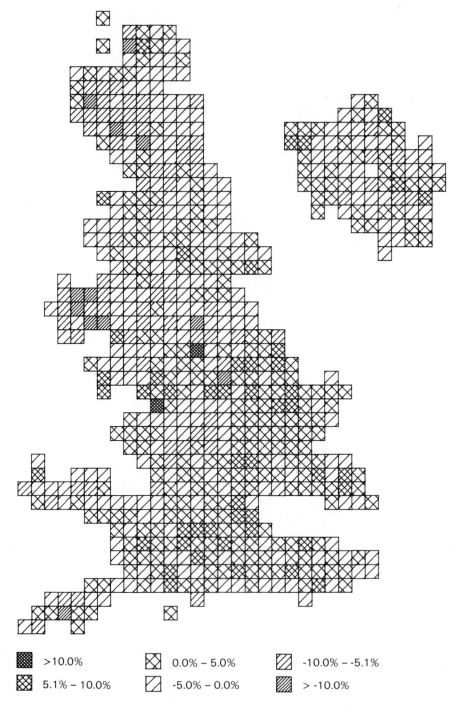

| >10.0% | 0.0% – 5.0% | -10.0% – -5.1% |
| 5.1% – 10.0% | -5.0% – 0.0% | > -10.0% |

Figure 1.17 The changing geography of the Conservative vote, 1979–1987.

shire South) recorded Conservative increases of ten points or more but a substantial number, the great majority of them in the south and east of England, recorded increases of between five and ten points. Its losses were, not surprisingly, greatest in the areas where Labour did relatively well over the period – throughout much of Scotland, on Merseyside, in Devon and Cornwall and in South Wales.

The picture that we gain from Figures 1.16 and 1.17 is of a growing divide between the north and west of Great Britain on the one hand and the south and east on the other in their support for the two parties that dominated British politics in the three decades after the Second World War: as Curtice and Steed (1982) expressed it, the north and west have shifted increasingly towards Labour, which was already strongest there, and the south and east have moved even further towards the Conservative party. But what of the new political force of the 1980s, the Alliance?

Figure 1.18 shows that the Alliance vote in 1983 was more than five percentage points higher than that recorded by Liberal candidates in 1979 in nearly every constituency: not surprisingly, it was less than the Liberal vote then in only six of the 633 constituencies. The major gains were concentrated in the south of England, but also in Scotland and Wales, especially in those parts of the two countries where the Liberal party was traditionally weak (as was the case also in parts of Birmingham and the Black Country). Even in the north of England, a minority of constituencies recorded an Alliance gain of only five percentage points or less. Between 1983 and 1987 the Alliance vote fell nationally, but this decline (Table 1.5) was not uniform across the country. In London, for example, 23 of the 84 constituencies experienced an increase in the Alliance vote, a situation which was quite common throughout the southern regions – especially south of the Thames (Figure 1.19). Further north, a decline was more usual, though far from universally the case, with the Alliance doing particularly badly in 1987 in many of those areas where it did so well in 1983; it lost votes in 61 of the Scottish seats, for example, and in 24 of those in South Wales.

The net result of the major increase in Alliance support from 1979 to 1983 followed by the slight decline to 1987 was a geographical pattern of polarisation not dissimilar to that for the Conservative party (compare Figure 1.20 with Figure 1.17). Only fourteen constituencies recorded an Alliance vote in 1987 which was less than the Liberal percentage in 1979, and several of these reflected special circumstances (as in Orkney and Shetland, Truro, and the Isle of Wight where the Liberal MPs of 1979 were not standing eight years later). In general, the Alliance apparently did better over the period as a whole in the south than in the north (excluding Scotland and Wales), but it requires closer statistical analysis to indicate whether that intuitive interpretation is valid.

The Changing Patterns of Votes: A Regional Analysis

Tables 1.6 and 1.7 provide the data on which such a closer analysis can be based. Looking first at the *geographical regions* (Table 1.6), very clear evidence of

Figure 1.18 The changing geography of the Alliance vote, 1979–1983.

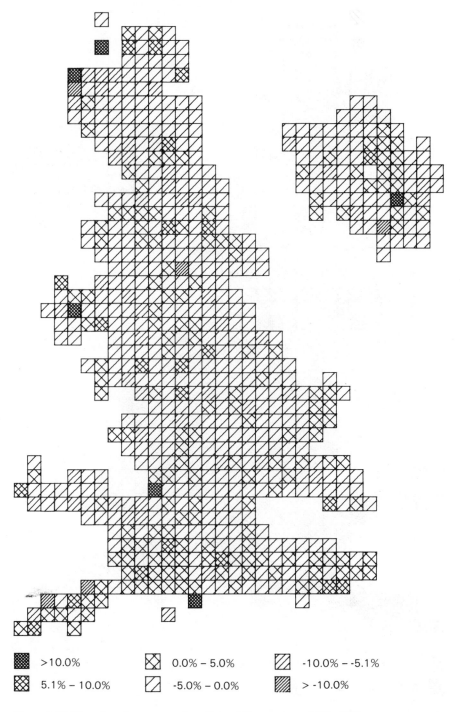

| | >10.0% | | 0.0% – 5.0% | | -10.0% – -5.1% |
| | 5.1% – 10.0% | | -5.0% – 0.0% | | > -10.0% |

Figure 1.19 The changing geography of the Alliance vote, 1983–1987.

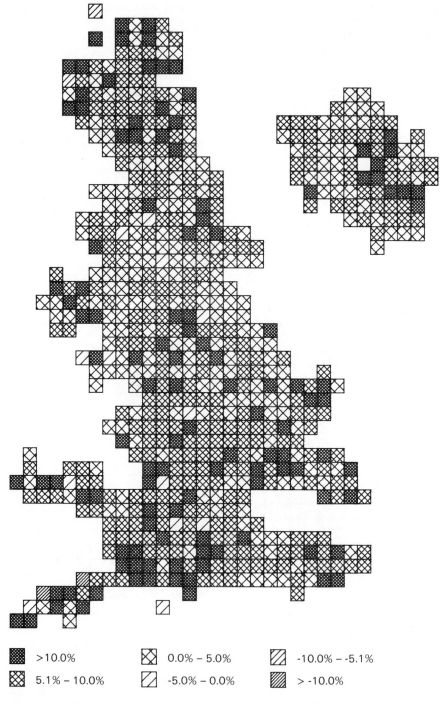

Figure 1.20 The changing geography of the Alliance vote, 1979–1987.

Table 1.6 The Percentage of the Electorate Voting for the Conservative, Labour and Alliance (Liberal in 1979) Parties, 1979–1987, by geographical region

	Conservative			Labour			Alliance		
	1979	1983	1987	1979	1983	1987	1979	1983	1987
Strathclyde	19.5	16.2	13.8	35.0	31.1	41.6	3.9	15.1	11.1
E. Scotland	20.8	19.9	19.0	30.2	25.7	33.6	6.1	18.0	14.7
Rural Scotland	22.7	22.4	22.1	14.7	10.7	15.9	10.7	18.8	19.8
Rural North	35.0	34.8	35.2	25.7	18.6	22.3	13.1	19.3	18.4
Industrial Northeast	24.4	22.1	20.9	39.5	30.9	38.2	7.9	17.5	15.1
Merseyside	29.7	24.7	21.2	33.1	28.6	36.2	9.7	16.5	17.2
Greater Manchester	30.9	26.9	27.8	33.8	27.4	32.0	10.2	17.0	15.2
Rest of Northwest	35.7	33.2	33.6	29.4	23.8	28.7	9.8	17.2	15.1
West Yorks	27.9	26.4	28.3	33.9	25.7	31.3	10.7	18.5	15.7
South Yorks	21.8	19.1	17.7	41.3	33.4	41.2	7.9	15.8	13.3
Rural Wales	26.1	26.0	26.7	24.6	17.8	23.9	11.5	17.6	17.4
Industrial South Wales	22.7	20.1	20.8	40.8	32.3	42.5	6.3	16.4	12.2
West Midlands Conurbation	32.4	29.0	30.4	32.8	26.6	29.5	5.6	14.3	12.4
Rest of West Midlands	35.8	36.1	37.3	25.7	18.3	20.6	11.6	19.9	19.1
East Midlands	35.0	34.7	37.5	28.8	20.8	23.5	10.1	17.7	16.1
East Anglia	37.5	37.9	40.0	24.3	15.5	17.0	11.8	21.1	19.8
Devon and Cornwall	40.1	39.3	38.2	14.8	8.0	12.3	19.8	28.2	26.2
Wessex	38.3	38.2	40.0	20.1	12.4	13.5	15.3	23.2	24.1
Inner London	25.5	21.7	24.2	31.7	24.3	27.5	6.3	14.1	14.0
Outer London	37.5	34.3	38.0	26.1	17.2	18.8	10.0	18.3	16.0
Outer Metropolitan	40.3	39.9	42.7	20.6	12.2	13.3	12.5	21.0	19.8
Outer Southeast	40.4	40.0	41.8	18.9	11.1	12.4	13.1	21.2	21.5
National	32.3	30.7	31.8	27.7	20.5	24.6	10.2	18.5	17.1

polarisation is present. In most of the northern regions, the percentage of the electorate which voted Conservative fell between 1979 and 1983, in most cases only by one or two percentage points, but substantially more in Strathclyde, Merseyside and Greater Manchester. In several, it then recovered in 1987 to approximately the 1979 level, slightly exceeding it in a few cases. In others, either the decline in the Conservative vote continued over the two inter-election periods, as in all of the Scottish regions (notably Strathclyde), in the Industrial Northeast and South Yorkshire, and on Merseyside. Further south, the 1979–1983 fall was only slight (and indeed absent in two cases) and the 1983–1987 recovery was to a level in excess of that for 1979; only Devon and Cornwall and Inner London departed from this. Thus over the period the Conservative party has become increasingly a party with its major support in the South.

The pattern for Labour is largely the complement of that for Conservative, as would be expected. The percentage of the electorate who voted Labour fell in every region between 1979 and 1983, much more so in the southern regions where up to 40 per cent of the 1979 support was lost. All of those southern regions then experienced an increase in Labour support between 1983 and 1987, but in no case did the 1987 level even approach that of 1979. In the northern and western regions, on the other hand, the 1979–1983 decline was followed by a recovery sufficient that the 1987 percentage of the electorate voting Labour exceeded the 1979 figure in five cases – three of them in

Scotland and one in Wales. Here again is evidence of the country shifting substantially away from Labour in the south and east over the full period, but sustaining its support for that party elsewhere.

Between 1979 and 1983 the Alliance vote more than doubled in some regions and increased very substantially in all. In general it performed better in the south, but fell below 15 per cent in only one region (the West Midlands Conurbation) and above 20 in only four. In all but four (Rural Scotland, Merseyside, Wessex, and Outer Southeast) its percentage declined between 1983 and 1987, but in every case its 1987 performance far exceeded its 1979 vote.

Turning to the *functional regions*, the same general picture emerges (Table 1.7). The Conservative party lost votes (relatively) in all but four regions between 1979 and 1983 (the exceptions were the Recent Growth, Southern Urban, Rapid Growth, and Agricultural regions, predominantly southern in location and relatively protected from the unemployment growth of that period); the Labour percentage fell in every region, being matched by Alliance growth everywhere. Over the following four years, the Conservative vote in-

Table 1.7 The Percentage of the Electorate Voting for the Conservative, Labour and Alliance (Liberal in 1979) Parties, 1979–1987, by functional region

	Conservative			Labour			Alliance		
	1979	1983	1987	1979	1983	1987	1979	1983	1987
I.C./Immig.	23.6	20.5	23.5	35.9	29.0	31.6	5.7	13.2	11.9
Ind./Immig.	27.8	25.1	26.4	36.6	29.9	34.3	6.7	14.0	11.8
Poorest Immig.	20.8	17.3	18.8	38.1	33.5	38.2	4.8	11.7	6.9
Intermed. Ind.	28.3	26.6	27.5	37.2	29.2	33.7	8.8	17.3	15.5
Old Indust/Mining	22.3	19.9	21.2	43.4	35.4	42.5	7.1	14.6	11.5
Textile	29.4	27.6	28.9	34.7	28.1	32.8	11.1	17.7	15.1
Poorest Domestic	13.8	11.2	11.6	41.4	33.0	43.6	3.5	11.7	11.0
Conurb. L.A.	25.3	22.1	21.7	39.1	31.3	37.5	6.9	15.2	12.7
Black Co.	27.3	25.1	27.7	37.2	30.9	33.1	4.2	13.3	11.1
Maritime Ind.	25.5	22.1	21.1	39.9	31.3	38.7	6.6	16.6	14.0
Poor I.C.	15.6	13.3	14.2	36.8	30.1	34.5	5.7	13.5	12.9
Clydeside	16.2	12.1	10.3	36.5	31.4	42.8	4.0	13.2	9.5
Scott. Ind.	17.2	16.0	13.9	35.1	31.8	41.4	1.9	14.7	10.7
Scott. Rural	25.4	25.1	25.2	12.7	8.7	12.1	13.0	21.5	22.1
High Status I.M.	35.7	30.3	32.6	23.3	17.7	21.1	8.3	14.7	13.0
I.M.	25.7	21.3	23.3	33.1	26.5	30.5	6.1	13.5	12.8
Outer London	42.0	38.8	42.2	20.7	12.5	14.5	11.6	19.8	18.0
Very High Status	44.9	42.9	44.7	16.2	9.0	10.7	14.1	21.4	20.6
Conurb. W. Collar	37.9	33.9	35.0	22.8	15.5	18.9	11.8	20.1	19.5
City Service	33.4	30.0	30.1	30.2	22.5	27.0	9.1	17.6	18.0
Resort/Retirement	41.6	40.7	41.9	14.4	8.1	10.2	16.2	22.3	22.9
Recent Growth	31.5	32.4	33.6	27.7	20.9	24.6	8.5	19.5	18.1
Stable Ind.	33.5	32.5	34.2	32.5	24.5	28.1	8.5	18.4	15.9
Small Towns	37.9	37.5	38.7	24.0	16.0	18.6	12.6	20.3	20.1
Southern Urban	40.5	40.8	43.1	20.5	12.1	12.9	12.2	21.6	21.4
Modest Aff.	40.0	38.5	39.4	25.7	17.2	20.3	10.9	20.2	19.1
Met. Ind.	34.9	33.9	37.3	30.1	20.4	23.2	8.9	18.6	15.4
Modest Aff. Scot.	32.3	30.5	30.1	22.7	18.5	26.9	9.4	20.1	16.4
Rapid Growth	39.6	41.3	44.0	16.9	9.1	11.0	14.7	22.7	21.2
Prosperous/No Ind.	40.8	40.5	41.0	15.5	8.4	11.0	16.6	23.2	23.8
Agricultural	37.4	38.1	39.0	15.9	9.5	11.7	17.7	24.0	23.7
National	32.3	30.7	31.8	27.7	20.5	24.6	10.2	18.5	17.1

creased in 26 of the 31 regions, in eleven to a level in excess of the percentage won in 1979; of the last group, only the Black Country comprises a region not generally associated with Conservative relative success over this period.

Labour's 1987 percentage exceeded its 1979 share in only five regions, three of them (Clydeside, Scottish Industrial, and Modestly Affluent Scotland) in Scotland. In all others its percentage increased on the 1983 figure, but did not return to 1979 levels; in some, as the data on changes in Table 1.8 indicate, its vote was substantially down on the first figure. The Alliance continued to gain support in only four regions, but its 1987 vote was well above the 1979 level in every case.

Table 1.8 Inter-Election Changes in Percentage of the Electorate voting for each party, 1979–1987, by geographical region

	Conservative			Labour			Alliance		
	79–83	83–87	79–87	79–83	83–87	79–87	79–83	83–87	79–87
Strathclyde	-3.3	-2.4	-5.7	-3.9	10.5	6.6	11.2	-4.0	7.2
E. Scotland	-0.9	-0.9	-1.8	-4.6	7.9	3.3	11.0	-3.3	8.6
Rural Scotland	-0.3	-0.3	-0.6	-4.0	5.2	1.3	8.1	1.0	9.1
Rural North	-0.2	0.4	0.1	-7.1	3.7	-3.4	6.2	-0.9	5.2
Industrial Northeast	-2.3	-1.2	-3.6	-8.6	7.3	-1.3	9.6	-2.4	7.2
Merseyside	-5.0	-3.5	-8.5	-4.5	7.7	3.1	6.8	0.7	7.5
Greater Manchester	-4.0	0.8	-3.1	-6.3	4.6	-1.7	6.9	-1.8	5.1
Rest of Northwest	-2.5	0.4	-2.1	-5.7	4.9	-0.8	7.4	-2.1	5.3
West Yorks.	-1.4	1.8	0.4	-8.2	5.6	-2.6	7.8	-2.8	5.0
South Yorks.	-2.7	-1.4	-4.1	-7.9	7.8	-0.1	7.9	-2.5	5.4
Rural Wales	-0.1	0.7	0.6	-6.8	6.1	-0.7	6.1	-0.2	5.9
Industrial South Wales	-2.6	0.7	-1.9	-8.4	10.2	1.8	10.1	-4.2	5.9
W. Midlands Conurbation	-3.4	1.4	-2.0	-6.2	2.9	-3.3	8.7	-1.9	6.7
Rest of West Midlands	0.3	1.2	1.5	-7.4	2.3	-5.1	8.3	-0.8	7.5
East Midlands	-0.3	2.8	2.5	-8.0	2.7	-5.3	7.6	-1.6	6.0
East Anglia	0.4	2.1	2.5	-8.8	1.5	-7.3	9.3	-1.2	8.0
Devon and Cornwall	-0.9	-1.1	-2.0	-6.8	4.3	-2.5	8.4	-2.0	6.4
Wessex	-0.1	1.8	1.7	-7.8	1.2	-6.6	7.9	0.9	8.8
Inner London	-3.8	2.6	-1.2	-7.4	3.2	-4.1	7.8	-0.1	7.7
Outer London	-3.2	3.7	0.5	-9.0	1.6	-7.3	8.3	-2.3	6.0
Outer Metropolitan	-0.5	2.9	2.4	-8.4	1.1	-7.3	8.5	-1.2	7.2
Outer Southeast	-0.4	1.8	1.4	-7.7	1.3	-6.4	8.1	0.4	8.5
National	-1.7	1.1	-0.6	-7.2	4.1	-3.1	8.3	-1.4	6.9

To bring the pattern of change into full perspective, Tables 1.8 and 1.9 indicate the average change in the percentage of the electorate supporting each party, in each region. (The figures in Tables 1.6 and 1.7 are averages too, not the total for each.) Thus Table 1.8 clearly discriminates between the southern regions, where in most cases the Conservative average vote increased over the full eight years while the Labour vote declined, and those further north, where the reverse was the general case. Table 1.9 suggests that in terms of functional regions, growth in the Labour vote over the full period was confined to very few, largely, it seems, because of the relative success of the Alliance nearly everywhere.

Table 1.9 Inter-Election Change in the Percentage of the Electorate voting for each party, 1979–1987, by functional region

	Conservative			Labour			Alliance		
	79–83	83–87	79–87	79–83	83–87	79–87	79–83	83–87	79–87
I.C./Immig.	-3.2	3.0	-0.2	-6.9	2.6	-4.3	7.5	-1.4	6.2
Ind./Immig.	-2.6	1.3	-1.3	-6.7	4.4	-2.3	7.3	-2.2	5.1
Poorest Immig.	-3.5	1.5	-2.0	-4.6	4.7	0.1	6.9	-4.8	2.1
Intermed. Ind.	-1.8	0.9	-0.9	-8.1	4.5	-3.6	8.5	-1.8	6.7
Old Indust./Mining	-2.4	1.3	-1.1	-8.1	7.1	-1.0	7.5	-3.2	4.4
Textile	-1.8	1.3	-0.5	-6.6	4.7	-1.9	6.6	-2.6	4.0
Poorest Domestic	-2.6	0.4	-2.2	-8.4	10.6	2.2	8.2	-0.7	7.5
Conurb. L.A.	-3.3	-0.4	-3.7	-7.8	6.2	-1.6	8.2	-2.5	5.8
Black Co.	-2.2	2.6	0.5	-6.4	2.2	-4.1	9.1	-2.2	6.9
Maritime Ind.	-3.4	-1.0	-4.4	-8.6	7.4	-1.2	10.0	-2.7	7.4
Poor I.C.	-2.3	0.9	-1.4	-6.6	4.4	-2.2	7.8	-0.5	7.3
Clydeside	-4.1	-1.9	-5.0	-5.1	11.5	6.4	9.2	-3.7	5.6
Scott. Ind.	-1.2	-2.1	-3.4	-3.4	9.7	6.3	12.8	-4.0	8.8
Scott. Rural	-0.3	0.1	-0.2	-4.0	3.4	0.6	8.4	0.7	9.1
High Status I.M.	-5.4	2.3	-3.1	-5.6	3.4	-2.2	6.5	-1.7	4.7
I.M.	-4.4	2.0	-2.4	-6.6	4.1	-2.6	7.4	-0.7	6.7
Outer London	-3.3	3.4	0.2	-8.2	2.0	-6.2	8.3	-1.8	6.5
Very High Status	-2.0	1.9	-0.1	-7.3	1.7	-5.6	7.3	-0.7	6.6
Conurb. W. Collar	-4.0	1.0	-3.0	-7.3	3.4	-3.9	8.3	-0.6	7.7
City Service	-3.3	0.1	-3.3	-7.7	4.5	-3.9	8.5	0.4	8.9
Resort/Retirement	-1.0	1.2	0.2	-6.3	2.1	-4.3	6.1	0.6	6.7
Recent Growth	0.9	1.2	2.1	-6.7	3.7	-3.1	11.1	-1.4	9.6
Stable Ind.	-1.0	1.7	0.7	-8.0	3.6	-4.4	9.8	-2.5	7.4
Small Towns	-0.4	1.2	0.8	-8.0	2.6	-5.4	7.7	-0.2	7.5
Southern Urban	0.4	2.3	2.6	-8.4	0.9	-7.5	9.4	-0.2	9.2
Modest Aff.	-1.5	0.9	-0.6	-8.5	3.2	-5.3	9.2	-1.1	8.1
Met. Ind.	-1.1	3.4	2.4	-9.8	2.9	-6.9	0.7	-3.2	6.5
Modest Aff. Scot.	-1.8	-0.4	-2.2	-4.3	8.4	4.2	10.7	-3.7	7.0
Rapid Growth	1.7	2.7	4.4	-7.7	1.9	-5.9	8.0	-1.6	6.4
Prosperous/No. Ind.	-0.3	0.6	0.3	-7.1	2.5	-4.6	6.6	0.6	7.2
Agricultural	0.6	0.9	1.5	-6.5	2.2	-4.2	6.4	-0.3	6.1
National	-1.7	1.1	-0.6	-7.2	4.1	-3.1	8.3	-1.4	6.9

As a final stage in this descriptive exercise, analyses of variance were conducted on both the percentage figures reported in Tables 1.6 and 1.7 and the percentage points change figures of Tables 1.8 and 1.9. The analyses test for differences between the regions, and the results are summarised in two ways. The first, the results of which are not reported here, indicates whether the differences between regions in either their average percentage of the vote for a particular party or their average percentage points change in a party's vote are so substantial that they are unlikely to have come about by chance – i.e. by a random allocation of voters among the regions. In every case, the differences were of such a magnitude between the regions that statistical tests indicated they were very unlikely indeed to be the result of random processes. The second way is to express, using the multiple correlation statistic R^2, the amount of variation among the 633 constituencies that is accountable by the regional classification. If all of it were – i.e. if each region's average differed from every other region's and all constituencies were closer to their regional average than to any other – the value of R^2 would be 1.0. The closer it is to 1.0, the greater the regional differentiation.

Tables 1.10 and 1.11 give the R^2 values from the analyses of variance of both data sets, for each suite of regions. They show high levels of regional differentiation, especially for vote percentages (Table 1.10), and particularly for functional regions. There is, it is clear, considerable variation between the

Table 1.10 The R^2 values associated with analyses of variance of regional differences in voting percentages

	1979	1983	1987
Geographical Regions			
Conservative	0.49	0.56	0.61
Labour	0.43	0.49	0.57
Alliance	0.27	0.24	0.26
Non-Voting	0.31	0.38	0.35
Functional Regions			
Conservative	0.71	0.75	0.73
Labour	0.74	0.77	0.76
Alliance	0.44	0.34	0.39
Non-Voting	0.44	0.53	0.53

Table 1.11 The R^2 values associated with analyses of variance of regional differences in changes in voting percentages

	1979–1983	1983–1987	1979–1987
Geographical Regions			
Conservative	0.27	0.42	0.38
Labour	0.19	0.54	0.52
Alliance	0.11	0.15	0.06
Non-Voting	0.17	0.27	0.27
Functional Regions			
Conservative	0.28	0.22	0.26
Labour	0.17	0.41	0.36
Alliance	0.15	0.14	0.08
Non-Voting	0.29	0.18	0.27

functional regions, and, to a slightly lesser degree, between the geographical regions in support for the parties. The pattern of votes for the Conservative and Labour parties, and to a lesser extent that of the Alliance too, was regionally structured. Turning to the pattern of change (Table 1.11), two new features stand out. First, the level of regional structuring is much less, with R^2 values substantially lower than those just noted for the static patterns. Secondly, that structuring was more apparent for the geographical regions than it was for the functional regions.

Our preliminary conclusions from these analyses, therefore, which provide the context for the rest of the book, are that there has been a clear regional structure to Great Britain's electoral geography over the period under consideration, which reflects both the characteristics of the constituencies (their functional regional membership) and their spatial location (their geographical regional membership). Over the period, that pattern has altered somewhat, particularly with regard to the geographical regions; the net changes in the distribution of votes between 1979 and 1983, 1983 and 1987, and 1979 and 1987 have been substantially, if not very closely, correlated to the regional divisions of the country adopted here. Just why that is the case is the focus of the remainder of the book.

IN SUMMARY

This chapter has provided an introduction to the remainder of the book by establishing that the issue of *Dividing Britain* is indeed a real one, calling for detailed analysis. Our cartographic depiction and statistical analysis of the results of the 1979, 1983 and 1987 general elections in Great Britain, and of the changing pattern of voting over those eight years, has sustained the general contention of most observers of the British political scene: the country is becoming increasingly polarised between those parts that sustain Conservative MPs and those that return Labour representatives. The polarisation is not simply north:south, however, and it is necessary to incorporate functional as well as geographical regionalisations in order to convey the changing geography adequately.

Having established that the years 1979–1987 have been characterised by substantial shifts in the country's electoral geography, our task now is to account for them. This we do by exploring the nature of those shifts in greater detail, in the context of a review – provided in the next chapter – of current understanding of British voting behaviour.

2

THE INFLUENCES ON VOTING BEHAVIOUR IN GREAT BRITAIN: SOCIAL AND/OR SPATIAL?

Our initial analyses of the geography of voting in Great Britain in the preceding chapter have provided clear evidence that both the pattern of voting in 1979, 1983 and 1987 and changes in the pattern of voting over those eight years were regionally structured. The implications of those findings are that people are influenced in their choice of party by their environment, by the people they live among and by the economic and social conditions in their localities. For most students of British voting, however, the major influences on people's choices are national social and political issues, not local concerns. To them, the important factors are social – what occupations people are in, what sort of housing they occupy, and so on. To the extent that there is a geography of social conditions then an electoral geography will follow (hence the concentrations of Labour voters in the functional regions characterised by above-average percentages of council housing). Once that social geography has been taken into account, however, the electoral geography displayed in the maps of Chapter 1 will be fully understood.

Against this position, other analysts argue that social factors alone, operating uniformly across the whole of Great Britain (e.g. council tenants are as likely to vote Labour in Bournemouth as in Bolton; managers are as likely to vote Conservative in Barnsley as in Bath), are insufficient to account for the observed electoral geography. Other factors are operating at the local level, producing substantial variations around the national trends. Their work is directed at identifying and accounting for those variations.

According to the first group of analysts, therefore, the explanation of Britain's electoral geography is entirely social, whereas according to the second group it is both social and spatial. The argument between these two views provides the context for the analyses here: are the patterns that we have described accountable solely by national social factors, or is it necessary to incorporate spatial as well as social elements to our explanation? As an introduction to that context, the present chapter reviews the arguments about British voting behaviour.

ELECTORAL CLEAVAGES

One of the most influential attempts to systematise the study of voting patterns in Western European liberal democracies was the concept of an electoral cleavage introduced by Lipset and Rokkan (1967). In those countries, the contest for power is between parties, groups within society that wish to rule it along certain policy lines. Those parties require stability of support on which to base their appeal to the electorate at large; without such support, their approach to the electorate must start afresh at each election. Creation of a support base requires two salient factors. First, the party itself must be a relatively stable group of politicians committed to a core set of beliefs – an ideology – so that the party can be identified not just by the people who run it but also, and much more importantly, by the principles on which its policies are based. This core set of ideas ensures that people know where the party stands on all of the most important political issues of the day, and can also know, with some certainty, how the party will react to new circumstances; they can 'predict' how it will respond to unanticipated events. Secondly, the party must have a stable group of supporters, people who will normally vote for it because they agree with its principles (or core beliefs; see Scarbrough, 1984) and the policies (or action principles) that can be derived from them.

A simplistic interpretation of this argument would be that parties search the electorate for the main principles on which they are divided, and develop their own ideologies accordingly. This puts the parties in a relatively passive role, merely responding to the electorate. But they are much more active; indeed in many societies they have been major mobilisation forces, stimulating the development of ideologies within the population by their activities. Thus parties are agents of both education and mobilisation; they are formally-constituted groups within society that seek to mould opinion in ways favourable to the political programmes they wish to promote (Schattschneider, 1960). As a consequence, the electoral history of a country is very much a function of the relative success of the various education and mobilisation strategies, and major changes in its voting patterns can follow from a successful educational programme by a party seeking to promote a new (or radically rewritten) ideology.

A mobilisation strategy may be pitched at the entire population, or a large majority of it, seeking to convince people of the correctness of a certain ideology. In most cases, however, parties have developed by focusing their mobilisation efforts at certain groups within society, arguing that their policies are in the best interests of those groups. The viability of such a strategy depends on either the existence of conflicting groups within society, so that a party can promote the interests of one over another, or the ability of a party to create such a situation, usually by capitalising on a latent (i.e. unrealised) conflict between two groups. What, then, might those groups be?

Lipset and Rokkan suggested that there were four different conflicts within European societies that offered the bases for mobilisation strategies and the development of electoral cleavages. The first two were products of what they termed the national revolution (the establishment and growing power of the nation state), whereas the other two were consequences of the industrial revolution.

1. *Subject versus Dominant Culture.* The creation of many nation-states in Europe involved the construction of territorially-bounded societies, controlled by a state elite, that contained within them more than one separate local culture. Such cultures could be distinguished by a variety of characteristics, physical and social, and in many cases may formerly have been politically independent. Their incorporation into the new nation-state could well have been the result of defeat in war, so that they became the subjects of a more powerful, and usually more numerous, dominant culture.

Within many of these new states, the goal of the dominant culture was not just to subdue the subject cultures but rather to eliminate them, and thereby incorporate their members in the dominant culture. The minorities were to be assimilated, and to lose all traces of separate identity as they adopted a common language, legal system, cultural norms, and so on; this was the Anglicisation process that was attempted in Wales, Scotland and Ireland with varying degrees of success up to the nineteenth century. Where such assimilation was achieved, the subject cultures disappeared. Where it was not, and remnants of the pre-existing subject culture remained, then there was a potential for conflict. Political parties could capitalise on that potential, mobilising groups in the subject culture against the dominant group, thereby creating an electoral cleavage.

2. *Church versus State.* Before the advent of the modern nation-state, one of the main sources of ideological power within societies was organized religion, which advanced not just a mythology based on ideas concerning the origin and nature of life but also an entire ideology for the conduct of life. Such an ideology was promoted by the religious elite, whose spiritual power may have been attached to secular power; church and state were undivided. With the growth of the nation-state, however, pressures to divide spiritual from temporal power grew, and there were conflicts between religious and secular groups for control over the ideological power base (as, for example, with the issue of whether education should be organised by the churches or by the state).

This conflict offered the potential for political mobilisation by parties, seeking to advance particular views of the role of the state and its link to spiritual power. Parties linked to the churches, and thus seeking support from religious adherents, would argue for their religious norms to dominate the state's ideology, while secular parties would argue that the role of the churches should be restricted to spiritual matters and that their views should not be imposed on those within the state who rejected the religious ideology. The cleavage, therefore, was between those who saw a political role for the churches and those who did not.

3. *Primary versus Secondary Economy.* In this, the first of the cleavages consequent on the industrial revolution, the conflict is between those whose livelihood is linked to agriculture and those dependent on the production and sale of

manufactured commodities. The industrial revolution saw the growth of the latter, most of them concentrated in urban areas. Their interests, in particular those of the capitalists who invested in industrialisation, were not necessarily those of the agriculturalists. In some parts of nineteenth century Europe, for example, most agriculturalists wanted protection from foreign producers, whereas most industrialists wanted free trade so that they could sell their products abroad; in others, it was the industrialists who favoured protection. Such divisions offered the potential for the development of electoral cleavages, between parties which drew support from the countryside (and the small towns dependent on it) and those which mobilised the urban electorates.

4. *Workers versus Employers*. With the industrialisation processes under capitalism came the development of a clear division within the population between those who invested in production, and lived from the profits of their investments, and those who sold their labour power to the investors, in return for a wage on which they and their dependants had to live. There was conflict between these groups, largely involving the labourers demanding higher real wages, with the higher standards of living that would follow, and the investors demanding greater productivity. That conflict was at the level of the individual workplace, but became organised with the growth of trades unions to represent the labourers' interests in general against those of their employers, some of whom organised to counter the unions.

Trades unions were established to fight for labourers' rights at the workplace. They were also the base for a wider political movement advancing labourers' (or working class) interests over a much wider range of issues. Political parties developed on that base, and established an electoral cleavage that was countered by parties representing the interests of the employers and those associated with them.

These four cleavages represent the full range of political divisions that developed in Western Europe, according to Lipset and Rokkan. There are few countries there today where all four are reflected in the party structure: in most one or two dominate. Which cleavage dominates where is a function of local circumstances, both the social structure and the success of particular mobilisation strategies. In Britain, as we review below, it is the Workers versus Employers (or Class) cleavage that is assumed to be dominant.

Mobilisation and Socialisation

The process of *mobilisation* involves either political parties or other organisations creating a context within which voters can be convinced that they should give their support to a particular cause. With regard to some of the cleavages listed here, that context is already given, and may well be spatial (or territorial) in its structure. With regard to the subject versus dominant culture cleavage, for example, it is very likely that the subject group occupies (or is concentrated in) one part of the nation-state's territory only, providing a spatial context for the mobilisation process. (The boundaries of that context may be ill-defined, of course, and mobilisation might be promoted at a smaller spatial scale, focusing on particular communities and localities within the cultural domain: Agnew, 1984; Cooke, 1984.) Similarly, the primary versus secondary economy cleavage implies a spatial demarcation between town and countryside, although again the boundaries may be diffuse and each town and rural area an arena for separate political mobilisation efforts. And, finally, to the extent that workers are mobilised at their workplaces in the class cleavage, so each workplace is a spatially-defined context within which mobilisation can be organised (as Lipset, Trow and Coleman, 1956, demonstrated).

The process of mobilisation is reinforced and extended by that of political *socialisation*. Once a particular context has been created, whereby a set of attitudes and beliefs comes to characterise a majority of its members, with the consequent actions and behaviour patterns that follow such ideological predispositions, then its nature tends to be passed on to successive 'generations' of residents. Thus, for example, a factory workforce may develop a militant trade union stance against its employer in a particular dispute, and that stance will be the cultural context into which new workers at the factory are socialised; they will then carry the militancy into the next 'generation'. In a locality, too, the development of widespread support for a particular political party, underpinned by a strong organisation, will be the context in which new voters are socialised, both those who move to the area and those who grow up there. And at the scale of the home, the development of a clear ideology by parents provides a very intense context within which their children will be socialised (implicitly if not explicitly) to adopt that ideology too.

Political mobilisation, then, involves the creation of electoral cleavages whereby people in (usually unclearly) defined situations are stimulated to support a particular political party. That mobilisation strategy may well take place in localities, even though its aim is to affect everybody everywhere within the relevant (probably nation-state) territory, and to the extent that its success varies so the geography of support for the party will vary too. That geography of support then provides a mosaic of socialisation contexts, whereby people learn and relearn political ideologies through their local milieux. As they learn, so the milieux may change, and to influence the learning further mobilisation activity will occur. The outcome is a geography of political socialisation, a spatially-structured process of learning.

ELECTORAL CLEAVAGES IN GREAT BRITAIN

The history of electoral politics in Great Britain over the nineteenth and twentieth centuries is one dominated by a single cleavage – that of workers versus employers. Of the other three, two have played a small role in that history, and the other has been almost entirely absent.

By the time of the industrial revolution, spiritual and temporal power had been divorced in Britain, and the development of mass politics during the nineteenth century was influenced very little by any conflict between church and state. Minority religions did provide a slight base for local political cultures, but there was no development of a major party seeking religious control over the state in competition with one promoting secular control. There was an established church with a clear influence, notably through the House of Lords, the Crown, and the patronage powers of the Prime Minister, and although there have been differences in the twentieth century in the support for various parties by people of different religious persuasions (including people of no such persuasion: Butler and Stokes, 1974, p. 156) the religious issue has not been very important in British electoral politics (except inasmuch as it influenced the Irish question in the nineteenth century).

By the time of the industrial revolution, also, the British nation-state was clearly defined as a territorial entity, with the anglicisation of the peripheral Celtic cultures having proceeded over several centuries. Nevertheless, the subject cultures had not been fully integrated into the English and they provided a base for political mobilisation against the hegemony of English rule. This base was exploited by Irish political parties throughout the nineteenth century, leading to the eventual independence of much of Ireland in 1922. It was not substantially exploited in Scotland and Wales until the late twentieth century, however, creating a significant political issue from the mid 1970s on (Agnew, 1984; Cooke, 1984). Finally, the urban:rural cleavage was developed during the nineteenth century, with the Conservative party mobilising the urban voters and Liberal being more active in rural areas. (Note, however, Taylor's, 1984a, argument that the geography of mobilised support did not necessarily match the geography of policy implications.) That cleavage declined in importance, however, as the rural population decreased, the Conservative party began to mobilise in the countryside, and the Liberal party fell into decay, being replaced by Labour whose main support base was in the industrial towns.

This leaves us with the fourth cleavage, widely known as the class cleavage, which many writers in the mid-twentieth century saw as dominating British politics. Further, Great Britain was seen as the stereotypical example of an electoral system dominated by that cleavage. Thus, Alford (1963, p. 120) concluded his comparative analysis of four countries:

> that very little except class matters for politics in Great Britain. In addition, we have
> discovered little evidence of a decline of the association of class and party.

Others came to similar conclusions: how one voted in Britain, it seemed, depended very largely on what occupational class one belonged to.

This raises major issues concerning the definition of class, of course, issues that remain important to the present-day (Kavanagh, 1986). The original Marxist distinction between capitalists and proletariat is of little value, because the great majority of the population fall into the latter category, so recourse is usually made to the Weberian schema based on the income, status, and power associated with occupations. Thus voting Conservative is usually associated with people in the higher-status, better-paid (generally), white-collar occupations (administrative and managerial, professional, clerical and service) whereas voting Labour is linked to the lower-status, less well-paid, manual (or blue-collar) occupations, most (but not all) involving factory work.

Attempts to identify the major cleavages in Britain's electorate were only made possible on any major scale with the development of political opinion polling after the Second World War. The first large national surveys were not conducted until the 1960s, and published in the seminal book *Political Change in Britain* by Butler and Stokes (1969, 1974). This work is often seen as a major statement of the predominance of the class cleavage, but is actually a much more sophisticated analysis that shows the interplay of a variety of factors. Thus in the introduction to the chapter of the second edition entitled 'The dominant class alignment', Butler and Stokes (1974, p. 67) write

> There is . . . evidence that partisanship has followed class lines more strongly in Britain than anywhere else in the English-speaking world. Yet . . . the links between class and party are more complex than is often supposed

and they conclude it with

> The relation of class to party is not . . . a static one. Conceptions of the social order have changed in an age of relative affluence, and the balance of beliefs about class and party has inevitably been modified as older electors have died and younger ones have come of age (p. 94).

Any model of electoral cleavages must accept the necessity of change, as part of the operation of the political system. If a cleavage is deep and permanent, so the division of power within the society would be permanent, too, unless the balance of the electorate on either side of the cleavage altered. Thus the party representing the larger segment of the population (assuming a single cleavage) would always win elections. To the party of the minority, the only counter to this situation is to seek either to relocate the cleavage, so that it is now the party of the majority - i.e. to remobilise the electorate and create a major re-alignment in voting patterns (as has happened several times in the United States: Archer and Taylor, 1981) - or to compete across a relatively ill-defined cleavage for the votes of those electors who could be convinced to support either party if its appeal were attractive enough.

All of the available evidence suggests that there has been no major realignment in the British electorate since the 1920s (Johnston, 1983a; Johnston, O'Neill and Taylor, 1987). Thus changes in the support for the various political parties (as illustrated in Chapter 1) must be consequences of changes in their appeal to different class (or other) groupings. Those changes may be either permanent, a group is convinced to transfer its allegiance, or temporary: the weight of the evidence suggests the latter (see Curtice, 1986).

The Class Cleavage

Before looking at shifts in allegiance it is necessary to outline briefly the contours of the basic class cleavage. As expressed by Alford (1963), it involved

Table 2.1 The Class Cleavage in Great Britain, 1943–1962*

Year of Survey	Non-Manual			Manual		
	Con.	Lab.	Lib.	Con	Lab.	Lib
1943	53	37	10	28	60	12
1945	68	32	0	31	9	0
1950	75	25	0	35	65	0
1951	77	23	0	35	65	0
1955 (1)	70	23	6	32	62	6
1955 (2)	73	23	4	32	65	3
1957 (1)	63	24	13	24	67	9
1957 (2)	64	24	12	26	67	7
1958 (1)	67	26	7	25	67	8
1958 (2)	57	22	21	24	64	11
1959 (1)	72	19	9	27	63	10
1959 (2)	67	21	12	30	57	13
1962	49	22	29	24	57	19

* The data are from opinion surveys which asked people how they would vote if an election were to be held 'tomorrow'. The data show the percentages in each occupation class who said they would vote for each party.

Source: Alford (1963, pp. 348–349)

a straightforward division of the electorate into white-collar and blue-collar occupational classes, with only those who voted either Conservative or Labour considered in his computing of an 'index of class voting'. The data on which he drew are given in Table 2.1, and show the extent of the class cleavage over a two-decade period. Three points stand out. First, for much of the period each of the two dominant parties at the time obtained about two-thirds of the preferences of members of the occupational class to which they were closely linked. Secondly, in the late 1950s increased support for the Liberal party saw an erosion of the class cleavage. Finally, there was always considerable 'cross-class' voting with between one-quarter and one-third of manual workers voting Conservative and about one-quarter of non-manual workers voting Labour.

There has been much speculation about, and exploration of, the reasons for 'cross-class' voting. Working-class Conservatism is frequently associated with a deferential culture, whose origins are in the paternalistic, small enterprises of rural areas, whereby people from blue-collar backgrounds accept that members of the traditional elite, represented by the Conservative party, are the 'natural' governors; this is enhanced by Conservative claims to be a 'one nation' party, which represents the interests of all in its support for freedom of market forces and individuals. White-collar Labour voting is often seen as a by-product of social mobility, on the other hand, whereby people from blue-collar backgrounds retain their pro-Labour political affiliations despite their class shift. Although both cases have some force, they are unlikely to be complete. One reason is that they over-simplify the class structure by looking at a single blue-collar/white-collar (or working-class/middle-class, or manual/nonmanual) division of the electorate only. This is the basis of the argument of Dunleavy and Husbands (1985) and the debate over how class should be measured (Kavanagh, 1986; Dunleavy, 1987). Heath, Jowell and Curtice (1985) illustrated how extensive differences are within the two basic classes with their five-fold division used to analyse the survey data of the 1983 British Election Study (Table 2.2). Within the white-collar occupational class (the first three divisions) Conservative support varied by 25 percentage points and Labour voting in one division was double that in another; similarly, between the two divisions of the manual occupational groups Labour support differed by a factor of two. (Rose and McAllister, 1986, provide more illustrations of this point.)

Differences such as those presented in Table 2.2 illustrate how people in different segments of the British occupational class structure interpret the ideologies of the political parties. Greatest support for the Conservative party comes from those who benefit most from its ideology – employers and the self-

Table 2.2 Class and Voting in Great Britain, 1983

Class	Percentage Voting			
	Conservative	Labour	Alliance	Other
Petty Bourgeoisie	71	12	17	0
Salariat	54	14	31	1
Routine Non-Manual	46	25	27	2
Foremen and Technicians	48	26	25	1
Working Class	30	49	20	1

Source: Heath, Jowell and Curtice (1985, p. 20)

Definition of classes:
Petty Bourgeoisie – Farmers, own account (self-employed) manual workers, and small proprietors.
Salariat – Managers and administrators, supervisors of nonmanual workers, and professionals and semi-professionals.
Routine Non-manual – Clerks, salesworkers, and secretaries.
Foremen and Technicians – Blue-collar workers with supervisory functions.
Working Class – Rank-and-file manual workers.

employed – whereas Labour draws most voters from the mass of factory workers, the skilled, semiskilled and unskilled of the working class. Miller (1977, 1978) suggests that these two groups are what he terms the core classes within the British electorate, those 'responsible for the class polarization of Labour/Conservative partisanship' (1978, p. 277). He defines the first of those classes to align it with the census occupational category of 'Employers and managers', who he calls the 'controllers', those who benefit most from Conservative policies, by and large. The second core class he terms the 'anti-controllers', the manual workers who are members of trades unions. These are most likely to be aligned with the Labour party.

Each of these core classes is stable in its support for the relevant party, therefore; they are at the heart of the groupings on each side of the class cleavage. Around them, however, are other classes whose level of identification with a party (what Whiteley, 1986a, terms their affective evaluation; see p. 52) is less strong, and who can be wooed by either party. Thus, for example, many of the professional and semi-professional white-collar workers are employed in the public sector (in schools, hospitals and social services, for example) and could be attracted to Labour policies not just because in general Labour is favourable to a large public sector as part of the welfare state while the Conservative party, especially since 1974, has increasingly favoured the privatisation of public services, but also because Labour conceptions of equality and justice are ideologically linked to the provision of such services by the state. Although the professionals are mostly affluent, they can be ideologically committed to vote for a party that promotes the interests of the relatively deprived with whom many of them deal; as Robertson (1984, p. 137) describes them, they form a small affluent subculture (about seven per cent of the population) who support both liberalism and egalitarianism.

Whereas some of the professional class can be wooed by Labour egalitarian policies, and the less affluent nonmanual workers by its promotion of income and wealth redistribution, some manual workers can be won over to the Conservative camp as a result of their successes in the labour market. These, usually skilled workers, enjoy the fruits of the process of embourgeoisement. Their high levels of productivity are rewarded by high wages which they are encouraged to spend on major consumer goods, notably owner-occupied homes and private cars. Such people are more likely to vote Conservative, because that party is seen as the defender of individual property rights, as Garrahan (1977) and Johnston (1981, 1982) have shown. Context is important, however. In the 1960s and 1970s many coalminers were paid at least as much as car workers, but the former lived in close communities where owner-occupancy was unusual and there were strong ties to the Labour party. Most car workers were in relatively newer towns, where Labour organisation was much weaker and owner-occupancy the norm: as Crewe (1973) showed, the affluent miners were much less likely to vote Conservative than the affluent workers in modern factories.

Alignments such as these which are apparently deviations from the class cleavage are relatively permanent. They enhance the core of stable support for the parties. But each needs a wider electorate to vote for it if it is to win a majority of seats at a general election. How, then, do the parties compete for those extra votes?

Political Evaluation

The cleavage structure described above is assumed to be a relatively long-term feature of British society, involving people in different class positions being socialised into different attitude sets, including propensities to support different political parties. Such a structure provides what Sarlvik and Crewe (1983, p. 74) term the 'lockgates on the vote', the long-term party preferences comprising the relatively enduring features of people's lives which, often at the prompting of the parties themselves, produce a sense of collective interest and instil a certain set of values.

Some people will be so 'locked-in' to a particular set of values that they habitually vote for the same party, perhaps without much thought at the time of an election. But others may be prepared to desert their traditional party at a particular election if the conditions of the time and the relative appeals of the parties convince them that they should do so. This produces the 'flow-of-the-vote', the movement of voters between parties across a pair of elections.

Estimating the flow-of-the-vote, and thus the sources of one party's success and another's failure, has been a major concern of studies of the British electorate. Table 2.3, for example, shows the flow between the October 1974 and 1979 elections. The Conservative party (which gained the support of 27.4

Table 2.3 The Flow-of-the-Vote, October 1974–1979

Vote in October 1974	Con	Lab	Lib	Other	Did Not Vote	Left Electorate
Conservative	70.6	2.9	4.1	0.1	9.8	12.2
Labour	9.0	64.5	5.6	0.1	10.8	9.7
Liberal	27.2	11.2	37.6	0.1	15.2	7.2
Other	10.3	13.8	6.9	44.8	17.2	3.4
Did Not Vote	25.0	14.0	5.7	2.6	46.1	6.1
Entered Electorate	24.8	34.2	12.4	1.0	28.6	

Source: Derived from Sarlvik and Crewe (1983, p. 51)

per cent of the electorate in October 1974 and 34.6 per cent in 1979) defeated Labour (percentages of 30.0 and 29.0 respectively) because it retained more of its 1974 voters, lost fewer to Labour than it gained from it, and won many more converts over from the Liberal cause and those who abstained in 1974; these relative successes more than outweighed the greater loss of Conservative voters from the electorate (largely through death) and Labour's greater success with the first-time voters.

Why do these flows occur? The basic argument of all three major analyses using the British Election Study data files (Butler and Stokes, 1969, 1974; Sarlvik and Crewe, 1983; Heath, Jowell and Curtice, 1985) is that they result from differential evaluation of the parties, their policies, images and leaders, in the context of voters' interpretations of their own situations. Thus, for example, Butler and Stokes (1974) showed that voters who shifted to Labour in 1964 were more likely to perceive Wilson as a better leader than Home than were those who did not shift (p. 367), and also that those who considered that their personal economic situation had worsened over 1963–1964 were more likely to shift away from the Conservatives (p. 384). Sarlvik and Crewe (1983) emphasised the importance of people switching their opinions on salient issues as a major source of electoral shifts: between 1974 and 1979, for example, many of those switching from Labour to Conservative did so because they agreed with the latter on the issues of nationalisation and stricter trade union legislation (p. 262).

The overall picture that we gain of the British electorate from these surveys, therefore, is of a population divided into groups of relatively homogeneous voters according to their occupational class position, each of which has a different set of propensities to vote for the competing parties. Those groups and their political affiliations are the results of the twin processes of mobilisation and socialisation. The political parties create an image of themselves which is more attractive to some groups than to others, and then, with their agents and associates, mobilise those attracted to that image not just to vote for them at particular contests but to develop a long-term commitment to that image, to adopt it as an ideology, and to work for its promotion and electoral success. This ideology then becomes part of people's milieux, the environments of home, workplace, and social life: their commitment to the ideology and the party is reinforced by their implied membership of a group and the weight of politically-relevant information that circulates within it. That environment is a context for political socialisation, by which new generations of voters are convinced that they should adopt the same ideology and partisan choice; it is bolstered by the continued, remobilisation efforts of the parties.

Having been socialised into a particular set of political beliefs, people are then called upon to use these as the basis for their political decisions. For some, that process is straightforward and brief: they have been so completely socialised that they are permanently committed to a party, and always vote for it. For many, however, their socialisation is the context for their evaluation, but does not determine their voting. They will evaluate the parties and their policy offerings prior to an election in terms of their perceived relevance to both national and local issues of the day and the voters' own interpretations of their individual situations (past, present and future). Some may be convinced that they should vote for an alternative party to that usually supported, because it is offering the best potential solution to contemporary problems. Others may be convinced to change their beliefs – perhaps in part because their own situations in the occupational class structure have changed. Thus, depending on the context of the election, some people may make a shift and vote against the party which they have been socialised to support.

One of the fullest analyses of this process has been provided by Whiteley (1983, 1986a), whose major concern is the decline in support for the Labour party over recent years. He suggests that voting is influenced by four sets of factors:

1. Social attributes – the contexts for socialisation;
2. Affective evaluations – the strength of commitment to a party;
3. Retrospective evaluations – perceptions of the relative ability of parties to solve major problems; and
4. Prospective evaluations – perceptions of the best ways of tackling contemporary problems.

Thus, for example, people socialised into certain contexts are more likely to vote Labour; they are also more likely to identify strongly with Labour, and, if they do, even more likely to vote for that party. Similarly, those socialised in particular contexts are more likely to think Labour is best able to tackle certain problems and has the best policies; they will then vote accordingly. But these four sets of factors are not deterministically linked and Labour's vote loss is likely to come from those whose retrospective and prospective evaluations lead them to prefer another party (and, over time, probably to weaken their affective evaluations).

For the 1979 general election, Whiteley (1983) concluded that the evaluation variables were much better predictors of Labour voting than were the social attribute variables; it was what people thought of Labour rather than the context in which they were socialised that most influenced their voting. Of the evaluation variables, their relative importance was affective, then retrospective, and finally prospective: people most likely to vote Labour were those most strongly committed to the party and who believed it was best able to tackle major issues, in particular those relating to trade unions. Overall, he concluded that

> the retrospective evaluation indicators dominate the prospective evaluation indicators when it comes to predicting voting behaviour. Voters judge Labour on its record not on its future policies, apart that is from the trade union issue (p. 102)

This conclusion was reinforced by a more sophisticated statistical analysis of 1983 data (Whiteley, 1986a), leading him to the following:

> the sociological account of electoral behaviour is clearly obsolescent if the aim is to explain and predict electoral outcomes, although it is still interesting for the descriptive analysis of electoral behaviour . . . [Further] because subjective evaluations are much more volatile than objective social characteristics, the findings suggest that future research should be directed towards the analysis of the dynamics, particularly the short-term dynamics of partisanship (p. 98)

Other analysts have similarly looked at the importance of retrospective and affective evaluations. Sanders, Ward and Marsh (1987), for example, investigated the revival of Conservative party popularity within the electorate from mid-1982 on, which led to the 1983 election success. The party's popularity increased by eleven percentage points between April and May, 1982 (popularity was measured by the percentage indicating that they would vote Conservative if an election were called immediately). Crewe (1985a), Dunleavy and Husbands (1985) and others have linked this upsurge of support to the so-called 'Falklands factor', arguing that 'the war . . . gave an exogenous boost to government popularity that shifted it to a higher plane' (Dunleavy and Husbands, 1985, p. 154), where it stayed for the next year (as the graph in Sanders et al., 1987, p. 286 shows). Against this interpretation, Sanders et al. argue that the growth of support for the Conservative party was a function of a perceived upturn in the economy; if people are more optimistic about the future, they claim, then they are more likely to support the incumbent government. Their analyses sustain their case; personal expectations (the percentage who think that their household's financial situation will improve over the coming year, less the percentage who think it will get worse) provide an excellent predictor of Conservative popularity over the period, along with three objective indices of economic performance (the level of public borrowing, the exchange rate, and the rate of unemployment). The latter variables do not influence the electorate directly, but were widely covered in the media, most parts of which (notably the national press) congratulated the government on their achievements; as Sanders et al. (1987, p. 298) put it, 'the electorate does not need to be sophisticated in order to be affected by the 'more good news' or 'more bad news' interpretations which are offered by the mass media when they report on fluctuations in these macro-economic indices'.

The importance of the government's economic performance as an influence on voting intentions is also stressed by Clarke, Stewart and Zuk (1986). They argue, from the data of the 1983 British Election Study (Heath et al., 1985), that voters see that in the trade-off between unemployment and inflation (the classic Phillips curve phenomenon: Phillips, 1958) the Labour party is more concerned with the rate of unemployment and the Conservative party with the rate of inflation; the Alliance lies between the two, but closer to Labour. Thus, all other things being equal, as the unemployment rate rises Labour support should increase, as should Alliance support, though more modestly; as the rate of inflation rises, on the other hand, Conservative support should increase. Their analyses of Gallup time series data were consistent with some of these expectations; thus, 'every percentage point increase in inflation cost Labour slightly over one-third of a point in popularity' (p. 130) and every increase of one point in the unemployment rate cost the Conservatives two percentage points in popularity. (Unemployment increased by 7.6 points over the period, so that if it were the only factor influencing popularity, Conservative support would have fallen by 15 points.)

Curtice's (1986) work expands on these findings, using a series of annual surveys since 1983. In these, people are asked a sequence of questions to determine the strength of their party identification: partisans are those who think of themselves as supporting a particular party; sympathisers are those who place themselves closer to that party than to any other; and residual identifiers are those in neither category but who would vote for the party if there were an election tomorrow. He shows that between 1983 and 1985 there was a substantial decline in Conservative partisanship, but very little change in the number of Labour and Alliance partisans. A reason for this decline in Conservative attachments was, he suggested, 'a particularly sharp downturn in economic expectations' (p. 47) among the self-employed. In addition, he identifies what he terms a

> clear shift to the left since the last election . . . the electorate has been moving significantly away from much of the ideological ground staked out by the present government (p. 52)

(This, of course, was written before the 1987 general election, which suggests that the shift may have been stronger in some regions than others.)

Heath, Jowell and Curtice (1987b) have presented a slightly different inter-pretation, based on an analysis of a panel of electors interviewed in 1986 as well as 1983 but again completed before the 1987 election; in the later year, respondents were asked how they would vote if a general election were held immediately. They found no significant change in voter attitudes over the three years (see also Heath, 1986), but clear shifts in voting intentions. The main correlate of those shifts was evaluation of the party leaders and of party images. Those who defected from the Conservative party between 1983 and 1986, for example, were much more likely to think that the party was 'good for one class only' than were those who stayed loyal, and similarly those who defected were much less likely to rate Mrs. Thatcher as the leader most likely to get things done and to look after all groups than were those who remained as Conservative supporters. Labour supporters in 1983 who thought their party too extreme were more likely to defect than those who didn't, and the Alliance lost the support of those who appeared to have lost confidence in the two party leaders. Thus, they conclude that 'Voters are looking for persons and policies who look as though they can competently and successfully manage the affairs of state' (p. 17).

Understanding the result of a particular election therefore involves knowl-edge not only of the basic influences on voting – the dominant cleavages that provide the context for socialisation – but also of the electorate's evaluations of party performance (past, present and future), in the context of their personal situation, and of the party leaders. The latter provide the variability that leads to changes of government. Some authors argue, however, that the long-term commitments to a party characteristic of the class cleavage model are increasingly obsolescent, and we turn to their case in the next section.

DEALIGNMENT AND THE END OF CLEAVAGES

Over the last decade, there has been increased awareness in a large number of western liberal democracies both that people are less tied to a particular party (in Whiteley's terms, affective evaluation is becoming weaker) and that mem-bers of the electorate are more volatile, more likely to shift their partisan preference between elections. This has led to increased use of the term *electoral dealignment* to indicate the weaker ties between voters and parties; it implies that socialisation is becoming less important as an influence on partisan choice, and evaluation is becoming more so. Two types of dealignment have been identi-fied, according to Dunleavy and Husbands (1985). The first involves cleavage dealignment, as people in different social locations (occupational classes in Britain) weaken their links to parties. The second is termed partisan dealignment. It is a function of declining party membership; fewer people are very closely linked to any party and so an increasing proportion are more likely to vote against the party they generally identify with because of its position on the issues of the day – they are 'more tolerant of lack of fit between supporting a party and dissent from its individual issue positions' (p. 12), which allows them to vote against in certain situations and thereby produces a more volatile electorate.

The existence of partisan dealignment in Britain is clearly suggested by the title of Sarlvik and Crewe's (1983) book on the 1970s – *Decade of Dealignment*. They argue that there was no realignment for there was no 'definite shift of party loyalties within any easily definable sector of society' (p. 332). Rather, 'none of the major occupational groups now provides the same degree of solid and consistent support for one of the two major parties as was the case in the earlier post-war era' (p. 332). Crewe (1985b) does not anticipate that this dealignment will eventually lead to a realignment, with the creation of a new set of electoral cleavages, but rather (metaphorically)

> the two major party icebergs will continue to melt. From time to time one or other will lose a substantial chunk. More and more loose ice will float about in the electoral sea. Some will re-attach itself to the big icebergs; the rest will form a soft-packed third iceberg precariously floating alongside, but dwarfed by, its bigger rivals (p. 144)

Not all agree with Crewe. Heath, Jowell and Curtice (1985) argued that

> class differences, whether with respect to objective inequalities, subjective values or support for the political parties, remained at much the same level throughout the postwar period (p. 39)

(See also Crewe, 1986a; Heath, Jowell and Curtice, 1987a; Dunleavy, 1987). And Dunleavy (1979) argued that there has been a realignment, as parties remobilise support around a consumption sector cleavage, with Labour promoting itself as the party for those who obtain their major consumption goods (notably housing and transport; to a lesser extent, health care and education) from the public sector, whereas the Conservative party represents the interests of those who obtain them through the private sector.

Those who accept the dealignment thesis argue that it is a consequence of major social, economic and political changes in recent decades. In a major review of the evidence from a number of countries, Dalton, Flanagan and Beck (1984, p. 5) note that

> fundamental changes are taking place in democratic political systems . . . stable party alignments are fragmenting, and the traditional sociopsychological bonds between voters and parties are weakening.

They suggest that these 'fundamental changes' are the consequences of six inter-related factors.

1. Embourgeoisement.   With greater economic prosperity the overlap in material standards between the two main occupational classes has increased, reducing the potential for a deep class cleavage.

2. Social mobility.   There is now much greater inter-generational mobility than in the past, so that more people are living in contexts (spatial as well as social) different from those in which they were politically socialised.

3. Mass society and community disintegration.   Primary group cohesion is

now much less than it was in the past, with the decline of community, and the mass media have replaced personal networks as sources of political information.

4. Cognitive mobilization. A better-educated electorate is more sophisticated, more able to question the arguments of the political elite and less ready to follow the dictates of others.

5. Ageing party systems. As traditional party ideologies become less relevant to contemporary situations, the salience of those ideologies for the electorate declines, and voters are more likely to act pragmatically.

6. Value changes. Rapid social change means that many of the traditional values defended by ageing parties are no longer seen as relevant by large sections of the electorate, who as a consequence are less likely to become firmly committed to a party.

These are general arguments, and some of the points are more relevant to the British situation than are others.

One of the first major critiques of the class cleavage concept as it applies to the British electorate was developed by Rose (1974, 1982), who focused on the decline of what he termed the ideal-typical class descriptions. Thus (Rose, 1982, p. 150):

> In Britain, an ideal-type manual worker, in addition to a manual occupation, is expected to have left school at the minimum leaving age, to belong to a trade union, live in a state-owned council house, and subjectively identify as working class. Reciprocally, a middle-class person, in addition to having a nonmanual occupation, is expected to have more than a minimum of education, to be a homeowner, not belong to a trade union, and subjectively identify with the middle class.

In 1964, only 14 per cent of the electorate fitted that description of the working class, and 12 per cent fitted the middle class definition; in 1979 the percentages were 4 and 10, so that over 85 per cent of the electorate could not be clearly identified with the stereotypes – let alone with Miller's (1977) 'core classes'.

Rose's arguments were taken up in a detailed study by Franklin (1985) of *The Decline of Class Voting in Britain*. His model of the propensity to vote Labour contains six independent variables: parents' class; parents' party; voter's education; voter's occupation; voter's housing (council or not); and whether the voter was a member of a trade union. In 1964, these variables together were able to account for 38.7 per cent of the variation in Labour voting (i.e. there was a bit better than a one in three chance of correctly predicting a Labour vote given knowledge of the six variables); by 1974 this had fallen to 28.4 per cent (nearly a one in four chance). The main decline over the decade was in the influence of parents' class (a major socialisation context) and voter's occupation (suggesting class dealignment): union membership and residence in a council house became slightly more influential over the period (though by 1983 the effect of the former had declined substantially: Johnston, 1986a). Franklin's conclusion (p. 125) is thus that class is no longer the basis of British politics:

The explanatory power of variables most central to the concept of social class (parents' class and respondent's occupation) had declined so extensively by 1974 that supportive variables [housing, union membership etc.] which used to reinforce those central influences are now essentially propping up a structure that has lost its backbone

It was replaced, from 1970 on, by 'issue voting' whereby the major influences on party choice were the respondent's party identification and political attitudes, both of which are only partly influenced by the traditional class variables. With attitudinal variables added, the probability of correctly predicting a Labour vote increased to 0.76.

According to this analysis, voters develop political attitudes as they are socialised, and they then re-evaluate their beliefs in the context of economic, social, and political change. Those attitudes are now less strongly linked to the social contexts in which they were socialised than was so in the past, which is why class voting has declined: previously socialisation led to the development of a political ideology that clearly directed the voter's party choice; today the link between context and ideology is much weaker, and there is much less solidarity in the support for any party.

Heath, Jowell and Curtice (1985), Robertson (1984), Scarbrough (1984), and others have recently explored the nature of the attitudes that British voters hold. Heath et al. suggest that those attitudes can be summarised by two dimensions only. The first is best described as the typical left-right ideological dimension in British politics, with those supporting major state intervention in the economy at one extreme and those favouring a relatively-unfettered free market at the other. The second, with the anti-nuclear voters at one extreme

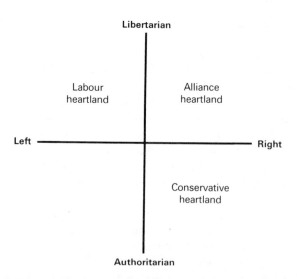

Figure 2.1 A two-dimensional map of the British Electorate according to attitudes. (Source: derived from Heath, Jowell and Curtice, 1985, pp. 119–120.)

and those favouring expansion of civil and military nuclear programmes at the other, suggests a continuum from the libertarians at one pole to the authoritarians at the other (see also Robertson, 1984). If those two dimensions form the coordinates of a map (Figure 2.1), then those in the northwest quadrant are most likely to vote Labour and those in the southeast are most likely to vote Conservative, whereas the Alliance draws its major support in the northeast; Labour voters in the northwest were most likely to stay loyal to the party between 1979 and 1983, as were Alliance voters in the northeast and Conservative voters in the southeast.

Discovery of these clear links between attitudes and voting led Heath et al. to propose that each party draws on a traditional heartland of support, a largely intuitive conclusion that has been confirmed by statistical analysis (Johnston and Pattie, 1988a). Note, however, that each party draws voters from all parts of the map: Robertson's (1984, p. 136) analyses suggest that upper class Labour supporters occupy positions in the far northwest of the 'map', whereas other Labour supporters lie due west of the intersection of the two dimensions, and so are neither liberal nor authoritarian: upper-class Conservatives are more right-wing than Tory supporters from other classes, but less authoritarian. There is thus a range of attitude types, as Johnston and Pattie (1988b) have shown; they differ in their social origins and their voting propensities. (An article in *The Economist* for August 1987 suggested that the Alliance leaders are scattered all across such a map: Anon, 1987.)

The importance of the link between attitudes and partisan choice has recently been challenged by Rose and McAllister (1986), who present evidence which they claim shows that

> How a person votes is a poor guide to what a person thinks about most issues today (p. 147)

The evidence is a table showing the percentage of Conservative, Labour and Alliance voters in 1983 respectively who agreed with 45 different attitudinal questions drawn from the 1903 British Election Study. They claim that this table shows that 'All three parties have most of their voters in agreement with one or both of their competitors on the great majority of issues' (p. 148), but differences are as great as 28 percentage points (e.g. 52 per cent of Alliance voters favoured stricter laws to regulate trade unions, as did 80 per cent of Conservative voters: the two sets of voters are said to agree). The implication is that one cannot predict how people will vote from knowledge of their attitudes: a discriminant analysis using the same data set has falsified that claim (Johnston and Pattie, 1988c).

The dealignment thesis, therefore, suggests that people have a clearly-defined set of political attitudes, but that which party they vote for is no longer so clearly determined by those attitudes as was the case in the past. Instead, they evaluate each party, its policies and its leaders, in the context of their attitudes and their interpretation of contemporary circumstances. Those contemporary circumstances may be spatially variable, and so produce spatially-varying evaluations and voting.

SPATIAL VARIATIONS IN VOTING PATTERNS

Most political science analysts of British voting patterns focus on the processes of mobilisation, socialisation, and evaluation with little or no reference to locational issues; it is implicit in their work that the processes operate uniformly over the country as a whole (Johnston, 1986d). The conclusion to be drawn from this is that geography does not matter, that there are no significant locational variations in the intensity of those processes and the relative success of the various parties. This is made explicit in a statement by Bogdanor (1983, p. 53) – which was apparently intended to apply to voting behaviour up to the 1960s only (Bogdanor, 1986; Johnston, 1986b):

> Electoral behaviour came to display a considerable degree of geographical homo-
> geneity since an elector in Cornwall would tend to vote the same way as an elector
> from a similar class in Glasgow regardless of national or locational differences.

And yet the classic study by Butler and Stokes had demonstrated just the opposite for the 1960s; they identified 'substantial variation . . . [in] class support for the parties' (1974, p. 127) across the eleven standard geographical regions of Great Britain in 1963–1966 and showed even greater variations between different functional regions (in mining seats, only 50 per cent of the middle class voted Conservative in 1970, compared with 80 per cent in the resorts; Labour voting percentages among the working class in the two types were 79 and 48 respectively). This led them to conclude (1974, pp. 129–130) that

> A good deal of empirical support can be found for the principle that once a partisan
> tendency becomes dominant in a local area processes of opinion formation will draw
> additional support to the party that is dominant. If this is true, perceptions of class
> interest may impart to an area a political tendency that is exaggerated still further by
> the processes that form and sustain a local political culture, thereby altering the
> pattern of support within classes.

In terms of the concepts used here, mobilisation is a locality-based strategy, at least in part. Where it succeeds in creating a local environment very much skewed toward support for one party, then the ongoing processes of socialisation will sustain that party's dominance, across all classes.

Butler and Stokes suggest that geography does matter, therefore, because the processes that control the lockgates on the vote are spatially variable; they also suggest that this is true for the processes of evaluation that lead to the flow-of-the-vote (see 1974, pp. 141–151) – though not the processes of retrospective/prospective evaluation. This has long been recognised by some other writers, notably Pelling (1969), whose *Social Geography of British Elections 1885–1910* demonstrated the many peculiarities of the various regions of Britain during the period following major reforms in both the franchise and the organisation of elections. His discussion of those regional peculiarities focuses on many of the reasons for their creation, as particular features of the local context influenced the mobilisation and socialisation processes. (Others similarly point to particular local features. See, for example, Pugh's, 1985, p. 123, reference to support for Conservative in Bolton at the end of the nineteenth century.)

Only Miller (1977) has followed up Pelling's portrayal of the electoral geography of Britain in a systematic way (though interestingly he referred to Pelling only once: the peculiarities of particular constituencies are now represented in the brief sketches of their characteristics provided by Crewe and Fox, 1984, and Waller, 1987). Miller undertook statistical analyses of voting patterns, by constituencies or groups of them, for the period 1918–74, with detailed work focusing on the 1966 election; census data were set alongside voting data to relate the characteristics of the constituencies to the voting behaviour there. He showed that the class structure of a constituency was the major influence on its voting pattern, with the rural-urban cleavage having a slight additional effect; there were some religious influences early in the period but these declined in importance thereafter (see also Crewe and Payne, 1976, on the 1970 result).

In part, these findings are what one would expect, since they simply imply that the electoral geography of the country matches the social geography. What is most important about Miller's work, however, is his finding about the nature of that match. He concludes from his analysis of 1966 (Miller, 1977, p. 65) that

> At a minimum, the class characteristics of the social environment have more effect on constituency partisanship than class differences themselves, perhaps much more. The partisanship of individuals is influenced more by where they live than what they do.

Thus, in a constituency where a party was expected to poll well, according to the social structure, it polled even better; where it was expected to poll badly, it did even worse. Figure 2.2 expresses this, using regressions for individual voters, irrespective of where they lived, and for constituencies.

Why this polarisation? Why are members of the middle class more likely to vote Conservative when their local environment is predominantly middle class than they are when it is predominantly working class? Miller (1977, p. 65) suggests that it results from a contagion process:

> The effect of the social environment may be explained by contact models: those who speak together vote together.

He relates this to the distribution of the core classes (see p. 49 above). The controllers and the anti-controllers tend to be firm in their partisan commitment – the former for the Conservative party and the latter for Labour. Those lying between these two groups are more susceptible, more likely to be converted by the weight of local opinion, hence the findings indicated in Figure 2.2. This is the classic neighbourhood effect – a process of conversion by contagion in localities – which has long been favoured by electoral geographers (Taylor and Johnston, 1979). The nature of the process is far from clear, however, and has been subject to a scathing attack by Dunleavy (1979: see also Johnston, 1986c, 1986d); attempts are now being made to provide alternative explanations for an empirical pattern that 'will not go away' (Johnston, 1983b;

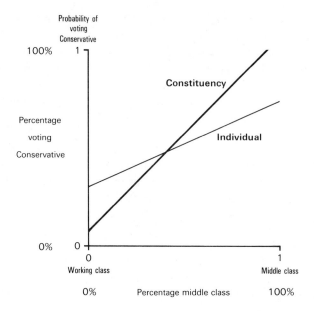

Figure 2.2. The relationship between class and voting, 1966, using individual and constituency data. The regression for individuals shows the difference in Conservative voting between working class (0.3) and middle class (0.74) survey respondents. The regression for constituencies shows the relationship between the percentage middle class and the percentage voting Conservative.

Taylor, 1985a, 1985b). (See also the suggestion by Warde et al., 1987, that members of other classes in constituencies with large percentages of controllers may be drawn to vote Conservative not by contact with the controllers but rather to defend the high property values that are a consequence of the characteristics of their local milieux.)

Following on from Miller's work, Johnston (1985a) has produced a detailed analysis of the 1983 general election in England, using a recently-developed statistical procedure (described in Chapter 5 below) to produce estimates of voting by occupational class in each constituency. He shows, for example, that the percentage voting Labour among the semi- and unskilled manual occupational class varied from 22 to 58 across the 519 constituencies, and a range from 1 to 32 for Labour voting among the professional and administrative classes. These variations were closely aligned to the social characteristics of the constituencies, in exactly the same way that Miller showed. Johnston's account for those variations does not favour the neighbourhood effect, however, and instead focuses on likely spatial variations in the mobilisation and socialisation processes, and to a lesser extent those of evaluation.

Complementing these constituency-level analyses, explorations of survey data for 1983 have been used to support the argument for spatial variations. Johnston (1986a, 1987d) has shown substantial interregional and urban:rural differences in the propensity of members of the working class (variously defined) to vote Labour. McAllister (1987a, 1987b) has argued against this interpretation, claiming that once various aspects of voters' social positions and their attitudes have been held constant, the spatial variations largely disappear. (Johnston and Pattie, 1988c, have countered this, on the grounds that since attitudes may be created via spatial processes of socialization they should not be held constant but rather should be taken as part of the spatial variation.)

McAllister's case has been presented in a number of other ways. For example, in an analysis with Rose of the 1983 general election (McAllister and Rose, 1984) it is argued that regional cultural variations had a slight influence on the pattern of voting only. This was based on predictions of what each region's voting should have been, derived from the national pattern by class. It produced the result that (pp. 93–4)

> In most regions of England there are limited but noteworthy differences between the predicted and the actual share of the vote . . . The regional differences do not exceed seven per cent, Labour's shortfall in the unfavourable regional culture of the South of England . . . where the [Conservative] party does five per cent better than would be predicted solely on the basis of social structure.

This differs very substantially from Johnston's (1985a; see also p. xii above) similar analysis of the same election; however, Rose and McAllister used four regions only, and Johnston analysed all 519 constituencies separately.

The Changing Spatial Pattern

All of the work reviewed so far offers accounts for spatial variations in voting patterns, but not for the spatial variations in voting pattern changes identified in Chapter 1 as the focus of the present book. The main approach to this issue was taken in a seminal paper by Curtice and Steed (1982). They identify 1955 as a key election in British post-war electoral history, arguing that (p. 256)

> Since that date the long-term change in the relative strength of the Conservative and Labour parties within constituencies has been marked by two major cleavages – between the North and the South, and between urban areas and rural ones. A North-South cleavage began to emerge in the 1955–59 swing . . . while the urban-rural cleavage became clearly evident in the 1959–64 swing.

In other words, the growing division of Britain that we identify for the period 1979–87 in Chapter 1 (and which Curtice and Steed, 1984, confirm for 1979–83) is a continuation of a well-established trend. (Note that Miller, 1984, also concludes that constituency-level polarisation increased between 1979 and 1983.)

Why should this trend have developed? Curtice and Steed review a number of possible explanations. First, it could simply result from a change in the class composition of constituencies in different parts of the country, in part as a function of *in situ* socio-economic change and in part as a result of selective in- and out-migration (see also Taylor, 1979). Undoubtedly these have happened, but they cannot account for the major shift away from Labour in certain areas between the two 1974 elections, for example. There must, Curtice and Steed (p. 263) argue, have been

> differences in the behaviour of otherwise similarly socially-situated voters according to some characteristics of the area in which they live
>   .

in line with Miller's findings. For rural areas, therefore, they suggest that the haemorrhage of Labour support reflects the weakness of trades unions there and the relatively atomized small workplaces of the rural areas and small towns; there are difficulties that Labour faces in organising and remobilising voters in such contexts, and workers lack the close contact with others that can reinforce pro-Labour sentiments. (One problem with this argument is that it implies that the organisational situation has changed. It hasn't; so why was Labour stronger in the rural areas prior to 1955?) Their third suggestion focuses on changes in economic and social well-being: economic decline accompanied by unemployment has been more substantial in the north than in the south, and in the inner cities rather than the small towns and rural areas. People in the relatively disadvantaged areas, from all social classes, have turned to Labour, whereas those in the more prosperous areas have increasingly favoured the Conservative party.

Finally, Curtice and Steed suggest that the growth of 'minor parties' – notably the Liberal party (up to 1979) and the two nationalist parties – can have influenced the geography of support for Conservative and Labour. They argue that both the Liberals and the SNP have tended to win most voters over from the weaker of the other two (Conservative and Labour) in a constituency – in part at least through processes of tactical voting; the Liberal advance in the south of England has done much to erode Labour support there, they claim. (A weaker party will then be less able to organise in a constituency during a general election campaign, with consequences for its advertising efforts there and its inability to mobilise support: see Johnston, 1987a, for evidence on the increasing importance of constituency campaign spending in election results.) Thus Curtice and Steed (p. 266) conclude that

> the change in the spatial distribution of the two-party vote during the last quarter of a century reflects three sorts of changes, each reinforcing the other – change in the distribution of social and economic characteristics of the electorate, the differential behaviour of voters of the same social group according to where they live, and the local political impact of third parties. The first trend, very probably, will continue; the impact of the current recession, which has badly affected the North of Britain, could well produce a continuation of the second change, while, on current electoral evidence, there does not seem to be any reason to anticipate a significant fall in the Liberal and SNP vote – if anything, the opposite.

Events since 1982 bear out their forecasts, which lead us to speculate in the next chapter on reasons for the trends identified in Chapter 1.

Curtice and Steed's thesis is of major voting differences within England, as well as between England on the one hand and Scotland and Wales on the other (as is the argument in, for example, Hechter, 1975; Madgwick and Rose,

1982; and Miller, 1981). In a later essay, Steed (1986) has developed this argument, arguing that England has a major political core-periphery within it, which was a matrix within which electoral choices were mobilized. He concludes (p. S102):

> By the end of the 19th century peripheral Britain had been mobilized solidly (except western Lancashire) for Gladstonian Liberalism, and core Britain for Unionism. In the 20th century Labour and Conservative have reflected the same dichotomy (with Labour taking western Lancashire but losing the Southwest).

The core is *lowland* England, focused on London, the core of Tory support, and its growing support, in 1987. (If Steed is correct, then 1945 and, to a lesser extent, 1949 and 1951 were aberrant elections because of Labour success in the core. Thus 1955 – the watershed election identified by Curtice and Steed, 1982 – was really a return to the situation in the 1930s: Johnston and Doornkamp, 1982.)

Curtice and Steed's conclusions have been followed up by Bodman (1985) in an analysis using the same set of geographical regions employed in this book. (Unfortunately, the procedure he uses to describe regional variations has been strongly criticised – Johnston and Taylor, 1987 – so it is not clear how valid his findings are in detail.) He argues that there was no increased regional polarisation over the period 1950–1983, because

> Both parties [Conservative and Labour] gained support in some of the regions where they had been weak and both exhibited negative trends where they had previously enjoyed high levels of support (p. 293)

The Conservative party's performance improved in every non-metropolitan region in the south, but Labour has not similarly improved throughout the north (except in Scotland). This suggests to Bodman that

> the simple North:South distinction used previously to describe electoral variation misses some of the regional subtleties (p. 294)

What those subtleties are, and why, we hope to identify here.

IN SUMMARY

Whether or not the British electorate has become more sophisticated over the last few decades, there can be no doubt that analysis of that electorate has. A simple class cleavage certainly does not exist now, and possibly never did. Instead, the electorate is portrayed as one that is mobilised in particular social contexts to affiliate (ideologically if not formally) with a particular political party, but those affiliations are then eroded by the competing claims of the parties to promote certain policies and the voters' evaluations of the veracity of those claims.

For some analysts, the processes of mobilisation, socialisation and evaluation are not spatially differentiated; they are uniform across the national territory. Dunleavy and Husbands (1985, p. 20) express this view clearly, arguing that most people most of the time act instrumentally to further the interests of their social location. They do not undertake an analysis of their individual household situation but rather act to promote the collective interests of their social location, as these have been defined in their society.

To others, such as Whiteley, however, those bonds to social locations are increasingly being broken, as they evaluate parties in terms of their personal circumstances. For Miller, and for Curtice and Steed, that process of evaluation appears increasingly to be related to people's spatial rather than social location, and it is that environmental influence in recent years that we turn to in the next chapter.

3

THE ELECTORAL CONTEXT, 1979-1987

The works reviewed in Chapter 2 illustrate one of the major features of developments in contemporary social theory. As Thrift (1983) describes it, much theory until recently has been *compositional*, arguing that behaviour is a function of social position. Thus, knowledge of individuals' characteristics on key variables allows them to be categorised (allocated to a particular niche within the, usually national, social structure), and it is assumed that they will also display the attitudes and behaviour typical of their category. The class cleavage in voting studies is a clear example of such a compositional theory. Against this a few writers posit *contextual* theories, contending that it is spatial and not social location that is the major influence, if not determinant, of behaviour.

Contemporary developments in social theory suggest the necessity for a fusion of the compositional and contextual approaches. People learn the meaning of a social location, they argue, in a particular spatial context where they are socialised into an appreciation of both the meaning of the characteristics they possess and those that others have. To the extent that spatial contexts vary, so will interpretation of social structure and niches within it. Few studies of voting in Britain have accepted this (as Johnston, 1986d, argues), and yet without recognition that Britain is itself a complex mosaic of local cultures appreciation of why people vote in the ways that they do is likely to be partial. Geography matters, according to strong arguments (e.g. Massey, 1984a, 1984b), arguments that we accept here. To explore how it has mattered with regard to recent trends in voting within Britain, we need to explore what the relevant geography has been.

CHANGING GEOGRAPHICAL CONTEXTS

The weight of the evidence reviewed in the previous chapter suggests the following summary:

1. The major cleavage within British society around which the two main

political parties (Conservative and Labour) mobilised support up to 1983 was occupational class.

2.   The success of those mobilisation efforts was spatially variable reflecting particular local circumstances. The result was that the contexts in which people have been politically socialised have varied substantially, sustaining a major pattern of geographical variation of voting behaviour. In general, each party is stronger where it has a more substantial electoral base, according to the occupational class structure of constituencies.

3.   Increasingly, when making their electoral choices people are taking account of the relative performance of the parties, their own perception of the future, and their views on how the parties and their leaders might influence the future if they were in power.

4.   Spatial variations in voting patterns have increased in recent decades, so that the electorate is more polarised by geographical and functional regions, as well as by class, than was the case.

Our task here is to link these conclusions to a study of the 1979–87 period, which requires a brief survey of those eight years.

The Conservative party won the general election of 1979 from a Labour government which had experienced major economic difficulties, had presided over substantial increases in the rates of inflation and of unemployment (countering the traditional view – p. 54 – that there is a trade-off between the two), and, in its last months, had to deal with a series of major strikes in the public sector that affected the lives of many people during a particularly hard winter. The Conservative slogan 'Labour isn't working' was used to focus on the unemployment problem, whereas the description of the early months of 1979 as the 'winter of discontent' drew attention to the strikes of that period, suggesting that Labour was no longer credible in its claim that it was the best party for dealing with the unions. The Conservatives offered to restore prosperity, by dealing firmly with the unions, by reducing inflation through control of the money supply, and by encouraging job creation via policies to reward enterprise and investment. As Sarlvik and Crewe (1983) explain it, this campaign was particularly successful in winning over working class Labour voters to the Conservative cause.

During the period of the first Conservative government under Margaret Thatcher (from 1979 to 1983), the rate of inflation was rapidly reduced, after an initial increase largely caused by the switch from income tax to VAT, but the level of unemployment continued to rise. By 1982, the party's popularity with the electorate was very low (below 30 per cent said they would vote Conservative at the beginning of the year, according to the Gallup polls). But Labour was experiencing great difficulties in convincing the electorate that it was a credible alternative, because of major internal debates over party organisation and policy; by December 1981 its rating in the polls was as low as that of the Conservatives. As a consequence of that bitter, public debate, several leading members of the Labour party broke away and in March 1981 formed the Social Democratic party. Later in that year this party formed an electoral Alliance with the Liberals which by December had a very substantial lead in the opinion polls. But then, from April 1982 on, there was a resurgence of support for the Conservative party based, as reviewed above (pp. 53-54), on more optimistic economic forecasts by voters following government success in controlling inflation though not in reducing the unemployment rate. Thus the Conservatives were re-elected in 1983 with a massive majority, despite a decline in their percentage of the vote. The divided opposition enabled this, for, according to Butler and Kavanagh (1984, p. 293), it was a grudging victory, given to the Conservatives more as a way of keeping Labour out than as an expression of support for much of what the Conservatives proposed to do. Opinion polls, they reported,

> found that voters' expectations were lower than those which greeted the Conservatives in 1979. In 1983 there was more pessimism about the government's ability to improve matters in relation to taxes, jobs, living standards, or the unions: there was more confidence only over handling the EEC and controlling inflation.

Over the next few years, that confidence was rewarded with continued falls in the level of inflation and with relative success in EEC negotiations. But unemployment continued to rise, and over three million were registered as such in the run-up to the 1987 election. Many new jobs were being created, in service industries especially, but in insufficient numbers to provide for all the potential workforce, especially the young. During this period, too, the government initiated major changes in the welfare state, notably in education, and argued for much more private involvement; many state assets were sold off (privatised) and increasingly the Conservative party presented itself as presiding over a radical revolution, producing an economy and society better able to compete in the world-economy. It won another convincing electoral victory in 1987, again despite a widespread feeling in the electorate (as reported by Curtice, 1986) that the shifts were too radical; the Labour party revived from the nadir in its fortunes in 1983, though it still failed to convince the electorate of its credibility on certain issues; the Alliance advance faltered badly.

During the 1983-1987 period the Conservative government also carried forward its plans to reduce the power of the trades unions, and especially what it identified as unaccountable and unrepresentative union leaderships. Laws were introduced requiring compulsory ballots for the regular re-selection of union executives with voting rights in union affairs and on the decision to raise a political levy. These were part of the campaign, as it was often presented, to 'destroy socialism', and were backed by arguments claiming that the majority of union members voted Conservative in 1983 (in fact a majority voted other than Labour but, according to Dunleavy and Husbands, 1985, p. 132, the Conservative and Labour parties each got 34 per cent of the votes of union members and the Alliance got 32). Labour was no longer the 'natural party' of the stereotype working class voters, it seemed (though Dunleavy and Husbands' figures dispute this; Labour won a substantial majority of votes among manual workers in both sectors but the Conservatives won an even bigger majority among private-sector non-manual unionists), because many unionists now realised that the Conservatives were best able to control the militant minorities who won control and led unions undemocratically.

The Conservative campaigns to reduce union power and win support from trade unionists were linked during the period of their second government to two major disputes. The first was the year-long National Union of Mineworkers' strike in 1984–1985 and the second the dispute over the opening of News International Ltd's new printing works in Wapping, from which their Gray's Inn Road and Fleet Street printing workers and unions were excluded. Both were marked by scenes of violence that were widely shown on television and used by Conservatives to promote their policies regarding both law and order and control of the unions. The Labour party was presented as unable to cope with either of these problems, because the unions dominated, and substantially financed, it.

Dealing with the unions was just part of the Conservatives' economic strategy; to some extent it could be seen as 'gaining revenge' on the unions for their role in engineering the downfall of the Heath government in 1974, but it was presented as one element of a larger package designed to promote economic restructuring. The rhetoric underlying that package focused on the belief that British industry was inefficient, as a consequence of three interacting factors: the strength of the unions meant that many industries were over-manned and had low productivity as a consequence; the size of the state-controlled sector was too large, because those industries were not accountable in the same way that private sector firms were; and the size of the welfare state meant that state borrowing in the money markets was much too large, with consequences on the level of investment in research and development. The Conservatives' goal was to make British industry more productive and efficient – 'leaner and fitter' – and thus better able to compete in world markets. To achieve this, they argued that it was necessary to: reduce public spending and borrowing, thereby reducing the cost of money and encouraging investment; place nationalised industries and parts of the welfare state in the private sector, thereby making them more accountable to market forces and hence more efficient; reduce the power of the unions; and withdraw support from inefficient industries. The result was a major restructuring of the economy, as detailed below, not so much because of direct government action as because of the removal of a whole range of protective measures for what were seen as inefficient outfits.

This major change could not be achieved very rapidly, nor even in one Parliament (though a comparable shift was achieved in New Zealand in less than three years: James, 1986). Thus it was necessary for the Conservative party to promote a new ideology that glorified inventors and investors (such as Sir Clive Sinclair), people who were prepared to put money into new ventures and to develop new ways of working. This required an environment conducive to such activities, and creating it involved a number of linked policies. Higher education institutions were criticised, in a government Green Paper, for example, for sustaining an 'anti-business culture' and steps were taken to reduce their dependence on state funding and reorient their research and teaching towards government perceptions of 'national needs'; similar moves with regard to the school system were indicated in the 1987 Conservative election manifesto. People who made fortunes in the city were fêted and honoured by the government, which sought to involve the population more directly in the market operations by promoting share ownership; the sales of government-owned enterprises were oriented towards the 'small shareholders', such that whereas in 1983 56 per cent of all shareholders were in the higher status white-collar occupations, four years later the percentage was only 29; among skilled manual workers, the percentage increased from 12 to 26 (*The Observer*, 26 October, 1987, p. 68).

Whilst the Conservative government was advancing this radical programme it was aided in the period prior to the 1983 general election by the dissension within the Labour party. After 1983, Labour regrouped its forces under a new leadership, but was particularly vulnerable to Conservative attacks on the defence issue, because of internal divisions between unilateralist and multilateralist nuclear disarmers, and on the left-wing policies of some local governments with Labour councils. The Alliance declined somewhat, largely because of a division between the two leaders which gave some the impression that it lacked a sense of purpose.

THE SPATIAL CONSEQUENCES I: UNEMPLOYMENT

Over the period that we are concerned with, therefore, the Conservative governments led by Margaret Thatcher have presided over a series of major economic changes that have had substantial social consequences. These changes and consequences have been spatially very variable. This is shown, for example, in the geography of unemployment. Depicting this geography, and its change, is made somewhat difficult by the alterations in definitions adopted by the government's statistical agencies over the period (see SEEDS, 1987). Nevertheless, the two cartograms here of unemployment as defined (a) by the 1981 Census and (b) by the government's *Employment Gazette* for December 1986 (Figures 3.1 and 3.2) clearly show a well-defined spatial structure.

Unemployment was greatest in 1981 in four main areas: the West Midlands, especially parts of Birmingham; Merseyside, especially Liverpool and its eastern suburbs; Tyne and Wear and Co. Durham; and Strathclyde, mainly Glasgow. All four of these concentrations were in the older industrial areas, whereas in much of southeastern England, and especially in London's commuter belt, unemployment rates were below 10 per cent (Figure 3.1); even within London itself, only three constituencies recorded unemployment percentages in excess of 15.0, although 22 exceeded the national figure of ten per cent. Most of South Wales, too, recorded unemployment rates above the national average.

Four years later, the same pattern was recorded, though with some additional 'black spots' (Figure 3.2). In addition to the four concentrations of constituencies with high percentages of unemployed, additional nodes in

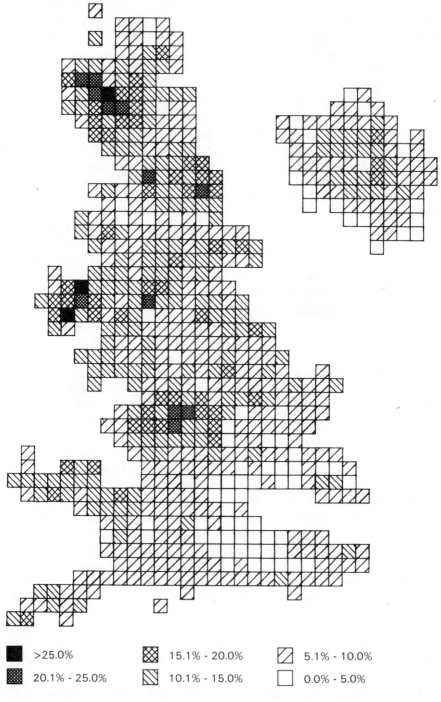

Figure 3.1 The geography of unemployment, by constituency, according to the 1981 Census.

Legend:

- ████ >25.0%
- ▓▓▓▓ 20.1% - 25.0%
- ▒▒▒▒ 15.1% - 20.0%
- ◺◺◺◺ 10.1% - 15.0%
- ⁄⁄⁄⁄ 5.1% - 10.0%
- □□□□ 0.0% - 5.0%

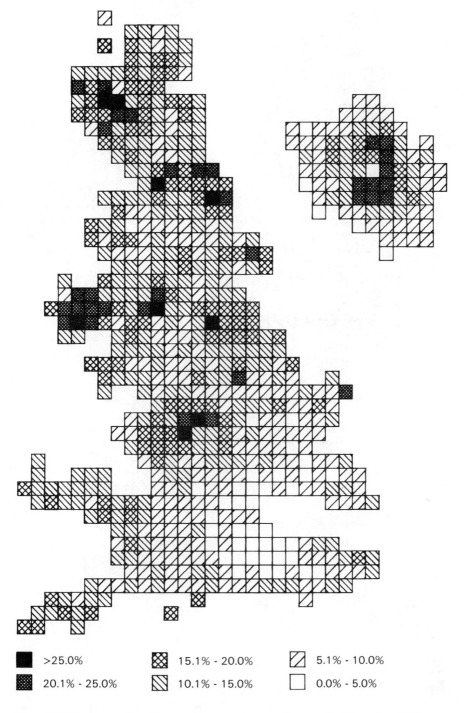

Figure 3.2 The geography of unemployment, by constituency, in December 1986.

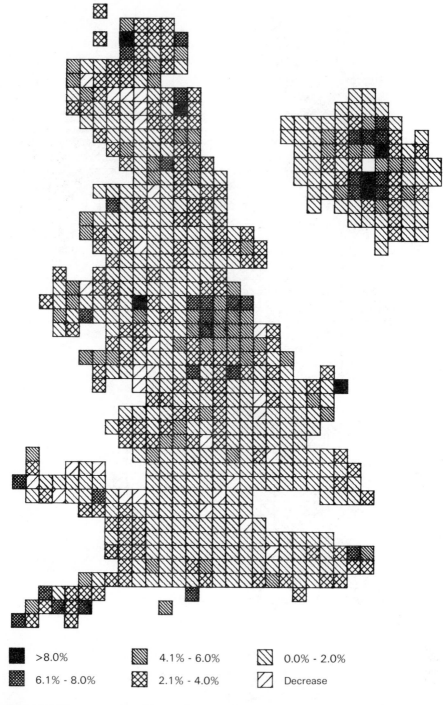

Figure 3.3 The geography of unemployment change, 1981–1986.

Greater Manchester, South Yorkshire, North Humberside and Inner London stand out, again in marked contrast to the low percentages (compared to the national average of 12.5 per cent) in most of the southeast (where only the resorts of North Thanet and the Isle of Wight, plus Portsmouth South, recorded more than 15 per cent unemployed).

These changes are brought into sharper focus by Figure 3.3, which shows the differences between the two previous maps. (As already noted, changes in the definition of unemployed make comparisons over the period difficult, but the relative shifts shown here are undoubtedly faithful reflections of the changing geography of unemployment.) The largest block of constituencies experiencing well-above-average growth in unemployment is in South Yorkshire, particularly the adjacent Metropolitan Districts of Barnsley, Rotherham and Sheffield where there was major decline of the steel industry. Devon and Cornwall, too, experienced major growth in unemployed numbers, as did Inner London and many of those parts of Scotland (including Edinburgh) that had relatively low unemployment in 1981.

Table 3.1   The Changing Geography of Unemployment, 1981–1986, by geographical region

	Mean Unemployment Rate (%)		Mean Unemployment Change	
	1981	1986	Percentage Points	Per Cent 1981
Strathclyde	15.8	17.8	2.0	12.6
E. Scotland	10.0	13.8	3.8	38.0
Rural Scotland	9.0	13.1	4.1	45.5
Rural North	9.2	11.7	2.5	27.1
Industrial Northeast	14.6	17.6	3.0	20.6
Merseyside	16.4	19.3	2.9	17.7
Greater Manchester	11.9	14.2	2.3	19.3
Rest of Northwest	10.2	12.5	2.3	22.5
West Yorks.	10.5	12.7	2.2	21.0
South Yorks.	11.3	17.5	6.2	54.9
Rural Wales	11.8	14.5	2.7	22.9
Industrial South Wales	13.7	14.2	0.5	3.6
West Midlands Conurbation	14.3	16.8	2.5	17.5
Rest of West Midlands	9.0	10.6	1.6	17.8
East Midlands	8.6	11.2	2.6	30.2
East Anglia	7.7	9.9	2.2	28.5
Devon and Cornwall	9.7	13.8	4.1	42.2
Wessex	7.4	9.5	2.1	28.4
Inner London	11.8	17.1	5.3	44.9
Outer London	6.8	8.5	1.7	25.0
Outer Metropolitan	5.9	6.6	0.7	11.9
Outer Southeast	7.4	9.6	2.2	29.7
National	10.0	12.5	2.5	25.0

Table 3.2 The Changing Geography of Unemployment, 1981–1986, by functional region

	Mean Unemployment Rate (%)		Mean Unemployment Change	
	1979	1986	Percentage Points	Per Cent 1981
I.C./Immig.	11.3	14.9	3.6	31.8
Ind./Immig.	14.1	16.5	2.4	17.0
Poorest Immig.	21.1	25.2	4.1	19.4
Intermed. Ind.	10.6	13.2	2.6	24.5
Old Indust./Mining	11.9	14.1	2.2	18.5
Textile	11.0	11.9	0.9	8.2
Poorest Domestic	16.7	18.4	1.7	10.2
Conurb. L.A.	14.2	17.5	3.3	23.2
Black Co.	15.8	17.9	2.1	13.3
Maritime Ind.	17.2	19.5	2.3	13.4
Poor I.C..	18.2	24.3	6.1	33.5
Clydeside	17.4	19.9	2.5	14.4
Scott. Ind.	13.6	16.0	2.4	17.6
Scott. Rural	8.3	12.1	3.8	45.8
High Status I.M.	9.8	14.0	4.2	42.9
I.M.	12.2	18.3	6.1	50.0
Outer London	5.6	6.7	1.1	19.6
Very High Status	5.3	5.9	0.6	11.3
Conurb. W. Collar	7.8	11.2	3.4	43.6
City Service	10.8	14.8	4.0	37.0
Resort/Retirement	9.0	12.5	3.5	38.9
Recent Growth	10.3	13.2	2.9	28.2
Stable Ind.	9.1	10.8	1.7	18.7
Small Towns	8.2	10.9	2.7	32.9
Southern Urban	6.0	7.6	1.6	26.7
Modest Aff.	7.7	9.0	1.3	16.9
Met. Ind.	7.8	9.3	1.5	19.2
Modest Aff. Scot.	8.2	10.9	2.7	32.9
Rapid Growth	5.7	6.3	0.6	10.5
Prosperous/No Ind.	6.4	8.3	1.9	30.0
Agricultural	7.9	10.3	2.4	30.4
National	10.0	12.5	2.5	25.0

Inspection of these cartograms suggests that both the levels of unemployment and the rates of change in those levels were spatially extremely variable, and this is confirmed by Tables 3.1 and 3.2 which summarise the geographies of unemployment by geographical and functional regions, as well as the pattern of unemployment change as it can best be described by comparing the two data sets (Figure 3.3). At the geographical regional scale (Table 3.1), the differences between the south and north of Great Britain in 1981 are clearly illustrated: in the former all but Inner London had a rate below the national level, whereas this was the case with only two regions (Rural Scotland and Rural North) further north. In the intervening five years, two of those regions were among those with the highest increases in unemployment, bringing Rural Scotland in line with the rest of that country and further accentuating the divide between Inner London and the rest of the southeastern area. The other two large rises (both absolutely and relatively) saw Devon and Cornwall apparently detached from the relative prosperity of the southern half of Britain plus a massive increase in South Yorkshire, consequent upon the major cutbacks in the steel industry there. Overall, however, the north–south differential was maintained.

Turning to the functional regions (Table 3.2) we see a much greater range in unemployment rates, from levels approximately half the national value in the Very High Status region to those double it in the Poorest Immigrant areas. Once again there is a clear general division between the relatively deprived regions (towards the top of the table) and the more affluent. Some of the latter experienced above-national average increases in unemployment over the five years in relative terms, because of their low 1981 base, and some of the hardest hit regions in 1981 suffered only relatively small increases to 1986. But the differentials were narrowed only slightly and there remains no doubt that certain functional regions suffered much more than others in the shake-out that was supposed to result in a leaner, fitter, more competitive British industry.

THE SPATIAL CONSEQUENCES II:
CHANGES IN OCCUPATIONAL STRUCTURE

Just as unemployment has been spatially concentrated over the period, so has the pattern of new job creation, the source of prosperity for some. As Hall (1987) demonstrates, during the late 1970s and early 1980s there was a major decline in manufacturing industries (1.8m jobs lost between 1978 and 1983) that was only partly countered by a growth in the service sector (621,000 jobs created in the same period, mainly in the information sector). Within the manufacturing sector there have been substantial shifts, however, with employment declines ranging from 16 per cent in chemicals to 53 per cent in metals (Keeble, 1987). The main growth (relatively if not absolutely) has been in the high-technology industries associated with electronics and, especially, defence.

There have been substantial changes to the geography of economic activity as a consequence of the net changes summarised here. Figure 3.4 shows this with regard to the geography of manufacturing activity over the two decades 1965–1985. Six of the ten standard regions in Great Britain (i.e. excluding Northern Ireland) experienced declines in their percentage of the country's manufacturing jobs, whereas the other four – the Southwest, the Southeast, East Midlands, and East Anglia – experienced increases, clearly indicating a north to south shift in the relative prosperity of the manufacturing sector. (The regions that lost shares were those which were covered, in part or totally, for all or part of the period, by various regional policy programmes to aid development areas: maps of these areas are provided in Townsend, 1987. Moore, Rhodes and Tylor, 1986, have estimated that these programmes led to the es-

Figure 3.4 The changing geography of manufacturing: regional percentage shares of UK manufacturing employment, 1965–1985. (Source: Keeble, 1987, p. 13.)

tablishment of 450,000 jobs that were still extant in 1981, with a multiplier effect producing a further 180,000. And yet, as they note on p. 12, 'For regional policy to have solved the regional problem in the decade of the 1960s, policy would have had to be two to three times more effective than it actually was. For regional policy to have solved the problem of the 1970s, regional policy would have had to have been about three times more effective'. Much was done to try and sustain the north relative to the south, but even more was necessary to stop the growing polarisation in terms of manufacturing-industry induced prosperity. The degree to which this shortfall represents a lack of political will remains an open question: see, for example, Sharpe, 1982. The reduction in both the volume of regional aid and the number of areas qualifying for it – Townsend, 1987 – was part of the Conservative party's programme of withdrawing support from inefficient industries and forcing restructuring.)

These inter-regional shifts are very substantial, but so too are the intra-regional net movements, especially within the four expanding regions of the south and east. Nationally, the U.K. lost 23.5 per cent of its manufacturing jobs between 1971 and 1981. The eight conurbations lost 34.3 per cent, the more urbanized counties (e.g. Lancashire, Cleveland) lost 16.2 per cent, the less urbanized counties 15.4 per cent and the more rural counties only 11.3 per cent (Keeble, 1987, p. 10). The fastest growing places were the medium-sized towns of the southeast, by and large. Of the twenty towns with the fastest employment growth between 1971 and 1981, only one – Aberdeen (the focus of oil-related industries) – was outside those four regions, and none of the other nineteen had a population much in excess of 100,000 (Begg and Moore, 1987, p. 55). Thus prosperity based on manufacturing jobs in recent decades has been focused on the small and medium-sized towns of the Southeast and Southwest, the East Midlands, and East Anglia.

The relative success of those four regions is a function of several factors. First, they contain relatively small proportions of the industries that have declined most in recent years, and so should have remained relatively buoyant. In addition, however, as Damesick's (1987) statistical analysis of the 1978–81 period shows, those four regions have also experienced less decline in the industries concentrated there than has been the case nationally. They contain within them the M4 high-tech corridor, the major developments around Cambridge, and most of the country's defence contractors, for example, focused on the major routeways that radiate from London, Heathrow airport, and a large number of government, private sector, and university/polytechnic research establishments (see, for example, Cooke, 1987). Thus, as Damesick (1987, p. 27) describes it:

> many less urbanized areas of Southern England . . . have benefited from a particular conjunction of attributes and influences which have helped them to develop new sources of growth, especially in the more technologically advanced sectors of industry. If national industrial regeneration and employment creation are, in line with current government hopes . . . , to be strongly based in the exploitation of new technologies and the expansion of new and small businesses, then this will tend to favour areas where conditions have already proved to be most conducive to innova-

tion and new firm foundation and growth. Present indications are that these areas are predominantly located south and east of a Severn-Wash divide.

Alongside these changes in manufacturing employment have been shifts in the service sector. Over the decade 1971–1981, employment in services increased by 15.3 per cent in Great Britain but, as Figure 3.5a shows, the largest growth was in the four regions that also experienced least manufacturing decline (Southeast, East Anglia, East Midlands, and Southwest). Services can be divided into those serving consumers (mainly wholesale and retail distribution) and those serving producers (insurance, banking, finance and other business services). Both increased their employment over the decade to 1981, but producer services at twice the rate of consumer services (35.9 and 17.6 per cent respectively). And, as Figures 3.5b and 3.5c show, the growth in that most buoyant sector of the economy has been much greater in the three southern regions (excluding Greater London) but most new jobs have been provided in the office developments along the M4 corridor. Gillespie and Green's (1987) analyses of the changing geography of employment in producer services (insurance, banking, advertising, accountancy, legal services, R and D, etc.) by types of labour market between 1971 and 1981 clearly shows this. London dominates, in that producer services are a larger proportion of employment there than elsewhere, but growth there over the decade, at 14.7 per cent, was less than half the national figure of 35.5. Places like Portsmouth, Southend, Norwich, Wellingborough and even Penzance have experienced much more rapid growth overall, but different services have different geographies: R and D clearly decentralized over the decade into the Outer Southeast region, for example, whereas insurance has remained concentrated in major regional centres (such as Edinburgh).

In terms of new jobs, therefore, it is the south and east of England that have been the most buoyant parts of Great Britain. Other smaller nodes of relative prosperity have developed, in parts of Cheshire, for example, and those sectors of Central Scotland known as Silicon Glen, but the main trend is for an emphasis of the north:south divide. As manufacturing has been restructured and the service industries have grown, so the regions that were the core of Britain's nineteenth century industrial prosperity have declined.

Together these two geographies, of unemployment and of new job creation, provide a firm base for suggesting that there should be geographical variations in response to the government at the ballot box. In the areas with high and continuing unemployment one would expect much less confidence in the government as able to stimulate job creation and prosperity than in the areas with low unemployment and many new jobs. In terms of the retrospective and prospective evaluation processes described by Whiteley and others (see p. 52), one would expect greater credit for and optimism in the government in some areas than in others. This would be in line with Curtice and Steed's argument which has as yet been untested with survey or other data.

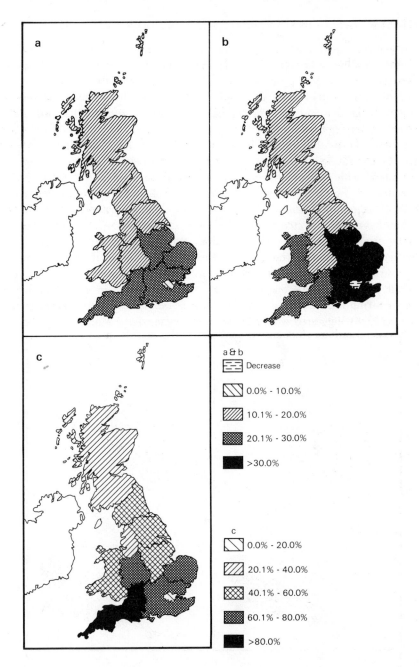

Figure 3.5 The changing geography of service employment, 1971–1981: a – all services; b – consumer services; c – producer services. (Source: data from Damesick, 1987.)

THE SPATIAL CONSEQUENCES III: PROPERTY VALUES

A further consequence of the government's econonomic restructuring policies and the new geographies of employment has been a substantial spatial polarisation in changing property prices. There are two causes of this. The first is the differential geography of supply and demand; in the areas of relative prosperity, the demand for housing has been greater and this has stimulated increased inter-regional differentials in property prices (as Hamnett, 1983, has illustrated). Those differentials have been exacerbated by two further factors. First, in the southeastern regions the booming financial services sector has been linked with extremely high incomes for those involved in, for example, successful dealing on the money markets and stock exchanges of the world. As Thrift, Leyshon and Daniels (1987) have shown, these substantial discretionary incomes have been directed towards major consumer goods, including housing, thereby stimulating house price inflation: this is particularly focused at the upper end of the market, both within London itself and in the large homes of its suburbs and exurbs, but has filtered down through the entire system. Secondly, the relatively poor prospects for investment in many sectors of manufacturing industry have stimulated the search for alternative strategies; as Harvey (1978) suggested would be the case, some of this money has gone into

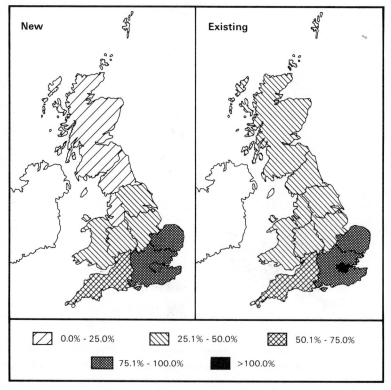

Figure 3.6 The changing pattern of house prices, 1983–1987. (Source: data from the Halifax Building Society).

the built environment, further fuelling the house price inflation in the London area, where most of the investment has been directed.

The consequences of these shifts, at the macro-scale, are illustrated in Figure 3.6, which shows changes in the prices of new houses (as computed by the Halifax Building Society) over the period 1983–1987. The differences across the Severn:Wash, north:south divide are clear, with prices increasing almost four times faster in Greater London than in the North. In the third quarter of 1987, the average price of a detached house in Greater London was £147,716, compared to £49,720 in Wales; for a terraced house, the average purchaser in the North paid £22,058 and in Greater London £76,343. Differences between towns were even greater, leading a journalist to note that 'a home buyer in Mansfield or Doncaster can buy five semi-detached houses for the price of one in London' (*The Independent*, 9 October, 1987, p. 5). These shifts not only result in greater interregional differences in people's equity holdings but also reduce the possibility of people moving from the areas of job shortage to those of relative plenty.

It is widely appreciated among psephologists and others that owner-occupiers of housing are more likely to vote Conservative than are tenants, because the free-market ideology of the Conservative party is consistent with their wish to reap the capital gains that they receive from property value increases. (This is part of the case for a consumption-sector cleavage developed by Dunleavy, 1979.) The greater the rate of inflation in property values, the greater that support is likely to be, from owner-occupiers who have more to lose from any political actions (probably introduced by a Labour government) that would threaten those values. To the extent that the inflation varies regionally, therefore, so the desire to vote to sustain it will vary; owner-occupiers where property values are low and rising only slowly have less to lose than those with expensive, rapidly-appreciating investments. Johnston (1987b) has tested this hypothesis on 1983 survey data, and found it valid.

A further change in the housing market since 1979 has been the government's insistence that council tenants should have the right to buy their homes from the local authorities that were renting them. In part, the take-up of this right has reflected the characteristics of the dwellings – houses have been much more popular than flats among buyers, for example. But there are also major spatial variations, as Dunn, Forrest and Murie (1987) have shown for England (Figure 3.7). In general, sales have been greatest in southern areas; Dunn et al. show that the authorities with the largest percentages of sales have been those with most houses (rather than flats), most young families, fewest male unemployed and with Conservative control of the local authority. To the extent that several of these variables (notably low unemployment, houses rather than flats, and Conservative control) are regionally differentiated they suggest regional differentials in embourgeoisement and its political effects (p. 56). Further, they weaken the pro-Labour solidarity of the council house estates (which is weaker in rural areas in any case: Johnston, 1987a), that is reflected in the geography of voting by council house tenants (Johnston, 1987b).

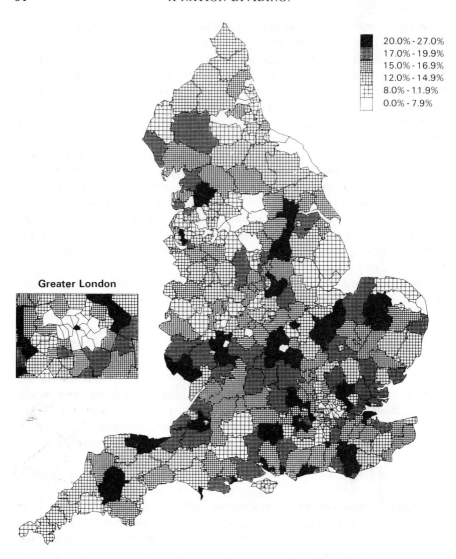

Figure 3.7 Spatial variations (by local authority) in the sale of council houses. (Source:
Dunn, Forrest and Murie, 1987.)

THE SPATIAL CONSEQUENCES IV:
CENTRAL AND LOCAL GOVERNMENT

Apart from the economic restructuring policies, several other aspects of government policy have had spatially differentiated impacts. Important among
these has been the attempt to control and reorganise local government spending. As part of the strategy of reducing inflation, the Conservative governments have been determined to curb local government spending and the
central contribution to it (largely through the Rate Support Grant), thereby to

reduce the Public Sector Borrowing Requirement, limit the public sector demand for capital in the money markets, produce lower interest rates, and stimulate borrowing for investment in new jobs. This has involved continuing attempts to control what are seen to be unnecessary levels of expenditure by local governments, not only on social services but also on a wide range of other activities. Labour-controlled local governments have been under considerable attack for such policies, leading to the characterisation of some by Conservative politicians as being under the control of the 'loony left'.

A major element in this campaign has been a series of attempts to reduce the amount of money made available by central government to local governments to meet necessary expenditure and equalise for differences in the resource on which local finance is raised, property values. Limits to Rate Support Grant were imposed in the early 1980s (see Bennett, 1982) and these were followed by rate-capping legislation which limited, by law, what each local government could spend initially without raising local rates substantially (which, it was hoped, voter reaction at local elections would limit), and then by straight central government order. This produced much conflict between the two arms of the state apparatus, and in 1985 led to near-revolts by several councils over whether to set a local rate. Liverpool City Council was much in the headlines over this, as it approached bankruptcy; eventually a large number of its councillors were found guilty of maladministration and debarred from holding office, and several of them were expelled by the Labour party. These actions did not all have the anticipated impact, however. Sheffield City Council, for example, raised its rates and won more seats at the next election; at the election after the removal of Labour councillors in Liverpool, that party won a majority again. Local campaigns against the central government – which was accused of retaining money which by rights should have been allocated to the local governments – mobilised voters to support local against central government, though they were clearly more successful in some places (such as Liverpool and Sheffield) than in others (such as parts of Greater London).

In 1985 the government also got a bill through the Commons and (with much difficulty) the Lords which led to abolition of the Greater London County Council (GLC) and the six Metropolitan County Councils (Tyne and Wear, Merseyside, Greater Manchester, West Yorkshire, South Yorkshire, and the West Midlands) on 1 April, 1986. Analysts differ over the real reasons for this. The rationale provided by the government for abolition proposals covered two areas (Secretary of State for the Environment, 1983). First, the GLC and the metropolitan counties were excessive spenders and provided their overtaxed ratepayers with poor value for money: the links with other aspects of Conservative policy towards local government, discussed above, are clear. Second, the GLC and the metropolitan counties provided only a limited number of services: they had failed to find a function. Abolition, it was argued, would remove a superfluous layer of bureaucracy at considerable savings to the public purse, and would thus considerably simplify urban government. However, these claims were challenged even before the legislation had passed through Parliament. The government failed to provide detailed costings of the savings it expected to be associated with abolition. An analysis of the likely outcome undertaken by a leading accountancy firm on behalf of the threatened authorities suggested that, first, the case for excessive expenditure was poorly argued: much of the increase in spending experienced by the metropolitan counties was the result of high levels of inflation for the goods and services provided by them. Second, far from providing savings, abolition of the authorities was likely to lead to increased local spending (Coopers and Lybrand, 1983, 1984). Furthermore, the metropolitan authorities provided essential strategic services which could only be provided on a metropolitan-wide basis (Bristow, 1984). In fact, many of these functions were to remain in the hands of non-elected city-wide joint boards after abolition: clearly, the metropolitan authorities did have a role (Duncan and Goodwin, 1985; O'Leary, 1987). It is difficult to find reasons for abolition in the economic and administrative arguments advanced by government, therefore.

For many commentators, mainly drawn from the political left, abolition was an attempt to remove a troublesome vestige of working-class political power. At the time of abolition, all of the metropolitan counties and the GLC were controlled by the Labour party and several (most notably the GLC and South Yorkshire) had come to be closely associated with the new urban left (Gyford, 1986; Gurr and King, 1987) and more generally, it has been argued that local government is more open to working class control than is central government (Duncan and Goodwin, 1982; Byrne, 1982). As a result, local authorities can provide a daily reminder that alternatives exist, not only to government policy but also to capitalism. For Duncan and Goodwin, the 'fear of locally expressed alternatives reached its extreme with the legislation to abolish the GLC and the Metropolitan Councils' (1985, p. 30). However, they emphasise that this fear is by no means limited to the present government. Ironically, it has been argued that the metropolitan authorities were first established as a result of a similar wish to loosen working class control of urban local government through restructuring (Dearlove, 1979; O'Leary, 1987). Saunders (1984) sees the abolition proposals as a means of completing this restructuring process.

However, as O'Leary (1987) points out, a number of abolished authorities changed hands regularly in the past. Indeed, he argues that, had it not been for the controversy which surrounded the abolition debate, the surge in support enjoyed by the London Labour party in 1985 and early 1986 (see also Husbands, 1985) would not have occurred and the Conservatives would have been likely to regain control of the GLC at least in the next round of local elections (a round which did not occur, thanks to abolition). The argument that abolition was an attempt to disenfranchise the left is not clear-cut. Indeed, in many respects, the enactment of the abolition legislation was extremely damaging for the government, particularly in the metropolitan areas (Husbands, 1985: however, the rally in Labour support at this time seems to have had more to do with opposition to abolition than with positive support for Labour, since, in London at least, it evaporated over the subsequent year). For O'Leary, abolition has its roots partly in the economic nostrums of the government (curbing local spending) and partly in the political confrontation between the local Labour left and the Conservative government. However, he goes further to find explanations peculiar to the operation of the Thatcher cabinet. Abolition 'emerged on the Prime Minister's agenda because of the need to disguise the failure of the first Thatcher government promise to abolish rates . . . [A]bolition [was] offered as a sop to the Prime Minister' (O'Leary, 1987, p. 213; Pickvance, 1986; Duncan and Goodwin, 1985; for the importance of rate reform to the Conservatives under Margaret Thatcher, see King, 1979). It was a stop-gap measure, then, not a fully-considered policy and as such it was a late addition to the Conservative's 1983 election manifesto (Gurr and King, 1987). This explains why the economic, administrative and political explanations for abolition outlined above are at best partial: abolition was not the only solution to these problems open to government, particularly in the context of the ratecapping powers of the central state. O'Leary argues that abolition was a folly, in that members of the government realised that it would cause serious political problems and was not the only policy open. It was adhered to, however, for two reasons, he claims. First, the closed nature of the Conservative Cabinet silenced opposition to the policy at the outset and the Conservatives' massive Parliamentary majority, gained in 1983, lulled the government into an overestimate both of its political power and of its public popularity. Second, the confrontational, conviction-style politics espoused by Mrs. Thatcher (the 'resolute approach') made an about-turn on abolition unthinkable, despite the massive adverse criticism. The style with which the government proposed abolition, as much as the content of its proposals, served to rally opposition, both inside and outside Parliament (O'Leary, 1987; Husbands, 1985; Duncan and Goodwin, 1985).

The geography of the central government:local government conflict during this period is a complex one, because it has involved several issues. In general, it was greatest in relatively deprived urban areas, though not in all of them by any means, since local councils, indeed local councils run by the Labour party, differed greatly in the degree to which they were prepared to challenge central authority. The main centres of conflict were in those councils where the Labour party was controlled by what has become known as the 'New Urban Left' (Gyford, 1986), largely militant young professionals who won control of ward parties and, when elected, become virtually 'full-time' politicians. They were typical of the libertarian egalitarians identified by Robertson (1984; see p. 59 above) and many, such as Ken Livingstone and David Blunkett (Boddy and Fudge, 1984), used their positions to mobilise support for the Labour party centrally as well as locally. Their attempts to develop local economic strategies (see Young and Mason, 1983) were promoted as counters to the run-down of manufacturing industry that followed central fiscal policies, and they instituted other policies, such as nuclear-free zones (Figure 3.8), which also provided rallying-points for local Labour parties against the central power of the Conservatives.

One area of Great Britain that became the focus of several central government initiatives during 1979–1987 was Scotland, and these actions had considerable political impact. Immediately prior to the 1979 election, a referendum

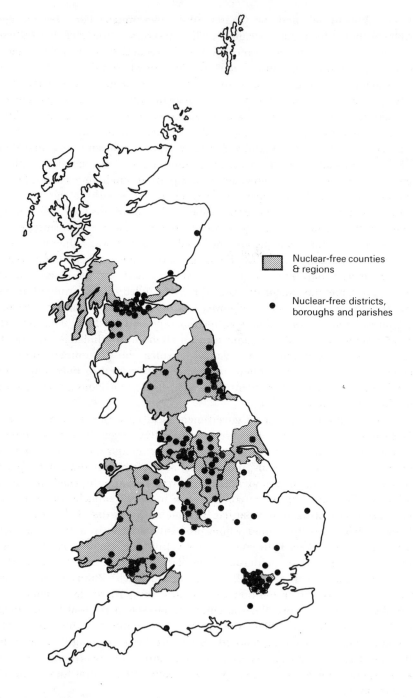

Figure 3.8 Nuclear-free counties and districts in Great Britain, 1981. (Source: Winn and McAuley, 1987, p. 55.)

had been held in both Scotland and Wales on limited devolution. It was lost in both; although a majority of those voting in Scotland were in favour, a majority of the electorate was necessary for the proposition to be carried, and this was not achieved. In Wales, the vote against devolution was substantial, and the issue didn't reappear on the political agenda over the next eight years. In Scotland, however, although there was little debate on devolution in the early years of the Conservative governments the issue clearly was not going to go away.

Scotland differs from Wales in that under the Act of Union of 1707 (much later than the union with Wales) it retained several aspects of its cultural identity, such as its own legal and educational systems. This was followed in 1885 by the establishment of a separate Scottish Office with executive responsibility over several important topics covered by separate departments in England and Wales (such as housing, roads, and education). Wales is much more integrated into England, however, and the Welsh Office was only established in 1964 (Kellas and Madgwick, 1982). Thus to a considerable extent Scotland is ruled from Edinburgh, but since 1979 by a minority of Scottish MPs, since the Conservatives won only 23 seats there in 1979, 21 in 1983, and 10 in 1987. In itself this is a cause of much political debate and the focus of dissent against the Conservative party. (Interestingly, there is little doubt that Scotland has more MPs than its population would seem to entitle it to, as was recognised by a House of Commons Select Committee in 1987. In 1985, the average Scottish constituency contained 55,100 voters while its English counterpart housed 68,700; in rural areas, the over-representation of Scotland is understandable, because so much of it is sparsely populated. But Scottish urban constituencies are much smaller than their English counterparts too: Johnston, 1985b. The Committee was not prepared to recommend that this be changed, however, arguing that 'In our judgement it would not be feasible on political grounds to change the Rules . . . we believe that Scotland and Wales would successfully resist any change in the numbers of seats which was sought in the interests of electoral parity'; Home Affairs Committee, 1987, p. vii.)

It was the area of local government finance that became a particular focus of conflict within Scotland, over two issues. The first was the rate-capping legislation and the penalties imposed on several councils. Midwinter, Keating and Taylor (1983) have discussed the penalties imposed on seven local councils in 1981–2 for 'excessive and unreasonable' expenditure and argue that, on the four criteria taken into account by the Secretary of State, the cases against them lacked intellectual credibility; all seven councils penalised were Labour-controlled. The implication was that the selection was politically motivated, thereby eroding the credibility of the procedure and exacerbating central-local frictions.

The second issue was over reform of the rating system. That part of their income that local governments raise themselves is nearly all the result of a levy on properties, for which the base is an imputed rental value. In 1985 there was a revaluation of all property values in Scotland; the first for two decades. A consequence of this was that some property-owners found that, because their revaluation was greater than the average for the district in which they lived, they faced very substantial increases in their rate bills. This was a cause of much criticism of the government, including within the Conservative party itself. It was the focus of debate at the Scottish Conference of the party in 1985, when members warned the government of the problems in store.

The Conservative party has long been committed to replacing the rates system for financing local government by something that they consider more equitable. In 1987, they settled on a community charge, which is a per capita levy on all resident adults in a district (and hence is often known as the poll tax). A commitment to introduce this was made in the 1987 manifesto. Prior to that, however, it had been decided that this new system, which has not proved popular in conception with the mass of voters, would be introduced in Scotland in 1988, and legislation was passed accordingly in 1987.

We have focused on Scotland here because the policies enacted there are so readily identifiable (see Denver, 1987). But there are many other government actions over the period that could have had an influence, perhaps indirectly, on how people voted. For example, the government's acceptance of the need to impose quotas on milk production promulgated by the EEC led to considerable hardship in those areas where dairy farming dominated, especially for small, marginal farms that had few other sources of income. And the search for a site at which low-level nuclear waste could be dumped led to the nomination of four villages where trial drilling would take place, and not surprisingly generated considerable local opposition which could have been carried through into a vote against the government. (Interestingly, work at the four sites – three of which were in constituencies held by government ministers, including the Chief Whip – was abandoned just before the election.) All of these particular local circumstances could have influenced voting at one or more of the elections. In many cases, the issues were not salient enough to sufficient people for them to come through in the regional patterns described in Chapter 1, but in some cases the impact of a policy may have been substantial enough to produce a noticeable warping of the country's electoral topography.

IN SUMMARY

In this and the previous chapter we have reviewed the literature on voting behaviour in Britain and the events of the period 1979–1987, as a background to analyses of the changing patterns of voting described in Chapter 1. There is clearly no general consensus, and all we can do in summary is highlight what we see as the major elements of contemporary accounts of who votes what, where, as a guide to our analyses in the rest of the book.

Of all the factors that influence how people vote, the most important still is their occupational class, since this influences the sort of home and locality environment in which they are initially socialised, the sort of education they receive, and the type of workplace they earn their living in. From those class backgrounds, which can vary quite substantially in their political orientations according to the success of the political parties in mobilising support and creating organisations that sustain the socialisation processes, they may move both socially and spatially, and be placed in situations where they encounter cross-pressures to vote for different parties. They must resolve those by deciding which to follow, and the probability is that they will be most influenced by the strongest pressures at home, in their communities, and at work.

Such pressures, which complement those that reach the voters via the mass media, will usually involve attempts to get people to evaluate the parties and their offerings; have they performed well in the past?, are they the best able to tackle contemporary problems?; have you done well under their rule in the past?, are you, and the country, likely to do well under them in the future? In evaluating these questions, voters will possibly take account not just of national and personal issues but also those relating to their local home areas and their neighbours. Thus, to the extent that government policies have differential direct and indirect spatial impacts, so one might get differential responses in the form of voting patterns.

Our discussion here has clearly indicated the existence of spatial variations in the impact of government policies over the period 1979–1987, with the implication that this can account for spatial variations in voting patterns. In assessing whether this is a valid account, our first task is to establish the veracity of those variations, that the spatial polarisation we described in Chapter 1 is not simply a mapping of social differences. This is the purpose of the next two chapters. We turn then to an analysis of the reasons for the geography that they reveal.

4

THE GEOGRAPHY OF VOTING AND THE GEOGRAPHY OF REPRESENTATION

The discussion in the previous two chapters has reviewed recent analyses of the influences on voting behaviour in Great Britain and has suggested why one of those influences might be the growing spatial variability in social well-being that voters are encountering. The analyses differ quite substantially in the pictures they present of how people are influenced as they make their voting decisions. Thus a simple model, that assimilates most of the findings reviewed, cannot be constructed. All we can present is a general structure, that the analyses in this and the next chapters will seek to fill in.

Our starting point is the class cleavage, which was clearly the dominant element in British voting in the 1950s. People were socialised into different (occupational) class locations, in which they learned the typical interpretations of those situations, the attitudes that went with them, and the parties to which they were linked. In part that socialisation was a uniform process over the whole of Great Britain, but in part it was not one but a large number of linked, local processes. Similar places may have developed different local political cultures, as a consequence of differential mobilisation activity. Thus, it was not necessarily the case that somebody socialised into one coal-mining community (in South Wales, say) was raised in exactly the same sort of milieu, focused on militant trade unionism with strong links to Labour party politics, as somebody in a similar community elsewhere (such as the Dukeries of north Nottinghamshire: Johnston, 1986a). In general, it was the case that the more homogeneous a community, the more likely it was that members of all occupational classes would vote for the political party (in most cases either Labour or Conservative) with the strongest links to the largest class.

We begin, then, with a geography of local milieux which both sustain and, to some extent, counter the national processes of mobilisation. People learn their political attitudes in those milieux. Many then leave them, both socially and spatially, and are placed in cross-cutting situations where the influences of their past socialisation are in conflict with those of their current situation. Some will jettison the past and develop new political ideologies; some will hold fast to their original attitudes and political affiliations; and others will retain their attitudes as the foundations on which they base their evaluations of parties at election times, because their ties to a particular party have been much weakened but the attitudes remain central to their personal ideologies.

It is this last group that we are particularly interested in, since they are the ones likely to have most impact on the pattern of voting at a single election, simply because they are the most impressionable and most ready to switch from one party to another (or to decide not to vote at all). The literature that we have reviewed here suggests that they make their minds up by considering three sets of factors: the records of the parties with regard to the salient issues; the prospects for the economy and for themselves; and the relative credibility of the party leaders. All of these evaluations can be made in the context of a national (i.e. Great Britain-wide) campaign and consideration, but they can be influenced, as we argue here, by the local context.

Take the evaluation of party performance, or likely performance. Whiteley (1984) has shown that very good predictions of whether or not people voted Conservative in 1983 were obtained by their identification of which party they believed was best able to make Britain more prosperous, to reduce unemployment, and to keep prices down. To a considerable extent, those beliefs would have been conditioned by the set of political attitudes that they developed as they were socialised and by media presentation of the success or otherwise of government policies (as Sanders, Ward and Marsh, 1987, indicate). But in part they may have been conditioned by evaluating the parties in a local rather than a national context so that, for example, a voter in a region where unemployment increased much more rapidly than the national average would be much less likely to vote Conservative in 1983, all other things being equal, than another voter, of the same background, living in a region where unemployment had increased much less than the national average.

Whiteley also showed that people who were optimistic about the country's economic future and their own financial situation were more likely to vote Conservative in 1983 than were those who were more pessimistic. Again, their interpretation may have been influenced by national data only, as presented via the mass media, but they could have been influenced by local issues; people in some regions may have been more optimistic than those living elsewhere, because of their local experience with regard to job prospects and so on, and so much more prepared to vote Conservative.

What we have, then, is a tentative rationale for the regional patterns that we described in Chapter 1. Before we can proceed to test the validity of that rationale, however, we need to establish more firmly than we have as yet that the spatial polarisation we described is 'real' and not an artificial construct of our analysis. In Chapter 1 we paid no attention whatsoever to the influences on voting that most people assume are present, and it may be that (as McAllister, 1987a argues) once they have been taken into account there is very little spatial variation left to explain. Thus in the rest of this chapter we investigate the degree to which spatial polarisation did exist, as indicated by the difference between predicted and actual election results, and in the next we present further analyses of its detailed pattern. Only with the details of the geography established can we then turn to an account of why it is present and has the form that it does.

SPATIAL VARIATIONS IN THE CLASS CLEAVAGE

As we have indicated earlier, the concept of class is one that has generated a great deal of debate over definitions. Many analyses have used a single index of class position only, that of occupation, and even with this how one classifies occupations has stimulated considerable controversy (see Heath, Jowell and Curtice, 1985; Dunleavy and Husbands, 1985; Kavanagh, 1986; Rose and McAllister, 1986). Rose (1982), Franklin (1985) and others have argued the necessity of studying at least six 'objective' indices of class position (parents' occupation; parents' party; education experience; housing tenure; occupation; and union membership) plus one 'subjective' measure – people's self-assigned class. Even then, they suggest, one gets poor results when correlating class position against vote.

Most of the analyses quoted above are based on survey data, so that the researchers can have considerable control over the questions asked and the way in which the responses are coded. Our work draws on the same sources, but in addition is dependent on census data, because we want to look at the characteristics of voters in individual constituencies. Unfortunately, no surveys are big enough to allow that kind of fine-grained spatial analysis at anything but the simplest level, because they contain insufficient voters in any one geographical or functional region for anything other than two- or three-variable cross-tabulations. Surveys tell us a lot about the national electorate (although, as both Miller, 1984, and Warde, 1986, argue, as spatial polarisation increases so the reliability of the surveys declines), but we can learn very little from them about spatial variability.

To investigate the geography of voting, at more than the initial, relatively superficial level of Chapter 1, we must turn to other data sources that can be combined with survey data. For this, the decennial Census of Population and Dwellings offers most scope, since it reports on the characteristics of the population (though not the electorate) and their homes in each of the Parliamentary constituencies. Unfortunately, not all of the relevant variables are collected by the Census, so that we have no information on trade union membership or parents' class and political affiliations, for example. We must make do with what is available, and paint as full a picture as we can from the information provided.

For the work that we are reporting here, no special surveys of the electorate were conducted, so we have been dependent on the data made available from other studies. We needed comparable surveys for each of the three elections that we are investigating (1979, 1983, 1987), which asked the sorts of questions that would give us some of the insights we needed to the problem we are addressing. For this, we selected the surveys conducted by the Gallup organisation for the BBC (in collaboration with Professor Ivor Crewe) at election time (on the day before and election day itself). These were of 2434,

4146, and 4887 respondents in 1979, 1983 and 1987 respectively. The full data sets were deposited in the Economic and Social Research Council's Data Archive at the University of Essex, and we have been able to gain access to them and develop our own analyses.

For the work that we report here, then, we are constrained by the data available to us in the BBC/Gallup surveys and the 1981 Census. With each, the questions asked and the way in which certain answers were coded (e.g. on occupation) limited what we could do. We were further constrained by the Census data since these refer to a snapshot in time, half-way between the 1979 and 1983 general elections and six years distant from that held in 1987. No account could be taken of changing occupational composition of constituencies over the eight-year period, therefore, and we have had to assume that, relative to each other, the constituencies have remained similar in their characteristics. In general, this is not too unreasonable, though some constituencies have clearly changed more than others as a consequence of, for example, major industrial closures, the construction of new housing estates, and gentrification processes. As an approximation, however, the Census allows us to develop insights that we could not otherwise gain (though with another census in 1991 a sequel to this book would be able to take the analysis much further). The next section describes the first stage in that development.

Occupational Class and Voting Predictions

Surveys give an overall picture of the pattern of voting at an election, and cross-tabulations of voting by occupational class indicate the extent of a class cleavage (as in Table 2.2). There are problems with the surveys, however, in that the patterns they report rarely fit precisely into the patterns indicated by, for example, the election result itself. For example, it is commonplace for survey respondents to under-report abstention – more people say that they have voted, or intend to vote, than turns out to be the case, either because of faulty memory (unlikely in our case because the survey was taken on election day), good intentions that were thwarted (probably the case with a small number) or unwillingness to admit the fact. Thus, from the survey data, one may not have an entirely accurate picture of the voting; as a result one cannot predict the actual result.

To illustrate this point, take a very simple hypothetical situation. We have an electorate of 2500 people, who could vote for party X or party Y. The result was 1200 votes for X and 800 for Y, with 500 abstaining. Those 2500 people are divided into two occupational classes, with 1300 in A and 1200 in B. A survey of 250 is taken, 130 in A and 120 in B, and their reported voting, in percentages, is

	X	Y	Abst.
A	40	50	10
B	60	25	15

If we use these percentages to predict the pattern of votes, however, we get

	X	Y	Abst.	Total
A	520	650	130	1300
B	720	300	180	1200
Total	1240	950	310	2500

The number of abstainers is substantially (190 out of 500) understated, whereas the number of voters for each party is overstated (especially for Y). The survey, then, is not an entirely accurate representation of the real result.

In order to conduct the analyses that we report here, it is necessary to obtain an exact representation. This is done by a statistical smoothing procedure (called Mostellerisation by Sarlvik and Crewe, 1983, p. 360, after the statistician who introduced it) that modifies the survey data, as little as possible, to get them to fit the result; the column and row sums are fixed, and only the internal cells of the table change. The procedure changes the percentages in a standard way to retain their relative sizes (i.e. more members of class B than of class A will abstain) in order to get the required fit, to within a predetermined tolerance level. The result of applying this procedure to our hypothetical matrix is (total number of voters, with row percentages in brackets)

	X	Y	Abst.	Total
A	522 (40)	558 (43)	218 (17)	1298
B	678 (56)	242 (20)	282 (23)	1202
Total	1200	800	500	2500

The voting result is reproduced exactly, and only two voters are wrongly located by class. The inter-class differentials are slightly altered, in order to produce the correct number of abstainers, but the proportions remain very similar. (In the original data, the ratios A/B were: party X, 0.67:1.00; party Y, 2.00:1.0; Abst., 0.67:1.00. In the 'smoothed' data, they are: 0.71:1.00; 2.15:1.00; and 0.74:1.00.)

This smoothing procedure was applied to each of the matrices that we obtained from the Gallup/BBC surveys, cross-classifying occupational class by vote. (One further issue that we faced was that the total number of people for whom occupational class was reported in the Census was not the same as the size of the electorate. To cope with this, we took the percentage in each class in each constituency and applied it to the electorate at the election in question, to give the number in each class. The relative size of each class in the electorate, and in the national population, was thus retained. Further, the samples were weighted, with Scotland and Wales over-represented in order to estimate nationalist voting; our smoothing eliminated the impact of that weighting.) Six classes were used, three on each side of the manual/non-manual divide: in the manual group, the usual distinction according to skill was applied; in the non-manual group, the distinctions were between role as well as skill.

Table 4.1 shows the three resulting matrices, as the best available representatives of the national class cleavage. They indicate that the relative differences between classes did not alter much over the eight-year period. The

Table 4.1 Voting by occupational class (in percentages)

	Con-servative	Labour	Alliance	Nation-alist	Other/Non-Voting
1979					
Professional	42.9	18.0	17.1	1.7	20.3
Administrative/					
Managerial	50.0	13.0	10.2	1.3	25.6
Routine Non-Manual	39.5	19.9	14.7	1.7	24.3
Skilled	27.1	36.8	8.2	1.7	26.2
Semiskilled	23.8	44.7	8.6	1.4	21.6
Unskilled	17.2	43.8	9.3	1.8	27.8
1983					
Professional	42.8	11.2	23.4	1.0	21.5
Administrative/					
Managerial	48.8	9.7	18.9	0.6	22.0
Routine Non-Manual	37.5	17.0	17.4	1.0	27.0
Skilled	31.0	31.7	24.6	1.6	33.3
Semiskilled	20.9	27.8	19.8	1.6	29.8
Unskilled	15.9	31.7	16.5	1.3	34.5
1987					
Professional	40.4	16.1	27.6	0.9	14.9
Administrative/					
Managerial	49.7	10.0	18.8	0.8	20.7
Routine Non-Manual	36.1	20.2	17.4	1.5	24.8
Skilled	27.0	26.2	16.9	1.6	28.3
Semiskilled	21.7	40.6	15.3	0.9	21.5
Unskilled	17.8	32.5	13.2	1.6	34.9

administrative and managerial class was the most pro-Conservative at each election, and the semiskilled and unskilled manual classes were the most pro-Labour. The ratio of voting Conservative between the managerial and the unskilled classes was 2.91 in 1979, 3.07 in 1983, and 2.79 in 1987; for voting Labour, the respective ratios between the unskilled and the managerial were 3.37, 3.27, and 3.25: together, these provide little evidence of any substantial class dealignment, in a relative sense (see, however, Dunleavy, 1987).

In 1979, the Liberal party (Alliance) gained much more support among the non-manual than the manual classes, especially from the Professional grouping. Four years later, following the creation of the Alliance, support differed little between the two groups, though within each one occupational class (the Professionals and the Skilled Manual) were more supportive of the Alliance than the other two. In 1987, the pattern of support was almost exactly the same in relative terms as in 1979, though of course the Alliance got many more votes in 1987 than the Liberals did eight years previously.

Given this pattern of class voting, the important question for us is whether it was repeated in every constituency, which would be the case (with some small variation as a function of sampling error in the surveys) if some of the arguments reviewed in Chapter 2 were true. If Britain has a national political culture, so that people in particular class positions vote the same way wherever they live, then those matrices should have been virtually the same everywhere. (There is one caveat to that. The nationalist parties only stood in Scotland and Wales, so a small percentage of the vote was available in the English constituencies for distribution among the other three parties, plus abstentions. And the Liberals did not stand in 13 constituencies in 1979.)

As a preliminary test of that argument, we use those matrices, plus the Census data and the election result, to 'predict' the result in each constituency. The procedure can be illustrated by a simple example. Take a constituency in which party X got 2000 votes, party Y got 1500, and 500 voters abstained. There are two classes only, A and B, whose national voting patterns (in percentages) were:

	X	Y	Abst.
A	50	30	20
B	40	50	10

The constituency has 2500 voters in class A and 1500 in class B.

If the national pattern were applied to that constituency, the election result should have been:

X	1250	(from class A: 50% of 2500)		
	+ 600	(from class B: 40% of 1500)	=	1850
Y	750	(from class A: 30% of 2500)		
	+ 750	(from class B: 50% of 1500)	=	1500
Abst.	500	(from class A: 20% of 2500)		
	+ 150	(from class B: 10% of 1500)	=	650

Thus whereas the actual pattern of voting, in percentages, was

X 50%   Y 37.5%   Abst. 12.5%

the pattern if the national class matrix applied would have been

X 46.25%   Y 37.5%   Abst. 16.25%

Compared to the national patterns, therefore, party X did better in the constituency, and there were relatively fewer abstainers. The difference between the observed and the expected voting can be shown by expressing the actual percentage voting for a party (or abstaining) as a percentage of the predicted value. This would give

X 108.1   Y 100.0   Abst. 76.9

Party X's performance was 8 per cent better than would have been the case if the pattern of voting by class was the same in the constituency as it was nationally, whereas the number of abstainers was only about three-quarters of the expected.

Using this straightforward procedure, therefore, we can predict what the pattern of voting should have been in each constituency, at each of the three elections, and compare this with the national pattern. It is that comparison that we focus on here. If the electorate in each constituency was, to all intents and purposes, a representative sample of the national electorate, then each of the comparative percentages (the observed vote as a percentage of the expected) should be almost exactly 100.0. (There would be some variability because of sampling error, and some because of the absence of nationalist candidates in England but their presence in Scotland and Wales.) To the extent that the *comparative percentages* vary from 100.0, so we have evidence of spatial variability in the voting behaviour of the members of the six occupational classes.

Our expectations are not only that we would get evidence of spatial variability but also that the extent of that variability would increase over time. Figure 4.1 illustrates how this would appear. At the first election, virtually all of the 633 constituencies fall into the central two categories, with only 13 having a percentage less than 75 and 20 a percentage exceeding 125. Four years later, 100 of the constituencies fall outside the central two categories, so that in about

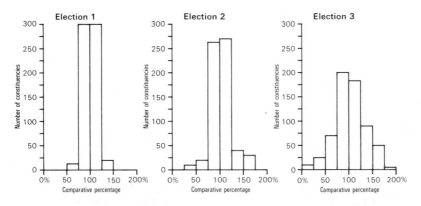

Figure 4.1 A hypothetical set of comparative percentages for one party at three elections in 633 constituencies, illustrating what would occur if spatial variability in voting increased over time.

15 per cent of them the predictions for the party concerned were more than 25 per cent out. And then at the third election the degree of variability increased yet again, with only about 60 per cent of the constituencies in the central two categories and 15 where the actual result was 75 per cent or more different from that predicted.

Figures 4.2 and 4.3 provide the data for the Conservative, Labour, and Alliance parties, and for Non-Voting. For the Conservative party (Figure 4.2) there is some indication of growing polarisation, but not a great amount. At each of the three elections, just under 300 of the constituencies record comparative percentages of between 100 and 125, with a small, but increasing over time, number with values in excess of 125: for about half of the constituencies, the actual Conservative vote was larger than predicted, but in very few by more than 25 per cent. To the left of that dominant category, over the three elections the number of constituencies in the 75–100 category declined whereas the number in the other three (0–24, 25–49, 50–74) increased slightly, again evidence of growing spatial variability. In 1987 the Conservative vote deviated more from the predicted, on average, than it did in 1979.

Turning to the Labour party (Figure 4.2), we find much more evidence of spatial variability, and of its increase over the eight years. In 1979, the largest category (percentages of 100–125) contained about 230 constituencies; in 1983 the largest was the 125–150 category, with less than 150 constituencies in it; and in 1987 the same category contained less than 125. The spread of values increased very considerably over time, with an increasing number of constituencies where the actual vote was as much as twice that which would have been recorded if members of each occupational class had voted in the same way in every place. Clearly, the geography of voting Labour by class became spatially more variable between 1979 and 1987.

For the Alliance (Figure 4.3) the pattern is one of quite considerable spatial variability in 1979 (for the Liberal party alone), of a substantial reduction in that variability in 1983, and then a return to greater variability again in 1987. In the first of those years, the comparative percentage in about half of the constituencies was between 50 and 100, with slightly more having less than 75 than having greater than that figure. In a lot of places, the Alliance underperformed by up to half of what it might have done if it had attracted votes in the same proportion from each class everywhere; this was countered by about 75 constituencies where its vote was at least half as much again as the predicted value. In 1983, however, the Alliance seems to have attracted votes in roughly similar proportions in the great majority of constituencies, with many fewer recording comparative percentages either below 50 or above 125. In 1987 its dominant category had shifted leftwards, so more constituencies were in the 50–74 class than any other, and there were again many more with values of 150 or greater. The Liberal party had a spatially polarised base in 1979, it seems; in 1983, the Alliance was much more a national party, but in 1987 it again picked up many more votes than would be expected from the national pattern in some places than in others.

For Non-Voting (Figure 4.3), finally, we see little evidence either of great

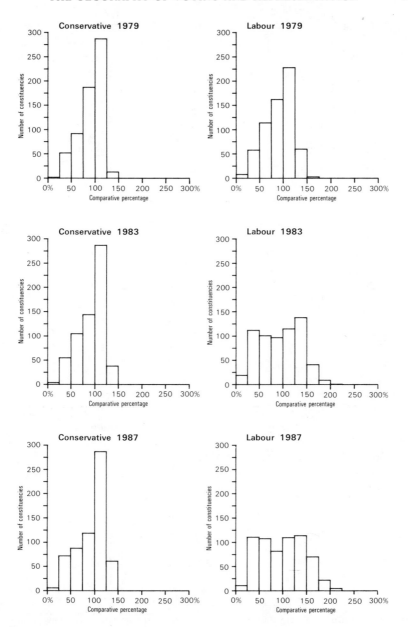

Figure 4.2 Comparative percentages for voting for the Conservative and Labour parties, using occupational class as the predictor, 1979–1987.

spatial variability at any one election or of an increase in that variability over the period. The level of abstention in each constituency is reasonably well-predicted from the national pattern which implies either that proportionally abstention was the same in each class in each place or that where it was higher in one class than was the case nationally it was lower in another.

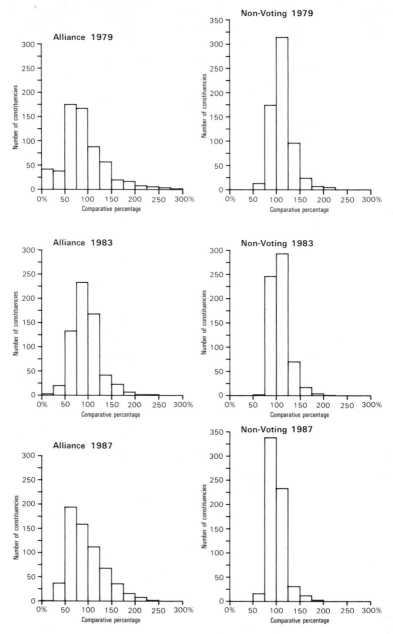

Figure 4.3 Comparative percentages for voting for the Alliance and for Non-Voting,
using occupational class as the predictor, 1979–1987.

The simplest way to summarise these graphs, and to gain a single quantitative statement of the changing degree of spatial variability, is to use the
Coefficient of Variation statistic (CV). This expresses the standard deviation of

the distribution as a percentage of the mean. The mean is the average value; the standard deviation is a measure of the average variation around that mean, such that 68.3 per cent of all values are within one standard deviation of the mean. The greater the value of the standard deviation (i.e. the wider the range of values necessary to incorporate just over two-thirds of all the constituencies), relative to the mean, the greater the degree of spatial variability.

Table 4.2 gives these summary statistics for each party across the three elections. The values of CV indicate a greater spread of values about the mean at the end of the period than at the beginning for both Conservative and Labour; the major shift is the much greater range of values (i.e. much greater spatial polarisation of votes relative to what was expected) for Labour between 1979 and 1983. For the Alliance, there was a very substantial decrease in the spatial variability in its vote-winning between 1979 and 1983, followed by a return to greater variability (though only one-third of the way to the 1979 level) in 1987. For Non-Voting, there was a clear, but slight, shift to less variability over time.

Table 4.2 Summary Statistics (CV) for the Comparative Percentage Distribution, using voting by occupational class as predictor

	1979	1983	1987
Conservative	25.8	28.5	31.4
Labour	31.7	45.3	46.6
Alliance	60.2	31.6	39.9
Non-Voting	19.8	18.0	17.8

Regional Variations

We have shown that spatial variability in the comparative percentages increased from 1979 to 1987, especially for the Labour party. From our knowledge of the national pattern of voting by class we are less able to predict each party's vote in the individual constituencies in 1987 than in 1979. But where? Given our descriptions in Chapter 1, we would expect there to be regional variations in the comparative percentages; in some geographical and functional regions, for example, the Labour vote should be much greater than predicted (i.e. comparative percentages exceeding 100.0, on average) whereas in others it should be less than predicted. If this were so, then we would have clear indirect evidence of regional differences in the propensity of people in the various classes to vote Labour.

Tables 4.3 – 4.6 provide evidence of substantial spatial variations in the comparative percentages, by both geographical and functional regions. The data for *geographical regions* are in Tables 4.3 and 4.4, and show the anticipated pattern, with the average percentages greater than 100.0 for Labour in most of the northern regions and for Conservative in most of those further south. The R^2 values (see p. 38) are high, too, showing that the regional patterns were both strong and increasing in importance (the R^2 for Conservatives increased from 0.53 to 0.64 over the period, while that for Labour grew from 0.42 to 0.59; for a discussion of the interpretation of R^2 values, see p. 39). For the Alliance and Non-Voting the fits are less substantial, indicating greater intra-regional variability, relative to the inter-regional differences.

For the Conservative party (Table 4.3), one of the salient features is that in most of the regions where its average was less than 100.0 in 1979, it was even less in 1987, whereas in those where the value exceeded 100.0 at the first date there was an increase by 1987. Clearly this indicates that where the party was initially strong, getting more votes than would be expected from the national pattern of voting by class, it became even stronger, whereas in places where it was initially weak it became even weaker. The biggest shifts away from the

Table 4.3 The Average Comparative Percentages for Conservative and Labour Voting, using occupational class as the predictor, by geographical region

	Conservative			Labour		
	1979	1983	1987	1979	1983	1987
Strathclyde	56.9	52.8	43.5	105.4	138.1	163.4
E. Scotland	59.3	62.8	58.3	96.9	119.2	137.6
Rural Scotland	65.0	69.2	66.5	48.8	50.4	65.6
Rural North	100.1	106.3	104.3	84.4	84.7	89.7
Industrial Northeast	75.6	73.7	67.2	121.9	134.3	146.7
Merseyside	88.7	79.2	65.3	101.6	123.5	137.1
Greater Manchester	90.8	85.2	85.1	107.4	122.5	125.4
Rest of Northwest	103.6	103.4	106.6	96.1	108.6	114.8
West Yorks.	82.4	84.0	87.1	108.6	115.7	123.3
South Yorks.	67.2	63.5	56.8	124.5	142.6	154.8
Rural Wales	74.8	79.2	79.2	86.1	86.1	102.1
Industrial South Wales	67.6	64.6	64.8	127.3	144.1	167.2
W. Midlands Conurbation	97.8	95.4	96.9	97.9	114.4	110.6
Rest of West Midlands	102.3	110.5	110.6	85.5	84.6	84.4
East Midlands	103.0	109.7	114.7	93.0	93.7	93.1
East Anglia	106.6	115.5	118.4	83.0	73.4	70.6
Devon and Cornwall	110.3	115.1	108.8	52.7	39.4	53.8
Wessex	106.4	113.6	116.2	70.7	59.6	57.2
Inner London	73.1	66.5	73.2	106.7	113.0	111.1
Outer London	101.3	98.8	107.7	95.4	84.8	82.0
Outer Metropolitan	107.7	113.4	119.1	76.7	61.8	59.4
Outer Southeast	111.3	117.7	120.0	67.3	54.6	53.7
R^2	0.53	0.60	0.64	0.42	0.50	0.59

party were in Strathclyde and Merseyside, and these were countered by even larger shifts in the comparative percentages for Labour. Overall, the movements involving Labour were much larger than those for Conservative, again with the party becoming much stronger where it was already strong and weaker where it was initially weak. In three regions (Eastern Scotland, Rest of Northwest, and West Midlands Conurbation) Labour shifted from performing less well than the national figures predicted in 1979 to better than predicted (by at least ten per cent) in 1987, suggesting an ability to win support in areas of growing relative economic decline (see Chapter 3). There were no regions where the Conservative party similarly shifted from a position of performing

Table 4.4 The Average Comparative Percentages for Alliance and Non-Voting, using occupational class as the predictor, by geographical region

	Alliance			Non-Voting		
	1979	1983	1987	1979	1983	1987
Strathclyde	37.0	71.4	64.1	125.1	115.4	97.6
E. Scotland	56.2	93.1	83.6	122.8	113.4	97.0
Rural Scotland	101.3	97.4	112.7	146.5	134.0	111.5
Rural North	122.1	98.9	103.2	104.3	101.2	96.7
Industrial Northeast	76.2	89.4	87.0	111.7	106.5	100.0
Merseyside	90.0	85.0	98.3	108.5	109.1	98.9
Greater Manchester	93.7	87.2	85.9	99.9	104.4	98.9
Rest of Northwest	90.9	87.9	84.8	99.6	95.3	90.8
West Yorks.	101.1	94.5	89.3	109.6	107.5	97.6
South Yorks.	77.5	80.0	76.3	115.6	115.2	108.1
Rural Wales	108.8	91.5	98.9	116.1	110.9	82.4
Industrial South Wales	59.6	84.7	69.9	104.1	103.7	87.2
W. Midlands Conurbation	53.9	72.9	70.9	114.4	109.0	108.9
Rest of West Midlands	107.6	101.5	107.1	107.5	95.7	92.8
East Midlands	96.3	90.3	91.1	103.6	98.3	91.3
East Anglia	109.2	107.8	111.0	105.9	95.0	94.2
Devon and Cornwall	179.5	145.2	146.1	100.6	92.2	95.3
Wessex	137.2	118.9	133.1	105.2	98.1	91.6
Inner London	55.6	73.4	80.5	146.2	144.8	135.4
Outer London	85.7	94.2	87.6	105.6	114.0	111.6
Outer Metropolitan	109.6	107.7	107.1	106.7	102.5	100.9
Outer Southeast	115.9	108.7	118.8	111.2	104.3	99.6
R^2	0.26	0.24	0.25	0.30	0.49	0.36

worse than expected to one of performing better than the national data predicted, a situation which applied to the Alliance as well (Table 4.4). Indeed, there were two regions where the Alliance's relative position moved the other way, in West Yorkshire and Rural Wales; where Liberal strength in 1979 was apparently not capitalised on in 1983 and 1987. Over all 22 regions there were few consistent trends in the Alliance performance; its major strength in two regions (Devon and Cornwall, and Wessex) was eroded, especially in the former, but only in Rural Scotland was there any major increase in its drawing power well above the percentage of votes expected.

With the *functional regions* (Tables 4.5 and 4.6), the R^2 values (see p. 39) were even higher than those just discussed, indicating very significant inter-regional (relative to intra-regional) variations. For the Conservative party (Table 4.5) there was continued erosion of support in the regions where it was initially weak (notably Poorest Domestic, Poor Inner City, Clydeside, and Scottish Industrial) and, somewhat surprisingly, it moved from a position of winning more votes than expected in the Conurbation White Collar constituencies (places such as Surbiton, Twickenham, and Wimbledon) in 1979 to less in 1987. In every other region where it had an average of over 100.0 in 1979 its performance increased by 1987, indicating growing polarisation in its areas of strength, and it also moved to an above 100.0 average in the Recent Growth, Stable Industrial, and Metropolitan Industrial regions, indicative of its ability to win over votes in areas of relative prosperity during the early 1980s. La-

Table 4.5 The Average Comparative Percentages for Conservative and Labour Voting, using occupational class as predictor, by functional region

	Conservative			Labour		
	1979	1983	1987	1979	1983	1987
I.C./Immig.	72.5	67.6	75.5	112.6	127.3	120.0
Ind./Immig.	88.4	86.7	88.2	108.5	127.0	125.8
Poorest Immig.	67.9	62.6	65.5	105.1	136.1	132.7
Intermed. Ind.	86.3	87.1	87.2	118.2	130.0	132.2
Old Indust./Mining	70.8	68.3	70.0	123.6	150.3	158.6
Textile	89.5	90.3	91.3	109.4	124.7	127.5
Poorest Domestic	44.9	40.2	40.1	117.2	130.1	159.8
Conurb. L.A.	80.5	75.6	71.8	117.6	133.2	140.2
Black Co.	87.2	88.8	94.2	105.4	128.0	120.1
Maritime Ind.	82.1	77.3	71.0	116.7	130.9	142.0
Poor I.C.	51.3	47.8	49.2	104.4	122.9	122.2
Clydeside	49.4	41.9	34.4	104.9	134.1	161.4
Scott. Ind.	50.0	53.2	44.7	104.9	141.8	163.6
Scott. Rural	73.1	77.7	75.7	43.3	42.0	50.9
High Status I.M.	92.8	83.3	89.2	94.5	96.2	99.2
I.M.	74.6	66.2	71.1	113.6	124.7	124.8
Outer London	109.3	107.2	114.6	82.5	67.1	69.0
Very High Status	114.6	116.1	119.1	66.3	49.6	51.9
Conurb. W. Collar	101.2	96.2	97.5	87.8	80.9	86.0
City Service	97.6	94.2	92.0	101.2	104.5	109.9
Resort/Retirement	113.0	117.7	118.4	53.2	40.7	44.8
Recent Growth	91.9	102.4	102.9	89.6	95.6	98.5
Stable Ind.	97.7	102.2	104.0	106.8	112.7	114.4
Small Towns	108.9	115.3	115.4	81.6	75.5	77.5
Southern Urban	110.3	118.9	122.1	75.3	60.7	58.0
Modest Aff.	110.0	113.0	112.8	93.1	85.9	89.6
Met. Ind.	99.7	103.7	111.2	104.3	97.2	97.8
Modest Aff. Scot.	87.0	86.9	84.5	89.3	98.5	127.2
Rapid Growth	108.1	120.5	125.2	61.9	46.2	48.9
Prosperous/No Ind.	108.7	115.0	114.2	59.2	44.0	50.0
Agricultural	103.0	111.8	111.3	57.3	47.4	51.4
R^2	0.64	0.69	0.66	0.66	0.73	0.71

bour, too, strengthened its performance in its areas of pre-existing strength, with very substantial increases in the average comparative percentage in each of the first thirteen regions in the table. Complementing those shifts, its performance weakened in eleven of the 14 regions where its 1979 average was below 100.0; the main exception to this was in the Modestly Affluent Scotland grouping, where its average increased by almost half, from 89 to 127. In general, then, the polarisation between Conservative and Labour which was present in 1979 was accentuated by 1987, but there were a few regions where one of the parties was able to turn the tide against it.

The Alliance lost ground in nearly every region in which it had an average

Table 4.6 The Average Comparative Percentages for Alliance and Non-Voting, using occupational class as predictor, by functional region

	Alliance			Non-Voting		
	1979	1983	1987	1979	1983	1987
I.C./Immig.	53.5	68.3	69.0	139.0	134.1	129.3
Ind./Immig.	65.6	71.7	69.2	114.7	110.6	106.5
Poorest Immig.	48.4	60.1	41.1	141.0	131.4	138.5
Intermed. Ind.	84.1	88.6	88.9	101.6	97.8	91.2
Old Indust./Mining	71.4	74.4	66.8	102.2	105.3	92.9
Textile	106.5	90.4	86.6	98.8	96.9	91.4
Poorest Domestic	35.4	60.4	65.8	135.1	135.3	109.8
Conurb. L.A.	68.2	77.6	74.2	113.6	112.9	108.2
Black Co.	43.0	67.3	65.1	121.4	111.1	107.9
Maritime Ind.	65.0	85.4	82.2	110.3	106.4	99.7
Poor I.C.	56.1	69.8	77.9	165.1	150.8	144.4
Clydeside	38.9	68.9	56.6	131.3	132.9	108.3
Scott. Ind.	18.2	75.9	62.0	126.6	110.7	92.0
Scott. Rural	124.4	111.2	126.0	138.6	126.6	109.0
High Status I.M.	67.1	76.7	69.7	129.0	141.1	138.7
I.M.	53.5	70.4	73.0	138.4	140.0	130.6
Outer London	98.1	102.4	97.5	102.2	110.5	105.4
Very High Status	119.0	109.3	109.4	100.1	104.2	102.7
Conurb. W. Collar	98.7	103.4	105.0	108.8	114.9	110.0
City Service	82.9	91.0	102.2	108.3	109.0	98.6
Resort/Retirement	142.9	115.3	126.6	110.5	108.9	102.8
Recent Growth	79.6	99.7	102.2	127.0	99.2	93.9
Stable Ind.	80.6	93.6	89.6	98.8	89.4	85.3
Small Towns	117.3	103.6	112.8	99.6	94.5	85.6
Southern Urban	108.5	110.5	117.2	107.5	96.9	93.2
Modest Aff.	98.2	103.0	104.5	92.7	90.9	87.0
Met. Ind.	80.3	95.5	86.1	102.9	99.9	95.7
Modest Aff. Scot.	81.6	103.8	88.9	112.0	100.3	85.8
Rapid Growth	130.7	116.2	115.7	115.6	101.4	98.6
Prosperous/No Ind.	145.3	119.3	129.6	107.6	104.7	100.1
Agricultural	163.6	123.4	132.4	107.7	100.0	95.3
R^2	0.41	0.34	0.36	0.41	0.49	0.49

exceeding 100.0 in 1979, the only exception being the Southern Urban region (places such as Buckingham, Fareham, and Daventry: Table 4.6). In many of the areas where it was initially relatively weak it was able to strengthen its vote-winning, however, and in four it was able to shift to a position where it won more votes than it would if the national pattern had applied; against this, however, its initial drawing power in the Textile Towns was eroded. Despite the general reduction in the spatial polarisation of its support, the Alliance nevertheless remained a dominant force in a few functional regions only – notably Rural Scotland, the Resort and Retirement Towns, the Prosperous Towns without Industries, and the Agricultural Areas.

The Parliamentary Impact

The discussion so far has concentrated on the percentage of the votes that each
party would have won in each constituency if the pattern of voting by occupational class had been the same everywhere. It has shown major spatial variations in the ability of the parties to win the number of votes that would be
expected if Great Britain had a uniform political culture. But as yet nothing
has been said about the impact of those variations in terms of the measure that
really matters; what influence did it have on the ability of the parties to win
seats?

   Given that the simple procedure we have applied here allows us to predict
the percentage of the electorate who would have voted for each party under
certain assumptions, it is easy to take the next step and inquire which party
would have won each constituency. The answer is given in Table 4.7 and can
be very easily summarised; the Conservative party would have won each

Table 4.7 The Predicted Number of Seats Won by Each Party in 1979, 1983 and
1987 using occupational class as the predictor

	Conservative	Labour	Alliance
1979	478	155	0
1983	632	1	0
1987	617	16	0

election by a landslide, indeed virtually a whitewash in 1983 and 1987. If
people in the six occupational classes had voted the same way wherever they
lived, then the Alliance and the nationalist parties would have won no seats,
and Labour very few after 1979. The class structure of almost all British
constituencies is such that Labour has no chance of success, let alone the
Alliance, unless it is able to capture many more votes in some, if not all,
classes in some places than it did on average in 1983 and 1987.

Table 4.8 Predicted and Actual Seats Won, using occupational class as predictor

Seats Predicted to be Won By	Seats Won By			
	Conservative	Labour	Alliance	Nationalist
1979				
Conservative	354	112	9	3
Labour	6	148	0	1
1983				
Conservative	397	208	23	4
Labour	0	1	0	0
1987				
Conservative	376	213	22	6
Labour	0	16	0	0

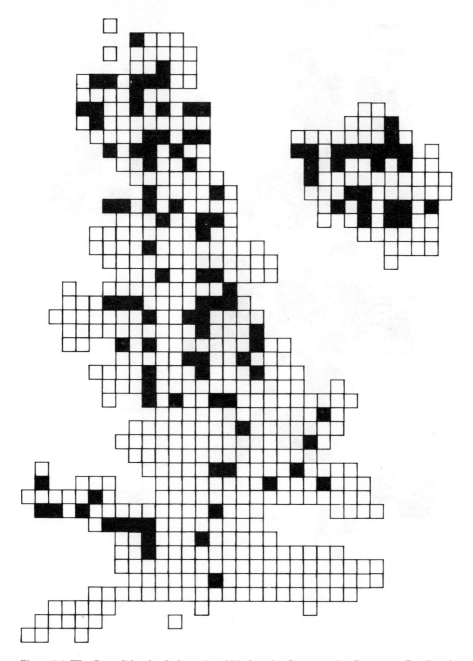

Figure 4.4 The Seats Won by Labour in 1979 that the Conservative Party was Predicted to Win, using occupational class as the predictor.

Clearly Labour did this, although not successfully enough to present a close challenge to the Conservative party at any of the three elections. Table 4.8 shows the extent of that success. In 1979, Labour won 112 constituencies

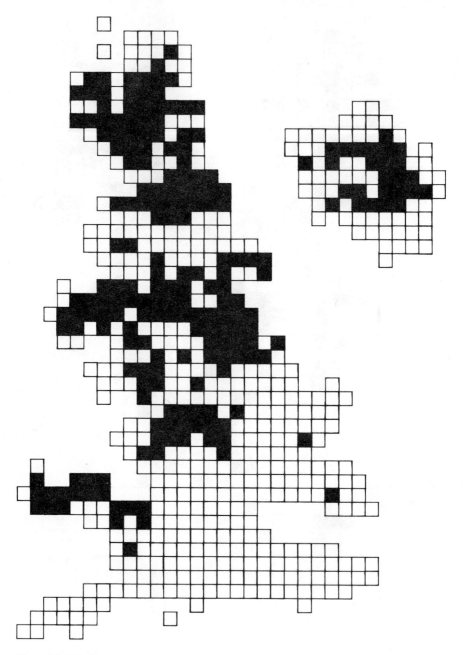

Figure 4.5 The Seats Won by Labour in 1983 that the Conservative Party was Predicted
to Win, using occupational class as the predictor.

where the Conservatives had a 'natural' majority according to the occupational
class structure – though Labour lost six to the Conservatives that it should
have won. In 1983, it won nearly twice as many 'unexpected' victories – 208 –

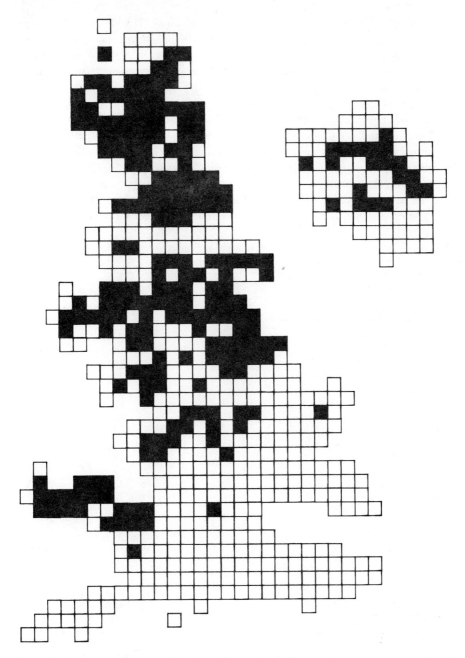

Figure 4.6 The Seats Won by Labour in 1987 that the Conservative Party was Predicted to Win, using occupational class as the predictor.

as well as holding on to the only seat it was predicted to win (Glasgow Provan) – and it won slightly more again in 1987. Labour's 'natural' source of votes is in the manual occupational classes, but at present it wins insufficient of their support nationally to obtain a Parliamentary majority; if it did not win much more support from them in some constituencies than in others, it would gain hardly any seats at all.

Where are those seats? Clearly, since Labour's success is increasingly in the northern regions they are there, and Figures 4.4 – 4.6 illustrate that. Interestingly, in 1979 it won several seats in southeastern England that the Tories were predicted to hold, but only three there in each of 1983 and 1987.

Regional analyses provide further insights into where the occupational class structure was such as to give Labour a victory in 1979, when it still won over 40 per cent of the votes cast in the manual classes, and in 1987, when its performance improved from the nadir in 1983. By geographical region (Table 4.9) its strength was clearly in the industrialised urban regions, though only in the Outer Southeast was there no seat that it should have won in 1979.

Table 4.9 Distribution of Seats that Labour was Predicted to Win, using occupational class as the predictor, by geographical region

	1979	1983	1987	Total Number of Constituencies
Strathclyde	16	1	3	32
E. Scotland	4	0	0	19
Rural Scotland	2	0	0	21
Rural North	7	0	0	26
Industrial Northeast	16	0	0	27
Merseyside	9	0	2	17
Greater Manchester	11	0	1	27
Rest of Northwest	6	0	0	29
West Yorks.	10	0	0	23
South Yorks.	9	0	2	15
Rural Wales	1	0	0	15
Industrial South Wales	11	0	0	23
W. Midlands Conurbation	20	0	5	32
Rest of West Midlands	4	0	0	26
East Midlands	11	0	0	41
East Anglia	1	0	0	20
Devon and Cornwall	1	0	0	16
Wessex	1	0	0	32
Inner London	9	0	3	32
Outer London	2	0	0	52
Outer Metropolitan	4	0	0	61
Outer Southeast	0	0	0	47

Merseyside, South Yorkshire, Strathclyde, and the West Midlands Conurbation were the only four where it was predicted to win half of the seats, however. By functional region (Table 4.10) in 15 of the 31 regions the 1979 predictions suggest no Labour victory, and in 1987 its 16 predicted wins were concentrated in eight regions (with half of them in two only, Poor Inner City and Clydeside).

Table 4.10 Distribution of Seats that Labour was Predicted to Win, using occupational class as the predictor, by functional region

	1979	1983	1987	Total Number of Constituencies
I.C./Immig.	2	0	0	8
Ind./Immig.	15	0	1	17
Poorest Immig.	4	0	2	4
Intermed. Ind.	6	0	0	30
Old Indust./Mining	29	0	0	34
Textile	6	0	0	18
Poorest Domestic	7	0	1	7
Conurb. L.A.	23	0	1	26
Black Co.	9	0	2	9
Maritime Ind.	15	0	1	15
Poor I.C.	12	0	5	12
Clydeside	12	1	3	17
Scott. Ind.	9	0	0	25
Scott. Rural	0	0	0	17
High Status I.M.	0	0	0	9
I.M.	0	0	0	14
Outer London	0	0	0	24
Very High Status	0	0	0	31
Conurb. W. Collar	0	0	0	24
City Service	1	0	0	24
Resort/Retirement	0	0	0	29
Recent Growth	4	0	0	19
Stable Ind.	1	0	0	26
Small Towns	0	0	0	27
Southern Urban	0	0	0	24
Modest Aff.	0	0	0	26
Met. Ind.	0	0	0	30
Modest Aff. Scot.	0	0	0	5
Rapid Growth	0	0	0	16
Prosperous/No Ind.	0	0	0	19
Agricultural	0	0	0	47

Turning to the seats that Labour won against a predicted Conservative victory, Table 4.11 indicates a clear north:south divide. Further, it also shows that Labour's ability to defeat a 'natural' Conservative majority was increasingly concentrated in the north, with declining success rates over time in Wessex, and Inner and Outer London. (Of the six seats that Labour should have won, but did not, three were in the West Midlands Conurbation.) In other regions, Labour's ability to gain sufficient votes to win seats where the occupational class structure favoured the Conservatives improved, notably in all three Scottish regions, in West Yorkshire, Industrial South Wales, and the East Midlands. At the scale of the functional regions (Table 4.12) this seat-winning ability is focused on only a few such as the Textile Towns, and the Conurbation White-Collar constituencies (including seats such as Cardiff Cen-

Table 4.11 Distribution of Seats won by Labour which the Conservative Party was Predicted to Win, using occupational class as the predictor, by geographical region

	1979	1983	1987
Strathclyde	12/16	25/31	27/29
E. Scotland	9/15	13/19	15/19
Rural Scotland	2/19	2/21	5/21
Rural North	4/19	8/26	9/26
Industrial Northeast	8/11	22/27	23/27
Merseyside	1/8	11/17	9/15
Greater Manchester	4/16	15/27	15/26
Rest of Northwest	4/23	9/29	9/29
West Yorks.	6/13	10/23	14/23
South Yorks.	5/6	14/15	12/13
Rural Wales	3/14	4/15	5/15
Industrial South Wales	8/12	16/23	19/23
W. Midlands Conurbation	1/12	18/32	12/27
Rest of West Midlands	3/22	4/26	5/26
East Midlands	7/30	8/41	11/41
East Anglia	2/19	1/20	1/20
Devon and Cornwall	0/14	0/16	0/16
Wessex	3/31	1/32	1/32
Inner London	13/23	18/32	13/29
Outer London	12/50	8/52	7/52
Outer Metropolitan	3/57	1/61	0/61
Outer Southeast	2/47	1/47	1/47

tral, Newcastle upon Tyne Central, Birmingham Edgbaston and Manchester Withington). The Labour party lost ground, on the other hand, in the City Service grouping (including seats such as Greenwich, Woolwich, and Portsmouth South), the Stable Industrial Towns (Bury North and Nuneaton, for example) and the Metropolitan Industrial group (Bury South, Ealing North, and Edmonton among them).

Finally, what of the Alliance, which would have won no seats if the national pattern of voting by occupational class had held everywhere? As Table 4.8 indicates, all of the seats won by Alliance candidates were predicted as Conservative successes at each of the three elections. Tables 1.3 and 1.4 have shown that those victories were concentrated in a few regions only, with the Scottish Rural areas providing by far the best contexts for Alliance vote-winning strategies.

THE GEOGRAPHY OF THE FLOW-OF-THE-VOTE

The analyses reported above have provided clear indirect evidence of geographical variability in the pattern of the class cleavage, since if that pattern were spatially invariant, and the national pattern then held everywhere, the Conservative party would have won in nearly every constituency. What those

Table 4.12 Distribution of Seats Won by Labour which the Conservative Party was Predicted to Win, using occupational class as the predictor, by functional region

	1979	1983	1987
I.C./Immig.	5/6	6/8	7/8
Ind./Immig.	2/2	13/17	13/16
Poorest Immig.	0/0	4/4	2/2
Intermed. Ind.	20/24	21/30	19/30
Old Indust./Mining	4/5	30/34	30/34
Textile	7/12	8/18	10/18
Poorest Domestic	0/0	6/7	6/6
Conurb. L.A.	1/3	20/26	21/25
Black Co.	0/0	9/9	6/7
Maritime Ind.	0/0	13/15	13/14
Poor I.C.	0/0	10/12	5/7
Clydeside	3/5	15/16	14/14
Scott. Ind.	16/16	24/25	25/25
Scott. Rural	2/17	1/17	1/17
High Status I.M.	0/9	0/9	1/9
I.M.	12/14	11/14	11/14
Outer London	0/24	0/24	0/24
Very High Status	0/31	0/31	0/31
Conurb. W. Collar	0/24	0/24	4/24
City Service	10/23	4/24	6/24
Resort/Retirement	0/29	0/29	1/29
Recent Growth	3/15	2/19	3/19
Stable Ind.	11/25	7/26	7/26
Small Towns	1/27	1/27	1/27
Southern Urban	0/24	0/24	0/24
Modest Aff.	2/26	1/26	2/26
Met. Ind.	12/30	1/30	3/30
Modest Aff. Scot.	0/5	0/5	1/5
Rapid Growth	0/16	0/16	0/16
Prosperous/No Ind.	0/19	0/19	0/19
Agricultural	1/47	1/47	2/47

analyses cannot take account of, however, is the long-term stability in voting patterns. Most of the places that Labour won in 1979, 1983 and 1987 it had represented at elections over the previous decade, so its recent victories did not signify a new ability to mobilise the electorate in certain areas more readily than in others; that differential had long been present. Nevertheless, the material in Chapter 1 suggests that the differential has been accentuated, that over the three elections studied here Labour has lost ground relatively in some regions but gained it in others.

To analyse the extent of the shift, we need to look at short-term fluctuations in support. These are summarised, at the national level, by flow-of-the-vote matrices such as that in Table 2.3. If the national pattern of shifts is the same everywhere – i.e. if a party loses the same percentage of its support to another in all constituencies – then the result at the second election should be predictable from that at the first, plus knowledge of the flows nationally. We can use the same method as earlier in this chapter to investigate geographical variability in short-term flows.

Flow-of-the-vote matrices can be constructed in one of two ways. First, they can be derived from what are known as panel surveys, whereby the same electors are interviewed at the time of each election and asked how they voted then; new voters (immigrants plus those who have recently achieved voting age) will have to be added, as relevant. Secondly, voters surveyed at the time of one election can be asked how they voted at a previous contest. The former is the more desirable, since it avoids the problems of recall that can lead to much misreporting in the second type, but panels are very difficult to sustain, because of voter mobility. Consequently most flow-of-the-vote matrices are constructed using the second method. This invariably produces distortions so that the flow from the known pattern of votes at one election doesn't produce the result of the second; again, the major problem is under-reporting of abstentions. (And, of course, one cannot survey those who have left the electorate, most of them through death, and has to estimate how they voted at the first contest.) Such matrices thus have to be 'Mostellerised' (see p. 96; Sarlvik and Crewe, 1983) to produce the best estimate of the gross pattern of stability and movement.

Flow-of-the-vote matrices have been constructed for our analyses for each of the inter-election periods (1979–1983 and 1983–1987), using the BBC/Gallup survey data. In them, we have omitted both those who left the electorate and those who joined it. The former are assumed to have voted the same way as the electorate at large in each constituency (e.g. if 40 per cent of the electorate in constituency x voted Labour in 1979, it is assumed that 40 per cent of those who died between 1979 and 1983 did too). We cannot test the veracity of that assumption, but it is the best that we can make with the data at our disposal.

Table 4.13 National Flow-of-the-Vote Matrices, 1979–1983 and 1983–1987

1979	1983 Conservative	Labour	Alliance	Nationalist	Non-Voting
Conservative	72.6	3.2	9.7	0.4	14.1
Labour	5.1	63.8	17.6	0.4	13.0
Alliance	11.9	8.2	67.1	0.2	12.6
Nationalist	5.4	10.4	25.3	47.2	11.7
Non-Voting	15.2	9.2	10.5	0.3	65.1

1983	1987 Conservative	Labour	Alliance	Nationalist	Non-Voting
Conservative	77.1	5.1	8.0	0.3	9.4
Labour	4.3	77.3	7.2	0.7	10.5
Alliance	13.1	15.8	60.0	0.9	10.6
Nationalist	5.8	11.1	5.3	60.8	17.0
Non-Voting	16.3	14.9	6.7	0.6	61.5

For new voters, we assume that they vote in the same way as non-voters at the first election of the pair. This is almost certainly not the case, but as far as we can tell the amount of error introduced by this assumption, across the 633 constituencies, is not great. (We could, by using the Census age tables, have estimated the number of new voters in each constituency, but decided not to. Further research is needed on this, but at this stage we are satisfied that the errors on assumptions introduced are not gross and do not distort the spatial variability that we seek to display.)

The two matrices are presented in Table 4.13, in which the flows are presented as percentages of the row totals. Thus between 1979 and 1983, a major difference between the Conservative and Labour parties was in their ability to retain the support of those who voted for them in 1979, a difference that was not present in the 1983–1987 period. The Alliance, on the other hand, held on to more support in the first period than in the second. The inter-party flows show a major haemorrhage from Labour to the Alliance in 1979–1983, and also from the nationalist parties to the Alliance, but the shift away from the Alliance in 1983–1987 was relatively equally balanced between Conservative and Labour, with the latter having a slight advantage only.

On the assumptions that these matrices are reliable estimates of the national flow patterns and that each constituency is a representative sample of the national population, it should be possible to predict the result in the constituencies. For the 1979–1983 period, for example, multiplying the distribution of votes in a constituency in 1979 by the flow-of-the-vote matrix will provide an estimate of what the result would have been in 1983. This estimate can then be compared with the actual distribution, producing comparative percentages in the same way that the estimates produced by the occupational class multiplications were derived above.

How good are those predictions relative to the actual results? We answer this question again by using comparative percentages, the actual result for a party as a percentage of the predicted value; the closer this figure is to 100.0, the more accurate the prediction. Figures 4.7 and 4.8 give the frequency distributions for 1983 and 1987, respectively. For 1983, we see that only with the Labour party was there a substantial number of constituencies which fell outside the values of 75 and 125 for the comparative percentages; most of the predictions of Conservative, Alliance and Non-Voting were reasonably accurate but in a substantial number of constituencies Labour did much less well than predicted, balanced by the largest category where it did a little better than predicted. Much the same picture is presented for 1987 (Figure 4.8), except that there is greater variability for the Alliance then than was the case four years earlier.

The summary statistics for the histograms in those two figures are given in Table 4.14. The CV values suggest little change over the two periods, with very slight shifts towards greater spatial variability in the Conservative and Alliance results but none at all for Labour. This suggests that between each pair of elections the spatial pattern of voting remained very consistent in relative terms.

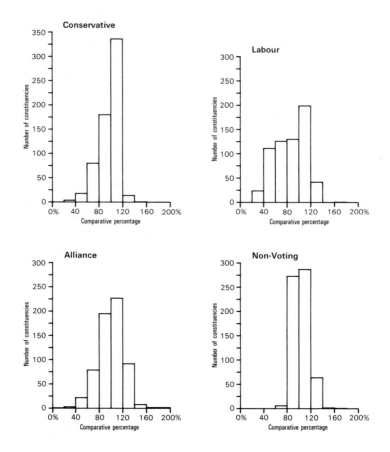

Figure 4.7 Comparative percentages for voting at the 1983 general election, using the 1979–1983 flow-of-the-vote matrix as the predictor.

To test whether, despite the apparent stability implied by Figures 4.7 and 4.8 and Table 4.14, there were spatial variations in the flow-of-the-vote, Tables 4.15 and 4.16 give the average comparative percentages according to the regional structures applied here. They show clear regional shifts within the overall apparent stability.

With regard to *geographical regions* (Table 4.15), there was a substantial shift against the Conservatives over the second period, relative to the first, in all of Scotland, in much of northern England (excluding Greater Manchester, the Rest of the Northwest, and West Yorkshire) and in Devon and Cornwall. Countering this, there were substantial shifts to the Conservative party in both Inner and Outer London. The Labour party did much better in Scotland and the whole of northern England, with the partial exception of Greater Manchester, from the 1983–1987 flows than it did from 1979–1983, as well as in Industrial South Wales and in Devon and Cornwall. For the Alliance, major relative gains in Rural Scotland were balanced by losses in Eastern Scotland. Further south, it gained ground substantially in Merseyside, Rural Wales and

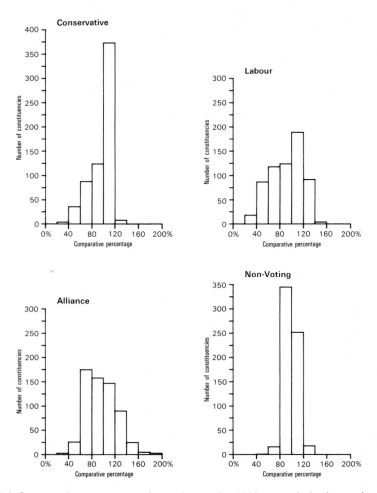

Figure 4.8 Comparative percentages for voting at the 1987 general election, using the 1983–1987 flow-of-the-vote matrix as the predictor.

Table 4.14 Summary Statistics (CV) for the Comparative Percentage Distributions, using flow-of-the-vote matrices as predictors

	1983	1987
Conservative CV	17.6	19.1
Labour CV	30.4	30.2
Alliance CV	22.9	27.3
Non-Voting CV	12.3	11.6

Table 4.15 The Average Comparative Percentages, using flow-of-the-vote matrices as predictors, by geographical region

	Conservative		Labour		Alliance		Non-Voting	
	1983	1987	1983	1987	1983	1987	1983	1987
Strathclyde	71.5	61.1	114.0	127.0	92.1	71.6	104.7	92.1
E. Scotland	86.1	76.5	102.0	113.3	100.6	84.9	103.0	91.7
Rural Scotland	86.5	79.4	61.6	76.3	92.3	109.4	111.1	93.9
Rural North	106.2	99.8	81.9	88.7	97.7	101.5	100.7	99.4
Industrial Northeast	87.4	79.9	105.4	117.6	99.4	89.3	106.2	101.0
Merseyside	83.7	72.3	107.2	113.5	89.5	105.9	109.3	98.4
Greater Manchester	90.6	93.6	103.5	105.0	90.1	89.6	107.7	99.6
Rest of Northwest	101.0	100.0	99.6	104.3	96.4	90.4	97.8	96.3
West Yorks.	94.6	96.3	97.8	107.3	97.4	89.7	105.7	97.1
South Yorks.	80.1	73.4	108.8	119.4	88.4	82.8	111.7	104.1
Rural Wales	96.4	93.4	80.7	98.0	86.2	101.1	103.6	79.2
Industrial South Wales	80.5	82.1	105.2	126.7	94.9	75.2	104.4	88.3
W. Midlands Conurbation	94.0	98.4	105.1	100.1	90.2	81.9	104.7	107.2
Rest of West Midlands	109.2	104.0	81.9	85.0	106.0	105.1	93.7	98.2
East Midlands	107.3	108.0	87.2	91.0	97.3	94.4	98.9	95.6
East Anglia	111.3	107.9	73.6	77.4	112.5	105.1	93.9	99.5
Devon and Cornwall	108.1	98.7	50.9	73.6	127.5	118.9	92.0	103.5
Wessex	109.8	106.8	63.9	65.5	113.4	120.4	96.3	94.7
Inner London	78.8	89.3	96.4	96.6	87.4	92.5	122.4	110.5
Outer London	100.2	108.9	77.0	80.4	102.0	91.9	111.1	105.4
Outer Metropolitan	110.7	110.7	64.3	65.5	111.8	105.2	98.4	101.0
Outer Southeast	110.4	107.5	62.2	64.8	111.2	114.8	99.3	99.5
R^2	0.52	0.59	0.48	0.51	0.18	0.24	0.30	0.27

Wessex, but lost in Industrial South Wales, the West Midlands Conurbation, East Anglia, Devon and Cornwall, Outer London and the Outer Metropolitan zone.

What we see in the geographical regions, therefore, is that there were substantial differential shifts in the success of the parties. In general terms, in the 1979–1983 flows, the Conservatives and the Alliance did relatively well in the southern regions, because their votes were on average greater than predicted, whereas the Labour party did relatively well in the north. Over the next four years, although this general pattern was sustained there were some notable shifts, with each party losing ground in areas where it was initially strong and gaining it where it was weak, as well as building on some of its strengths. The regional map has been in a state of considerable flux, but the increase in the R^2 values suggests that inter-regional variations have been crystallised over the period.

Turning to the *functional regions*, Table 4.16 shows a very clear regional pattern. In 1983, the average comparative percentage for Labour exceeded 100.0 in each of the first 13 regions in the table, and also in the Inner Metropolitan category; this was balanced by averages below 100.0 in each of those regions for both Conservative and Alliance, and above 100.0 in virtually every other for both of those parties. Non-Voting tended to have averages above 100.0 in the regions where Labour did too, and below 100.0 in the regions where the the Conservative and Alliance averages exceeded that value. Thus, compared to the national pattern, the net flows to Labour and Non-Voting were greater than average in the less prosperous functional regions and the net flows to Conservative and the Alliance exceeded the national figure in the more prosperous parts of Great Britain. Of all the data presented so far in this book, this is probably the clearest evidence of growing regional polarisation in the country's electoral geography.

Between 1983 and 1987 the changes were not as consistent. One of the most salient features is that in all four regions whose constituencies are all in Scotland the net flow to Conservative was less than expected according to the national pattern; in Clydeside, in Scottish Industrial, in Scottish Rural, and in Modestly Affluent Scotland the 1987 comparative percentage average was substantially lower than that for 1983, so the shifts away from the Tories were, in relative terms, great. The Labour party clearly benefited from this in all four regions, with substantial increases in its average; this was already over

Table 4.16 The Average Comparative Percentages, using flow-of-the-vote matrices as predictors, by functional region

	Conservative		Labour		Alliance		Non-Voting	
	1983	1987	1983	1987	1983	1987	1983	1987
I.C./Immig.	80.5	93.0	104.9	101.7	81.7	83.6	117.9	111.9
Ind./Immig.	91.8	94.7	108.6	109.2	83.6	80.1	108.8	105.2
Poorest Immig.	74.2	82.0	115.9	111.5	73.2	52.8	116.3	121.8
Intermed. Ind.	96.2	95.0	104.5	108.9	96.0	93.1	100.9	96.5
Old Indust./Mining	82.7	85.9	111.5	119.6	83.4	75.9	108.6	94.9
Textile	96.5	97.6	106.4	108.7	91.3	87.9	101.0	96.8
Poorest Domestic	58.4	61.2	104.2	125.7	72.2	88.8	120.6	94.7
Conurb. L.A.	85.4	83.3	107.7	114.4	88.6	87.5	111.4	106.1
Black Co.	92.8	100.4	110.5	103.5	86.1	77.0	103.6	107.5
Maritime Ind.	85.9	81.1	105.8	117.9	98.7	84.9	107.5	101.8
Poor I.C.	64.2	67.4	105.8	104.5	83.3	87.1	122.9	117.7
Clydeside	59.8	53.1	110.9	129.0	79.4	66.3	118.7	95.1
Scott. Ind.	78.3	65.0	116.0	125.5	93.9	71.2	99.1	86.8
Scott. Rural	93.4	86.5	54.6	64.1	101.4	111.7	107.8	94.4
High Status I.M.	91.4	101.0	86.3	88.0	87.4	84.8	122.3	112.0
I.M.	79.4	88.5	102.6	103.5	82.9	86.7	122.5	109.5
Outer London	104.8	111.0	68.2	74.2	108.3	100.0	107.3	108.8
Very High Status	110.1	109.6	56.9	62.1	110.7	108.7	101.3	100.6
Conurb. W. Collar	98.6	100.7	78.3	84.4	107.0	105.6	109.6	101.9
City Service	96.2	96.4	94.7	100.9	100.2	108.2	107.7	97.3
Resort/Retirement	109.2	105.7	53.5	59.6	108.5	118.0	103.4	100.4
Recent Growth	106.5	100.2	91.6	95.3	114.0	100.0	90.0	97.5
Stable Ind.	103.5	103.0	96.8	100.3	105.1	91.6	91.6	94.4
Small Towns	109.6	105.7	77.4	83.3	104.6	107.6	95.9	91.5
Southern Urban	113.3	110.0	65.8	67.5	115.5	112.2	93.2	97.3
Modest Aff.	108.9	105.9	81.5	89.9	110.0	104.2	94.3	93.6
Met. Ind.	105.7	109.3	86.0	93.1	106.3	88.2	100.3	98.8
Modest Aff. Scot.	100.6	95.9	93.8	114.2	110.0	91.4	94.4	85.4
Rapid Growth	115.4	110.7	55.3	62.8	115.4	107.8	94.2	99.7
Prosperous/No Ind.	110.7	104.2	54.2	66.9	111.4	120.9	100.4	98.6
Agricultural	109.4	103.2	58.2	64.8	110.0	116.6	96.2	97.7
R^2	0.67	0.59	0.69	0.61	0.25	0.34	0.44	0.26

100.0 in Clydeside and the Industrial areas in 1983, and it switched to above 100.0 also in the Modestly Affluent constituencies (such as Ayr, Stirling, and Edinburgh Pentlands). In the Scottish Rural areas the Alliance was clearly a substantial beneficiary, but in the other three it did less well at attracting votes in 1987 than in 1983, so that outside the rural areas Scotland clearly shifted very substantially away from Conservative and Alliance and towards Labour. Interestingly, the four Scottish groupings also recorded a decreasing flow into the Non-Voting category, with all having averages below 100.0 in 1987, suggesting that the shift to Labour was accompanied by a greater willingness to vote (notably against the incumbent government).

Outside Scotland there were no uniform shifts in the apparent net flows. Compared with the 1979–1983 situation, for example, Labour did even better in 1983–1987, relative to the national pattern, in the Old Industrial and Mining group (including all three Barnsley seats, Wigan, and Workington), in the seven constituencies forming the Poorest Domestic Conditions category (Newham South, Liverpool Walton, Hull West, Cynon Valley, Merthyr Tyd-fil, Rhondda, and Western Isles), in the Maritime Industrial group (places such as Bootle, Hartlepool, and Great Grimsby), and in the City Service (Wallasey, Tynemouth and Exeter, for example) and Stable Industrial (Rother Valley, Congleton, and Wellingborough, among others) groups. But else-where, its ability to win over converts, and to retain the votes of Labour loyalists, was less than in 1983, although its average remains above 100.0. For the Conservative party, in those regions where its average was below 100.0 in 1983 it improved its relative performance in twelve, but lost ground in six. Where its average was over 100.0 in 1983 it remained so in 1987, with the exception of the Modestly Affluent Scottish group; it performed better in 1987 than 1983 in only two, however, so that although some regions apparently became even stronger Labour groups this was not countered by a similar hardening of Conservative vote-winning strength in certain areas. In part this was because of the activities of the Alliance. Where it was relatively weak at winning votes in 1983, the Alliance was in general even weaker in 1987. Where it was relatively strong in 1983, however, it was able to sustain that strength in many cases, winning more net converts than it did nationally. In the City Service grouping, in the Resort and Retirement centres (Southport and Torbay, for example, and Bournemouth and Blackpool), in the Prosperous Non-Industrial constituencies (such as Bath and Cheltenham, Tunbridge Wells and Harrogate) and in the Agricultural areas the net flows to the Alliance were apparently greater in the second period than in the first. As it became a more regional party (see Chapter 1), largely in competition with the Conservatives, so it cut into the latter's ability to attract floating voters and sustain the loyalty of its previous supporters.

Flows and Seats

The analyses reported in this section take the differential pattern of voting by occupational class implied by the earlier discussion in this chapter as given.

(Thus in 1983, for example, we assume that people in each class are more likely to vote Conservative in some constituencies than in others.) The flows in each constituency start from those differential bases. Thus it would be unlikely that spatial variations in the flow-of-the-vote would produce as many variations from the predicted (on a national basis) distribution of seats as in the first analysis (Table 4.8), and this was indeed the case (Table 4.17). In 1983, only 65 of the 633 constituencies were not won by the party predicted to do so from the national flow matrix, and in 1987 the number fell to 55.

Table 4.17 Predicted and Actual Seats Won, using flow-of-the-vote matrices as the predictor

1979–1983

Seats Predicted to be Won By	Seats Won By			
	Conservative	Labour	Alliance	Nationalist
Conservative	390	31	12	1
Labour	7	178	4	2
Alliance	0	0	7	1

1983–1987

Seats Predicted to be Won By	Seats Won By			
	Conservative	Labour	Alliance	Nationalist
Conservative	370	21	16	5
Labour	6	208	4	1
Alliance	0	0	2	0

Tables 4.18 and 4.19 show the regional distribution of the seats that were won, according to predicted winner. (The small number of seats – seven in 1983 and two in 1987 – that the Alliance was predicted to win are excluded, as are the four in 1983 and six in 1987 won by the nationalist parties.) These show that Labour's loss of seats that it should have won was concentrated in the East Midlands and Industrial South Wales in 1983, but distributed across seven functional regions, suggesting that it was regional rather than functional issues that led to Labour's failures; in 1987, the six seats that Labour 'lost' to the Conservatives were spread across six geographical regions, and though two were in the Intermediate Industrial grouping there was no obvious concentration in functional type either.

Turning to the larger number of seats won by Labour when the national flow trends suggested a Conservative victory, Table 4.18 shows that in 1983 one-quarter of these were in the West Midlands conurbation. (Four years later, Labour retained its hold on seven of these, but lost one back to the Conservative party.) Another major block was in the Yorkshire/Lancashire groups of

Table 4.18 Distribution of Seats Won according to Predicted Winner, using flow-of-the-vote matrix as predictor, by geographical region

| Predicted Winner | 1983 | | | | | | 1987 | | | | | |
| | Conservative | | | Labour | | | Conservative | | | Labour | | |
Actual Winner	C	L	A	C	L	A	C	L	A	C	L	A
Strathclyde	5	2	1	0	24	0	2	3	0	0	27	0
E. Scotland	5	0	1	0	13	0	3	2	1	0	13	0
Rural Scotland	11	0	2	0	2	1	5	1	6	0	4	0
Rural North	17	1	0	0	7	0	16	1	1	0	8	0
Industrial Northeast	4	1	1	0	21	0	4	1	0	0	22	0
Merseyside	5	2	1	0	9	0	4	0	2	0	11	0
Greater Manchester	11	2	0	0	13	0	10	1	0	0	15	1
Rest of Northwest	24	4	0	0	5	0	19	0	0	1	9	0
West Yorks.	10	2	1	1	8	1	9	3	0	0	11	0
South Yorks.	1	1	0	0	13	0	1	0	0	0	14	0
Rural Wales	7	0	1	0	4	0	4	1	3	0	4	0
Industrial South Wales	5	2	0	2	14	0	4	3	0	0	16	0
W. Midlands Conurbation	14	8	0	0	10	0	14	0	0	1	17	0
Rest of West Midlands	22	0	0	0	4	0	21	1	0	0	4	0
East Midlands	30	2	0	3	6	0	30	2	0	0	9	0
East Anglia	18	1	1	0	0	0	18	1	0	1	0	0
Devon and Cornwall	14	0	1	0	0	1	14	0	2	0	0	0
Wessex	30	0	1	0	1	0	30	0	1	0	1	0
Inner London	12	3	0	0	15	2	12	0	0	1	16	3
Outer London	44	0	0	0	8	0	44	0	0	1	7	0
Outer Metropolitan	59	0	0	1	1	0	60	0	0	1	0	0
Outer Southeast	46	0	1	0	0	0	46	1	0	0	0	0

regions, with ten in Merseyside, Greater Manchester, Rest of Northwest and West Yorkshire. There is evidence of a concentration of these seats in functional regions too (Table 4.19), not only in the Black Country but also in the Industrial group with Immigrants, the Intermediate Industrial towns, the Textile Towns, the Inner Metropolitan constituencies and the City with Service Industries grouping. Four years later, Labour clearly retained its hold on most of these seats, although two in the Intermediate Industrial group were unexpectedly won by the Conservative party. The Labour victories where Conservative success was expected were concentrated in Scotland, West Yorkshire, Industrial South Wales and the East Midlands; functionally, most of them were in either the Conurban White-Collar or the City Service grouping.

Alliance successes were mainly in the rural areas, especially Scotland, when the expected victor was Conservative. Its victories over Labour were very much concentrated in Inner London.

Table 4.19 Distribution of Seats Won according to Predicted Winner, using flow-of-the-vote matrix as predictor, by functional region

Predicted Winner	1983 Conservative			Labour			1987 Conservative			Labour		
Actual Winner	C	L	A	C	L	A	C	L	A	C	L	A
I.C./Immig.	2	0	0	0	6	0	1	0	0	0	7	0
Ind./Immig.	3	5	0	1	8	0	2	2	0	1	12	0
Poorest Immig.	0	0	0	0	4	0	0	0	0	0	4	0
Intermed. Ind.	9	4	0	0	17	0	9	0	0	2	19	0
Old Indust./ Mining	3	2	0	1	28	0	4	0	0	0	30	0
Textile	8	3	1	0	5	0	6	2	0	1	8	1
Poorest Domestic	0	0	0	0	6	0	0	0	0	0	7	0
Conurb. L.A.	4	2	0	1	18	1	4	1	0	0	21	0
Black Co.	0	5	0	0	4	0	0	0	0	1	8	0
Maritime Ind.	1	1	1	0	12	0	0	1	1	0	13	0
Poor I.C.	1	0	0	0	10	1	1	0	0	0	10	1
Clydeside	0	1	0	0	15	0	0	0	0	0	17	0
Scott. Ind.	1	1	0	0	23	0	0	1	0	0	24	0
Scott. Rural	10	0	2	0	1	1	5	0	6	0	1	0
High Status I.M.	9	0	0	0	0	0	8	1	0	0	0	0
I.M.	2	3	1	0	8	0	2	0	0	1	11	0
Outer London	24	0	0	0	0	0	24	0	0	0	0	0
Very High Status	31	0	0	0	0	0	31	0	0	0	0	0
Conurb. W. Collar	24	0	0	0	0	0	20	4	0	0	0	0
City Service	17	3	1	1	1	1	15	3	1	0	3	2
Resort/ Retirement	28	0	1	0	0	0	28	0	1	0	0	0
Recent Growth	14	0	2	1	2	0	15	1	1	0	2	0
Stable Ind.	19	0	0	0	7	0	19	0	0	0	7	0
Small Towns	24	1	1	1	0	0	24	0	1	0	1	0
Southern Urban	24	0	0	0	0	0	24	0	0	0	0	0
Modest Aff.	24	0	0	1	1	0	24	1	0	0	1	0
Met. Ind.	29	0	0	0	1	0	27	2	0	0	1	0
Modest Aff. Scot.	5	0	0	0	0	0	4	1	0	0	0	0
Rapid Growth	16	0	0	0	0	0	16	0	0	0	0	0
Prosperous/No Ind.	19	0	0	0	0	0	19	0	0	0	0	0
Agricultural	39	0	2	0	1	0	38	1	5	0	1	0

IN SUMMARY

In this chapter we have provided substantial indirect evidence that the geography of voting in each of Great Britain's 633 constituencies in 1979, 1983 and 1987 was not just a replication of the national pattern. Knowledge of the pattern of voting by occupational class derived from national surveys did not allow for very exact predictions of the distribution of votes between the parties in the individual constituencies. To produce the actual results, and thereby to prevent landslide Conservative victories, the Labour and Alliance parties must have won many more votes from all classes in some places than they did in others. Further, the growing polarisation of the electorate suggests that this differential ability increased rather than decreased over time.

People do not come to each general election with a completely open mind, unaffected by their behaviour at previous contests. Thus the differences just summarised, once present, are the starting point for the next campaign; parties seek to convince people who voted for them previously to remain loyal and to convert others who voted for a different party to switch. This relative success is summarised in a flow-of-the-vote matrix which shows the gross pattern of shifts between parties. Such matrices are also constructed from national surveys. Our analyses here suggest that they are not faithful reproductions of the situation in the individual constituencies, so that, although the differences between predicted and actual winners were fewer than in the analyses of occupational class, we were again unable to predict the distribution of votes in many places very accurately. Regional analyses showed not only that each party achieved greater net gains in some parts of Great Britain than others but also that there were considerable differences between 1979–1983 and 1983–1987 in the geography of vote-winning.

What our analyses so far have done, therefore, is to enhance the conclusions of Chapter 1 with regard to the importance of the regional dimension to an understanding of the changing pattern of voting in Great Britain. Constituencies differ very substantially in the ability of parties to win votes in the different occupational classes, and then to retain those votes, because knowledge of the national pattern of voting does not allow very successful prediction of the results by constituency, neither in terms of the percentage of the votes won by each party nor even in terms of which party would win the seat. Having established this important conclusion, we can now move to clearer analyses of the reasons for it.

5

A CHANGING ELECTORAL GEOGRAPHY?

Two major implications can be drawn from the findings reported in Chapter 4. First, because the occupational class composition of each constituency proved to be an unreliable predictor of the election results there, it is clear that people in the same occupational class voted differently in different places; the class cleavage is spatially variable in its amplitude, at least. Secondly, since the results in each constituency could not be very accurately predicted using the national flow-of-the-vote matrix showing voter shifts between elections, it is similarly clear that both party loyalty and inter-party movements must vary spatially. Our concern here is to explore these two sets of spatial variations, and to chart their changing geographies.

How can one analyse such details about elections? The needed data refer, of course, to individual voters, cross-classifying their party choice at one election with both their choice at previous elections and their socio-economic characteristics. But such data are not available as part of any major collection, certainly not those collected during the electoral process itself, because of the secrecy inherent in the ballot. All that is known in Great Britain are (i) the number of people registered as electors in each constituency (and this is not an accurate statement at most dates, because changes – notably deaths and migrations – are not necessarily notified to the returning officers, who complete the rolls in October of each year; Todd and Dodd, 1982) and (ii) the number of votes cast for each candidate. The latter are reported at the constituency scale only; not only are no data released for smaller areas, they are not even compiled, because the law requires that all ballot papers in a constituency be put together prior to counting the votes for each candidate. (There is a prior count of votes cast at each polling booth, but this total is not published.) For full details of how many votes were cast for each candidate, therefore, we cannot study at scales below that of the constituency.

To complement the official counts with details of the electorate, the techniques of opinion polling have been developed over the last half-century. These use statistically-selected samples of the electorate, and so necessarily incorporate some error factors that result from the use of sampling procedures. (Those errors are typical of all samples and, if the sample is properly taken and is a true random sample of the population, are relatively small – even with a sample of only a few thousand to represent the entire British electorate – and can be computed. The problem for most surveys, however, is knowing whether they do have a random sample of the electorate, as both Butler and Stokes, 1969, 1974, and Heath, Jowell and Curtice, 1985, indicate.) Such surveys use questionnaires that can collect a range of factual and attitudinal data, and provide insights to how different sections of the electorate not only vote as they do, but why.

Opinion polling has been developed to serve three main purposes. The first is to inform the political parties about the ways the electorate are thinking about issues, and how they are likely to respond to various policy proposals. Thus the party of an incumbent government will poll the electorate to obtain feedback on its actions and to gauge when it might sensibly call an election. Opposition parties will similarly conduct polls to inform them what is popular and unpopular in what the government is doing and the opposition are proposing. Such polls, the results of which are usually kept secret by the parties, are very important during an election campaign, aiding parties to pitch their message towards the voters they think could be persuaded to vote for them.

The second type of poll is that conducted by the media, both to inform and, in some cases, to influence. Opinion polls at any time give statements of what people think about issues, parties and individual politicians, and are considered useful adjuncts to news coverage in journals, newspapers, radio and TV. At election time, they are of particular interest, since they chart the progress of the campaign. In recent years, as Crewe (1986b) shows, the number of such polls has increased greatly. The reasons lie in the roles that the media have developed, and their need for apparently important new information on the course of a campaign. Thus Crewe proposes that

> However static public opinion actually is, the polls enable the media to maximise the impression of flux and change (p. 249)
> However clear the outcome and trend, polls allow the media to hedge their bets (p. 250)

and thus retain reader/listener/viewer interest.

> The more improbable a poll finding, the more likely the media will give it prominence (p. 251)

Further

> Poll reports are a lazy editor's godsend; a reliable filler on a good day (p. 251)

and

> The more polls there are, the more likely they are to become an election issue (p. 252)

For the media, then, polls provide ready 'news' material with which to generate interest, so that if one part of the media is reporting frequent polls others will need to commission theirs also, in order to keep pace in the contest for reporting latest opinion about the ongoing contest. For some, this is the sole reason for using polls; for others there is the ulterior motive of using (if not abusing) the poll findings to promote a particular political line. (In Britain this refers only to newspapers, since control of broadcasting prevents partisan presentation of material in other than a balanced way, although the rules devised by the broadcasting companies favour established parties: see Munro, 1986.) Whether the publication of poll results does influence how people vote is as yet an incompletely answered question (see Whiteley's, 1986b, claim that polling aided the Alliance in 1983); if it does, then clearly there is great potential for manipulating the electorate, both locally and nationally.

The third type of polling is that undertaken for academic analyses, in which the surveys (both the questionnaires and the samples) are designed to provide information that can be used to answer a wide range of questions about electoral behaviour rather than a few readily digested facts for immediate use only. Such surveying was initially developed in the U.S.A.; in Britain, the various waves of the British Election Study have produced major analyses of each general election since 1959 (Butler and Stokes, 1969, 1974; Sarlvik and Crewe, 1983; Heath, Jowell and Curtice, 1985).

Virtually all of these studies are designed to provide information about the electorate as a whole. (Most of the exceptions are polls of particular places or, more likely, particular types of places, such as marginal constituencies.) Usually they comprise 2000–4000 respondents only, which is sufficient to provide a good general picture of the national position but insufficiently large to allow analyses of particular geographical or functional regions (as Johnston, 1986a, 1987d, shows). For this reason, survey data alone are insufficient for the tasks that we have set here.

So what alternatives are there? The one that has been widely used, particularly by geographers (as reviewed in Taylor and Johnston, 1979), involves combining two sets of aggregate data into what are known as ecological analyses. The two sets are the election results and the census data, by constituencies. Statistical analysis of these two allows inferences to be made such that, for example, if there is a positive correlation between percentage voting Labour and percentage unemployed it can be inferred that (i) the unemployed are more likely to vote Labour and (ii) that where unemployment is high, those in employment are likely to vote Labour (see Brown and Payne, 1986). Such inferences need to be theoretically-based otherwise spurious correlations could be translated into apparently meaningful relationships: why, for example, should people who live in houses without internal WCs be more likely to vote Labour (Rasmussen, 1973)? Sensitively used, as in Crewe and Payne (1976), ecological analyses can shed a great deal of light on the possible influences on voting patterns, and suggest hypotheses worthy of testing with other data.

Ecological analyses, because they are based on place-specific data, such as those for constituencies, allow the geography of voting to be explored in ways that survey analyses do not. Recently, procedures have been developed to combine the two, and it is these which are the focus of our discussion here. The next section provides a brief exposition of the methods that we use.

THE ENTROPY-MAXIMISING APPROACH

In Chapter 4, we combined survey, census and electoral data to produce predictions of what the election result would have been in each constituency if the relationships described by the survey data held everywhere. The results clearly indicated that the assumption was invalid. Thus we have to ask an alternative question: to what extent must the relationships between, for example, occupational class and vote vary between constituencies, in order to produce the observed election results, given the constituency occupational class structures as portrayed by the census?

A means of answering this question has been provided by Johnston and Hay (1982), who have adapted a method developed for predicting traffic flows. The full details of the procedure are laid out in their paper, and in an appendix to Johnston's (1985a) use of them to explore the geography of voting in England in 1983. We will not repeat those technical details here, but simply provide a brief overview of the procedure.

Take the very simple hypothetical situation of an electoral system divided into three constituencies. For each of those constituencies we know: (a) the number of votes cast for each party; and (b) the number of people in each of the four occupational classes. We have no knowledge of the number of people in each occupational class who voted for each party in each constituency. This gives the pattern of knowns (K) and unknowns (U) in Table 5.1. Our task is to estimate the values of U. We know that for each row, the sum of all the U

Table 5.1 The Knowns (K) and Unknowns (U) in the Pattern of Voting by Occupational Class in a Hypothetical System of Three Constituencies

*Constituency x**

Occupational Class	Vote for Party				
	I	II	III	IV	Total
A	U	U	U	U	K
B	U	U	U	U	K
C	U	U	U	U	K
D	U	U	U	U	K
Total	K	K	K	K	K

* x = 1,3

values must equal the K value, and similarly for each column. But there is a very large number of possible values for each U, given that the K values are not small.

Only knowing the K values for each of the constituencies, it is possible to produce estimates of the U values, using the techniques of mathematical

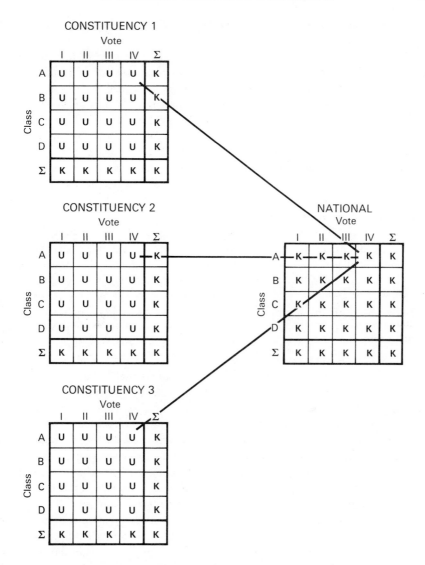

Figure 5.1 A hypothetical national electoral system comprising three constituencies, illustrating the data used in the entropy-maximising procedure.

programming. But these estimates are not particularly realistic. Knowledge of one further set of K values allows much better estimates to be computed. We take a survey of all voters in the system and estimate the values of U; people are asked how they voted and what occupational class they belong to, and with that information we can produce a national class-by-vote matrix. That matrix is derived from a sample, but we can then inflate it so that it provides estimated voting for the whole population (e.g. if we took a five per cent sample, we multiply the cell values by 20 to get estimates of the national values). Figure 5.1 illustrates what we now know and what remains unknown, on the assumption that our sample provides an accurate representation of the population as a whole.

With our national sample survey, we now know the sum of each set of U values; we know, for example, the total number of people in class A who voted for party IV (as Figure 5.1 indicates). This gives an extra, important piece of information on which to base an estimation procedure. Thus we know:

1)   That in each constituency, the sum of all of the U values in any row must equal the K value for that row (i.e. the total of people in a class voting for each party must equal the total for that class in the constituency);

2)   That in each constituency, the sum of all of the U values in any column must equal the K value for that column (i.e. the total of people voting for each party across the four classes must equal the total number of votes cast for that party in the constituency); and

3)   That across all constituencies, the sum of all the U values in any class x party cell must equal the K value for that cell in the national matrix (i.e. the total number of people in a given class voting for a given party must sum to the total for that class x vote combination for the system as a whole). With these three constraints, it is possible to use the entropy-maximising procedures, developed for estimating traffic flows, to provide the best estimates of the U values, such that they fit the class and voting patterns in each constituency and the class-by-vote pattern for the system as a whole. (The technical term for those estimates is maximum likelihood: Johnston, 1985a.) They indicate the minimum amount of variation around the national matrix that is consistent with the class structure and pattern of voting in each constituency.

Given that we have the electoral and class data for each constituency (as described in Chapter 4), plus survey estimates of the national pattern of voting by occupational class, production of the maximum-likelihood estimates is a relatively straightforward task, conducted using specially-written computer programs. They provide us with reliable estimates of that which we need to know for analyses of spatial variability in the class cleavage, and also in the flow-of-the-vote. (The latter are produced in exactly the same way, except that the rows in Figure 5.1 are parties, and not classes.) Just how reliable the estimates are is as yet unexplored for British data (though see Johnston, Hay and Rumley, 1983, 1984, for critical evaluations using Australian data). Given the data available to us, they are the best possible estimates that we can derive; further, as already stressed, they are conservative estimates, indicating the minimum amount of spatial variability that is consistent with the results. The geography that they describe must exist at least to that degree; if the variability in one component is exaggerated (voting for party II by class B, for example) then if that variability were reduced the variability in others would have to be increased in compensation.

The remainder of this chapter describes and analyses various aspects of the geography of voting in Britain over the period 1979–1987 using the procedure outlined here to produce the needed data. What we are portraying is the most likely spatial variability in voting within Britain, to the extent that the data allow.

VOTING BY CLASS

As indicated above (p. 94), there is much discussion in the psephological literature on the proper definition of classes for voting studies. While accepting the cases made by some in this context (notably Heath, Jowell and Curtice, 1985), we are constrained here by the data available to us, particularly from the BBC/Gallup Surveys. Thus we use the system of six occupational classes also employed in Chapter 4, as follows:

1) Professional;
2) Administrative and Managerial;
3) Routine Non-Manual;
4) Skilled Manual;
5) Semiskilled Manual; and
6) Unskilled Manual.

The descriptions are reasonably self-explanatory, though clearly there can be considerable debate as to the correct class location for many occupations (and, of course, about the best classification; see Heath, Jowell and Curtice, 1985; Kavanagh, 1986; Dunleavy, 1987). Since the survey data were already pre-coded, we had to accept the decisions made, which were consistent with the six-fold occupational classification obtained from the 1981 Census.

For each of the three elections (1979, 1983, 1987) we have produced estimates of the number of votes cast by members of each occupational class for each party (including abstainers, with whom are included those who voted for parties other than Conservative, Labour, Alliance, Plaid Cymru and Scottish Nationalist). Thus for each of the 633 constituencies we have three class (6 rows) by vote (5 columns) matrices, for each of the three elections. In the next section we describe these matrices in summary form, and follow that with analyses of the variations in their contents. First, however, we look at a few maps showing their distributions. (With six occupational classes, four voting possibilities – Conservative, Labour, Alliance and Non-Voting – and three elections, the total number of possible maps is 72; we show only a small selection, and focus on the two end-dates, 1979 and 1987.)

The first four maps focus on the Administrative and Managerial occupational class which, as Table 4.1 indicates, gives more support to the Conservative party than does any other. (It is our equivalent of Miller's, 1977, core class of controllers.) Figures 5.2 and 5.3 show voting by that class for the Conservatives in 1979 and 1987 respectively and show that despite its overall apparent predilection for the Tory candidates there has been very substantial variation in the level of support they have obtained. In 1979, most of southern England (outside Greater London) had at least 45 per cent of this class voting Conservative; eight years later, many of those reporting lower figures previously had joined the general pattern (constituencies such as Slough and Swindon) and there is a definite block of what can only be described as solid Tory country there (with Portsmouth South and Yeovil the only exceptions). Conversely, further north, and especially in parts of South Wales, Merseyside,

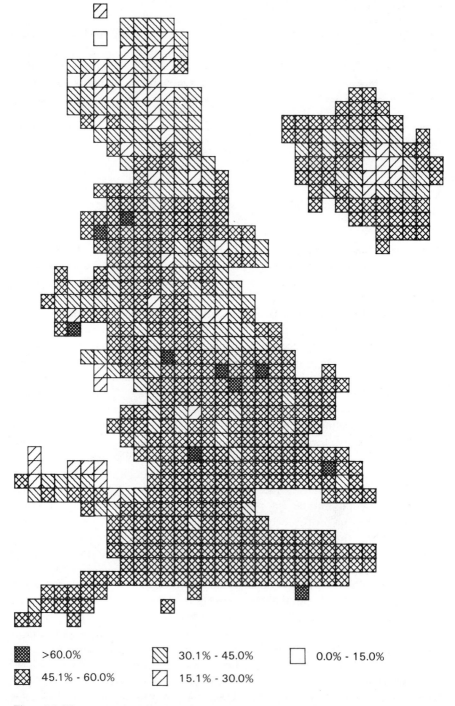

Figure 5.2 The geography of voting Conservative by the Administrative and Managerial occupational class, 1979.

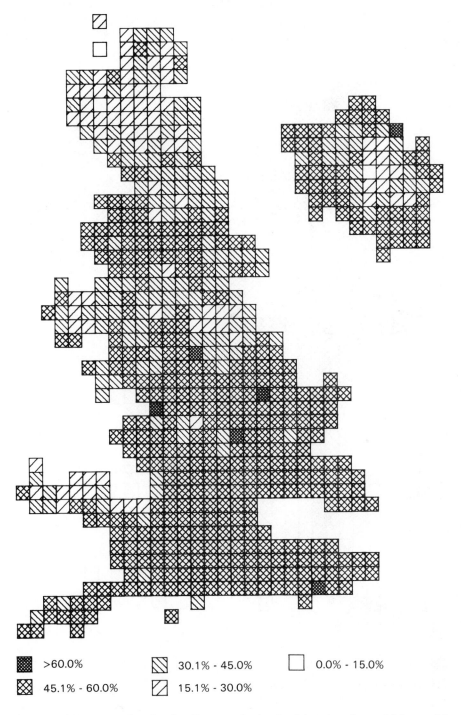

Figure 5.3 The geography of voting Conservative by the Administrative and Managerial occupational class, 1987.

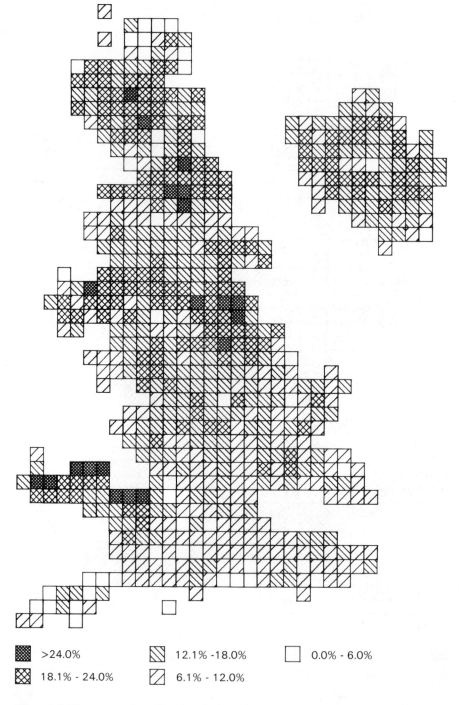

■ >24.0%	◩ 12.1% -18.0%	□ 0.0% - 6.0%
▧ 18.1% - 24.0%	◪ 6.1% - 12.0%	

Figure 5.4 The geography of voting Labour by the Administrative and Managerial occupational class, 1979.

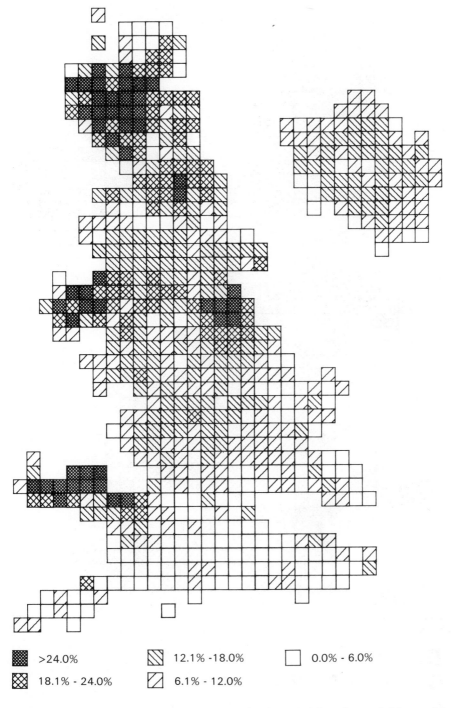

▓ >24.0%	◫ 12.1% -18.0%	☐ 0.0% - 6.0%
▩ 18.1% - 24.0%	◪ 6.1% - 12.0%	

Figure 5.5 The geography of voting Labour by the Administrative and Managerial occupational class, 1987.

Figure 5.6 The geography of voting Labour by the Unskilled Manual occupational class, 1979.

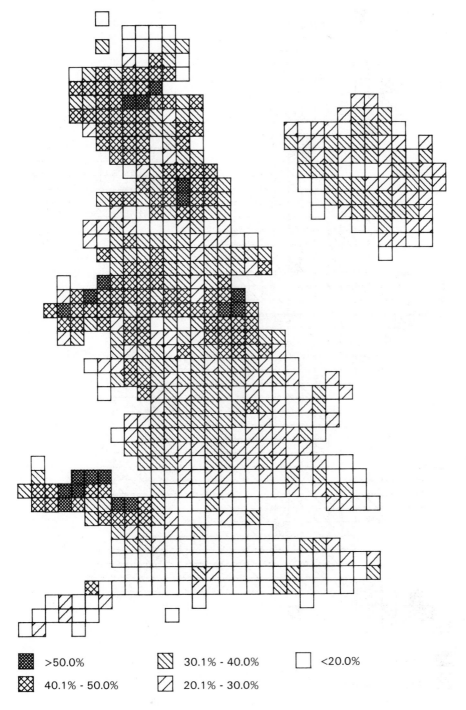

Figure 5.7 The geography of voting Labour by the Unskilled Manual occupational class, 1987.

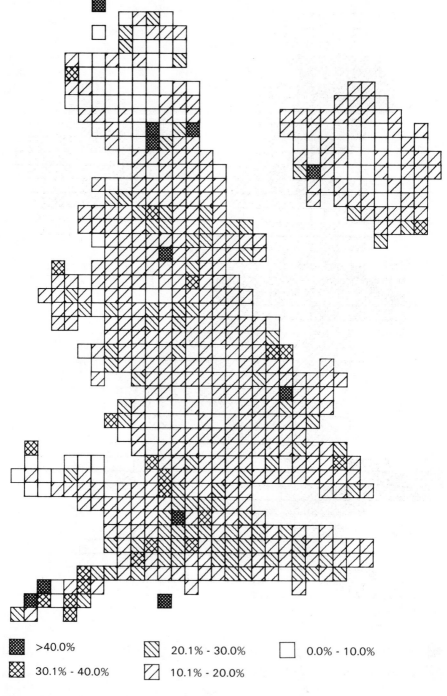

<table>
<tr><td>■</td><td>>40.0%</td><td>◨</td><td>20.1% - 30.0%</td><td>□</td><td>0.0% - 10.0%</td></tr>
<tr><td>▨</td><td>30.1% - 40.0%</td><td>◪</td><td>10.1% - 20.0%</td><td></td><td></td></tr>
</table>

Figure 5.8 The geography of voting Alliance by the Professional occupational class, 1979.

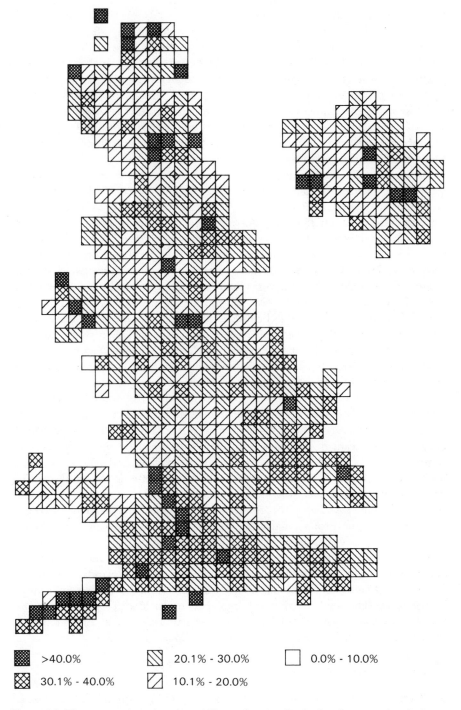

Figure 5.9 The geography of voting Alliance by the Professional occupational class, 1987.

South Yorkshire and much of Scotland, the percentage of Administrators and Managers voting Conservative fell to below 30, especially in 1987. In contrast, those are the parts of Britain where upwards of 18 per cent of the class have voted Labour; in 1979 (Figure 5.4) those blocs were less apparent than in 1987 (Figure 5.5) when the concentrations of constituencies recording 24 per cent or more voting Labour in those four areas, plus Tyneside, make a very clear impression. In 1987, however, that northern concentration is countered by the increased number of constituencies in the south, including many Outer London suburbs, recording Labour percentages below 6 for the Administrative and Managerial occupational class.

Turning to our closest approximation to Miller's other core class (the anti-controllers), Figures 5.6 and 5.7 show voting Labour by the Unskilled Manual occupational class in 1979 and 1987. Again, an increased polarisation is immediately apparent. In 1979, Labour obtained the votes of more than 50 per cent of the members of that class in a substantial number of constituencies; most were in South Wales, northern England and Scotland, but there were some in the Home Counties too, where several others recorded between 40 and 50 per cent (Figure 5.6). Eight years later, many fewer constituencies recorded over 50 per cent, and they were all in one of five blocs; South Wales, Merseyside, South Yorkshire, Tyneside, and Scotland. Further, there were also many fewer with between 40 and 50 per cent, and there were none of those at all in the southeast of England, including London (Figure 5.7). Indeed, the southeastern regions are marked by a very poor Labour performance (below 20 per cent) among its core class in the majority of constituencies.

The final pair of maps shows a continuing pattern of spatial polarisation also, this time in Alliance voting within the Professional occupational class. In 1979, the Liberal party (the only component of the Alliance then in existence) got over 40 per cent of the votes from the Professionals in only a handful of constituencies, of which half were in southern England and half were much further north (Figure 5.8). In general, the party did better in the south than in the north; its performance was more variable in the former that in the latter, however. Eight years later, not only had the Alliance consolidated its voting strength within the Professional grouping but it had also become much more uniform in its success throughout the southeast (Figure 5.9). Further north, its performance was much more variable. There were small concentrations of relative success on Merseyside, in the Southern Scottish Uplands, and in the Scottish Highlands and Islands, as well as, for example, success in coastal Lincolnshire. The south:north divide remains, but is less clear-cut than is the case for the Conservative and Labour voting patterns discussed above. So to what extent has there been spatial polarisation over the period?

Class-by-Vote: Spatial Summaries

In Chapter 4 we used the coefficient of variation (CV) to summarise the spatial variation in the distribution on any characteristic; the larger the CV the greater the spread of values, relative to the average. Given the context of this

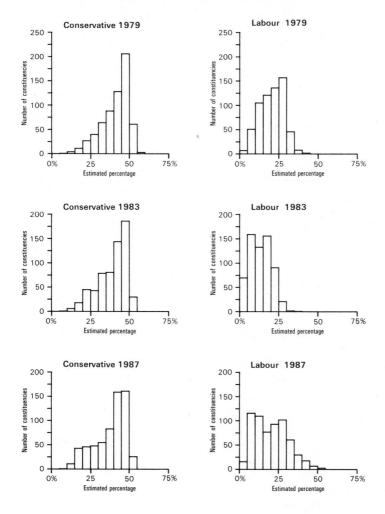

Figure 5.10 Estimates of Conservative and Labour voting by the Professional occupational class.

book, we would expect the values of CV to increase over time, as evidence of spatial polarisation in support given to the parties by the different classes.

Figures 5.10–5.21 give the distributions of the estimated values for all classes and parties. Figure 5.10 focuses on the Professional class, and its voting for the Conservative and Labour parties. In each case, there is clear evidence of growing variability in support across the 633 constituencies. With regard to Conservative voting, for example, there is a major shift from the situation in 1979 with one single very tall column, indicating over 200 constituencies where the party won support from between 45–49 per cent of the electorate, to that in 1987 where there was both an equal number of constituencies in the 40–44 and 45–49 per cent categories plus a much wider spread of values (over 50 constituencies in the categories 10–19 per cent in 1987 compared to fewer than 20 in

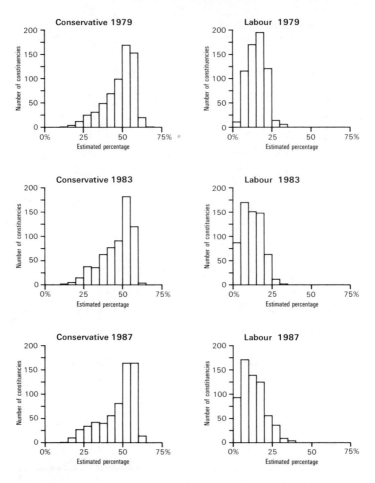

Figure 5.11 Estimates of Conservative and Labour voting by the Administrative and
       Managerial occupational class.

1979). Such a change is even more apparent in the support given by that class
to Labour. In 1979, the great majority of constituencies had estimated percentages of between 10 and 29 for Labour support among the professional class; in
1983, there was a substantial shift leftwards on the graph, indicating reduced
support in most places; and then in 1987 the spread of values increased very
significantly, with a much greater number recording greater than a 30 per cent
vote for Labour in 1987 than in 1979, and at the same time many more
recording less than 10 per cent support for the same party.

   For the Administrative and Managerial class, the histogram for voting
Conservative changed very little over the eight-year period; at each election the
main categories, comprising about 300 constituencies in total, were those
covering the range between 50 and 59 per cent, with very few recording more
Conservative votes but a substantial 'tail' to the left of the graph ranging down
to 15 per cent. Few constituencies were predominantly Conservative for this

class; most had a majority of the electorate voting Tory, however. For Labour, the great majority of constituencies recorded percentages below 25 (Figure 5.11); in 1987, however, there was a longer 'tail' to the right of the graph, indicating up to 29 per cent of the electorate in the 'controller' class voting Labour, whereas in 1979 there was virtually no tail (although, reflecting the larger vote for Labour overall, the main block of constituencies was in the range 5–24 in 1979 but 0–19 in 1987). Labour lost votes in this class over the period, but retained support better in a few places than in the majority.

Turning to Conservative and Labour voting in the third white-collar occupational class – the Routine Non-Manual, encompassing the great majority of non-professional workers in service industries – Figure 5.12 suggests little overall change in the pattern for Conservative but a substantial alteration for Labour. With regard to the first, all three graphs show a substantial concentra-

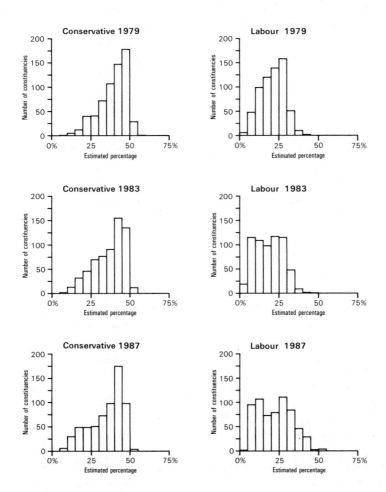

Figure 5.12 Estimates of Conservative and Labour voting by the Routine Non-Manual occupational class.

tion of constituencies in the 40–49 per cent range with a longish 'tail' to the left but virtually none to the right; the Conservative party rarely did outstandingly well, and was more likely to perform quite badly, but for the class as a whole its performance was very consistent. For Labour, however, the 1987 histogram is much flatter than that for 1983, which in turn is flatter than that for 1979. Over the period, Labour's performance in this class has become spatially much more variable. Exactly the same set of patterns is shown for the Skilled Manual occupational class (Figure 5.13). In the Semiskilled and Unskilled Manual occupational classes, too, Labour voting became spatially much more variable over time (Figures 5.14 and 5.15); there was a clear peak to each graph in 1979 but by 1987 a very flat distribution, indicating a much greater variation in the ability of Labour to win votes from groups one of which is generally considered its core class. The histograms for Conservative voting by these two classes changed much less, though again both graphs indicate increased variability with a wider spread of scores and a lower peak.

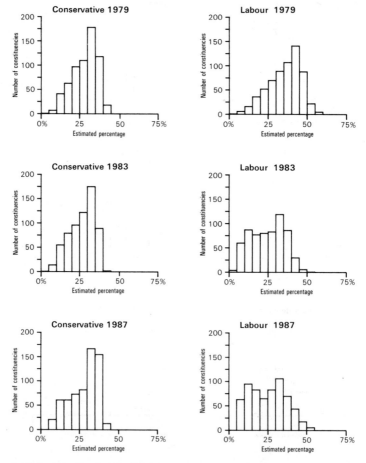

Figure 5.13 Estimates of Conservative and Labour voting by the Skilled Manual occupational class.

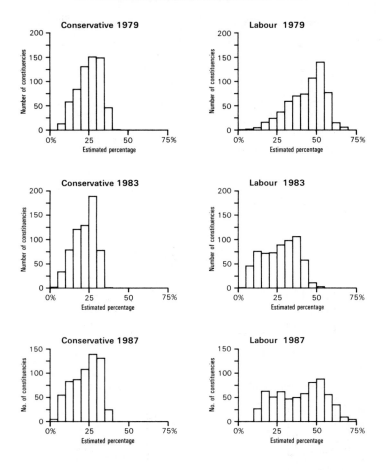

Figure 5.14 Estimates of Conservative and Labour voting by the Semiskilled Manual occupational class.

For the *Alliance* parties, the Professional class shows a major shift over the three elections (Figure 5.16). In 1979, the Liberals won between 10 and 19 per cent of the votes of the electorate in that class in the great majority of constituencies; they got less in about 100, and more than 20 per cent in another 150 or so (over 30 per cent in very few). Four years later, the Alliance average was about ten percentage points higher but the overall shape of the histogram had not changed; the great majority of constituencies recorded support for the Alliance between 15 and 24 per cent. By 1987, however, the average was about the same but the distribution was much flatter; a few constituencies were even estimated to have more than half of the members of this class voting Alliance then. Once again, spatial variation has clearly increased. This is less true with the Administrative and Managerial class, however, which overall gave relatively little support to the Alliance; there was more variability in 1987 than 1979, but not to the same extent as with the Professionals. With the Routine

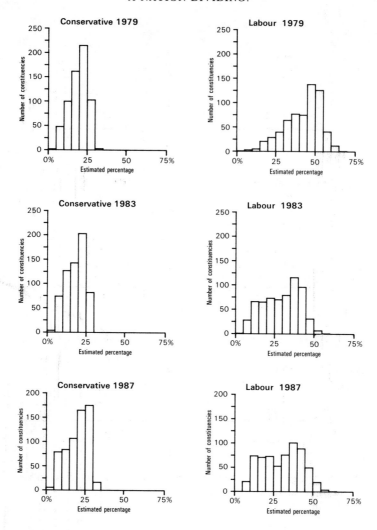

Figure 5.15 Estimates of Conservative and Labour voting by the Unskilled Manual
            occupational class.

Non-Manual occupational class (Figure 5.17) the spread was greatest in 1979,
least in 1983, and increased again slightly for 1987. The same was true for the
Skilled Manual grouping, though for it the peak of support in 1987 (about 200
constituencies in the 10–14 range) was much less than that for 1979 (almost
350 in the 5–9 group) so that overall variability increased over time. The other
two manual occupational classes show exactly the same patterns (Figure 5.18).

Finally, with regard to *Non-Voting*, the distributions for the Professional,
Administrative/Managerial, Routine Non-Manual and Skilled Manual occupational classes (Figures 5.19–5.20) all show an increased concentration in a
narrow band (only 10 percentage points wide) of values. This is not so,
however, with the Semiskilled and Unskilled Manual classes (Figure 5.21), for

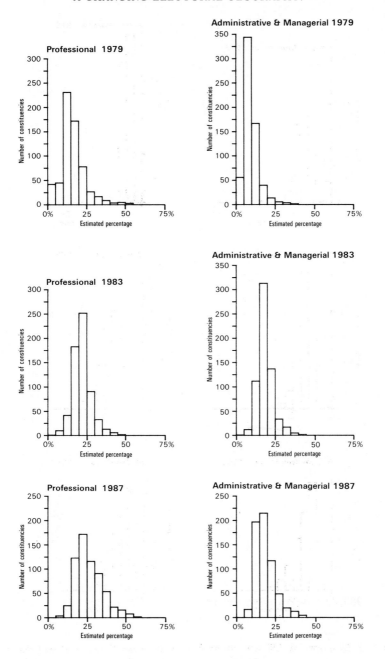

Figure 5.16 Estimates of Alliance voting by the Professional and the Administrative and Managerial occupational classes.

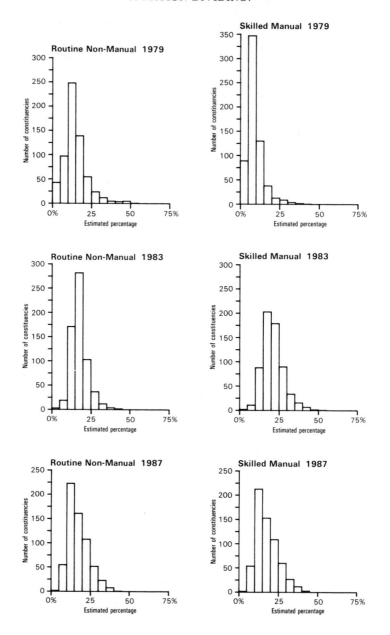

Figure 5.17 Estimates of Alliance voting by the Routine Nonmanual and the Skilled
Manual occupational classes.

both of which the spread of values increases over time while the height of the
peak value declines. Thus whereas for most occupational groups geographical
variations in Non-Voting appear to have declined, for these two they have
increased.

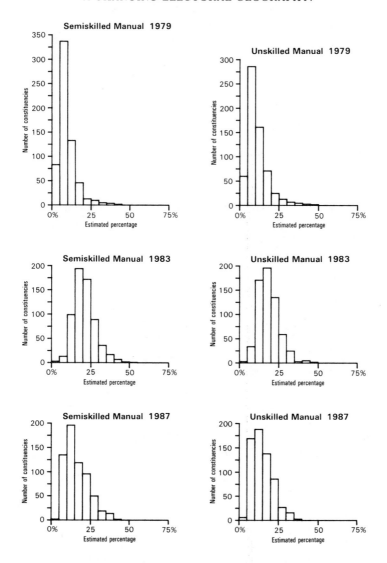

Figure 5.18 Estimates of Alliance voting by the Semiskilled Manual and the Unskilled Manual occupational classes.

Summaries of all of the 72 histograms (six occupational classes; four voting categories – excluding nationalists; and three elections) are given in Table 5.2. Several important conclusions can be drawn from the CV values there.

1) First, there is a general tendency that for each party the CV is higher, in any year, for the occupational classes where it won fewest votes on average. In each year, for example, the lowest CV for the Conservative party was for the Administrative and Managerial class, whereas the highest was in either the Semiskilled or the Skilled Manual class (see Table 4.1 for the national pattern

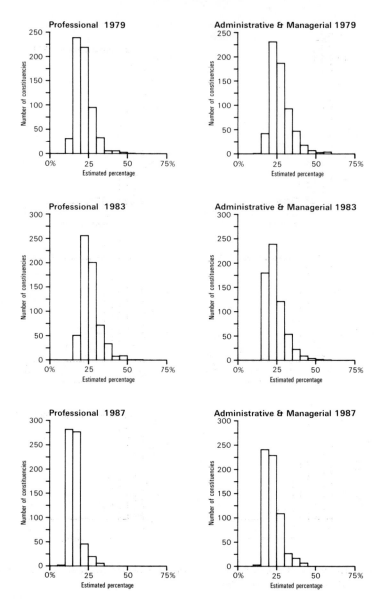

Figure 5.19 Estimates of Non-Voting by the Professional and the Administrative and
            Managerial occupational classes.

of voting by class). The implication is that support for a party is much less
variable in the classes on which it draws most heavily than in those where it
performed less well; in the latter, it was able to do much better in some constituencies than it was in others.

2)   Secondly, voting for the Labour party was spatially more variable, than

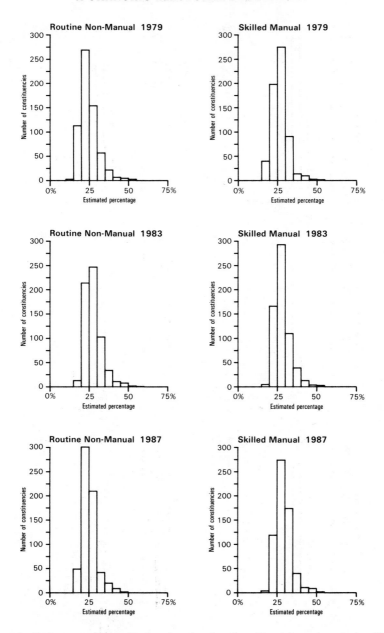

Figure 5.20 Estimates of Non-Voting by the Routine Non-Manual and the Skilled Manual occupational classes.

was voting for the Conservative party, in every occupational class in 1983 and 1987, but only in the three non-manual classes in 1979. Over the period, therefore, support for Labour has become more differentiated, geographically, within classes than was the case at the outset.

3) For both Conservative and Labour, but especially so for Labour, the

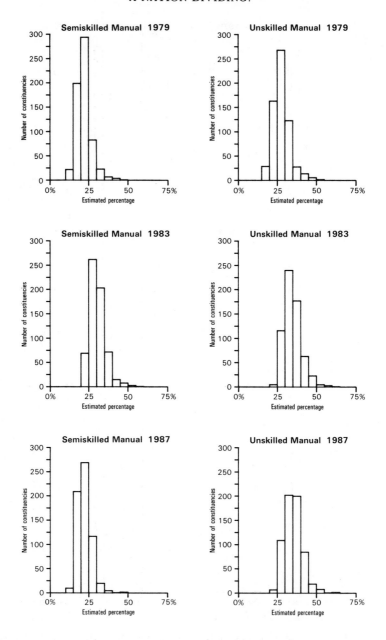

Figure 5.21 Estimates of Non-Voting by the Semiskilled Manual and Unskilled Manual occupational classes.

degree of spatial variability in support increased in every class across the three elections. The average increase in the CV for the Conservative party between 1979 and 1987 was just over six percentage points (or a 25 per cent increase on the initial average value of 25.5); for Labour, the average increase was 17

Table 5.2 Spatial Polarisation in Voting by Occupational Class

	CV for Election in		
	1979	1983	1987
Professional			
Conservative	22	24	28
Labour	37	51	53
Alliance	53	27	33
Non-Voting	26	23	23
Administrative and Managerial			
Conservative	20	22	24
Labour	38	53	59
Alliance	57	28	35
Non-Voting	25	26	24
Routine Non-Manual			
Conservative	22	27	31
Labour	36	47	49
Alliance	54	31	39
Non-Voting	24	20	19
Skilled Manual			
Conservative	29	30	33
Labour	29	43	46
Alliance	65	33	40
Non-Voting	19	18	17
Semiskilled Manual			
Conservative	29	33	38
Labour	27	42	47
Alliance	68	34	47
Non-Voting	22	17	21
Unskilled Manual			
Conservative	31	34	37
Labour	27	40	42
Alliance	66	37	45
Non-Voting	20	16	16

percentage points, or a 52.5 per cent increase on the average 1979 CV of 32.3. This is very convincing evidence that Labour's support especially has become increasingly concentrated in particular areas over the period. The main increase came between 1979 and 1983; as Labour's vote fell to its nadir in 1983, so it became geographically more variable, and the partial recovery in 1987 was slightly more variable still.

4) In 1979, the Liberal party had by far the greatest set of CV values, indicating very significant spatial variability in its vote-winning ability. With the launch of the Alliance, in 1983 its ability to win support became spatially much more even, with the average CV falling from 60.5 in 1979 to 31.7 in 1983; in the latter year, its support was much less variable than was Labour's in all classes, but especially in the three white-collar groupings. But then in

1987 geographical concentration increased again, with an average CV of 39.8; its CV was still less than that for Labour in four of the six classes, however. 5) Non-Voting has remained very stable in its overall geography, with no substantial shifts in the CV values.

Overall, then, we see that in 1979 the Alliance (i.e. the Liberal party) had the greatest geographical variability in its support within each occupational class, but by 1983 it had been replaced in this position by Labour. Of the three parties, the Conservatives were most consistent in drawing support in similar proportions in all constituencies. Even so, Table 5.2 and the figures that it summarises indicate substantial geographical shifts in voting for it too. There is clear evidence that not only have people in the same occupational class voted differently in different places but also that the geography of those differences has itself changed quite substantially. It is to an analysis of those changes that we now turn.

Continuity and Change

In any electoral system characterised by a well-developed cleavage, the basic theme in any study of a sequence of elections will be continuity (Archer and Taylor, 1981). This can be observed at both the individual and the aggregate scale. At the individual scale, the majority of voters will remain loyal to one party; at the aggregate scale, the proportion of the voters (in a constituency, say) choosing a particular party will be highly correlated from one election to the next. Analyses of British elections have demonstrated this aggregate stability (see Johnston, 1983a).

For the present study, the aggregates that we are focusing on are not the total votes cast for a party in each constituency (as percentages of the electorate), but the votes cast for each party within each occupational class. Here again, we would expect stability in the pattern over time so that, for example, the constituencies with high percentages of Professionals voting Conservative in 1979 should also be the constituencies with similar high percentages in 1983 and 1987. In other words, the relative relief of the map of voting (to use a topographical analogy) should be the same at each election.

Although the relative relief will be the same, the absolute relief may not be. To stick with the example of Professionals voting Conservative, between 1979 and 1987 the average percentage fell by three points (Table 4.1), as about 7 per cent of former Conservative voters in that class shifted their preference to one of the other parties. According to the continuity hypothesis, this fall should be the same everywhere. But was it? All the evidence that we have presented so far in this book suggests not.

We can investigate the geography of change relative to the continuity hypothesis very simply, using the technique of linear regression analysis. This takes a scatter-plot of the values for each observation on two variables, and fits a straight-line through that scatter of points to minimise the total sum of squared deviations between the individual points and the line. (Most introductory texts illustrate this point: see Johnston, 1978, Chapter 2.) Figure 5.22

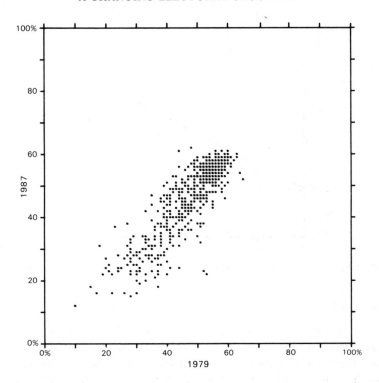

Figure 5.22 Scatter-plot of the Relationship between Voting Conservative at the 1979 and 1987 elections, for the Administrative and Managerial occupational class.

shows one such scatter-plot, for the relationship between the percentage of the Administrative and Managerial class voting Conservative in 1979 and 1987.

Linear regression analysis provides us with three statistical parameters which describe the relationship between the two variables.

1) *The slope of the regression.* This is displayed by the *b* parameter, which indicates the steepness of the slope; the larger the value of *b*, the steeper the slope.

2) *The intercept of the regression.* This is indicated by the parameter *a*, and marks the point on the vertical axis where the regression line intercepts it.

3) *The fit of the regression.* This is indicated by the parameter r^2, and is a measure of the closeness of all the points to the regression line. The larger the value of r^2, the closer the fit: an r^2 of 0.0 indicates a random scatter of points, whereas 1.0 indicates that all the points are on the line.

Figure 5.23 illustrates the nature of the *a* and *b* parameters. There are two variables, X and Y, of which Y is the dependent variable (the effect) and X is the independent (the cause: X is always shown on the horizontal axis and Y on the vertical). The relationship between the two variables is shown by the regression line. The general formula for such a line is

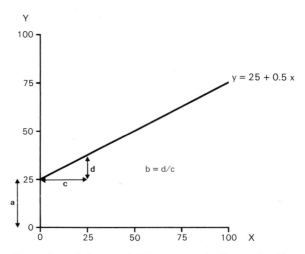

Figure 5.23 An illustration of the *a* and *b* Parameters in Regression Equations.

$$Y = a + bX$$

with *a* indicating the value of Y when X equals 0.0 and *b* the increase in the value of Y for every increase of 1.0 in the value of X. As the diagram shows, *a* is 25.0. The slope coefficient, *b*, is derived as the ratio *d/c*, the amount of increase in Y for a given increase in X; in this case *c*, the increase in X, is 25.0, and *d*, the increase in Y over that distance, is 12.5, giving a value for *b* of 0.5. Thus the formula for this particular regression line is

$$Y = 25 + 0.5X$$

so that, for example, when X = 0, Y = 25; when X = 50, Y = 25 + 0.5X = 25 + 25 = 50; and when X = 75, Y = 25 + 0.5X = 25 + 37.5 = 62.5. (Note that *b* can be negative, indicating that as X increases, Y decreases. The value of *a*, too, can be negative. Strictly, this means that Y has a negative value for certain values of X, which may be meaningful. In other situations, it may be the case that a negative value of *a* means that Y does not appear until X reaches a certain threshold value; if Y = -10 + 2X, then Y does not get a positive value until X = 5.)

The goodness-of-fit statistic, r^2, varies according to the scatter of points; the closer all the points are to the regression line, the closer the r^2 value will be to 1.0. The usual interpretation of r^2 is the proportion of the variation in Y accounted for by the variation in X. If r^2 = 1.0, then all the variation in Y is accounted for; all of the observations are exactly on the regression line. If r^2 = 0.5, half of the variation in Y is accounted for by X, but there is a residual half unaccounted for, which suggests either that Y is a function of additional variables to X or that part of its pattern is a function of random forces only. If r^2 = 0.0, the distribution of Y is entirely random with regard to X, and one cannot predict values of Y with any certainty at all from knowledge of values of X; the larger the value of r^2, the better one's predictions of Y from knowledge

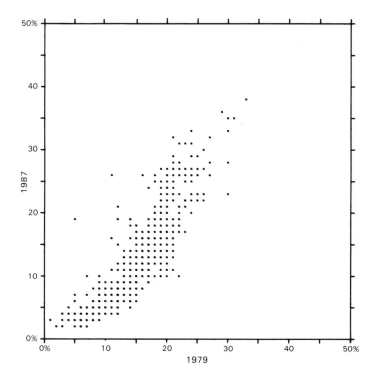

Figure 5.24 Scatter-plot of the Relationship between Voting Labour at the 1979 and 1987 elections, for the Administrative and Managerial occupational class.

of X (e.g. if Y is percentage voting Labour and X is percentage employed in mining, the larger the value of r^2 the better able we are to predict the Labour vote in a constituency from knowledge of its mining population).

Our purpose here is to identify the degree of continuity in voting patterns by members of each occupational class. If continuity were great, then the r^2 values would be very high; the pattern of voting at one election would be accurately predicted from the pattern at a previous election. The scatter of points in Figure 5.24 is an example where predictability is clearly high; the r^2 value of 0.76 indicates that three-quarters of the variation in the percentage voting Labour in 1987 among the Administrative and Managerial class can be accounted for by the percentage voting that way in 1979. The majority of constituencies cluster around a linear structure, through which the regression line passes, but there are some constituencies (such as the one where Labour got about 7 per cent of the votes in 1979 but 20 in 1987) where the percentage in 1979 is a relatively poor predictor of the 1987 figure. (The term 'relatively poor' is critical here: what is important is that that constituency stands outside the main scatter; the more that do that, the lower the value of r^2 and the poorer the predictive power.)

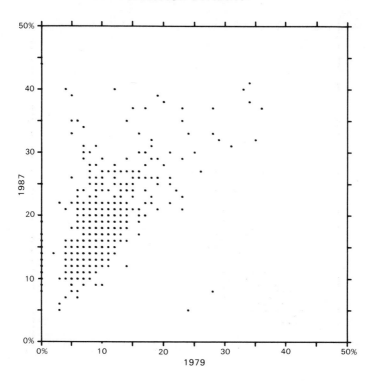

Figure 5.25 Scatter-plot of the Relationship between Voting Alliance at the 1979 and
           1987 elections, for the Administrative and Managerial occupational class.

What do the values of *a* and *b* tell us in this context? For our example of
Figure 5.24, the regression line formula is

Y = -4.29 + 1.14X

which we interpret as follows.
1)   The value of *a* is -4.29, which implies that with some values of X, Y will
be below zero. Since a negative percentage of the electorate voting Labour is
nonsensical, this clearly is not a valid interpretation. What the *a* value indicates is that the average percentage voting Labour in that class fell between
1979 and 1987; the 1987 value, on average, is below the 1979 value. (A few
constituencies did have below 4 per cent voting Labour in 1979, so a negative
percentage would be predicted for them in 1987. Because this is impossible, the
relationship shown in Figure 5.24 is slightly curved, so that all 1987 percentages are positive, as they must be. Technically, it is possible to correct for such
nonlinearity. We do not do so here, partly because it is relatively trivial in this
context, and partly because the linear regressions are much easier to interpret;
the technical breach of the statistical rules is not a serious one.)
2)   The value of *b* is greater than 1.0, which indicates that as the 1979
percentages increase, so the 1987 percentages increase even more. Take the

following seven hypothetical constituencies, where X = 5.0, 10.0, 15.0, 20.0, 25.0, 30.0 and 35.0 respectively. Fitting the equation we get:

$$
\begin{aligned}
Y &= -4.29 + 1.14X \\
&= -4.29 + 1.14(5.0) &&= 1.41 \\
&= -4.29 + 1.14(10.0) &&= 7.11 \\
&= -4.29 + 1.14(15.0) &&= 12.81 \\
&= -4.29 + 1.14(20.0) &&= 18.51 \\
&= -4.29 + 1.14(25.0) &&= 24.21 \\
&= -4.29 + 1.14(30.0) &&= 29.91 \\
&= -4.29 + 1.14(35.0) &&= 35.61
\end{aligned}
$$

For the first six, the value of Y is less than that of X; Labour did less well in 1987 than in 1979. But in the seventh it did better. Clearly, the interpretation is that the swing away from Labour was greatest in those seats where it was weak in 1979, whereas in those where it was strong then, there was a swing towards it in 1987. Any value of b greater than 1.0 indicates a polarisation of voting for the party in question, whereas one less than 1.0 indicates the opposite, a more even spread of its votes across the constituencies at the second election than at the first. With a b exceeding 1.0, the polarisation may be relative, with no constituency actually experiencing an increase in its vote at the second election. This depends on the size of the negative value of a relative to that of b; the value of X at which the value of Y is greater is found by dividing a by $(b - 1.0)$, which in this case is

$-4.29/(1.14 - 1.0) = -4.29/0.14 = -30.64.$

The sign can be disregarded; 30.64 is the value of X above which the Labour percentage was greater in 1987 than in 1979. (If a is positive, of course, then a value of b greater than 1.0 necessarily indicates a relative polarisation of the voting pattern.)

With the three parameters of the linear regression equations, then, we can get a clear indication of the changing geography of voting. This has been done by taking the percentage in each occupational class voting Conservative, Labour and Alliance and also Non-Voting and regressing: the 1983 figure against that for 1979; the 1987 figure against that for 1983; and the 1987 figure against that for 1979. The first two regressions show the changes in each separate inter-election period; the third shows the change over the period as a whole. The full results are given in Table 5.3, and the following paragraphs highlight its salient features.

1) The r^2 values are highest, in all classes, for the Conservative and Labour parties (with the one exception of the Unskilled Manual class in 1979–1983, when the Alliance r^2 exceeded that for Labour). This indicates, not unexpectedly given the context, greater continuity in the geography of Conservative and Labour support than in that for the Alliance. Interestingly, the geography of Non-Voting was not very consistent over time, with no r^2 value exceeding 0.7.

Table 5.3 The Parameters of the Continuity Regressions

Class and Vote	1979–1983			1983–1987			1979–1987		
	a	b	r^2	a	b	r^2	a	b	r^2
Professional									
Conservative	-0.46	0.96	0.83	-2.56	1.03	0.88	-3.09	1.00	0.74
Labour	-3.41	0.82	0.86	-0.16	1.54	0.91	-5.10	1.26	0.76
Alliance	13.39	0.52	0.53	0.12	1.20	0.67	15.23	0.68	0.43
Non-Voting	7.33	0.86	0.64	5.00	1.32	0.69	5.86	1.00	0.45
Administrative and Managerial									
Conservative	0.48	0.96	0.85	-1.66	1.05	0.90	-0.00	1.00	0.75
Labour	-3.34	1.02	0.86	-0.77	1.13	0.91	-4.29	1.14	0.76
Alliance	11.98	0.67	0.49	-0.46	1.01	0.65	11.32	0.72	0.36
Non-Voting	3.21	0.76	0.69	1.74	0.99	0.75	6.46	0.93	0.54
Routine Non-Manual									
Conservative	-2.67	1.00	0.82	-3.74	1.05	0.92	-6.75	1.06	0.77
Labour	-3.85	1.07	0.86	0.23	1.20	0.92	-4.23	1.27	0.79
Alliance	9.75	0.57	0.52	-1.23	1.05	0.71	8.51	0.59	0.46
Non-Voting	9.20	0.74	0.62	5.58	0.87	0.56	6.87	0.70	0.32
Skilled Manual									
Conservative	-0.09	0.94	0.89	-1.17	1.10	0.93	-1.12	1.03	0.82
Labour	-8.28	0.93	0.82	-0.20	1.03	0.91	-7.98	0.94	0.71
Alliance	12.41	0.97	0.65	-1.26	0.89	0.74	9.70	0.88	0.50
Non-Voting	8.81	0.72	0.52	6.12	0.75	0.55	9.29	0.59	0.33
Semiskilled Manual									
Conservative	-0.91	0.91	0.89	-2.79	1.16	0.92	-4.06	1.07	0.84
Labour	-11.70	0.88	0.85	4.87	1.30	0.90	-10.16	1.13	0.76
Alliance	12.09	0.94	0.66	-3.12	0.92	0.76	7.70	0.90	0.55
Non-Voting	14.06	0.74	0.49	11.83	0.83	0.55	8.86	0.58	0.29
Unskilled Manual									
Conservative	-1.12	1.00	0.89	-0.55	1.13	0.93	-1.73	1.13	0.82
Labour	-9.76	0.93	0.63	0.25	1.02	0.90	-9.01	0.93	0.72
Alliance	9.59	0.80	0.69	-0.90	0.85	0.77	7.14	0.68	0.54
Non-Voting	13.95	0.74	0.53	9.18	0.72	0.56	10.18	0.49	0.27

2) For both Conservative and Labour, the r^2 values were greater, in all classes, for 1983–1987 than for 1979–1983, indicating that the main shifts occurred between the first two elections. To the extent that a new geography of voting Conservative and Labour was created over the period, it happened mainly prior to the 1983 contest.

3) Over the full period, 1979–1987, the average predictability was 79 per cent for Conservative and 75 for Labour, indicating substantial changes in their electoral geographies during the first eight years of Tory rule under Margaret Thatcher.

4) For the Alliance, there was a substantial change in the geography of support between 1979 and 1983, as the new grouping succeeded the Liberal party and spread its campaigning more widely. The average r^2 then was only 0.59, with the three lowest values being for the non-manual occupational classes; the geography of 'working-class' Alliance support had more continuity then than did the geography for the 'middle class'. Between 1983 and 1987 the average r^2 of 0.72 indicates greater continuity; again, it was greatest in the

manual occupational classes. Over the full period, however, the map of Alliance support changed very substantially.

5) For 1979–1983, only two values of b exceeded 1.0, suggesting that relative polarisation was not the operative process; no party garnered more votes, relatively, where it was initially strong, on average, with this being balanced by greater losses than average where it was initially weak. The impact of the Alliance was clearly to generate shifts away from the traditional patterns. Between 1983 and 1987, on the other hand, the majority of the b coefficients were greater than 1.0, indicating growing polarisation in support for all parties in most classes. The largest coefficients, indicating the greatest polarisation, were for the Labour party, especially in the three white-collar occupational classes. Over the eight-year period as a whole, there was a spatial polarisation of Labour support, especially among the white-collar occupational classes, and of Conservative support in the manual classes; the two parties that dominated British politics in the fifty years up to the mid-1970s were increasingly winning votes in certain areas only, especially among the occupational classes from whom they traditionally have got least support. For the Alliance, on the other hand, the period 1979–1987 witnessed a deconcentration of its support; Non-Voting, too, became spatially more uniform in its occurrence, especially among the manual classes.

Putting these five sets of salient features in Table 5.3 together we see that the period 1979–1987 was characterised by a substantial erosion of the long-lasting continuity in Britain's electoral geography; between 20 and 30 per cent of the variation in the voting for Conservative and Labour in 1987 could not be accounted for by the variation eight years previously. Over that period, too, within the general pattern of continuity both of those parties has experienced increased concentration of its support in the areas where it was already strong, relative to the decline in those constituencies where it was initially weak. Meanwhile the Alliance has expanded outwards from the Liberal heartlands of the 1970s, increasing its support where it was initially weak more than in the areas of traditional strength.

The Correlates of Change

If continuity is no longer the predominant feature of Britain's electoral geography, we must turn to an examination of what aspects of the country's economic and social geography can account for the residuals, the deviations from the continuity. This we do in two parts. First, in this section we look at the impact of six constituency characteristics; secondly, in the next we incorporate geographical and functional regional variations.

The six constituency characteristics that we have chosen to analyse are based on a wide range of research findings concerning the correlates of voting patterns in Britain. A number of studies (such as Crewe and Payne, 1976; Miller, 1977; and Johnston, 1985a) have suggested that the Conservative party does better in agricultural areas than does Labour, all other things being equal, whereas the position is reversed in mining areas.

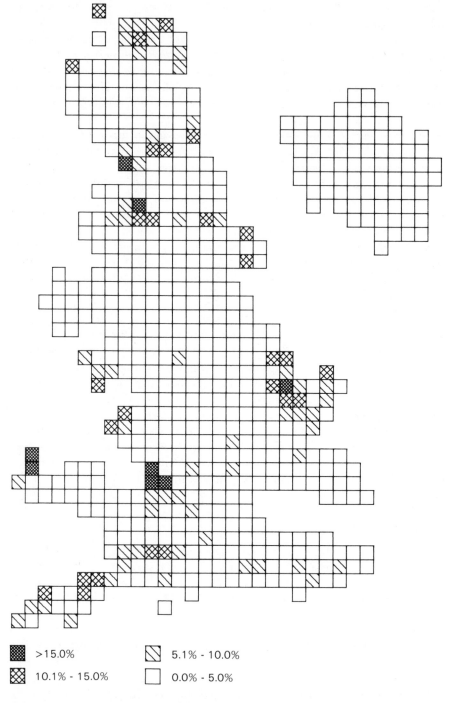

>15.0%   5.1% - 10.0%

10.1% - 15.0%   0.0% - 5.0%

Figure 5.26 The Geography of Agricultural Employment, 1981.

Most British constituencies had less than 5.0 per cent of their workforce employed in *agriculture*, according to the 1981 Census (Figure 5.26); conversely, only eight of the 633 had 15 per cent or more so employed, with another 27 recording between 10 and 14 per cent. The main concentrations were in Norfolk and Lincolnshire, in parts of Somerset, Devon and Cornwall, in Southwest Wales, in much of the Welsh Marches, on either side of the English:Scottish border, and in the far north of Scotland. In these areas, it is suggested, the erosion of Conservative support will have been less than in otherwise comparable constituencies (i.e. with the same Conservative support in 1979), because of the party's traditional strength in rural areas among all classes.

Coal-mining areas traditionally have provided Labour with some of its safest seats; our findings above suggested that Labour's vote-winning was increasingly concentrated in the constituencies where it was already strong, and we suggest here that it did even better in those safe seats that were in mining areas than it did in comparable seats elsewhere. Unfortunately, we cannot get constituency data on coal-mining employment alone from the census; the only category available is *energy*, which includes mining. Virtually all of the constituencies with more than 5 per cent of their workforce in the energy industry are in the coalfields; the exceptions are a few with major power stations, as in North Kent and northern Scotland (Figure 5.27). The main concentrations are in South Wales, Yorkshire/Derbyshire/Nottinghamshire, and parts of northeast England and East-Central Scotland.

The third of the variables we consider here is *unemployment* (the geography of which is depicted in Figures 3.1 and 3.2). To the extent that people in areas of high unemployment (and not just the unemployed themselves) blame the incumbent government for that situation, so they are likely to vote against it. Thus areas of high unemployment are likely to experience greater erosion of support for the Conservative party than are areas of similar initial Conservative strength but lower unemployment.

Our fourth variable is percentage of households who rent homes from local authorities. Various studies have shown that, holding class constant, *council tenants* are more likely to vote Labour than are people in other tenures, especially owner-occupancy (e.g. Johnston, 1987b). Dunleavy (1979; see also Dunleavy and Husbands, 1985) has argued that this is because the Labour party is increasingly associated with the public sector side of what he terms the consumption cleavage. Consequently, in areas where people's occupational class and housing tenure are both pro-Labour one would expect Labour to do better than when the latter is absent; council tenants are more likely to stay loyal to Labour because it mobilises their support and there is greater potential pro-Labour solidarity on council estates than in other housing tenure districts.

Scotland has the highest percentage of its households in council tenancies (Figure 5.28), with no other part of Great Britain having comparable concentrations. Only in Inner London are there any English constituencies where more than 80 per cent of households were council tenants in 1981; there were concentrations of 60 per cent plus in the West Midlands, Merseyside,

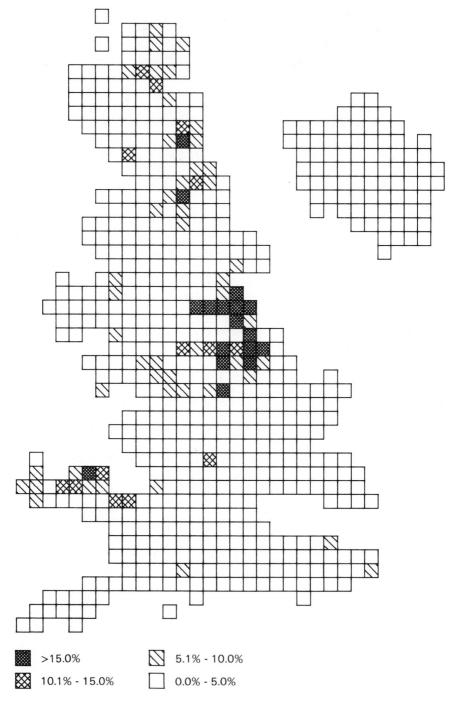

Figure 5.27 The Geography of Employment in the Energy Industry, 1981.

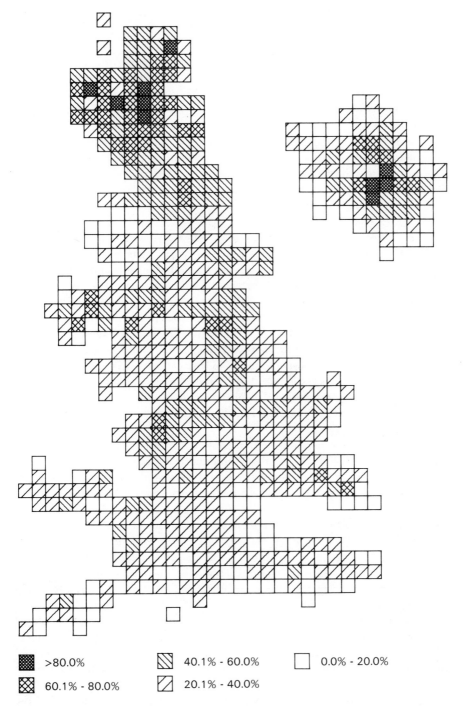

Figure 5.28 The Geography of Council Tenancies, 1981.

Greater Manchester, South Yorkshire and Tyne and Wear metropolitan areas, but not in West Yorkshire; much of industrial Lancashire, too, had relatively low levels of council tenancy.

The class-by-vote matrices (Table 4.1) indicate that the Alliance gets most support from the professional occupational class. This contains the most highly trained and qualified segments of the British population, which can be characterised from the Census by those with *degrees* (Figure 5.29). A small number of constituencies (including Bristol West, Oxford West, and Sheffield Hallam in England, and Glasgow Hillhead and Edinburgh Central and South in Scotland) had percentages of graduates exceeding 15 in 1981. In general, the constituencies in the south and east of England (excluding eastern London) had more highly qualified people than was the case further north and west, and it was in these that the Alliance was expected to do particularly well in 1983 and 1987.

Finally, we turn to the population of Afro/Caribbean and Asian ethnic origin. It is widely believed that in recent years members of this group, especially those coloured people from Africa, the Indian subcontinent, and the Caribbean, plus their descendants, are strongly pro-Labour. The geography of these groups is best shown with census data using the category 'households whose heads were born in the New Commonwealth or Pakistan' (*NCWP*). They are concentrated (as Figure 5.30 shows) in much of London and the West Midlands, with very few constituencies outside those areas having more than 8 per cent of their household heads in that category. (The main exception is Leicester.) Our expectation is that in those areas Labour will have done relatively better over the period than it did in areas with similar initial Labour support but few NCWP households, because of the solidarity for Labour among the NCWP.

Our analysis in the previous section showed that there was a shift in voting patterns between 1979 and 1987 that could not be entirely accounted for by the continuity factor. We have suggested here that six other variables could account for that residual variation, because the parties would have done better in certain types of areas than others. (We could have included a seventh, the social class composition of the constituency; following Miller, 1977, we found that the greater the percentage of a constituency's workforce in the Administrative and Managerial occupational class, the greater the Conservative vote in 1979, in all occupational classes. Thus, the class structure was already incorporated in our analyses, since it underpinned the 1979 pattern; we could not include it twice.)

To incorporate these six further variables, we use the technique of multiple linear regression analysis, which is an extension of the simple regression procedure used above. Instead of having one cause (the independent variable) and one effect (the dependent variable), we now have one dependent variable but seven independents. For each of the latter, we have a *b* value, a slope coefficient which shows the relationship between the dependent variable and the independent variable, assuming no variation in all the other independents. In other words, if our dependent variable is percentage Professionals voting La-

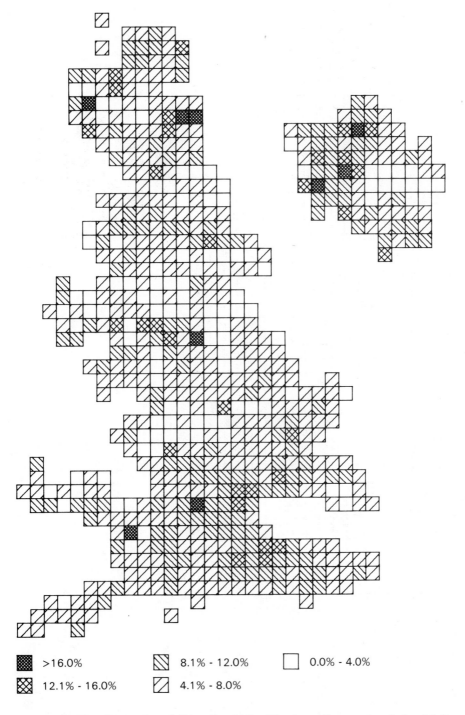

Figure 5.29 The Geography of Educational Qualifications: Percentage of the Adult Population with a Degree, 1981.

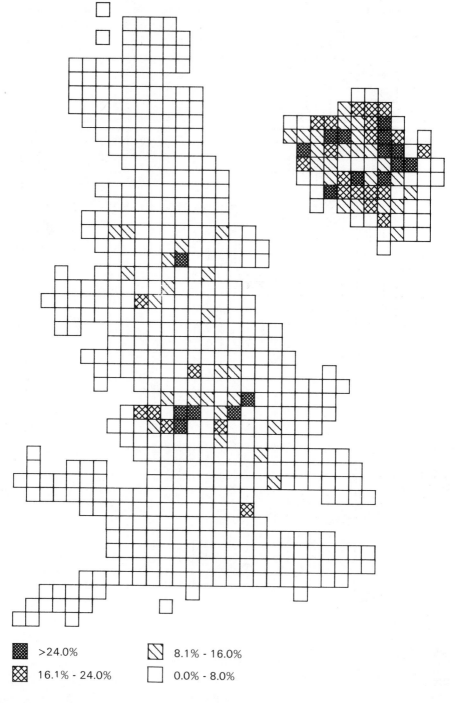

Figure 5.30 The Geography of NCWP-headed Households, 1981.

bour in 1983 the b for Percentage in Agriculture shows the slope of that relationship across the 633 constituencies assuming that there is no variation in the percentage Professionals voting Labour in 1983, the Percentages in Energy, Unemployed, Council Tenants, with Degrees, and in NCWP Households; the variation in these six is statistically controlled – or 'held constant' – to see if Percentage in Agriculture had any independent influence on the voting pattern in 1987. We assess whether it did have an influence, not just by the slope of the relationship itself (the b value) but also by its 'statistical significance', which is a measure of its goodness-of-fit; in the present context, an independent variable is assessed as having a statistically significant influence on the dependent if, in statistical terms, the probability of it being different from zero by chance alone is less than 0.05.

As well as evaluating the goodness-of-fit for each of the separate variables, we can also evaluate the goodness of fit of the entire set, using the statistic R^2, which is interpreted in exactly the same way as r^2. Clearly, if each of the six additional factors is influential, in a multiple regression equation containing seven independent variables in all (those six, plus the relevant vote at the first date of the period being examined), then:

1) the value of R^2 should be larger than that of r^2; and
2) each of the b values should be statistically significant.

The results of these analyses are given in Tables 5.4–5.8, in which only the b coefficients (the regression slopes) assessed as statistically significant are included. The R^2 values are also given as, for purposes of comparison, are the r^2 values from Table 5.3. In every case, the R^2 value is greater than that of r^2 (though only marginally so in several of the analyses of the changing pattern of Alliance voting: Table 5.6), indicating that the changing electoral geography of the country has been linked to aspects of Britain's economic and social geography, as hypothesised.

In reporting the results of the regression analyses, the b coefficients are interpreted assuming 'all other influences are held constant' – or *ceteris paribus*. Every b coefficient indicates the trend in the relationship between the dependent variable and the relevant independent variable, as if there were no variations at all in any of the other independent variables (so that they had no influence at all on the dependent variable). Thus, for example, a positive b value for the relationship between percentage voting Conservative and percentage employed in agriculture means that, when the effects of all other independent variables on the percentage voting Conservative have been taken into account (statistically), there is a significant link between the two; whatever other influences occur, it remains the case that the more people employed in agriculture, the more votes for the Conservative party. Alternatively, a positive value of b for percentage employed in agriculture could be interpreted as a *relative* swing towards the Conservative party in the more agricultural areas – with a negative value of b indicating a relative swing away.

With the regressions relating to the *Conservative* party (Table 5.4), of the 108

Table 5.4 Regression Slopes for the Six Additional Variables as Influences on Conservative Voting

	1979–1983 b	1983–1987 b	1979–1987 b	1979–1983 b	1983–1987 b	1979–1987 b
	Professional			*Administrative and Managerial*		
Agriculture	0.29	–	0.26	0.29	–0.11	0.22
Energy/Mining	–0.13	–	–	–0.15	–	–
Unemployment	–0.43	–0.29	–0.61	–0.43	–0.30	–0.62
Council Tenants	–0.05	–	–0.06	–0.03	–	–0.05
Degree	–0.28	–0.14	–0.35	–0.27	–0.21	–0.42
NCWP	–0.07	0.21	0.16	–0.05	0.19	0.16
R^2	0.89	0.90	0.81	0.89	0.92	0.81
(r^2)*	(0.83)	(0.88)	(0.74)	(0.85)	(0.90)	(0.75)
	Routine Non-Manual			*Skilled Manual*		
Agriculture	0.35	–0.12	0.26	0.16	–0.12	–
Energy/Mining	–0.21	–	–9.13	–0.10	–	–
Unemployment	–0.51	–0.30	–0.67	–0.34	–0.27	–0.54
Council Tenants	–0.05	–	–0.07	–	–	–0.03
Degree	–0.25	–0.20	–0.36	–0.23	–0.19	–0.37
NCWP	–0.09	0.17	0.11	–0.04	0.13	0.10
R^2	0.90	0.94	0.86	0.92	0.95	0.87
(r^2)*	(0.82)	(0.92)	(0.77)	(0.89)	(0.93)	(0.82)
	Semiskilled Manual			*Unskilled Manual*		
Agriculture	–	0.09	0.14	0.12	–0.08	0.08
Energy/Mining	–0.07	–0.06	–0.07	–0.09	–	–
Unemployment	–0.31	–0.28	–0.52	–0.28	–0.22	–0.45
Council Tenants	–0.02	–	–	–0.01	–	–0.02
Degree	–0.27	–	–0.28	–0.19	–0.14	–0.30
NCWP	–0.03	0.10	0.09	–0.04	0.09	0.06
R^2	0.92	0.94	0.89	0.92	0.95	0.88
(r^2)*	(0.89)	(0.92)	(0.84)	(0.89)	(0.93)	(0.82)

* taken from Table 5.3

coefficients only 21 were not statistically significant, so clearly the changing pattern of that party's support was closely linked to all six of the variables included. Least influential on Conservative voting overall was the Energy/Mining variable, with only half of the slope coefficients significant. Of those nine, six referred to the 1979–1983 period. All were negative, so under the first four years of Tory rule the party lost more votes, relatively, in the mining constituencies than in comparable areas on all other variables except employment in the energy and mining industries: the more miners in an area, the greater the swing away from the Conservative party. During the second four-year period, however, such a swing was observed among the Semiskilled Manual workers only; once all other influences had been held constant, the Conservatives did as well in the mining areas as elsewhere. With the absence of such a swing against it then, it is not surprising that over the full eight years there was a significant relationship in only one of the six occupational classes.

The Conservative party has traditionally performed badly in the coalfields, and the results in Table 5.4 suggest that it continued to lose votes there between 1979 and 1983. From then on, however, it appears that there was no further decline in the relative performance of Conservative candidates in mining areas; the swing against them in 1983–1987 was no worse there, on average, than elsewhere. It is not entirely clear why this should be so. Most likely it relates to the National Union of Mineworkers' strike in 1984–1985 which created divisions both within and between coalfields. In some mining districts (notably in Nottinghamshire: Johnston, 1986e) support for the strike was weak, whereas in others it was very strong. Since the NUM is a strong supporter of the Labour party, it could well have been the case that in 1987 the anti-strike areas were less likely to support Labour candidates than was the case in the pro-strike areas.

The Conservative party has long had major strength in the rural areas, and several analysts have shown that its vote tends to increase with the percentage of the workforce employed in agriculture. This was the case between 1979 and 1983 among all but one (Semiskilled Manual) of the occupational classes, and the coefficients for the three white-collar classes indicate how well the party did in the agricultural areas, all other things being held constant. Between 1983 and 1987, however, that trend was absent from all but one of the classes; indeed, in four the slope was negative, indicating a swing *away* from the Conservative party in the rural areas. Over the full eight-year period, the agricultural areas saw relative swings to Conservative – except among the Skilled Manual workers. Those swings were confined to the first four years, however. Just as the Tories appear to have reached the nadir of their fortunes in the coalfields in 1983 so they seem to have reached the peak of their success in the rural areas then. Table 5.6 suggests why; between 1983 and 1987 the agricultural areas displayed substantial relative swings to the Alliance.

Unemployment, not surprisingly, hit the Conservative vote; the higher its level in a constituency the greater the swing away from the party. The slopes suggest that this swing was greater in the first four years than in the second, especially among the white-collar classes, but the changes in the counting of unemployed workers make this conclusion a tentative one only. Clearly, however, the areas of high unemployment were substantially against the party of government, with an average of about a five percentage point decline in the Conservative performance for every increase of 10 percentage points in the number of unemployed.

Council tenants are traditionally few in their support for the Conservative party, and council estates have for long been major foci of local Labour party organisation. The swings against the Conservatives in the areas with more council tenants were small, however, and were not significant in 1983–1987 in any of the occupational classes. To some extent, this may reflect the success of the government's council house sale programme (Figure 3.7; see also Williams, Sewel and Twine, 1987) in eroding Labour's strongholds there (as Table 5.5 also suggests). Traditionally, too, the coloured immigrant population have been staunch Labour supporters. Tables 5.4 and 5.5 suggest that this remained

Table 5.5 Regression Slopes for the Six Additional Variables as Influences on Labour Voting

	1979–1983 b	1983–1987 b	1979–1987 b	1979–1983 b	1983–1987 b	1979–1987 b
	Professional			*Administrative and Managerial*		
Agriculture	–	–	–	–	–	–
Energy/Mining	0.20	–	0.23	0.18	–	0.14
Unemployment	0.37	0.29	0.60	0.37	0.17	0.41
Council Tenants	0.03	0.03	0.07	0.03	0.01	0.06
Degree	0.08	0.18	0.20	0.09	0.14	0.16
NCWP	0.03	–0.16	–0.14	0.04	–0.15	–0.13
R^2	0.91	0.93	0.85	0.91	0.94	0.85
$(r^2)^*$	(0.86)	(0.91)	(0.76)	(0.86)	(0.91)	(0.76)
	Routine Non-Manual			*Skilled Manual*		
Agriculture	–	–	–	–	–	–
Energy/Mining	0.24	–	0.22	0.32	0.09	0.31
Unemployment	0.46	0.27	0.58	0.63	0.28	0.66
Council Tenants	0.04	–	0.05	0.07	–	0.09
Degree	0.09	0.13	0.16	0.12	0.15	0.16
NCWP	0.04	–0.17	–0.16	0.06	–0.20	–0.17
R^2	0.91	0.94	0.86	0.90	0.93	0.84
$(r^2)^*$	(0.86)	(0.92)	(0.79)	(0.82)	(0.91)	(0.71)
	Semiskilled Manual			*Unskilled Manual*		
Agriculture	–	–	–	–	–	–
Energy/Mining	0.30	–	0.32	0.32	0.11	0.34
Unemployment	0.56	0.43	0.84	0.60	0.32	0.68
Council Tenants	0.03	0.04	0.09	0.06	–	0.08
Degree	–	0.27	0.21	–	0.15	–
NCWP	0.06	–0.21	–0.17	0.05	–0.21	–0.18
R^2	0.90	0.92	0.85	0.89	0.92	0.83
$(r^2)^*$	(0.85)	(0.90)	(0.76)	(0.63)	(0.90)	(0.72)

* taken from Table 5.3

the case in 1979–1983, with relative swings against the Conservatives and towards Labour in the constituencies with large percentages of NCWP residents. But in 1983–1987 there was a major shift, with very substantial pro-Conservative swings in those areas. Either the Conservative party won a lot more votes from the NCWP residents in 1987 than in 1983 or it won many more from the others among whom they lived, especially the white-collar workers; the latter is more likely, suggesting a white electoral backlash against both the disturbances in several inner city areas in previous years which were popularly linked to racial issues, and against the Labour party's selection of several NCWP candidates (including one who was de-selected shortly before the 1987 election). (See also, on this issue in 1983, Dunleavy and Husbands, 1985.)

Finally with regard to the Conservatives, the regression slopes for the relationship with Degree indicate that it lost votes very substantially, relatively and probably absolutely too, in constituencies with higher percentages of people with degree-level qualifications. Since most people with degrees work in white-collar occupations, the clear implications to be drawn are that (i) such people were less likely to vote Conservative, and increasingly less likely in 1987 than in 1983, than were people in comparable occupational situations but lacking the educational qualification, and (ii) that in constituencies with concentrations of such people, voters in all classes were apparently influenced by that growing anti-Conservative milieu. Those constituencies are of two main sub-types. The first are associated with Universities, Polytechnics and other institutions of higher and further education, whose staff members have traditionally been more pro-Labour than other professional groups. (Such constituencies include Sheffield Hallam, which had the highest percentage of professionally qualified workers – 33.9 – according to the 1981 Census, Bristol West, Glasgow Hillhead, Oxford West and Leeds Northwest.) The second are those suburban areas with high concentrations of professionals (constituencies such as St. Albans, Hampstead and Highgate, Richmond and Barnes, Epsom and Ewell), many of whom are imbued with the egalitarian views typically associated with the Labour party. (A full list of the constituencies in the 'top 50' is in Crewe and Fox, 1984, p. 386.) More recently (as Table 4.1 indicates) that group has been mobilised by the Alliance, and many professionals linked to the egalitarian wing of the Labour party (through, for example, the Fabian Society) shifted their allegiance to the Alliance after 1981 because they saw it as a better vehicle for advancing their goals than the increasingly left-wing domi-nated (as they interpreted it) Labour party. Table 5.6 suggests that this was indeed the case over the full 1979–1987 period as a whole, although Table 5.5 indicates that Labour, too, benefited from the swing away from the Conser-vative party in the constituencies being discussed here, especially among the white-collar classes. The implication is of an intellectual swing away from the Conservative party, from which both Labour and the Alliance have benefited.

In general terms, the pattern of regression slopes for *Labour* (Table 5.5) is, not unexpectedly, the reverse of that for Conservative (Table 5.4). There are some relationships (or the lack of them) that are worthy of comment, however. The first is the total lack of any relative swing against Labour in the more rural areas. Curtice and Steed (1982, 1984) have argued for a growing urban:rural polarisation of the country over the period 1955–1983, but our analyses provide no supporting evidence for that since 1979. Labour, it seems, has not suffered unduly in the rural areas. Its relative strength in the mining areas was dented in the 1983–1987 period, however, for it failed to do better there than expected in terms of the general continuity of voting alone. (Reasons for this are suggested above, p. 173.)

Labour's greatest relative gains have been in the areas of highest unemploy-ment, with particularly steep regression slopes in the three manual occupa-tional class analyses. All other things being held constant, for every increase of ten points in the percentage unemployed, Labour gained an additional average seven percentage points among manual workers and five among non-manual workers. The greater the depth of economic recession in a constituency, as measured by this indicator, the greater the electoral return to the Labour party. Labour also did relatively well, though to a lesser extent, in the areas with large percentages of council tenants. It lost quite substantially, however, in the areas of immigrant concentration between 1983 and 1987. (Note that, as Figure 5.30 shows, most of these constituencies were in either Inner London or the West Midlands Conurbation. It may be that we are picking up a regional effect rather than an immigrant effect. Nevertheless, at least part of any explanation of a shift against Labour in those regions would have to take account of the immigrant issue.)

Turning to the *Alliance* (Table 5.6), we find much less evidence of a changing pattern of vote-winning substantially linked to the six elements of the country's economic and social geography than was the case with Conservative and Labour. Of the 108 relationships, 49 were statistically insignificant for the Alliance, compared with 21 for Conservative and 28 for Labour. The R^2 values in Table 5.6, too, are much lower than those in Tables 5.4 and 5.5; for the 1983–1987 period in particular, the difference between the r^2 and R^2 figures is negligible, indicating that the six variables added very little to the statistical account of the pattern to be explained. Between 1979 and 1983 the Alliance did less well, in relative terms, in the more rural areas, in the coalfields, in the areas of high unemployment and in the constituencies with substantial concentrations of immigrants; it did slightly better than expected on the council estates. Its main appeal, it seems, was to 'middle Britain', those constituencies which were not characterised by high values for the main variables that have apparently influenced electoral behaviour in the past.

Over the next four years, as the Alliance consolidated its position as a 'third force', and lost some votes, it no longer did particularly badly in the coalfields, or among the unemployed and immigrants; it did lose white-collar votes in greater than expected numbers on the council estates between 1983 and 1987, however. Its main trend was a build-up of relative strength in the more rural areas, which suggests that its appeal was increasingly to both agricultural populations per se and the residents of the small, growing towns of exurbia. Because it lost votes relatively in those areas in 1979–1983, this pattern was not one that characterised the whole period. For 1979–1987, the main conclusion is that the Alliance did relatively badly in the coalfields but well in the areas with well-qualified electorates. Overall, it was shifting its locus of support to particular types of suburb and rural area, it seems.

Non-Voting produced 68 significant slope coefficients out of the possible 108, and in general the six variables added considerably to the statistical accounts provided (Table 5.7; the average increase between r^2 and R^2 was 0.053 (or 5.3 percentage points) for 1979–1983, 0.075 for 1983–1987, and 0.160 for 1979–1987). Several main trends stand out. First, non-voting increased relatively, over all periods and occupational classes, in areas with high percentages of households with NCWP heads, suggesting growing voter alienation in the inner city areas where immigrants were concentrated. Secondly, there were similar, and substantial, relative increases in non-voting in the constituencies with high percentages of professionally qualified people, over the period as a whole but especially during 1979–1983. This suggests similar alienation among

Table 5.6 Regression Slopes for the Six Additional Variables as Influences on Alliance Voting

	1979–1983 b	1983–1987 b	1979–1987 b	1979–1983 b	1983–1987 b	1979–1987 b
	Professional			*Administrative and Managerial*		
Agriculture	−0.13	0.27	–	−0.11	0.16	–
Energy/Mining	−0.13	−0.11	−0.23	−0.10	–	−0.11
Unemployment	−0.25	–	–	−0.18	0.11	–
Council Tenants	0.06	−0.04	–	0.06	–	0.03
Degree	–	0.15	0.28	–	–	0.22
NCWP	−0.13	–	−0.15	−0.10	–	−0.14
R^2	0.57	0.69	0.46	0.55	0.66	0.39
(r^2)*	(0.53)	(0.67)	(0.43)	(0.49)	(0.65)	(0.36)
	Routine Non-Manual			*Skilled Manual*		
Agriculture	–	0.14	–	−0.10	0.13	–
Energy/Mining	−0.15	–	−0.18	−0.22	–	−0.18
Unemployment	−0.24	–	–	−0.38	–	−0.15
Council Tenants	0.04	−0.03	–	0.03	–	–
Degree	–	–	0.15	–	–	0.14
NCWP	−0.11	–	−0.11	−0.13	–	−0.11
R^2	0.63	0.72	0.50	0.71	0.75	0.54
(r^2)*	(0.52)	(0.71)	(0.46)	(0.65)	(0.74)	(0.50)
	Semiskilled Manual			*Unskilled Manual*		
Agriculture	−0.14	0.25	0.15	–	0.11	–
Energy/Mining	−0.23	–	−0.22	−0.22	–	−0.17
Unemployment	−0.42	–	−0.20	−0.38	–	−0.17
Council Tenants	–	–	–	–	–	–
Degree	–	–	0.16	–	–	–
NCWP	−0.14	–	−0.09	−0.13	–	−0.10
R^2	0.73	0.78	0.61	0.75	0.77	0.59
(r^2)*	(0.66)	(0.76)	(0.55)	(0.69)	(0.77)	(0.54)

* taken from Table 5.3

the well-educated, but Table 4.1 shows that non-voting was particularly low among the Professionals. More likely it is picking up increased alienation among the student population, for many of the constituencies with high percentages of people with degrees also house substantial numbers of students and it is believed that the young in general are increasingly alienated from the political system. Thirdly, non-voting increased relatively, and quite substantially, in the areas of high unemployment, among the white-collar but *not* the blue-collar occupational classes; the latter, it seems, were more prepared to switch – or remain loyal – to Labour in such contexts than were the former.

Overall, these findings do not suggest a straightforward continuation of the trends suggested by Curtice and Steed (1982). Before presenting a full evaluation, however, we turn to an analysis of regional variations too.

Table 5.7 Regression Slopes for the Six Additional Variables as Influences on Non-Voting

	1979–1983 b	1983–1987 b	1979–1987 b	1979–1983 b	1983–1987 b	1979–1987 b
	Professional			Administrative and Managerial		
Agriculture	–	–	–	–	-0.06	-0.10
Energy/Mining	0.14	-0.05	–	0.13	–	–
Unemployment	0.31	0.06	0.18	0.32	0.19	0.33
Council Tenants	–	–	–	–	0.03	0.04
Degree	0.24	0.06	0.15	0.25	0.11	0.22
NCWP	0.15	0.11	0.17	0.12	0.11	0.18
R^2	0.70	0.74	0.59	0.74	0.80	0.69
$(r^2)^*$	(0.64)	(0.69)	(0.45)	(0.69)	(0.75)	(0.54)
	Routine Non-Manual			Skilled Manual		
Agriculture	–	–	–	–	–	-0.10
Energy/Mining	0.07	-0.07	–	–	-0.08	–
Unemployment	0.21	–	0.18	0.18	–	0.12
Council Tenants	–	–	–	–	–	–
Degree	0.25	–	0.20	0.22	–	0.17
NCWP	0.13	0.17	0.24	0.12	0.18	0.25
R^2	0.66	0.64	0.48	0.57	0.62	0.49
$(r^2)^*$	(0.62)	(0.56)	(0.32)	(0.52)	(0.55)	(0.33)
	Semiskilled Manual			Unskilled Manual		
Agriculture	-0.17	0.16	–	–	–	–
Energy/Mining	–	-0.15	-0.13	–	-0.13	-0.14
Unemployment	0.10	-0.13	–	–	-0.09	–
Council Tenants	-0.02	-0.02	-0.04	-0.03	-0.03	-0.05
Degree	0.14	–	0.16	0.18	–	0.15
NCWP	0.15	0.09	0.18	0.11	0.19	0.27
R^2	0.57	0.67	0.47	0.57	0.64	0.44
$(r^2)^*$	(0.49)	(0.55)	(0.29)	(0.53)	(0.56)	(0.27)

* taken from Table 5.3

Regional Patterns

The R^2 values in Tables 5.4–5.7 indicate that we can account for a great deal of the spatial variability in the voting pattern by any one occupational class, using that class's voting at a previous election plus six other variables (employment in agriculture and in energy and mining, unemployment, households which are in council-owned properties, people with degrees, and New Commonwealth plus Pakistan-headed households) as the predictors. This indicates that continuity plus certain key features of the country's economic and social geography are sufficient to account for most of the electoral geography that we described in Chapter 1. To the extent that those key features are regionally clustered (as Figure 3.1 and Figures 5.26–5.30 indicate), so we have accounted for the regional variations described earlier, not by analysing the regions themselves but by looking at certain characteristics of both geographi-

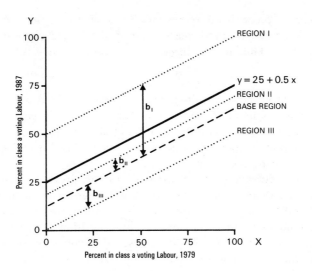

Figure 5.31 An illustration of the Regression Coefficients used in Regional Analyses.

cal and functional regionalisations. Are there, then, any other regional variations not encapsulated by the variables analysed in Tables 5.3–5.7?

To answer this question we have extended the multiple regression analyses by incorporating 51 further variables to represent the 22 geographical regions and the 31 functional regions. (There is no arithmetical mistake; two regions are omitted, for reasons outlined below.) For each of these 51, we also get a regression coefficient. This doesn't indicate a slope, however, but rather the distance between the average values for two regions. Figure 5.31 illustrates the procedure.

We have regressed the percentage in a class voting Labour in 1987 (Y) against the same percentage for 1979 (X), and obtained the equation

$$Y = 25 + 0.5X$$

This is shown by the solid line in Figure 5.31. We then turn to the 22 geographical regions, and select one of them to be what we will call the base region, against which we are going to compare all 21 others. The regression line for that region alone (i.e. fitted just to the constituencies in that region) is shown by the dashed line in Figure 5.31. It is (necessarily, given the technique that we are using) parallel to the solid line (which is the regression for all 633 constituencies) but lower, by 12.5 percentage points on the Y axis; the formula for the region is

$$Y = 12.5 + 0.5X$$

We then take all of the other regions and compare their regression lines with that for the base region. They must run parallel to each other and so the only piece of information that we need is their distance from the base region on the

Y axis. This is given by a regression (b) coefficient, which is simply the distance between the two (and can be read off the Y axis where the regression lines intersect it). Thus for the three regions shown their b values are

b_I + 32.5 b_{II} + 5.0 b_{III} -10.0

Thus, having taken the continuity factor into account, on average Labour won 32.5 percentage points more votes from class a in 1987 in region I than it did in the base region, which indicates a substantial swing to Labour in region I; by contrast it won 10 percentage points less on average in region III, clearly indicative of a swing against it.

   As with the regression slopes discussed in the previous section, we can enquire whether these b values are significantly significant; if they are (again we use the 0.05 level), this means that the constituencies in each region are grouped around its particular regression line, and don't overlap those of the base region very much. Figure 5.32 shows two hypothetical situations; in (a) the b_I value for region I will be statistically significant, whereas in (b) it will not, because of the much greater overlap in the distribution of the two sets of coefficients. Again, we only report the significant b values here, to focus on the major interregional differences.

   In our analyses, two base-line regions are used as comparators against which to evaluate trends elsewhere, one for the set of 22 geographical regions and the other for the 31 functional regions. In both cases we selected base-line regions where the Conservative party is traditionally strong, so that the regression coefficients compare all of the other regions *not* with the British average but with an extreme case; in this way we can evaluate shifts in the geography of voting relative to what we might term the 'Conservative heartland'. For the geographical regions, we selected the Outer Southeast; for the functional regions, we selected the Agricultural areas.

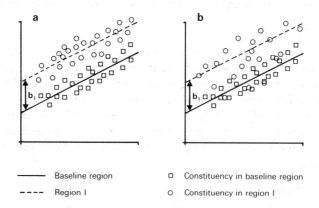

—— Baseline region	□ Constituency in baseline region
- - - Region I	○ Constituency in region I

Figure 5.32 The Difference between a Statistically Significant (a) and Statistically Insignificant (b) Regression Coefficient for Region I.

All of the significant regression coefficients for the 72 different analyses are given in Tables 5.8–5.23. These contain a massive volume of information, from which the following points identify the salient features.

1. In terms of accounting for the spatial variation, the R^2 values given in Tables 5.8, 5.9, 5.12, 5.13, 5.16, 5.17, 5.20 and 5.21 show that in every case addition of the 51 regional variables leads to an increase in the level of statistical explanation: by looking at geographical and functional regions, as well as the six variables evaluated in Tables 5.4–5.7, we get closer to providing a full account of the variability among the 633 constituencies. (The R^2 values in brackets in the tables are taken from Tables 5.4–5.7, so comparing them with the new values in Tables 5.8–5.23 indicates the extra statistical explanation provided. All of the R^2 values are corrected to take account of the number of independent variables being analysed.)

2. For the Conservative and Alliance parties, addition of the regional variables leads to an increase of R^2 of about 3–4 points on average, with very few smaller than 2 or larger than 5. The same is true for Labour when the 1979–1983 and 1983–1987 periods are looked at; for the full 1979–1987 period, however, the average increase in R^2 attributable to the regions is 0.07, or seven percentage points. This clearly implies that there has been a greater inter-regional variability in the pattern of Labour voting over the three elections than has been the case for the other two parties. With Non-Voting the average increases in R^2 are much greater, at 0.17 for 1979–1983, 0.08 for 1983–1987, and 0.15 for 1979–1987. The pattern of Non-Voting has become much more variable between geographical and functional regions over the eight years.

3. Looking at the coefficients, in general terms the geographical regions produce relatively more significant b values per analysis (i.e. column of a table) than do the functional regions, for each of the three parties. For Non-Voting, however, the functional regions contribute more than the geographical regions to the overall pattern. There are some interesting differences among the parties. With the Conservatives, there are more significant coefficients for the 1979–1983 analyses than for the 1983–1987 set (with the exception of functional regions for the Semiskilled Manual), suggesting that there was more inter-regional polarisation of the party's vote between the first pair of elections than between the second. The reverse was the case with Labour, on the other hand, with many more significant coefficients for 1983–1987 than for 1979–1983; for Labour, the regional polarisation came later than it did for Conservative. (This is somewhat at odds with the overall trends shown in Table 5.2; presumably between 1979 and 1983 the growing polarisation in the Labour vote was linked more closely to the six independent variables analysed in Tables 5.4–5.7 than was the case in 1983–1987.) For the *Alliance*, there was little difference between the two periods at the geographical scale, but with the functional regions the major period of patterning was 1983–1987. *Non-Voting* showed the same differentiation between periods as Labour.

The overall impression, then, is that, despite the sparsity of a few of the columns in the tables, the regional variables have added to our statistical account. The implication of this is that, having taken into account both the

Table 5.8 Regression Coefficients for Geographical Regions, White-Collar Occupational Classes Voting Conservative

	Professional			Administrative/Managerial			Routine Non-Manual		
	79–83 *b*	83–87 *b*	79–87 *b*	79–83 *b*	83–87 *b*	79–87 *b*	79–83 *b*	83–87 *b*	79–87 *b*
Strathclyde	−6.24	−3.53	−9.39	−6.70	−3.38	−10.21	−6.79	−4.10	−10.23
E. Scotland	−4.13	–	−5.54	−4.29	–	−5.69	−4.91	−2.56	−6.86
Rural Scotland	−4.60	–	−4.78	−3.68	–	−5.08	−5.27	−2.87	−7.55
Rural North	–	–	–	–	–	–	–	–	–
Industrial Northeast	−2.31	−2.51	−4.58	−2.82	−1.97	−4.73	−2.74	−2.54	−5.01
Merseyside	−3.42	−6.20	−9.14	−4.16	−5.73	−9.59	−4.06	−5.26	−8.81
Greater Manchester	−3.04	–	−3.55	−3.67	–	−3.59	−3.75	–	−4.24
Rest of Northwest	−1.48	–	−2.19	−1.81	–	–	−2.34	−1.19	−3.22
West Yorks.	–	–	–	−1.63	–	–	−1.74	–	–
South Yorks.	−2.91	−2.59	−5.02	−3.17	−2.51	−5.53	−3.27	−2.80	−5.42
Rural Wales	−3.58	–	−2.88	−2.95	–	–	−4.82	–	−5.51
Industrial South Wales	−4.31	–	−4.79	−4.82	–	−4.33	−4.84	–	−6.00
W. Midlands Conurbation	–	–	–	–	–	–	−1.64	–	−2.15
Rest of West Midlands	–	–	–	–	–	–	–	–	–
East Midlands	1.80	–	2.99	1.74	–	3.17	1.45	–	2.47
East Anglia	–	–	–	–	–	–	–	–	–
Devon and Cornwall	–	−2.65	–	–	–	–	–	−2.40	–
Wessex	–	–	–	–	–	–	–	–	–
Inner London	−2.62	1.92	–	−2.66	–	–	−2.56	–	–
Outer London	−1.67	1.75	–	−2.06	–	–	−1.65	–	–
Outer Metropolitan	–	1.44	–	–	–	–	–	–	–
R^2	0.92	0.92	0.85	0.92	0.93	0.85	0.93	0.96	0.91
(r^2)*	(0.89)	(0.90)	(0.81)	(0.89)	(0.92)	(0.81)	(0.90)	(0.94)	(0.86)

* taken from Table 5.4; refers to geographical and functional regions

continuity of the geography of voting and the polarisation linked to six salient constituency characteristics discussed in the previous section, there have been clear regional shifts in Britain's electoral geography over the three elections studied. We turn now to an evaluation of those shifts in more detail.

For the *Conservative* party, the dominant impression given by Tables 5.8 and 5.9 is of a north:south shift, with only a few notable deviations from that. (Recall that the coefficients in those tables indicate the average difference between constituencies in the named region and those in the Outer Southeast region, once continuity and all other variables have been accounted for.) The only region that clearly is distinctive in its behaviour in that context is the Rural North, which records only three significant coefficients out of the total of 27. The Conservatives did not lose support there (except among the Semi-skilled and Unskilled Manual classes in 1983–1987), in contrast to most of the rest of northern Britain; a consequence of this is the block of Conservative seats stretching from Blackpool to Scarborough, described in Chapter 1 (p.

Table 5.9 Regression Coefficients for Geographical Regions, Blue-Collar Occupational Classes Voting Conservative

	Skilled Manual			Semiskilled Manual			Unskilled Manual		
	79–83 b	83–87 b	79–87 b	79–83 b	83–87 b	79–87 b	79–83 b	83–87 b	79–87 b
Strathclyde	−4.38	−3.24	−7.42	−4.28	−4.51	−7.66	−3.56	−2.97	−6.22
E. Scotland	−2.95	−2.01	−4.82	−3.18	−3.53	−5.55	−2.69	−2.13	−4.46
Rural Scotland	−2.58	−2.55	−5.02	−3.78	−2.78	−5.25	−2.88	−2.48	−4.97
Rural North	–	–	–	–	−2.27	−1.83	–	−0.87	–
Industrial Northeast	−2.05	−2.03	−3.95	−1.59	−3.13	−4.24	−1.55	−1.84	−3.27
Merseyside	−3.60	−4.10	−7.38	−2.98	−4.92	−7.30	−2.69	−3.18	−5.63
Greater Manchester	−3.20	–	−3.61	−2.67	−1.98	−4.17	−2.52	–	−3.11
Rest of Northwest	−1.86	–	−2.61	−1.46	−2.73	−3.88	−1.66	−1.07	−2.59
West Yorks.	−1.47	–	–	−1.26	−1.19	−2.11	−1.21	–	−1.34
South Yorks.	−2.37	−2.33	−4.36	−2.05	−2.94	−4.22	−1.84	−2.00	−3.47
Rural Wales	−2.44	–	−2.72	−2.87	−2.01	−3.95	−2.69	–	−3.04
Industrial South Wales	−2.95	–	−4.08	−2.65	−2.78	−4.87	−2.32	−1.33	−3.71
W. Midlands Conurbation	−1.46	–	−1.89	−1.30	−1.19	−2.37	−1.31	–	−1.78
Rest of West Midlands	–	–	–	–	–	–	–	–	–
East Midlands	1.00	1.01	2.08	0.92	–	–	–	0.75	1.40
East Anglia	–	–	–	–	–	–	–	–	–
Devon and Cornwall	–	−1.92	−2.54	–	−2.39	−2.80	–	−1.94	−1.77
Wessex	–	–	–	–	–	–	–	–	–
Inner London	−1.66	–	–	−1.59	–	–	−1.34	–	–
Outer London	−1.14	–	–	−0.91	–	–	−0.79	–	–
Outer Metropolitan	–	–	–	–	–	–	–	–	–
R^2	0.94	0.96	0.91	0.94	0.96	0.93	0.95	0.96	0.92
$(r^2)^*$	(0.92)	(0.95)	(0.87)	(0.92)	(0.94)	(0.89)	(0.92)	(0.95)	(0.88)

* taken from Table 5.4; refers to geographical and functional regions

14). In addition, there was very little loss of relative support for the Conservatives in West Yorkshire among the three white-collar occupational classes (Table 5.8).

Over the full eight-year period, the relative swing against the Conservatives in the northern regions was both widespread and substantial, especially among the Manual groups. The greatest swings were on Merseyside and in Strathclyde, where the losses averaged nine percentage points more than expected in the white-collar occupational classes and seven percentage points in the blue-collar. For the latter groups, the whole of Britain to the north and west of a Plymouth to Hull line, except for the Rural North, experienced shifts in voter preferences away from the party in power at Westminster (as did London between 1979 and 1983 but not in the later years), relative to what was happening in the Outer Southeast region. The division between the two parts of the island – a spatial cleavage defined by the Plymouth-Hull line – was widening, with the East Midlands clearly joining the southeastern part of the country in its growing relative support for the Conservative party.

Table 5.10 Regression Coefficients for Functional Regions: White-Collar Occupational Classes Voting Conservative

	Professional			Administrative/Managerial			Routine Non-Manual		
	79–83 *b*	83–87 *b*	79–87 *b*	79–83 *b*	83–87 *b*	79–87 *b*	79–83 *b*	83–87 *b*	79–87 *b*
I.C./Immig.	–	–	–	–	–	–	–	–	–
Ind./Immig.	–	–	–	–	–	–	–	–	–
Poorest Immig.	–	–	–	–	–	–	–	–	–
Intermed. Ind.	–	–	–	–	–	–	–	–	–
Old Indust./Mining	–	–	–	–	2.24	–	–2.71	–	–
Textile	–	–	–	–	–	–	–	–	–
Poorest Domestic	–4.41	–	–	–4.49	–	–	–5.03	–	–4.60
Conurb. L.A.	–	–	–	–	–	–	–	–	–
Black Co.	–	–	–	2.89	–	5.20	–	–	–
Maritime Ind.	–	–	–	–	–	–	–2.23	–	–
Poor I.C.	–	–	–	–	–	–	–	–	–
Clydeside	–	–	–	–	–	–	–	–	–
Scott. Ind.	–	–	–	–	–	–	–	–	–
Scott. Rural	–	–	–	–	–	–	–	–	–
High Status I.M.	–	3.34	–	–	–	–	–	–	–
I.M.	–	–	–	–	–	–	–2.55	–	–
Outer London	–	–	–	–	–	–	–	–	–
Very High Status	–	–	–	–	–	–	–	–	–
Conurb. W. Collar	–	–	–	–	–	–	–	–	–
City Service	–	–	–	–	–	–	–	–	–
Resort/Retirement	–	–	–	1.89	–	–	1.64	–	–
Recent Growth	2.98	–	3.54	4.23	–	5.28	2.39	–	2.74
Stable Ind.	–	–	–	–	–	–	–	–	–
Small Towns	1.52	–	–	1.70	–	–	–	–	–
Southern Urban	1.97	–	–	2.65	–	–	–	–	–
Modest Aff.	–	–	–	2.01	–	–	–	–	–
Met. Ind.	2.23	–	3.61	2.93	–	4.90	–	–	–
Modest Aff. Scot.	–	3.85	–	4.63	4.56	9.43	–	–	–
Rapid Growth	3.07	–	4.19	3.81	–	4.57	2.97	–	3.11
Prosperous/No Ind.	–	–	–	–	–	–	–	–	–

With regard to the functional regions (Tables 5.10–5.11), the major trend is that there was a swing towards the Conservatives, relative to what was happening in the Agricultural region, in some of the relatively prosperous areas, especially during 1979–1983. The growing places (constituencies such as Milton Keynes and Peterborough in the Recent Growth group, and Wantage and Newbury in the Rapid Growth type) swung more to the Tories than did the more rural areas. Few types swung substantially against the party, however; the main exception was the region comprising constituencies with the Poorest Domestic conditions (Hull West, Cynon Valley and Liverpool Walton, for example), though in the Semiskilled Manual occupational class a number of the less prosperous functional regions shifted significantly against the government between 1983 and 1987 (Table 5.11). Overall, therefore, it was at the geographical rather than the functional regional scale that the Conservative voting pattern became increasingly differentiated.

Table 5.11 Regression Coefficients for Functional Regions: Blue-Collar Occupational Classes Voting Conservative

	Skilled Manual			Semiskilled Manual			Unskilled Manual		
	79–83 *b*	83–87 *b*	79–87 *b*	79–83 *b*	83–87 *b*	79–87 *b*	79–83 *b*	83–87 *b*	79–87 *b*
I.C./Immig.	–	–	–	–	-2.24	–	–	–	–
Ind./Immig.	–	–	–	–	-2.02	–	–	–	–
Poorest Immig.	–	–	–	–	–	–	–	–	–
Intermed. Ind.	–	–	–	–	-1.95	–	–	–	–
Old Indust./Mining	–	–	–	–	-1.94	-1.69	-1.13	–	–
Textile	–	–	–	–	-2.06	–	–	–	–
Poorest Domestic	-2.38	–	–	-1.79	–	-2.42	-1.95	–	-2.22
Conurb. L.A.	–	–	–	–	-1.84	-1.82	–	–	–
Black Co.	–	–	3.22	–	–	1.12	–	–	–
Maritime Ind.	–	–	–	–	-1.60	–	–	–	–
Poor I.C.	–	–	–	–	–	–	–	–	–
Clydeside	–	–	–	–	–	–	–	–	–
Scott. Ind.	–	–	–	–	–	–	–	–	–
Scott. Rural	–	–	–	–	1.91	–	–	–	–
High Status I.M.	–	–	–	–	–	–	-1.87	–	–
I.M.	–	–	–	–	-1.94	–	–	–	–
Outer London	–	–	–	–	–	–	–	–	–
Very High Status	1.35	–	–	1.19	–	–	–	–	–
Conurb. W. Collar	–	–	–	–	-1.93	–	–	–	–
City Service	–	–	–	–	-2.18	-1.63	–	–	–
Resort/Retirement	1.22	–	–	–	–	–	–	–	–
Recent Growth	2.73	–	3.43	2.26	–	–	1.53	–	1.97
Stable Ind.	1.35	–	–	1.48	-1.30	–	–	–	–
Small Towns	1.27	–	–	1.26	-1.13	–	–	–	–
Southern Urban	2.12	–	2.08	1.94	–	–	1.32	–	1.33
Modest Aff.	1.81	–	1.84	1.91	-1.59	–	–	–	–
Met. Ind.	2.15	–	3.13	2.02	–	–	1.01	–	1.51
Modest Aff. Scot.	2.77	–	4.44	–	–	–	–	–	–
Rapid Growth	2.80	–	2.99	2.27	–	2.06	1.92	–	1.95
Prosperous/No Ind.	–	–	–	–	–	–	–	–	–

For the *Labour* party, both sets of regions are important for describing the changing pattern of voting (Tables 5.12–5.15); the north:south divide stands out again with regard to the geographical regions, but in addition Labour did relatively better in many functional regions than it did in the Agricultural areas, especially during 1983–1987.

In contrast to its performance in the Outer Southeast, Labour picked up votes in virtually all of the geographical regions to the northwest of the Plymouth-Hull line, across all occupational classes and all time periods (Tables 5.12–5.13). During the first four years, the two Yorkshire urban regions, the West Midlands (Conurbation and the Rest) and two of the rural regions did not experience relative swings to Labour, but this was followed by substantial swings in the following four years, so that over the full eight years there was a significant swing to Labour in the first 13 regions in the table (i.e. all of Scotland and Wales, and northern England plus the West Midlands Conurba-

Table 5.12 Regression Coefficients for Geographical Regions: White-Collar Occupational Classes Voting Labour

	Professional			Managerial/Administrative			Routine Non-Manual		
	79–83	83–87	79–87	79–83	83–87	79–87	79–83	83–87	79–87
	b	b	b	b	b	b	b	b	b
Strathclyde	3.13	5.41	9.43	3.11	3.85	6.79	4.36	5.20	9.47
E. Scotland	2.33	3.90	6.32	2.24	2.38	4.06	3.37	3.74	6.33
Rural Scotland	–	4.69	5.65	–	2.83	3.73	–	3.79	4.97
Rural North	1.16	1.65	2.99	–	0.85	1.53	1.73	2.10	3.63
Industrial Northeast	–	3.67	4.89	–	2.57	3.24	–	4.25	5.54
Merseyside	3.29	3.78	8.42	2.83	3.10	6.13	4.35	4.75	9.40
Greater Manchester	2.30	2.26	5.15	1.93	1.34	3.17	3.00	2.63	5.54
Rest of Northwest	2.59	2.93	6.15	2.23	1.70	3.78	3.55	3.33	6.74
West Yorks.	–	2.84	3.30	–	1.73	1.87	–	3.25	3.86
South Yorks.	–	4.18	5.24	–	2.82	3.51	–	4.33	5.38
Rural Wales	–	3.98	5.44	–	2.57	3.48	–	3.92	5.54
Industrial South Wales	2.04	6.74	9.74	2.00	4.73	6.93	2.58	6.81	9.61
W. Midlands Conurbation	–	–	2.02	–	–	1.25	–	–	2.26
Rest of West Midlands	–	–	1.61	–	–	–	–	–	2.11
East Midlands	–	–	–	–	–	–	–	–	–
East Anglia	–	–	–	–	–	–	–	–	–
Devon and Cornwall	–	–	–	–	1.44	–	–	2.59	2.27
Wessex	–	–	–	–	–	–	–	–	–
Inner London	-1.39	–	-2.27	-1.05	–	-1.56	-1.66	–	–
Outer London	-0.97	–	–	–	–	–	-1.40	–	-1.64
Outer Metropolitan	–	–	–	–	–	–	–	–	–
R^2	0.93	0.96	0.92	0.93	0.96	0.93	0.93	0.96	0.92
(r^2)*	(0.91)	(0.93)	(0.85)	(0.91)	(0.94)	(0.85)	(0.91)	(0.94)	(0.86)

* taken from Table 5.5; refers to geographical and functional regions

tion) in the three white-collar occupational classes (Table 5.12), and in those 13 plus the Rest of the West Midlands, Devon and Cornwall, and the East Midlands among the Semiskilled and Unskilled Manual groupings. Labour's revival from its 1983 nadir was much greater in those parts of the country outside the London metropolitan region, East Anglia and Wessex than it was in Britain's prosperous regions. And those relative swings to Labour were substantial, being over 10 percentage points in the Semiskilled Manual grouping in all three Scottish regions, for example. (Table 5.15 shows that within Scotland the swings were even greater in some areas: Strathclyde had an average relative swing to Labour of 8.70 points between 1983 and 1987, for example; those Strathclyde constituencies in the Clydeside functional region – most of Glasgow – had an additional swing of 6.01 points, making a total of 14.71. The two sets of coefficients are additive, so that for any one constituency, predicting its Labour vote involves summing the two.)

In the functional regions, the swings towards Labour, relative to its perfor-

Table 5.13 Regression Coefficients for Geographical Regions: Blue-Collar Occupational Classes Voting Labour

	Skilled Manual			Semiskilled Manual			Unskilled Manual		
	79–83 b	83–87 b	79–87 b	79–83 b	83–87 b	79–87 b	79–83 b	83–87 b	79–87 b
Strathclyde	5.44	5.99	10.67	4.52	8.70	13.53	5.65	6.53	11.34
E. Scotland	4.87	4.48	8.01	3.39	8.05	10.95	4.75	5.24	8.72
Rural Scotland	2.97	4.61	6.85	–	9.93	10.83	–	5.68	7.34
Rural North	2.24	2.36	4.07	2.64	3.73	6.22	3.02	2.88	5.23
Industrial Northeast	–	4.70	5.96	–	5.96	7.68	–	5.17	6.84
Merseyside	4.87	5.00	9.62	5.41	5.45	11.70	5.54	5.43	10.53
Greater Manchester	3.49	3.02	5.99	3.86	3.99	7.99	3.87	3.54	6.79
Rest of Northwest	4.35	3.76	7.39	4.74	5.29	10.11	5.06	4.36	8.54
West Yorks.	–	3.74	4.29	–	5.47	6.19	–	4.47	5.40
South Yorks.	–	4.59	5.55	–	5.82	6.99	–	4.83	5.97
Rural Wales	2.21	5.02	7.30	–	9.26	10.51	2.33	6.44	8.75
Industrial South Wales	3.42	8.11	11.53	2.63	9.93	13.11	3.38	8.98	12.30
W. Midlands Conurbation	1.67	–	2.63	1.96	–	3.91	1.87	–	–
Rest of West Midlands	–	–	2.47	1.58	2.18	4.00	1.86	1.60	3.28
East Midlands	–	–	–	–	1.93	2.37	–	1.37	1.84
East Anglia	–	–	–	–	–	–	–	–	–
Devon and Cornwall	–	3.19	2.81	–	3.80	3.88	–	3.87	3.80
Wessex	–	–	–	–	–	–	–	–	–
Inner London	–	–	–	-2.08	–	–	-2.20	–	–
Outer London	-1.79	–	–	-1.98	–	–	-2.29	–	-2.03
Outer Metropolitan	–	–	–	–	–	–	–	–	–
R^2	0.93	0.95	0.92	0.92	0.95	0.92	0.92	0.95	0.91
$(r^2)^*$	(0.90)	(0.93)	(0.84)	(0.90)	(0.92)	(0.85)	(0.89)	(0.92)	(0.83)

* taken from Table 5.5; refers to geographical and functional regions

mance in the Agricultural areas, were largely confined to the less prosperous groupings among the white-collar occupational classes (Table 5.14), and there were relatively few in 1979–1983; among the blue-collar groups they were much more widely spread, especially in the later four-year period. Labour's post–1983 revival was, it seems, particularly marked among manual workers in many parts of the country other than the Agricultural, whereas among the white-collar workers, and especially those in the Administrative and Managerial occupational class, it was confined to a smaller number of functional regions. Even so, Labour picked up votes, relative to its performance in the Agricultural region, among the Professional and Administrative/Managerial classes, not only on Clydeside and in the Textile towns but also in the two Inner Metropolitan groups (containing constituencies such as Chelsea and Bristol West, Fulham and Glasgow Hillhead) and the Conurbation White-Collar constituencies (Sheffield Hallam and Cardiff Central, for example). Among the manual classes, it displayed no relative swing at all, in any period,

Table 5.14 Regression Coefficients for Functional Regions: White-Collar Occupational Classes Voting Labour

	Professional			Managerial/Administrative			Routine Non-manual		
	79–83 b	83–87 b	79–87 b	79–83 b	83–87 b	79–87 b	79–83 b	83–87 b	79–87 b
I.C./Immig.	–	2.74	–	–	1.74	–	–	3.47	3.40
Ind./Immig.	–	–	2.77	–	–	–	–	2.41	3.62
Poorest Immig.	–	–	–	–	–	–	–	–	–
Intermed. Ind.	2.36	–	3.36	1.75	–	1.59	3.34	1.64	4.54
Old Indust./Mining	2.70	1.68	4.96	2.23	–	2.84	3.43	1.99	5.23
Textile	2.29	–	3.62	1.66	–	1.83	3.22	–	4.55
Poorest Domestic	–	3.93	6.15	1.69	2.83	4.79	–	3.24	5.19
Conurb. L.A.	1.86	–	3.73	1.47	–	–	2.63	1.94	4.36
Black Co.	–	–	–	–	–	–	–	–	–
Maritime Ind.	–	2.03	3.75	–	–	2.15	–	2.55	4.40
Poor I.C.	–	–	–	–	–	–	–	–	–
Clydeside	–	5.32	7.32	–	3.40	5.05	–	3.81	5.67
Scott. Ind.	–	3.86	6.03	–	2.54	4.31	–	–	4.76
Scott. Rural	–	–2.69	–	–	–1.68	–2.40	–	–	–
High Status I.M.	–	5.01	6.72	–	2.34	3.56	–	4.73	6.35
I.M.	–	3.78	4.93	–	2.00	2.79	–	4.09	5.12
Outer London	–	2.25	2.57	–	–	–	–	2.60	3.09
Very High Status	–	2.21	–	–	1.02	–	–	2.30	–
Conurb. W. Collar	–	2.78	3.14	–	1.28	–	–	3.14	3.66
City Service	–	–	2.19	–	–	–	–	2.06	3.34
Resort/Retirement	–	–	–	–	–	–	–	–	–
Recent Growth	–	–	–	–	–	–	–	–	2.17
Stable Ind.	1.27	–	2.20	–	–	–	1.99	–	2.94
Small Towns	–	–	–	–	–	–	–	–	–
Southern Urban	–	–	–	–	–	–	–	–	–
Modest Aff.	–	–	–	–	–	–	–	1.55	–
Met. Ind.	–	1.90	–	–	–	–	–	2.54	3.09
Modest Aff. Scot.	–	4.04	4.18	–	–	–	–	4.41	4.78
Rapid Growth	–	–	–	–	–	–	–	1.64	–
Prosperous/No Ind.	–	1.84	–	–	–	–	–	2.00	–

in only four regions: two could have been anticipated (Resort and Retirement; Southern Urban), but two more probably not (Poorest Immigrant; Poor Inner-City: three of the four in the former are in inner Birmingham and, as we showed above, areas with immigrant concentrations shifted substantially away from Labour: p. 174). Overall, then, Labour's revival was much better in most functional regions than it was in the rural areas, and in the northern geographical regions than it was in the Outer Southeast.

Turning to the *Alliance* we find a very different picture, with only small numbers of significant coefficients; the implication is that shifts in voting for the Alliance were not homogeneous within regions, but were more specific to individual constituencies. With regard to the geographical regions, many of which are large, therefore, there are few salient features (Tables 5.16–5.17). The Rest of the Northwest region stands out as the one in which the Alliance consistently lost votes; it won them in Industrial South Wales among the white-collar workers in 1979–1983, but lost them across all occupational classes

Table 5.15 Regression Coefficients for Functional Regions: Blue-Collar Occupational Classes Voting Labour

	Skilled Manual			Semiskilled Manual			Unskilled Manual		
	79–83 b	83–87 b	79–87 b	79–83 b	83–87 b	79–87 b	79–83 b	83–87 b	79–87 b
I.C./Immig.	–	3.90	–	–	5.21	–	–	4.60	4.80
Ind./Immig.	–	2.62	4.08	–	3.22	5.38	–	3.01	5.10
Poorest Immig.	–	–	–	–	–	–	–	–	–
Intermed. Ind.	4.27	1.93	5.18	5.21	2.86	7.63	5.59	2.51	6.85
Old Indust./Mining	4.27	2.41	6.02	4.88	2.89	7.70	4.98	2.79	6.97
Textile	3.88	–	4.95	4.72	–	7.08	5.26	–	6.45
Poorest Domestic	–	3.64	6.60	–	4.75	7.55	–	3.87	6.61
Conurb. L.A.	3.51	–	4.84	4.20	2.79	6.84	4.30	–	5.73
Black Co.	–	–	–	–	–	–	–	–	4.11
Maritime Ind.	–	2.79	4.96	2.73	3.38	–	2.83	3.12	5.80
Poor I.C.	–	–	–	–	–	–	–	–	–
Clydeside	–	4.23	6.76	–	6.01	8.38	–	4.71	6.72
Scott. Ind.	4.14	3.35	7.04	–	5.67	8.95	3.72	4.04	7.31
Scott. Rural	–	–	–	–	-4.84	6.41	–	–	–
High Status I.M.	–	5.03	7.16	–	7.51	10.13	–	5.65	7.78
I.M.	–	4.44	5.80	–	6.20	7.87	–	5.15	6.58
Outer London	–	2.73	3.26	–	4.57	5.50	–	3.32	4.15
Very High Status	–	2.45	–	–	3.80	3.13	–	2.88	–
Conurb. W. Collar	–	3.32	3.87	–	5.20	6.06	–	3.94	4.78
City Service	–	2.20	3.67	2.68	3.52	5.84	2.89	2.88	5.06
Resort/Retirement	–	–	–	–	–	–	–	–	–
Recent Growth	2.12	–	2.82	2.72	–	4.60	3.35	–	4.31
Stable Ind.	2.67	–	3.49	3.35	–	5.27	3.87	–	4.78
Small Towns	–	–	–	–	2.00	3.08	–	–	2.66
Southern Urban	–	–	–	–	–	–	–	–	–
Modest Aff.	–	–	–	–	3.13	3.62	–	2.09	2.82
Met. Ind.	–	2.85	3.72	–	4.75	6.29	2.40	3.62	5.33
Modest Aff. Scot.	–	5.12	6.20	–	8.26	9.55	–	6.47	7.88
Rapid Growth	–	1.73	–	–	2.57	–	–	2.05	–
Prosperous/No Ind.	–	–	–	–	–	–	–	2.44	–

thereafter, as was generally the case in Devon and Cornwall, too. The Rural North was also a region where it performed badly relative to the situation in the Outer Southeast.

Among the functional regions, a small number stand out as areas of poor Alliance performance relative to its success in the Agricultural areas. In Modestly Affluent Scotland, for example, its performance was between 6 and 10 percentage points worse than it was in Britain's rural areas, with voters in constituencies such as Ayr and Stirling clearly moving away from the Alliance in substantial numbers in the later inter-election period. The Rapid Growth and Metropolitan Industrial regions also displayed consistent shifts away from the Alliance then, though at only half the volume (Tables 5.18–5.19). There were also substantial losses in some of the other urban regions, especially in 1983–1987, notably the High Status Inner Metropolitan grouping, Outer London, and the Very High Status areas.

Finally, with regard to *Non-Voting*, a number of interesting particular fea-

Table 5.16 Regression Coefficients for Geographical Regions: White-Collar Occupational Classes Voting Alliance

	Professional			Managerial/Administrative			Routine Non-Manual		
	79–83 *b*	83–87 *b*	79–87 *b*	79–83 *b*	83–87 *b*	79–87 *b*	79–83 *b*	83–87 *b*	79–87 *b*
Strathclyde	4.02	–	–	4.20	–	–	–	–	–
E. Scotland	–	–	–	3.32	–	–	–	–	–
Rural Scotland	–	–	–	–	–	–	–	–	–
Rural North	–	–	–3.29	–	–	–	–1.67	–	–2.41
Industrial Northeast	2.44	–	–	2.31	–	–	–	–	–
Merseyside	–	–	–	–	2.75	–	–	–	–
Greater Manchester	–	–	–	–	–	–	–	–	–
Rest of Northwest	–	–3.00	–4.78	–	–	–2.91	–	–1.96	–3.60
West Yorks.	–	–2.58	–	–	–	–	–	–	–
South Yorks.	–	–	–	–	–	–	–	–	–
Rural Wales	–	–	–	–	–	–	–	–	–
Industrial South Wales	3.90	–5.71	–3.46	3.85	–3.41	–	2.66	–3.82	–2.76
W. Midlands Conurbation	–	–	–	–	–	–	–	–	–
Rest of West Midlands	–	–	–	–	–	–	–	–	–
East Midlands	–	–	–2.94	–	–	–	–	–	–
East Anglia	–	–	–	–	–	–	–	–	–
Devon and Cornwall	3.92	–2.46	–	3.18	–	–	3.41	–	–
Wessex	–	–	–	–	–	–	–	–	–
Inner London	–	–	–	–	–	–	–	–	–
Outer London	–	–	–	–	–	–	–	–	–
Outer Metropolitan	–	–	–	–	–	–	–	–	–
R^2	0.61	0.73	0.50	0.59	0.69	0.42	0.66	0.75	0.54
(r^2)*	(0.57)	(0.69)	(0.46)	(0.55)	(0.66)	(0.39)	(0.63)	(0.72)	(0.50)

* taken from Table 5.6; refers to geographical and functional regions

tures stand out. Among the geographical regions, the two in Wales show much lower changes in the rates of non-voting than was the case in the Outer Southeast across most classes, and very substantially so in Rural Wales (Tables 5.20–5.21), whereas in general the three London regions (Inner and Outer London plus the Outer Metropolitan) have higher rates of abstention. Among the manual occupational classes, and in particular the Semiskilled and Unskilled, the 1983–1987 period has significantly lower Non-Voting rates in most of the northern regions (with the general exception of Scotland), suggesting that part of Labour's recovery then was the result of working-class voters there who abstained in 1983 being prepared to vote in 1987. Among the functional regions (Tables 5.22–5.23), the most substantial block of significant coefficients indicates lower Non-Voting rates in a number of the more prosperous groupings (Recent Growth, Stable Industrial, Small Towns, Southern Urban, Modestly Affluent, Metropolitan Industrial, and Modestly Affluent Scotland); whereas most functional regions had changing patterns of Non-Voting not

Table 5.17 Regression Coefficients for Geographical Regions: Blue-Collar Occupational Classes Voting Alliance

	Skilled Manual			Semiskilled Manual			Unskilled Manual		
	79–83 b	83–87 b	79–87 b	79–83 b	83–87 b	79–87 b	79–83 b	83–87 b	79–87 b
Strathclyde	–	–	–	–	–	–	–	–	–
E. Scotland	–	–	–	–	–	–	–	–	–
Rural Scotland	–	–	–	-3.34	–	–	–	–	–
Rural North	-2.21	–	-2.58	-2.26	–	-3.34	-2.30	–	-2.51
Industrial Northeast	–	–	–	–	-2.25	–	–	–	–
Merseyside	–	–	–	–	–	–	–	–	–
Greater Manchester	–	–	-2.64	–	–	-3.36	-1.73	–	-2.57
Rest of Northwest	-1.90	-1.86	-3.91	-2.03	-2.77	-4.81	-2.08	-1.76	-3.73
West Yorks.	–	–	–	–	-2.35	-2.64	–	–	–
South Yorks.	–	–	–	–	–	–	–	–	–
Rural Wales	–	–	–	–	–	-3.87	–	–	-2.69
Industrial South Wales	–	-3.43	-3.29	–	-4.11	-4.35	–	-2.94	-3.23
W. Midlands Conurbation	–	–	–	–	–	–	–	–	–
Rest of West Midlands	–	–	–	–	–	–	–	–	–
East Midlands	–	–	–	–	–	-2.27	–	–	–
East Anglia	–	–	–	–	–	–	–	–	–
Devon and Cornwall	3.51	–	–	3.61	-2.35	–	3.44	-1.78	–
Wessex	–	–	–	–	–	–	–	–	–
Inner London	–	–	–	–	–	–	–	–	–
Outer London	–	–	–	–	–	–	–	–	–
Outer Metropolitan	–	–	–	–	–	–	–	-1.21	–
R^2	0.73	0.77	0.58	0.76	0.81	0.66	0.78	0.79	0.63
$(r^2)*$	(0.71)	(0.73)	(0.54)	(0.73)	(0.78)	(0.61)	(0.75)	(0.77)	(0.59)

* taken from Table 5.6; refers to geographical and functional regions

significantly different from those in the Agricultural areas, in the relatively prosperous and growing districts abstention rates fell.

Together, all of these findings clarify the extent of the regional shifts in voting within Britain over the relatively brief period 1979–1987. The extent of these shifts should be neither magnified nor underestimated; they show, without any doubt, that during those eight years the country became increasingly divided among its geographical and functional regions in the partisan choices of people in ostensibly similar socio-economic situations. We evaluate that finding later, after an analysis of similar shifts in the flow-of-the-vote.

Table 5.18 Regression Coefficients for Functional Regions: White-Collar Occupational Classes Voting Alliance

	Professional			Managerial/Administrative			Routine Non-Manual		
	79–83	83–87	79–87	79–83	83–87	79–87	79–83	83–87	79–87
	b	b	b	b	b	b	b	b	b
I.C./Immig.	–	–	–	–	–	–	–	–	–
Ind./Immig.	–	–	–	–	–	–	–	–	–
Poorest Immig.	6.13	–	–	5.45	–	–	5.05	–	–
Intermed. Ind.	–	–	–	–	–	–	–	–	–
Old Indust./Mining	–	–	–5.08	–	–	–	–	–	–3.99
Textile	–	–	–	–	–	–	–	–	–
Poorest Domestic	–	–	–	–	–	–	–	–	–
Conurb. L.A.	–	–	–	–	–	–	–	–	–3.58
Black Co.	–	–	–	–	–	–	–	–	–
Maritime Ind.	–	–	–	–	–	–	–	–	–
Poor I.C.	–	–	–	–	–	–	–	–	–
Clydeside	–	–	–9.89	–	–	–7.46	–	–	–6.96
Scott. Ind.	–	–5.37	–7.74	–	–	–5.75	–	–	–5.54
Scott. Rural	–	–	–	–	–	–	–	–	–
High Status I.M.	–	–8.01	–12.70	–	–5.32	–9.25	–	–5.51	–9.36
I.M.	–	–	–	–	–	–	–	–	–
Outer London	–	–	–5.31	–	–	–3.92	–	–	–4.07
Very High Status	–	–	–4.81	–	–	–3.68	–	–	–3.65
Conurb. W. Collar	–	–	–	–	–	–	–	–	–
City Service	–	–	–	–	–	–	–	–	–
Resort/Retirement	–	–	–	–	–	–	–	–	–
Recent Growth	–	–	–	–	–	–	–	–	–
Stable Ind.	–	–	–	–	–	–	–	–	–
Small Towns	–	–	–	–	–	–	–	–	–
Southern Urban	–	–	–	–	–	–	–	–	–
Modest Aff.	–	–	–	–	–	–	–	–	–
Met. Ind.	–	–3.88	–4.91	–	–	–	–	–	–3.60
Modest Aff. Scot.	–	–7.13	–10.96	–	–5.06	–8.44	–	–4.84	–7.76
Rapid Growth	–	–	–4.28	–	–	–3.38	–	–	–3.21
Prosperous/No Ind.	–	–	–	–	–	–	–	–	–

THE FLOW-OF-THE-VOTE

Each inter-election period is characterised by a pattern of gross shifts in voting between parties (including Non-Voting as a 'party'); the resultant of all those shifts is the net gain or loss in votes for each party that produced the election result. Other analyses have shown that the gross flows vary significantly among the constituencies (Johnston, 1985a); in general, people are more likely to remain loyal to a party where it is electorally strong, and those deserting one party are likely to shift their allegiance to a strong party in the constituency rather than to a weak one.

Our interest here is not in the pattern of flows between each pair of elections (1979–1983; 1983–1987) but rather in whether those flows had the same geography in each period. If one accepts the general thesis of continuity in British voting patterns, then one would expect, for example, that those constituencies with high percentages of Conservative loyalists in the first period would also

Table 5.19   Regression Coefficients for Functional Regions: Blue-Collar Occupational Classes Voting Alliance

	Skilled Manual			Semiskilled Manual			Unskilled Manual		
	79–83 b	83–87 b	79–87 b	79–83 b	83–87 b	79–87 b	79–83 b	83–87 b	79–87 b
I.C./Immig.	–	–	–	–	–	–	–	–	–
Ind./Immig.	–	–	–	–	–	–	–	–	–
Poorest Immig.	6.08	–	–	6.02	–	–	5.37	–	–
Intermed. Ind.	–	–	–	–	–	-3.98	–	–	-2.91
Old Indust./Mining	–	–	-4.10	–	–	-4.62	–	–	-3.81
Textile	–	–	–	–	–	-3.67	–	–	–
Poorest Domestic	–	–	–	–	–	–	–	–	–
Conurb. L.A.	–	–	-3.73	–	–	-4.27	–	–	–
Black Co.	–	–	–	–	–	–	–	–	–
Maritime Ind.	–	–	–	–	–	–	–	–	–
Poor I.C.	–	–	–	–	–	–	–	–	–
Clydeside	–	–	-7.49	–	–	-7.17	–	–	-6.15
Scott. Ind.	–	–	-6.38	–	–	-5.96	–	–	-5.20
Scott. Rural	–	–	–	–	–	–	–	–	–
High Status I.M.	–	-5.54	-9.88	–	-6.31	-10.42	–	-4.91	-8.79
I.M.	–	–	–	–	-3.39	-5.03	–	–	–
Outer London	–	–	-4.15	–	-3.05	-4.69	–	-2.26	-3.88
Very High Status	–	-2.13	-3.73	–	-2.79	-3.81	–	-2.44	-3.41
Conurb. W. Collar	–	–	–	–	-2.81	-4.07	–	–	-3.15
City Service	–	–	–	–	–	–	–	–	–
Resort/Retirement	–	–	–	–	–	–	–	–	–
Recent Growth	–	–	–	–	–	–	–	–	–
Stable Ind.	–	–	–	–	–	–	–	–	–
Small Towns	–	–	–	–	–	–	–	–	–
Southern Urban	–	–	–	–	–	–	–	–	–
Modest Aff.	–	–	–	–	–	–	–	–	–
Met. Ind.	–	-2.59	-3.58	–	-3.60	-4.45	–	-2.42	-3.33
Modest Aff. Scot.	–	-4.93	-7.82	–	-5.56	-8.22	–	-4.34	-6.73
Rapid Growth	–	–	-3.23	–	–	-3.16	–	–	-2.83
Prosperous/No Ind.	–	–	–	–	–	–	–	–	–

experience high percentages in the second. If, on the other hand, and as suggested above, that continuity is breaking down, then one would expect inter-regional variations in levels of Conservative loyalty. The analyses reported in this section were designed to inquire whether there was such inter-regional variation.

For those analyses, we needed estimates of the flow-of-the-vote matrix in each of the 633 constituencies for both of the time periods, since these are not available from survey data. The entropy-maximising procedure described above (p. 130) was again used. The method was exactly the same as that employed for estimating constituency class-by-vote matrices, except that the rows represented the parties at the first election and the columns represented the parties at the second. (Thus Figure 5.1 would be adapted so that the four rows in each matrix, like the four columns, were parties I-IV.)

Table 5.20   Regression Coefficients for Geographical Regions: Non-Voting in White-Collar Occupational Classes

	Professional			Administrative/Managerial			Routine Non-Manual		
	79–83 *b*	83–87 *b*	79–87 *b*	79–83 *b*	83–87 *b*	79–87 *b*	79–83 *b*	83–87 *b*	79–87 *b*
Strathclyde	–	–	–	–	2.37	2.70	–	–	–
E. Scotland	–	–	–	–	–	–	–	–	–
Rural Scotland	4.39	–	–	4.71	–	2.61	3.99	–	–
Rural North	–	–	–	–	–	–	–	–	–
Industrial Northeast	–	–	–	–	–	–	–	–	–
Merseyside	–	–	–	–	–	–	–	–	–
Greater Manchester	1.75	–	–	1.87	–	–	1.41	–	–
Rest of Northwest	–	–	–	–	–	–	–	–	–
West Yorks.	–	–	–	–	–	–	–	–1.40	–
South Yorks.	2.18	–	–	–	1.79	2.54	1.81	–	–
Rural Wales	–	–3.70	–3.26	1.81	–4.33	–3.45	–	–7.03	–6.80
Industrial South Wales	–	–1.39	–1.23	–	–	–	–	–2.85	–3.05
W. Midlands Conurbation	–	–	–	–	–	–	–	–	–
Rest of West Midlands	–	–	–	–	–	–	–	–	–
East Midlands	–	–0.85	–1.00	–	–1.47	–1.67	–	–1.45	–1.62
East Anglia	–	–	–	–	–	–	1.55	–	–
Devon and Cornwall	–2.63	–	–1.33	–2.51	–	–1.55	–2.36	–	–1.82
Wessex	–	–1.05	–1.39	–	–1.24	–1.64	–	–1.44	–1.85
Inner London	3.34	–	–	2.93	–	–	3.62	–	1.91
Outer London	2.17	–	1.40	2.13	–	1.90	2.29	–	2.02
Outer Metropolitan	–	–	1.06	–	–	1.20	–	–	1.43
R^2	0.80	0.78	0.70	0.82	0.84	0.79	0.77	0.73	0.66
(r^2)*	(0.70)	(0.74)	(0.59)	(0.74)	(0.80)	(0.69)	(0.66)	(0.64)	(0.48)

* taken from Table 5.7; refers to geographical and functional regions

The national flow-of-the-vote matrices have been derived from the BBC/Gallup files (and Mostellerised so that they fit the row and column totals); they are shown in Table 4.13. The main differences between the two periods are the greater levels of Conservative and, especially, Labour loyalty between 1983–1987 than between 1979–1983, with a consequent drop in the volume of inter-party flows, especially from Labour to Alliance, as well as into Non-Voting. More Liberal voters remained loyal to the Alliance between 1979 and 1983 than was the case for Alliance voters as a whole over the ensuing four years; Labour was the major beneficiary of the movement away from the Alliance in the latter period.

Figures 5.33–5.41 show various aspects of the geography of the flow patterns. The first two focus on Labour loyalty and bring out two clear points: (1) the greater average level for 1983–1987 relative to 1979–1983; and (2) the very substantial north:south divide in both periods. Thus whereas between 1983 and 1987 the majority of northern constituencies recorded Labour loyalty rates

Table 5.21 Regression Coefficients for Geographical Regions: Non-Voting in Blue-Collar Occupational Classes

	Skilled Manual			Semiskilled Manual			Unskilled Manual		
	79–83 b	83–87 b	79–87 b	79–83 b	83–87 b	79–87 b	79–83 b	83–87 b	79–87 b
Strathclyde	–	–	–	–2.81	–	–	–3.17	–	–3.56
E. Scotland	–	–	–	–	–	–2.46	–	–	–
Rural Scotland	3.72	–	–	–	–	–	–	–3.06	–
Rural North	–	–	–	–	–1.71	–1.73	–	–1.61	–1.84
Industrial Northeast	–	–	–	–	–2.13	–2.09	–	–2.12	–2.25
Merseyside	–	–2.08	–2.23	–	–3.23	–3.50	–	–3.40	–4.05
Greater Manchester	–	–	–	–	–1.99	–1.50	–	–1.86	–
Rest of Northwest	–	–	–	–	–2.17	–2.41	–	–2.13	–2.73
West Yorks.	–	–1.62	–	–	–2.34	–1.92	–	–2.44	–2.06
South Yorks.	–	–	–	–	–1.54	–	–	–	–
Rural Wales	–	–7.65	–7.10	–	–6.19	–6.80	–	–9.55	–10.02
Industrial South Wales	–	–3.32	–3.53	–1.91	–4.04	–4.68	–2.25	–5.00	–5.96
W. Midlands Conurbation	–	–	–	–	–	–	–	–	–
Rest of West Midlands	–	–	–	–	–	–1.36	–	–	–
East Midlands	–	–1.58	–1.57	–	–1.51	–1.48	–	–1.84	–1.83
East Anglia	–	–	–	–	–	–1.52	–1.69	–	–
Devon and Cornwall	–3.09	–	–2.33	–3.22	–	–1.86	–3.02	–	–2.75
Wessex	–	–1.59	–2.15	–	–1.23	–1.84	–	–1.70	–2.36
Inner London	3.56	–	–	3.50	–	–	3.60	–	–
Outer London	2.41	–	2.44	2.35	–	2.04	2.79	–	2.73
Outer Metropolitan	–	–	1.64	–	–	1.41	–	1.20	1.84
R^2	0.71	0.72	0.65	0.70	0.76	0.67	0.71	0.74	0.66
(r^2)*	(0.57)	(0.62)	(0.49)	(0.57)	(0.67)	(0.47)	(0.53)	(0.64)	(0.44)

* taken from Table 5.7; refers to geographical and functional regions

of at least 80 per cent, and very few had less than 60, in much of the south of England loyalty rates less than 60 per cent were quite common. (Note, too, that only three Greater London constituencies recorded loyalty rates exceeding 80 per cent in that period.)

Turning to inter-party shifts, Figures 5.35–5.37 focus on three aspects of the 1979–1983 matrix. That for the movement of 1979 Labour voters to Conservative support in 1983 shows very clearly that the volume of such movement was much greater on average in southern England than it was elsewhere (Figure 5.35). Apart from a block of four constituencies in the north of England (Westmorland and Lonsdale; Ribble Valley; Richmond (Yorks.); and Skipton and Ripon) there is very little evidence of above-average Labour-to-Conservative shifts north of the Plymouth-Hull line; indeed, in much of Strathclyde, Merseyside and South Yorkshire the shift was less than 3 per cent, as it was also in much of South Wales and Inner London. Somewhat similarly, the average shift from Labour-to-Alliance was much greater in the south of

Table 5.22   Regression Coefficients for Functional Regions: Non-Voting in White-Collar Occupational Classes

	Professional			Administrative/Managerial			Routine Non-Manual		
	79–83 *b*	83–87 *b*	79–87 *b*	79–83 *b*	83–87 *b*	79–87 *b*	79–83 *b*	83–87 *b*	79–87 *b*
I.C./Immig.	–	2.72	–	–	–	–	–	–	–
Ind./Immig.	–1.53	–	–	–	–	–	–2.71	–	–2.43
Poorest Immig.	–	–	–	–	–	–	–	–	–
Intermed. Ind.	–	–	–	–	–	–	–2.31	–	–2.06
Old Indust./Mining	–	–	–	–	–	–	–	–	–
Textile	–2.52	–	–	–	–	–	–3.04	–	–
Poorest Domestic	–	–	–	4.10	–	–	–	–	–
Conurb. L.A.	–	–	–	–	–	–	–	–	–
Black Co.	–3.08	–	–	–2.66	–	–2.86	–3.33	–	–
Maritime Ind.	–	–	–	–	–	–	–	–	–
Poor I.C.	–	1.86	2.45	–	2.89	3.45	–	2.65	3.17
Clydeside	–	–	–	3.62	–	–	–	–	–
Scott. Ind.	–	–	–2.39	–	–2.60	–3.39	–	–4.25	–5.40
Scott. Rural	–	–	–	–	–	–	–	–	–
High Status I.M.	3.71	–	4.36	3.64	3.32	5.11	3.12	–	4.13
I.M.	–	–	–	–	–	–	–	–	–
Outer London	–	–	–	–	–	–	–	–	–
Very High Status	–	–	–	–	–	–	–	–	–
Conurb. W. Collar	–	–	–	–	–	–	–	–	–
City Service	–	–	–	–	–	–	–	–	–2.04
Resort/Retirement	–	–	–	–	–	–	–	–	–
Recent Growth	–4.92	–	–2.79	–4.78	–1.59	–4.01	–5.09	–	–3.90
Stable Ind.	–	–	–1.49	–2.66	–	–1.87	–3.94	–	–2.75
Small Towns	–	–	–1.49	–	–1.43	–1.99	–1.64	–1.76	–2.52
Southern Urban	–2.26	–	–1.35	–2.08	–	–1.78	–2.55	–	–2.17
Modest Aff.	–1.72	–	–	–	–	–	–2.08	–	–1.83
Met. Ind.	–2.38	–	–1.64	–2.16	–	–2.48	–2.73	–	–2.97
Modest Aff. Scot.	–	–	–	–	–3.47	–4.04	–	–3.83	–4.53
Rapid Growth	–	–	–	–	–	–	–	–	–
Prosperous/No Ind.	–	–	–	–	–	–	–	–	–

England than further north (Figure 5.36), though with some clear exceptions to this, such as Crosby (won at a by-election by the Alliance candidate, Shirley Williams, in 1981) and adjacent Southport in Merseyside and Caithness and Sutherland in the far north of Scotland. There was no clearly discernible spatial pattern to the Conservative-to-Alliance flows, however (Figure 5.37); across most of Britain, one was as likely to find a constituency with between 5 and 10 per cent of 1979 Conservative voters shifting to the Alliance as one with between 10 and 15 per cent (see also Figure 5.43).

Between 1983 and 1987 the regional variations in the shifts are even clearer. Figures 5.38 and 5.39 focus on the movements between Conservative and Labour, for example. With regard to shifts from Conservative to Labour, the north:south divide is starkly displayed (Figure 5.38). With only one exception (Devon North) there was no constituency in southern England (including all of Greater London) where more than 10 per cent of those who voted Conservative in 1983 transferred their support to Labour in 1987, and less than 5 per

Table 5.23 Regression Coefficients for Functional Regions: Non-Voting in Blue-Collar Occupational Classes

	Skilled Manual			Semiskilled Manual			Unskilled Manual		
	79–83 *b*	83–87 *b*	79–87 *b*	79–83 *b*	83–87 *b*	79–87 *b*	79–83 *b*	83–87 *b*	79–87 *b*
I.C./Immig.	–	–	–	–	-3.06	-3.29	–	–	–
Ind./Immig.	–	–	-2.59	–	-2.33	-3.25	-2.79	–	-3.83
Poorest Immig.	–	–	–	–	–	–	–	–	–
Intermed. Ind.	-1.94	–	-2.08	-2.25	-2.01	-3.03	-3.06	-2.04	-3.64
Old Indust./Mining	–	–	–	–	-1.89	–	–	–	-2.46
Textile	-2.86	–	–	-3.18	–	-3.16	-3.87	–	-3.84
Poorest Domestic	–	–	–	–	-2.53	–	–	–	–
Conurb. L.A.	–	–	–	–	–	–	–	–	–
Black Co.	–	–	–	–	–	-3.04	-3.40	–	-3.64
Maritime Ind.	–	–	–	–	–	-2.33	–	–	–
Poor I.C.	–	–	–	–	–	–	–	–	–
Clydeside	–	–	–	–	-3.71	–	–	-4.36	–
Scott. Ind.	–	-4.51	-4.74	–	-3.49	-4.28	–	-5.50	–
Scott. Rural	–	–	–	–	–	–	–	–	–
High Status I.M.	4.10	–	4.67	4.43	–	–	3.34	–	–
I.M.	–	–	–	–	-3.17	–	–	–	–
Outer London	–	–	–	–	–	–	–	–	–
Very High Status	–	–	–	–	–	–	–	–	–
Conurb. W. Collar	–	–	–	–	-1.83	–	–	–	–
City Service	–	-2.01	–	–	-2.67	-2.73	–	-2.79	-3.22
Resort/Retirement	–	–	–	–	–	–	–	–	–
Recent Growth	-4.61	–	-4.22	-4.64	-1.73	-4.18	-5.52	–	-5.15
Stable Ind.	-3.42	–	-2.75	-3.80	-1.56	-3.36	-4.64	–	-4.19
Small Towns	–	-2.09	-2.59	–	-2.09	-2.69	–	-2.63	-3.48
Southern Urban	-2.01	–	-2.26	-2.07	-1.47	-2.54	-2.57	–	-3.01
Modest Aff.	–	–	–	–	–	-2.23	–	–	-2.69
Met. Ind.	-1.84	-2.00	-2.82	-1.96	-2.47	-3.40	-2.58	-2.77	-4.15
Modest Aff. Scot.	–	-4.30	-4.11	–	-4.08	-4.09	–	-5.54	-5.81
Rapid Growth	–	–	–	–	–	–	–	–	–
Prosperous/No Ind.	–	–	–	–	–	–	–	–	–

cent did so in a majority of the constituencies there. But in that same part of Britain, for at least 6 per cent of those who voted Labour in 1983 transferring their allegiance to the Conservative party in 1987 was common, and over 9 per cent did so in a substantial number of places, whereas further north it was not uncommon for less than 3 per cent of the 1983 Labour voters to transfer their allegiance in that direction (Figure 5.39). In relative terms, therefore, the south was marked by Conservative-to-Labour shifts being outbalanced by Labour-to-Conservative moves, with the opposite in the north of Britain.

Finally, the flows away from Alliance voting in 1983 provide further evidence, at a gross, impressionistic scale, of the north:south divide. For the Alliance-to-Conservative shifts (Figure 5.40) in general the volume was greater in southern England than in northern England, and substantially more so than it was in either Scotland or Wales. In the more prosperous parts of Britain, it seems, those who decided they could no longer support the Alliance switched to the Tories, whereas in the less prosperous areas – notably South Wales, South

Figure 5.33 The geography of Labour loyalty, 1979–1983.

Figure 5.34 The geography of Labour loyalty, 1983–1987.

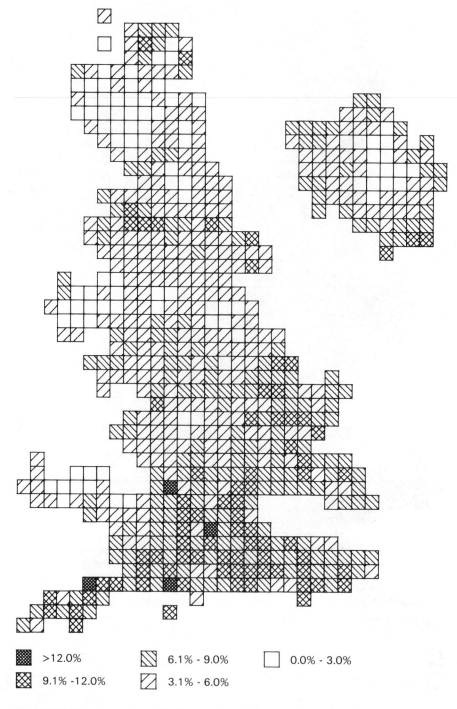

Figure 5.35 The geography of Labour-to-Conservative flows, 1979–1983.

Figure 5.36 The geography of Labour-to-Alliance flows, 1979–1983.

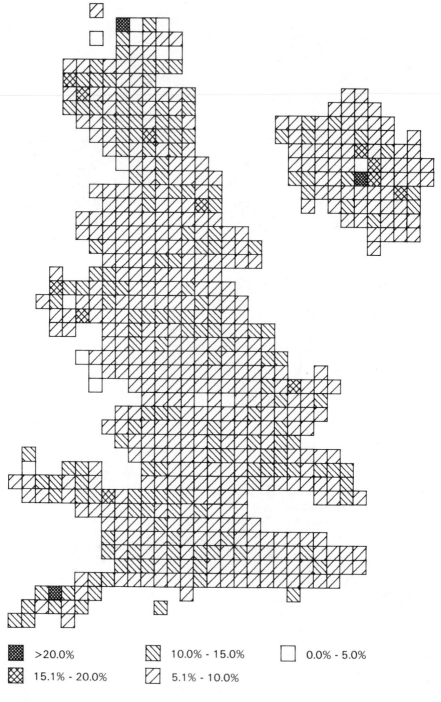

Figure 5.37 The geography of Conservative-to-Alliance flows, 1979–1983.

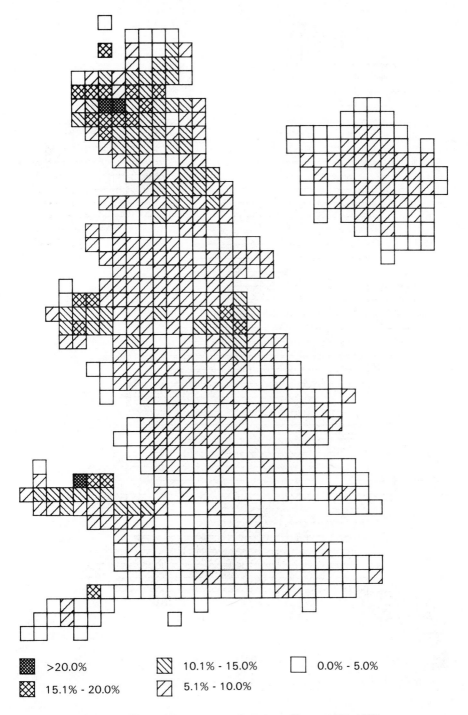

Figure 5.38 The geography of Conservative-to-Labour flows, 1983–1987.

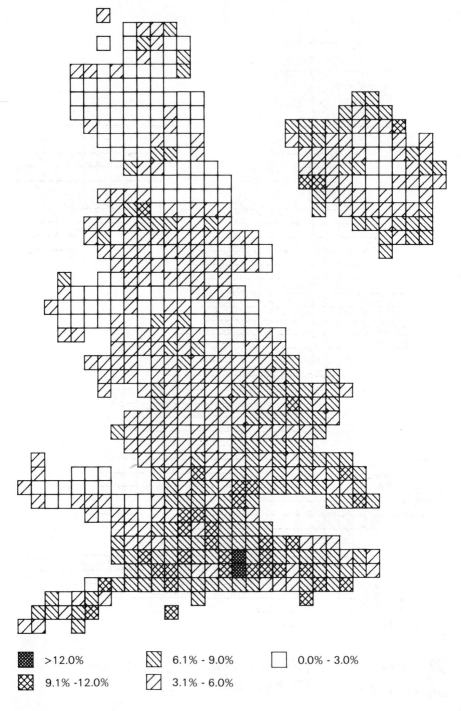

Figure 5.39 The geography of Labour-to-Conservative flows, 1983–1987.

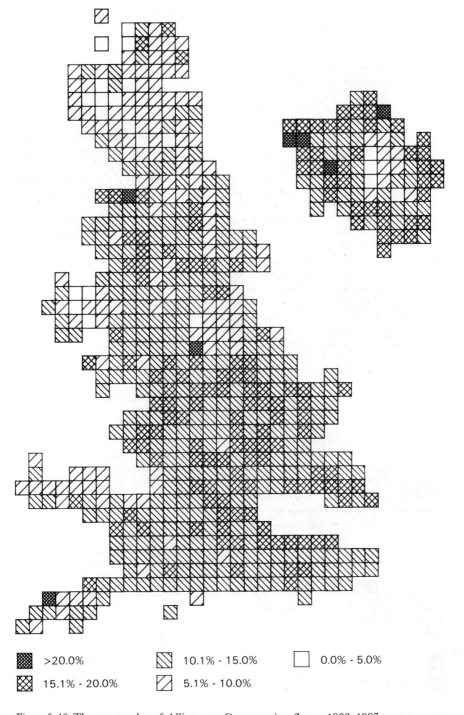

Figure 5.40 The geography of Alliance-to-Conservative flows, 1983–1987.

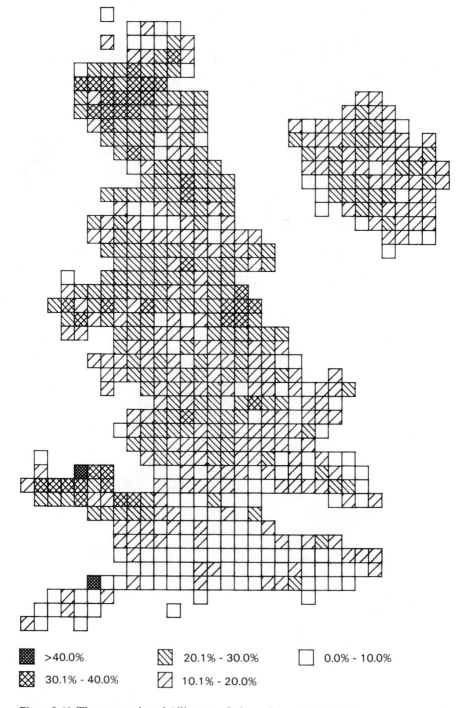

Figure 5.41 The geography of Alliance-to-Labour flows, 1983–1987.

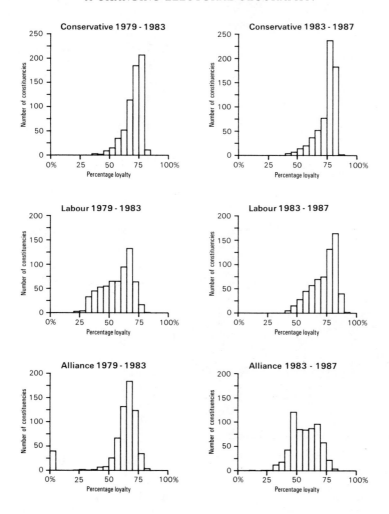

Figure 5.42 Estimates of Party Loyalty, 1979–1983 and 1983–1987.

Yorkshire, and Strathclyde – they were much more likely to switch to Labour (Figure 5.41). Britain was polarised in terms not just of the support for the various parties but also in the degree to which they switched from one to another.

The patterns displayed in that series of cartograms are summarised in Table 5.24, and Figures 5.42 and 5.43 show some of the frequency distributions of the flow percentages. The overall impressions are of greater variability in 1983–1987 than 1979–1983 in some of the flows, but less in others.

Figure 5.42 shows the frequency distribution of loyalty percentages for each of the three main parties. For both Conservative and Labour, the pattern is clearly greater concentration of the constituencies in a small range of values in the second period than in the first. For the Conservatives, about 400 constit-

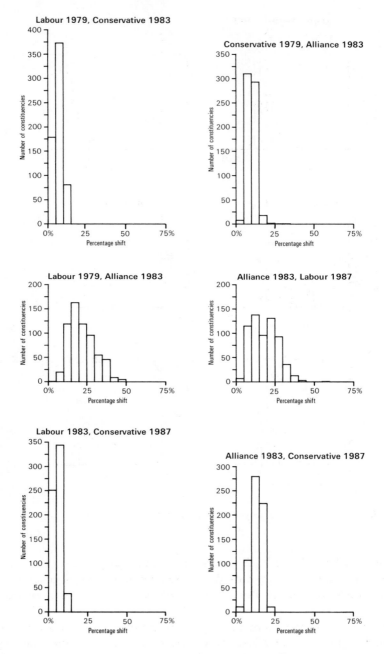

Figure 5.43 Estimates of Inter-Party Shifts, 1979–1983 and 1983–1987.

uencies recorded loyalty rates in the 70s between 1979–1983, whereas nearly
450 recorded between 75 and 84 in the second period. Nevertheless, there is a
not inconsiderable number with loyalty below 65 in each period, hence the lack

Table 5.24 Parameters of the 633 Constituency Flow-of-the-Vote Matrices

Flow		1979–1983			1983–1987		
From	To	Range	Mean	CV	Range	Mean	CV
Conservative	Conservative	37–84	70.2	10.7	42–86	74.4	10.9
Labour	Conservative	1–14	6.3	40.4	1–14	5.4	46.2
Alliance	Conservative	0–19	11.1	33.8	2–23	13.0	28.2
Non-Voting	Conservative	4–30	15.4	27.5	4–29	16.4	27.0
Conservative	Labour	1–11	3.47	53.5	1–22	6.5	59.0
Labour	Labour	22–81	56.3	22.5	40–93	72.5	14.6
Alliance	Labour	0–23	5.3	56.6	3–58	17.9	46.8
Non-Voting	Labour	2–25	8.2	40.0	3–36	15.0	39.4
Conservative	Alliance	2–31	9.8	25.5	1–34	8.1	39.9
Labour	Alliance	3–49	21.6	38.9	1–30	9.4	57.4
Alliance	Alliance	0–84	60.8	28.9	14–82	56.6	19.5
Non-Voting	Alliance	1–24	10.6	29.2	1–21	6.8	38.4

All flow values (range, mean) are expressed as percentages of the relevant row totals

of change in the CV value (Table 5.24). With Labour, however, the CV value for 1983–1987 is only two-thirds that for 1979–1983, and the very wide spread of loyalty values in the period prior to the 1983 election is followed by a much narrower one, though still with a substantial range, in the following four years. For the Alliance, on the other hand, a very peaked distribution for 1979–1983 is succeeded by a much flatter one for 1983–1987. (In this case, the lower CV for the later period is misleading. There were 17 constituencies without Liberal candidates in 1979, and so no flows from the Alliance between 1979 and 1983 there; these constituencies are clearly visible on the left of the frequency distribution for Alliance loyalty in 1979–1983.)

Many of the inter-party flow estimates are clustered into a very small range of values only (although because the means are low the CV values are still high); others are quite widely spread. Six are shown in Figure 5.43 to illustrate this difference. Those on the left-hand side of the figure are for flows in which the great majority of the constituencies fell within a very small range of values. Those on the right-hand side are much more variable. Thus between 1979 and 1983 the percentage of a constituency's Labour voters who shifted their allegiance to the Alliance ranged from 3 to 40, and there were over 100 constituencies recording shifts of 30 per cent or more. In the following four years, the shift back from the Alliance to Labour varied from 3 percentage points in one constituency to 58 in another; about one hundred were in each of the five categories 5–9, 10–14, 15–19, 20–24, and 25–29. The shifts from the Alliance to the Conservative party were spatially much less variable, however, so it was the movements between the Alliance and Labour which were spatially most distinct. Did they have the same spatial structure over each period, or were there changes to the geography?

Continuity

The first part of our analysis of the changing geography of the flow-of-the-vote matrix concentrates on the continuity factor. As in the earlier analyses, this involves regressing the 633 values for one of the elements of the matrix, Conservative loyalty say, in the second time period against the values for the same element in the first period. In the terms of Figure 5.23, therefore, the independent variable (X) on the horizontal axis would be the 1979–1983 flow and the dependent variable (Y) on the vertical axis the 1983–1987 flow. Fitting a regression line to the scatter of points (as in Figure 5.44) evaluates the level of continuity; the greater the value of r^2, the greater the continuity. If b is greater than 1.0, there has been spatial polarisation in the flow over time; if it is less than 1.0, the opposite has occurred.

The parameters of the sixteen regression equations are given in Table 5.25. Their goodness-of-fit is not very high overall, with an average r^2 of only 0.42; the largest values are all for flows involving either or both the Conservative and Labour parties, with only one of 0.6 or greater involving the Alliance. In general, then, the pattern of flows between 1983 and 1987 is not well predicted by the pattern between 1979 and 1983, suggesting a changed geography of changing partisan preferences between the two periods. In particular, the flows

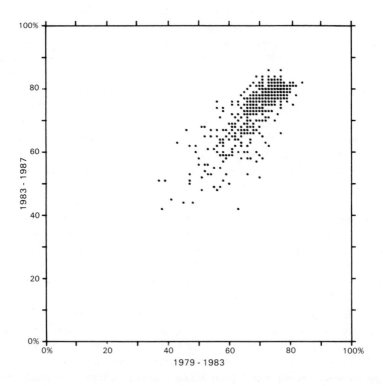

Figure 5.44 Scatter-plot of the Relationship between Conservative Loyalty 1979–1983 and Conservative Loyalty 1983–1987.

Table 5.25 Parameters of the Continuity Regression Equations

Flow From	To	a	b	r^2
Conservative	Conservative	13.5	0.87	0.65
Conservative	Labour	0.4	1.77	0.73
Conservative	Alliance	2.9	0.53	0.16
Conservative	Non-Voting	4.0	0.39	0.46
Labour	Conservative	−0.1	0.86	0.78
Labour	Labour	31.5	0.73	0.76
Labour	Alliance	−1.4	0.50	0.61
Labour	Non-Voting	3.1	0.57	0.30
Alliance	Conservative	6.8	0.56	0.32
Alliance	Labour	10.6	0.89	0.24
Alliance	Alliance	36.4	0.33	0.28
Alliance	Non-Voting	9.8	0.09	0.03
Non-Voting	Conservative	3.9	0.81	0.60
Non-Voting	Labour	3.6	1.40	0.60
Non-Voting	Alliance	2.3	0.43	0.25
Non-Voting	Non-Voting	49.1	0.18	0.04

to and from the Alliance have low correlations between the two periods, indicating that the patterns of gains and losses during its build-up of electoral strength in 1979–1983 were not closely matched by the later pattern of gains and losses as it consolidated its hold over one-quarter of the electorate in the following four-year period.

All but two of the b coefficients are less than 1.0, most of them substantially so. Only with the flows from Conservative to Labour and from Non-Voting to Labour was there substantial polarisation between the two periods, so that where Labour did well in 1979–1983 it did very much better in 1983–1987. For all other flows, although in every case the signs of the b coefficients indicate a continuity effect (with the large flows being in the same constituencies in 1983–1987 as in 1979–1983), there was a decline in the differentials between the two periods. With the Labour to Conservative flows, for example, in a constituency where the percentage of 1979 Labour voters shifting to Conservative in 1983 was 5, the same percentage for 1983–1987 was 4.2; where it was 20 in 1979–1983, it was 17.1 in the later period.

The relatively poor fits for the continuity regressions (compared to those reported in Table 5.3 for the class-by-vote regressions) suggests that the other variables used in our analyses – Agriculture, Mining etc. plus the geographical and functional regions – should be influential in providing statistical accounts of the changing geographies. Tables 5.26–5.30 suggest that this is so, although some of the final R^2 values (in Tables 5.28 and 5.30) are still fairly low. For the six constituency characteristics variables, the average increase from the r^2 of Table 5.25 is 0.13, with the largest for the flows involving either or both of the Alliance and Non-Voting and the smallest for the flows involving only

Table 5.26 Regression Slopes for the Six Additional variables as Influences on Flows

From	Conservative				Labour			
To	C	L	A	N-V	C	L	A	N-V
Agriculture	-0.13	-0.04	0.20	–	-0.04	-0.30	0.22	0.13
Energy/Mining	–	–	–	–	-0.03	0.11	–	-0.16
Unemployment	-0.36	0.16	0.14	0.19	-0.11	0.21	–	-0.21
Council Tenants	-0.07	0.03	–	0.03	-0.01	–	-0.02	-0.03
Degree	-0.21	–	0.19	–	–	-0.19	0.18	–
NCWP	0.26	-0.13	-0.06	–	0.05	-0.14	–	0.08
R^2	0.74	0.80	0.25	0.58	0.83	0.78	0.64	0.48
$(r^2)^*$	(0.65)	(0.73)	(0.16)	(0.46)	(0.78)	(0.76)	(0.61)	(0.30)

From	Alliance				Non-Voting			
To	C	L	A	N-V	C	L	A	N-V
Agriculture	-0.15	-0.54	0.53	-0.08	–	-0.15	0.17	–
Energy/Mining	–	0.38	-0.34	–	-0.05	0.18	–	-0.17
Unemployment	-0.27	0.49	-0.30	0.08	-0.30	0.28	–	–
Council Tenants	-0.03	0.11	-0.07	–	-0.06	0.04	-0.02	–
Degree	-0.22	-0.32	0.44	-0.11	-0.08	–	0.15	–
NCWP	0.13	-0.07	-0.17	0.15	0.07	-0.16	-0.04	0.21
R^2	0.49	0.61	0.44	0.27	0.71	0.70	0.39	0.16
$(r^2)^*$	(0.32)	(0.24)	(0.28)	(0.03)	(0.60)	(0.60)	(0.25)	(0.04)

*taken from Table 5.25

Conservative and Labour (including loyalty to those two parties). Exactly the same holds for the further increases in R^2 when the geographical and functional regions are introduced; the average increase is 0.10.

The *b* coefficients in Table 5.26 show shifts that in part are as expected, but in addition identify aspects of the changing geography of voting that have not yet been fully recognised. For example, the fall in the percentage of Conservative loyalists the greater the level of *unemployment*, and the increase in the flows from Conservative to Labour, Alliance and, especially, Non-Voting are in line with earlier findings, as are: the increasing percentage of Labour loyalists; the decreasing flow from Labour to Conservative; the increased flow from Alliance to Labour; and the increased flow from Non-Voting to Labour matched by a decreased flow to Conservative – all as unemployment increases. In addition, however, there was a decreasing flow from Labour to Non-Voting. Overall, the greater the level of unemployment, the greater the shift away from the party of government, and also from the Alliance, and the greater the shift to Labour, including many people who did not vote in 1983. The geography of unemployment has had a major influence on the changing electoral geography (there are few *b* coefficients in the rest of Table 5.26 as large as those in the rows for the unemployment variable).

With regard to the other variables, the coefficients make it clear that, compared to the 1979–1983 flows, the main beneficiary between 1983–1987 in the areas with large percentages employed in *agriculture* was the Alliance. It gained

Table 5.27 Regression Coefficients for Geographical Regions: Flows from Conservative and Labour

From	Conservative				Labour			
To	C	L	A	N-V	C	L	A	N-V
Strathclyde	-8.16	4.00	-	2.97	-2.40	5.71	-3.00	-3.76
E. Scotland	-5.94	2.52	-	1.72	-2.36	5.56	-2.98	-3.64
Rural Scotland	-	2.72	4.73	-	-2.74	5.46	-	-4.19
Rural North	-	0.85	-	-	-1.36	5.01	-1.79	-3.00
Industrial Northeast	-3.32	2.58	-	1.00	-1.52	6.47	-2.57	-3.11
Merseyside	-7.32	3.33	3.18	1.49	-1.63	3.88	-	-3.63
Greater Manchester	-	1.06	-	-	-0.79	3.96	-	-2.79
Rest of Northwest	-	1.38	-	-	-1.32	6.17	-3.00	-3.61
West Yorks.	-	1.46	-	-	-1.03	6.13	-2.51	-3.15
South Yorks.	-4.61	3.09	-	2.01	-1.50	6.03	-2.38	-2.58
Rural Wales	-	2.26	-	-2.68	-2.04	8.29	-2.98	-8.24
Industrial South Wales	-	3.71	-1.34	-	-1.90	9.01	-4.10	-5.10
W. Midlands Conurbation	-	-	-	-	-	-	-	-
Rest of West Midlands	-	-	-	-	-0.84	3.16	-	-1.71
East Midlands	-	-	-	-1.14	-	3.68	-1.73	-2.07
East Anglia	-	-	-	-	-0.54	3.74	-2.33	-1.80
Devon and Cornwall	-2.36	1.01	-	-	-1.11	3.64	-2.00	-
Wessex	-	-	-	-	-	-	-	-
Inner London	-	-	-	-	-	-	-	-
Outer London	-	-	-	-	-	-	-	-
Outer Metropolitan	-	-	-	-	-	-	-	-
R^2	0.79	0.88	0.33	0.66	0.87	0.82	0.70	0.66
$(r^2)*$	(0.74)	(0.80)	(0.25)	(0.58)	(0.83)	(0.78)	(0.64)	(0.48)

* taken from Table 5.26; refers to geographical and functional regions

substantially increased flows in the second period from both Conservative and Labour, both of which lost loyalists in such areas relative to the earlier period, and the Alliance also retained many more votes. In the later period, then, the Alliance consolidated its support in the rural areas, as well as in the constituencies with large percentages of the population having a *degree*, where exactly the same pattern held. Our earlier analyses suggested that the Alliance vote was less spatially concentrated in 1983 than in 1979, but then more concentrated again (though not to 1979 levels) in 1987. The results here show that the concentration in the later period was into two types of constituency; those with high percentages employed in agriculture or/and high percentages with degrees.

Labour's hold was consolidated in the *mining* areas, except with regard to flows from Conservative, and in the areas with large percentages of *council tenants* (although there was no increase in Labour loyalists in the latter). For the Conservatives, the main relative gains were in the inner city areas with large percentages of *NCWP* households, where it attracted greater flows from all

Table 5.28 Regression Coefficients for Functional Regions: Flows from Conservative and Labour

From	Conservative				Labour			
To	C	L	A	N-V	C	L	A	N-V
I.C./Immig.	–	2.44	–	–	–1.55	7.71	–	–4.51
Ind./Immig.	–	1.49	–	–	–1.10	4.87	–	–3.46
Poorest Immig.	–	2.03	–	–	–	–	–	–
Intermed. Ind.	–	–	–	–	–0.93	4.21	–	–3.33
Old Indust./Mining	–	–	–	–	–	3.70	–	–2.85
Textile	–	–	–	–	–1.01	–	–	–3.04
Poorest Domestic	–	4.33	–	–	–	–	–	–3.51
Conurb. L.A.	–	–	–	–	–0.75	–	–	–2.44
Black Co.	–	–	–	–	–	–	–	–
Maritime Ind.	–	–	–	–	–	4.61	–	–2.89
Poor I.C.	–	–	–	2.39	–	–	–	–
Clydeside	–	3.32	–3.44	–	–	–	–	–3.87
Scott. Ind.	–	1.58	–3.41	–2.67	–	–	–	–3.99
Scott. Rural	4.63	–2.05	–3.13	–1.87	–	–	–	–
High Status I.M.	–	2.35	–4.17	–	–1.56	11.33	–7.34	–4.01
I.M.	–	2.44	–	–	–1.35	9.10	–4.25	–4.76
Outer London	–	–	–	–	–0.83	6.71	–3.65	–3.30
Very High Status	–	–	–	–	–0.77	5.45	–3.13	–1.78
Conurb. W. Collar	–	1.31	–	–	–1.29	7.98	–3.67	–4.10
City Service	–	–	–	–	–1.10	4.91	–	–3.84
Resort/Retirement	–	–	–	–	–	–	–	–
Recent Growth	–	–	–	–1.24	–0.68	3.74	–2.16	–2.57
Stable Ind.	–	–	–	–	–0.66	3.97	–2.58	–2.67
Small Towns	–	–	–	–1.05	–0.71	3.55	–	–2.97
Southern Urban	–	–	–	–	–0.60	3.23	–	–2.31
Modest Aff.	–	–	–	–	–1.13	6.10	–2.97	–3.40
Met. Ind.	–	–	–	–1.33	–1.18	7.94	–4.20	–4.29
Modest Aff. Scot.	6.68	–	–4.61	–4.06	–	9.89	–5.67	–5.71
Rapid Growth	–	–	–	–	–	3.79	–2.43	–
Prosperous/No Ind.	–	0.89	–	–	–	–	–	–

other parties in the second period than in the first and retained more of its original vote. Flows into Non-Voting from Labour and Alliance also increased in these areas, as did Non-Voting 'loyalty'; increasingly, it seems, residents of these immigrant concentrations either voted Conservative or failed to vote at all.

Between 1979–1983 and 1983–1987, therefore, the coefficients in Table 5.26 suggest that Labour consolidated its support in the traditional areas of its support – the coalfields and the council estates; the Conservative party extended its vote-winning in the inner city immigrant areas; and the Alliance became focused in its vote-winning on the rural areas and those with educationally well-qualified populations. In addition, as Tables 5.27–5.30 show, there were inter-regional variations that both accentuated and supplemented these trends.

At the scale of the *geographical regions* (Tables 5.27 and 5.29) the dominant feature is the relative shift to Labour in most of the regions outside the Southeast of England, plus Wessex and the West Midlands Conurbation.

Table 5.29 Regression Coefficients for Geographical Regions: Flows from Alliance and Non–Voting

From	Alliance				Non-Voting			
To	C	L	A	N-V	C	L	A	N-V
Strathclyde	-3.64	6.48	–	–	-5.46	5.41	–	–
E. Scotland	-2.78	4.41	–	–	-4.59	4.66	–	–
Rural Scotland	-3.58	–	–	–	-4.75	5.47	–	–
Rural North	–	4.06	-4.44	–	–	2.61	–	–
Industrial Northeast	-1.51	5.68	–	–	-2.39	4.55	–	–
Merseyside	-3.18	5.11	–	–	-3.27	5.11	–	-3.13
Greater Manchester	–	4.71	–	–	–	3.14	–	-1.86
Rest of Northwest	–	6.75	-6.98	–	–	4.16	-1.26	-2.61
West Yorks.	–	4.71	-4.38	–	–	1.55	–	-2.79
South Yorks.	-1.87	6.09	–	–	-2.99	4.17	–	–
Rural Wales	–	6.23	-8.59	-3.58	–	7.91	–	-12.31
Industrial South Wales	–	11.60	-10.22	–	-1.94	8.49	-1.69	-6.13
W. Midlands Conurbation	–	–	–	–	–	–	–	–
Rest of West Midlands	–	–	–	–	–	1.47	–	–
East Midlands	1.51	–	–	–	1.38	1.50	–	-2.64
East Anglia	–	2.55	–	–	–	1.55	-1.04	–
Devon and Cornwall	–	–	–	–	-1.62	2.27	–	–
Wessex	–	–	–	-1.31	–	–	–	-2.14
Inner London	–	–	–	–	–	–	–	–
Outer London	–	–	–	–	–	–	–	–
Outer Metropolitan	1.00	–	–	0.96	–	–	–	–
R^2	0.57	0.76	0.53	0.35	0.76	0.82	0.45	0.46
(r^2)*	(0.49)	(0.61)	(0.44)	(0.27)	(0.71)	(0.70)	(0.39)	(0.16)

* taken from Table 5.26; refers to geographical and functional regions

Compared to what happened in the Outer Southeast, the level of Labour loyalty was significantly and substantially higher (averaging 5.4 percentage points) in all but five of the regions; the flows to Labour were significantly different from those for the Outer Southeast in 13 regions for shifts from the Conservatives, 12 from the Alliance, and 16 from Non-Voting, whereas flows from Labour were significantly less in 15 to the Conservatives, 12 to the Alliance, and 15 to Non-Voting. Compared to 1979–1983, therefore, the period 1983–1987 was one in which there was a greater shift towards Labour in virtually all of Britain outside the metropolitan heartland of England's southeast.

The dominance of the changing geography of Labour support at the geographical region scale is matched by the pattern in the *functional regions* (Tables 5.28 and 5.30). From the Conservatives, its relative success was in picking up more votes in some of the poorest constituencies plus urban Scotland; from the Alliance, it did better in all but three of the 30 regions relative to the flow in the Agricultural areas, and it also picked up more votes from Non-Voting in 1983–1987 than in 1979–1983, relative to the Agricultural areas, in all but seven regions (it lost in rural Scotland). With regard to Labour loyalists, the party did particularly well in the constituencies in the regions in the lower part

Table 5.30 Regression Coefficients for Functional Regions: Flows from Alliance and Non-Voting

From	Alliance				Non-Voting			
To	C	L	A	N-V	C	L	A	N-V
I.C./Immig.	–	6.04	–	–	–	4.60	–	–
Ind./Immig.	–	6.08	–	–	–	3.57	–	-3.29
Poorest Immig.	–	8.36	–	–	–	–	–	–
Intermed. Ind.	–	5.78	-6.40	–	–	3.18	–	-3.36
Old Indust./Mining	–	7.45	-8.21	–	–	3.54	–	-2.51
Textile	–	5.49	–	–	–	2.86	–	-2.94
Poorest Domestic	–	8.13	–	–	–	5.79	–	–
Conurb. L.A.	–	5.84	-7.22	–	–	2.34	–	–
Black Co.	2.86	4.41	–	–	–	–	–	–
Maritime Ind.	–	7.25	-6.80	–	–	3.55	–	–
Poor I.C.	–	–	–	–	–	–	–	-5.35
Clydeside	–	11.77	-11.92	–	–	5.73	–	–
Scott. Ind.	3.62	10.13	-11.34	–	–	5.13	-2.26	-7.81
Scott. Rural	2.99	–	–	–	4.23	-2.92	–	–
High Status I.M.	4.24	13.45	-19.61	4.19	–	5.51	-4.29	–
I.M.	–	9.64	-10.04	–	–	5.40	–	–
Outer London	2.07	5.46	-7.06	–	–	2.76	–	–
Very High Status	–	4.95	-6.23	–	–	2.09	-1.55	–
Conurb. W. Collar	–	7.45	-7.95	–	–	3.81	–	–
City Service	–	5.21	–	–	–	3.90	–	-4.23
Resort/Retirement	–	–	–	–	–	–	–	–
Recent Growth	2.12	3.92	–	–	–	1.90	–	-3.78
Stable Ind.	1.93	5.51	–	–	–	2.43	-1.55	-2.98
Small Towns	–	3.32	–	–	–	2.22	–	-3.68
Southern Urban	–	2.85	–	–	–	–	–	-2.38
Modest Aff.	–	4.85	-5.57	–	–	2.80	–	-3.02
Met. Ind.	2.79	6.89	-9.39	–	–	3.90	-1.78	-4.46
Modest Aff. Scot.	4.69	9.93	-16.27	–	4.00	6.13	-2.83	-9.12
Rapid Growth	–	2.93	–	–	–	–	–	–
Prosperous/No Ind.	–	3.85	–	–	–	1.77	–	–

of the tables – those where its electoral appeal was weakest in 1983 and 1987; compared to the Agricultural areas, Labour held on to more of its 1983 votes in affluent urban Britain, and lost fewer votes to the Conservatives and the Alliance. Thus the conclusions derived from Table 5.26 are confirmed and hardened in the regional analysis: the Conservative party increased its hold in the Outer Southeast and a few adjacent geographical regions, and also did relatively well in the second period in some inner city areas; the Alliance consolidated its electoral appeal in the agricultural areas.

IN SUMMARY

This chapter has provided a very substantial body of statistical evidence which confirms, without any doubt, that there has been a significant and substantial set of changes to the geography of voting in Britain over the period 1979–1987. At its simplest, that set of changes can be characterised as a growing

north:south divide but, as we have illustrated here, within that simple dichotomy there have been many other shifts. Some of them, such as the consolidation of Labour's strength on the coalfields and the council estates, continue
long-established trends, and others, such as the major swings to Labour on
Merseyside and in Strathclyde, accentuate such trends. But others are new
shifts, such as the movement away from the Conservatives and the Alliance in
Devon and Cornwall and the growing vote for the Conservatives in certain
inner city areas. And the establishment and consolidation of the Alliance as a
third party saw it increasingly concentrate its support in certain areas – rural
and well-educated – largely to the Conservative party's disadvantage since
Labour was already relatively weak there.

The amount of material presented here is very large, and no summary can
do it justice. Much of it remains only partly interpreted, and many more
analyses could be carried out. For the present purposes, however, what we
have discussed in this chapter establishes the important conclusions that we
have just drawn regarding the changing electoral geography of Britain, and it
is towards an appreciation of why that has happened that we now turn.

6

ACCOUNTING FOR THE REGIONAL TRENDS

The previous chapter has provided unequivocal statistical evidence that there have been major changes to Britain's electoral geography over the period 1979–1987. The analyses discussed there have been partial, in that the nature of the available data (especially from the census) precludes the inclusion of variables representing influences on voting other than occupational class, such as trade union membership (though this is no longer a major predictor of a Labour vote; Johnston, 1986a), parental occupational class and party identification, and housing tenure. (Earlier analyses of the 1983 general election in which voters were categorised by both occupational class and tenure – Johnston, 1985a – produced a finer-grained classification of the electorate, but generated very similar results from those using occupational class alone. Unfortunately, the survey data that we used here for 1979 did not include information on tenure, so a comparable data set for that year could not be compiled.) McAllister (1987a) has argued very strongly that once such variables are included, then there is little additional spatial variation; people in the same socio-economic position on a wider set of variables tend to vote the same way wherever they live. He concludes that

> Social context thus influences only a small and distinct minority within the electorate, and its effect is not consistent across all groups (p. 27)

We have countered that on a variety of grounds (Johnston, 1987e; Johnston and Pattie, 1987; see also Savage, 1987) but McAllister (1987b) has persisted, claiming that

> The regional impact of the vote – the alleged 'contextual effect' – is small and inconsistent (p. 353)

But he then continues

> The effects that emerge suggest less the influence of context than, inter alia, the significance of regional political traditions and patterns of party competition . . . The effect for Labour in 1983 points to the influence of local political culture and party competition on a party consigned to a regional hinterland (p. 353).

This is puzzling, since he argues first that context (regional location) is largely irrelevant and then contends that context (regional political culture) is the answer to the question 'why spatial variations?'.

The analyses that we have presented and discussed here provide, we believe, a more than adequate riposte to McAllister's claims. Not only is there a clear geography to voting patterns in Great Britain which suggests the influence of local context but, as we have focused upon, there has been a substantial change to that geography over the period studied. Denver (1987) has argued that 'the most striking feature of the election results' in 1987 was 'regional variations' (p. 451) and we have provided a very substantial body of material reiterating and expanding upon that observation. We must not, of course, over-accentuate the geographical elements of voting in Britain, but our data clearly indicate their existence, and increasing importance. The next step, therefore, must be to account for them.

A MODEL OF CHANGING VOTER CHOICE

The analyses in Chapter 5 suggested, at the aggregate scale, that the changing electoral geography of Britain during the years of the first two Thatcher governments was a function of three sets of factors:

1) A strengthening of party loyalty in areas where it has traditionally been strong. This has particularly been the case with Labour, with its growing relative strength on the coalfields and in the council estates;

2) The ability of parties to mobilise greater support in some functional regions than others. This was particularly so with the Alliance, with its greater appeal (especially in 1987) in the rural constituencies and in those with large percentages of educationally well-qualified people, but it also applied to the Conservative mobilisation of support in the inner-city areas with large percentages of immigrant households; and

3) The shift away from the government in areas of relative economic distress. This is seen particularly in the falling Conservative vote, matched by the improved Labour performance, in the areas of high unemployment. It has been accentuated by general regional shifts – as in the whole of Merseyside and in Devon and Cornwall as well as, most substantially, in Scotland and Wales.

Why should those shifts have come about? Interpretations of aggregate data are always prone to what is known as the 'ecological fallacy', the tendency to ascribe traits to individuals that are observed in (or inferred from) populations as a whole. Thus to explore the reasons for the patterns we have described, we need to turn to information on individuals, which we can get from the surveys that were called upon to provide needed information on the national patterns of both voting by occupational class and the flow-of-the-vote.

To structure that information, and provide a series of hypotheses that we can test against the survey data, we will develop a simple model of voting behaviour. The traditional model is that shown in Figure 6.1, in which Voting

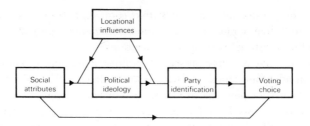

Figure 6.1 The traditional model of voting behaviour in Britain.

Choice is a product of Social Attributes, as mediated by Political Ideology and Party Identification. As people grow into adulthood having particular social attributes so they develop political ideologies linked to those attributes, as part of the socialisation process. Those ideologies, in turn, lead them to identify with particular political parties; again, this is usually part of the socialisation process, so that assuming the ideology of a particular social group involves, among other things, accepting that one particular party is linked to that ideology and is the one they should support. And finally, having identified with a particular party they then habitually vote for it.

The support for and strength of this model has been such that many commentaries and analyses omit the intermediate steps and proceed directly along the single link from social attributes to voting choice. People with similar characteristics will vote in the same way. But, as some of the 'geographical' studies reviewed earlier in this book indicate (notably those of Crewe and Payne, 1976; Miller, 1977, 1984; and Johnston, 1985a), that is very much an oversimplification. People with similar characteristics may vote in different ways, if they live in different places. It is not necessarily the case that people with ostensibly the same social attributes are socialised into the same political ideologies; in different places, class may be interpreted differently, for example, or greater stress may be placed on some issues rather than others. Similarly, people with comparable ideologies may differ in their party identification, because one party has mobilised support among those people in one place but another party has won their allegiance in another. These, then, are locational influences which interact with the political socialisation process at two points in the sequence (as Figure 6.1 indicates) and can produce locational variations in either or both of ideological development and party identification, leading to variations in voting choice also. Hence it is a very partial approach to British voting behaviour which studies the direct route from Social Attributes to Voting Choice only; to appreciate geographical variations in voting choice it is necessary to study all three of the links indicated in Figure 6.1, as they are subject to locational influences.

Introducing Dealignment

The simple model set out in Figure 6.1 encapsulates the received wisdom regarding British voting behaviour prior to the onset of dealignment in the

1970s. For the period since then it is insufficient, however, since the links from Social Attributes to Voting Choice have become weaker. Thus for the period that we are interested in here, we must introduce further variables to incorporate the dealignment process. This we do in Figure 6.2.

As the discussion in Chapter 2 indicated, British psephologists differ quite substantially in the explanations that they offer for voting patterns in the 1980s. They have introduced three further potential influences, and these are all incorporated to our model. We cannot be sure of their relative importance, and so will use them all in our analyses here.

The first two of the new variables are linked in the model to party identification, since it is suggested that people's partisan allegiances will clearly influence how they evaluate parties; people who profess an allegiance to the Labour party are more likely to think Labour has the best policies, for example, than are those who identify with the Conservatives. However, there could well be a recursive element here, in that people evaluate the policies before they decide on, or are prepared to declare, their party allegiance. The model suggests that party identification occurs prior to policy and leader evaluation, but for some voters at least – especially those whose socialisation did not produce a firm allegiance to one party – evaluation of policies may come first.

With regard to *party evaluation*, the implication is that people's choice of which party to vote for is predicated on their relative evaluation of the parties' offerings; which party, to them, is best able to tackle what they see as the salient political issues? We suggest in the model that four other variables influence that process of evaluation: party identification; general influences; economic optimism; and locational influences. For the first, as just indicated,

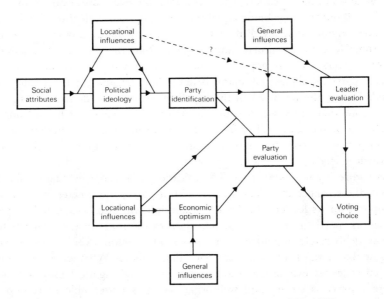

Figure 6.2 An expanded model of British voting behaviour, 1979–1987.

the more closely people identify with a party the more likely they are to consider its policies the best. The other three variables may counter that relationship, however. General influences are those that refer to the electoral context and the presentation of the parties – notably through the mass media. Thus, for example, a voter may be convinced both that law and order is a salient political issue and that the Conservative party has the best policies on that issue, not because he or she has close knowledge of either law and order problems or Conservative policies but because the weight of media coverage leads him or her to that conclusion. One particular way in which general influences can affect voter evaluations is via their economic optimism: as indicated in Chapter 2 (p. 53), when the great volume of mass media reporting is optimistic, people are likely to reflect that by being more favourably inclined towards the party in power.

Economic optimism is likely to be influenced by local as well as general factors, however. The mass media may suggest that the future is relatively rosy for Britain as a whole, but voters in some parts of the country may be less impressed by such claims than those in others; to the extent that there are spatial variations in levels of economic and social well-being, so one would expect similar variations in levels of economic optimism. Those variations would then feed through to produce spatial variations in party evaluation. Finally, locational influences may have some effect on the party identification:party evaluation link, as suggested in Figure 6.2. In regions where the Labour party is a strong socialising and mobilising force, for example, it is more likely to be able to convince Labour party identifiers that it has the best policies than in regions where the party's organisation is weak, and its ability to influence voters directly is poor.

Evaluation of party leaders is to a considerable event also evaluation of party policies; all other things being equal the most popular leaders will be those with the most popular policies. But this is not all, and many analyses have shown that some leaders are much more popular than the policies they stand for, whereas others are less popular. Thus, for example, a voter may prefer the Labour party's policies but many believe that, because of the quality of the party's leader, the promises in those policies will not be delivered; as a consequence, another party may get that person's vote, because it has a leader who is believed better equipped to fill the role of Prime Minister (perhaps irrespective of policies; leadership may be more important to some than the direction in which it leads!).

As Figure 6.2 indicates, party identification and leader evaluation should be linked; the stronger the identification with a party, the greater the probability of support for its leader. But leader evaluation will also be affected by general influences, particularly those emanating from the mass media which (whether or not deliberately intended to promote one person over another) tend to suggest that some leaders are stronger than others. Whether local influences also affect leader evaluation is less certain, although again it may well be that where a party is strong and well-organised it is better able to convince the electorate of the quality of its leader(s) than it is in other places where it is unable to make such a strong and persuasive showing. (On this, in the New Zealand context, see Johnston and Honey, 1988.)

Our model, then, suggests that voting choice is a function not only of social attributes (mediated through political ideology and party identification) but also party and leader evaluation, which are influenced by general and locational factors as well as social attributes. If, as the dealignment thesis suggests, the general influences (including economic optimism) are becoming more important, then the links between social attributes and voting choice should be declining in importance whilst the influences of other factors on party and leader evaluation should be increasing. Our particular interest, of course, is in locational influences; are they having a greater impact on voting choice via party evaluation now than in the past?

The model is a relatively complicated one, and all of its components cannot be evaluated in detail here – in part because we lack the necessary data. What we present in the remainder of this chapter is a series of straightforward tabulations of data taken from the three BBC/Gallup election surveys, as an exploration of the possible causes of the changing electoral geography of Britain we have described in previous chapters.

REGIONAL VARIATIONS

We begin this analysis by looking at regional variations in party identification, party evaluation, leader evaluation, and economic optimism, to explore the extent of differences that might account for the voting patterns that we have already described. To do this, we use data taken from the BBC/Gallup surveys. These constrain us in two ways. First, the range of questions asked varied between the three surveys so that on some issues it was not possible to get comparable data. Even when such data were available, slight differences in the wording of the questions requires care in interpretation. Secondly, we could only use the geographical regions, since the classification on which our functional regions are based used 1981 census data referring to the new constituency boundaries introduced in 1983; consequently, the 1979 constituencies could not be allocated to the regions. (In any case, with 31 regions the number of respondents in several was too small to provide useful material.)

Looking first at *party identification*, Table 6.1 shows the percentages in each region identifying with one of Conservative, Labour and Alliance, at each election. The question on which these percentages are based at each election was:

> "Leaving aside this particular election, would you say you *generally* think of yourself as Conservative, Labour, Liberal, SDP, Alliance [in 1983 and 1987], Nationalist, or what [other in 1983]?"

The first point to note from these figures is the relatively small amount of change overall in people's identification with particular parties. The national data, in the last row, show that the largest shift was of only six percentage points, in the Conservative identifiers between 1979 and 1983. The implication

Table 6.1 Party Identification by Geographical Region, 1979–1987*

	1979			1983			1987		
	C	L	A	C	L	A	C	L	A
Strathclyde	18	48	8	26	42	11	21	49	10
E. Scotland	29	41	6	25	42	16	27	39	14
Rural Scotland	27	31	17	33	28	13	24	29	17
Rural North	39	32	17	37	33	16	43	32	14
Industrial									
Northeast	26	50	10	34	50	8	27	42	19
Merseyside	41	46	5	31	38	22	28	43	21
Greater Manchester	22	44	19	38	36	15	30	44	12
Rest of Northwest	33	42	11	38	39	14	40	35	12
West Yorks.	20	55	10	33	38	11	26	39	19
South Yorks.	18	64	4	37	34	14	21	54	11
Rural Wales	16	21	0	40	39	7	34	36	12
Industrial									
South Wales	31	55	3	29	37	12	28	44	11
W. Midlands									
Conurbation	50	31	4	33	35	11	37	39	10
Rest of West									
Midlands	46	27	11	38	29	13	39	26	17
East Midlands	44	33	9	35	43	11	40	34	16
East Anglia	27	32	21	37	25	25	44	26	15
Devon and Cornwall	39	35	30	38	11	37	39	21	23
Wessex	35	23	20	48	21	21	39	23	21
Inner London	28	42	14	25	44	8	18	53	13
Outer London	36	35	14	41	32	13	32	36	17
Outer Metropolitan	41	28	21	54	20	18	39	23	19
Outer Southeast	54	21	12	57	18	16	47	22	18
National	31	38	12	37	33	15	33	35	18

* The data are percentages of all respondents. Key: C – Conservative; L – Labour; A – Alliance

is that people retain fairly stable party affiliations (as Crewe, Sarlvik and Alt, 1977, reported), which are not necessarily reflected in their voting behaviour; this conclusion is enhanced by the fact that at two of the three elections (1983 was the exception) more people identified with Labour than with Conservative, even though the latter won substantially more votes than Labour at each election.

Turning to the regional variations, the general pattern is consistent with the north:south division outlined in our discussions of voting, especially for the Conservative and Labour parties. Thus southern regions tend to have more Conservative identifiers than do northern regions, with the reverse for Labour identifiers. There are some intriguing exceptions, however. Merseyside had 41 per cent Conservative identifiers in 1979, for example, which was well above the national figure, and East Anglia had below the national figure for Tory identifiers in both 1979 and 1983; in Merseyside, the very low percentage of Alliance identifiers apparently accounts for the deviation, whereas for East Anglia the high Alliance percentages must have reduced the number of Conservative identifiers.

Between elections, the number of identifiers for each party varied quite substantially in some cases, in contrast to the national stability. Thus, for example, the percentage who were Labour identifiers in South Yorkshire fell from 64 to 34 (less than the Conservative figure) between 1979 and 1983, and then rose again to 54 in 1987. This suggests very considerable instability which is in line neither with general knowledge of South Yorkshire nor with our earlier findings regarding voting there. The probable explanation lies in the nature of the sample taken there in 1983. The samples were taken to fill national quotas of people from different types of constituency, not to provide a representative sample for each region. Thus the South Yorkshire sample of 1983 may fit well into the national mix, but is not representative of the socio-political structure of that county. This illustrates the care that needs to be taken in these explorations, for occasional 'maverick' results are possible.

Overall, relative stability is characteristic of most regions, with some interesting features that shed light on our findings on voting. The decline of Alliance support in Devon and Cornwall between 1983 and 1987, matched by the increase in Labour identifiers, squares with the voting shifts there, for example, as does the substantial growth in Conservative identifiers in East Anglia over the three elections.

Turning to *economic optimism*, the 1983 and 1987 surveys provide information on both retrospective and prospective evaluations of the financial situation, but that for 1979 covers one retrospective issue only. For the full three election periods we have data on people's perceptions of their household's economic fortunes over the last twelve months. The questions were:

1979   -"And do you consider that the financial situation of your household in the last 12 months has improved a lot, improved slightly, remained the same, deteriorated slightly, deteriorated a lot, don't know?"

1983/1987 -"And how does the financial situation *in your own household* compare with what it was twelve months ago? Has it got a lot better . . . , don't know?"

For 1983 and 1987, we also have data on:

1) Perceptions of the national economic situation over the last twelve months, with questions

1983/1987 -"How do you think the general economic situation in this country has changed over the last 12 months? Has it got a lot better, got a little better, stayed the same, got a little worse, got a lot worse, don't know?"

2) Perceptions of the likely trends in the national economic situation over the next twelve months, with questions

1983/1987 -"How do you think the *general* economic situation will develop over the *next* twelve months? Will it get a lot better . . . don't know?"

3) Perceptions of the household's likely economic situation over the next twelve months, with questions

Table 6.2 Perceptions of Changes in Personal Economic Situation over the Previous Twelve Months, by Geographical Region*

	1979				1983				1987			
	B	S	W	Ratio	B	S	W	Ratio	B	S	W	Ratio
Strathclyde	25	39	34	0.74	14	35	50	0.28	21	42	37	0.57
E. Scotland	28	34	36	0.78	22	35	43	0.51	27	46	27	1.00
Rural Scotland	25	38	36	0.69	30	33	35	0.86	29	46	24	1.21
Rural North	34	28	34	1.00	21	40	37	0.57	35	40	22	1.59
Industrial Northeast	36	39	23	1.57	24	43	33	0.73	27	37	33	0.82
Merseyside	33	26	33	1.00	14	41	44	0.32	20	43	36	0.55
Greater Manchester	28	47	25	1.12	28	35	37	0.76	13	51	35	0.37
Rest of Northwest	30	35	34	0.88	26	39	35	0.74	22	47	30	0.73
West Yorks.	45	20	35	1.29	26	36	37	0.70	22	49	25	0.88
South Yorks.	36	33	29	1.24	17	37	46	0.37	21	41	37	0.57
Rural Wales	16	37	47	0.34	20	47	33	0.61	29	48	22	1.32
Industrial South Wales	28	41	31	0.90	25	36	37	0.68	31	39	28	1.11
W. Midlands Conurbation	21	40	40	0.53	18	38	42	0.43	28	43	26	1.08
Rest of West Midlands	27	41	32	0.84	27	32	40	0.68	37	32	30	1.23
East Midlands	27	39	32	0.84	27	36	37	0.73	36	36	28	1.29
East Anglia	32	27	40	0.80	27	41	30	0.90	41	39	20	2.05
Devon and Cornwall	40	30	28	1.43	26	37	36	0.72	31	15	18	1.72
Wessex	23	34	41	0.56	29	36	34	0.85	27	44	28	0.96
Inner London	24	37	37	0.65	23	40	36	0.64	28	38	30	0.93
Outer London	22	30	47	0.47	25	38	36	0.69	27	45	28	0.96
Outer Metropolitan	31	32	36	0.86	30	38	30	1.00	38	33	28	1.36
Outer Southeast	27	32	39	0.69	34	44	20	1.70	36	43	21	1.71
National	28	36	35	0.80	25	37	37	0.65	29	42	28	1.04

* The data are percentages of the respondents reporting – B, got better; S, stayed the same; W, got worse. The ratio is B/W

1983–1987 -"And how do you think the financial situation *in your own household* will develop over the next 12 months? Will it . . . don't know?"

Table 6.2 presents the data on people's evaluation of changes in their (or their household's) financial situation over the last twelve months. In each survey, respondents were offered five categories: a bit better; a little better; about the same; a little worse; and a lot worse. For analysis here, the first two and the last two were combined to give three categories – better; same; worse – and the percentages responding in each category are given in Table 6.2 along with the better:worse ratio for each region.

In 1979, just over one-third of the respondents nationally stated that their situation had stayed the same and another third that it had got worse, and a little over one-quarter said that it had improved. The better:worse ratio was

0.8. In five regions, however, more respondents said things had improved then saw they had got worse; four were in the north (Industrial Northeast, Greater Manchester, West Yorkshire and South Yorkshire) suggesting that respondents there evaluated the policies of the Labour government positively, at least as far as they were concerned individually. Further south, in many regions the ratio was lower than the national figure, indicating that residents of such regions as Wessex, London and the Outer Southeast perceived that they had come out of the last year of the Labour government relatively badly. (It was not a simple north:south divide, however, because Scottish residents were also more likely to report a worsening personal situation than was the case nationally.)

By 1983, the position nationally had worsened quite considerably, with a better:worse ratio of only 0.65. And there were some substantial shifts in the geography of that ratio. In most of the southern regions (the only exception was Inner London) the better:worse ratio was higher than the national figure, whereas further north, and most especially in Scotland and Merseyside, the ratio was well below the national value of 0.65. After four years of Conservative rule, therefore, residents of southern Britain were more likely to think their personal situations were getting better than were their counterparts further north.

This position was made even clearer in 1987, when the national ratio indicated approximately equal proportions thinking their personal situations had either improved or deteriorated. In most southern regions (with the two in London the main exceptions, and then only marginally so) substantially more people thought things had got better than worse; in East Anglia, twice as many responded better than worse. Further north, the position was reversed, with a few exceptions. In the urban regions of Yorkshire, Lancashire, Northeast England and Strathclyde, many more people responded that their situation had worsened then reported that it had improved. In the rural parts of Scotland and the North, and throughout Wales, however, people were generally satisfied, it seems.

With regard to the next twelve months, Table 6.3 shows that in both 1983 and 1987 many more people thought their household situation would improve than thought it would get worse. There was considerable variation about the national ratios, however. In both years, people in the two southeastern regions outside London (Outer Metropolitan; Outer Southeast) were much more optimistic than were the respondents as a whole, whereas residents of Strathclyde were much less optimistic (though in all regions more people were optimistic than pessimistic). There were some notable deviations, however (which may in part be a product of sampling issues, as discussed above: p. 225). In 1983, for example, Merseyside residents were as optimistic about the future as the population as a whole, but four years later almost as many people there thought things would get worse as better. Conversely, West Yorkshire and East Midlands residents became increasingly optimistic.

Turning to interpretations of the national economic situation, again the general pattern is of a north:south divide – with the north relatively pessimistic and the south relatively optimistic – but with noteworthy exceptions. Regard-

Table 6.3 Perceptions of Changes in Personal Economic Situation over the Next Twelve Months, by Geographical Region*

	1983				1987			
	B	S	W	Ratio	B	S	W	Ratio
Strathclyde	27	38	21	1.29	31	38	14	2.21
E. Scotland	26	40	23	1.13	33	45	12	2.75
Rural Scotland	36	37	12	3.00	33	39	9	3.67
Rural North	32	43	16	2.00	36	42	8	4.50
Industrial Northeast	36	40	17	2.12	40	33	14	2.86
Merseyside	29	38	14	2.07	23	41	20	1.15
Greater Manchester	30	47	15	2.00	27	47	15	1.80
Rest of Northwest	29	46	14	2.07	27	41	16	1.69
West Yorks.	34	39	17	2.00	33	38	8	4.13
South Yorks.	29	43	20	1.45	21	53	13	1.62
Rural Wales	26	51	13	2.00	31	40	14	2.21
Industrial South Wales	32	40	11	2.91	34	41	13	2.62
W. Midlands Conurbation	27	39	10	2.70	30	46	8	3.75
Rest of West Midlands	32	40	14	2.29	41	35	12	3.42
East Midlands	40	33	17	1.08	42	35	8	5.25
East Anglia	33	45	9	3.67	34	44	9	3.78
Devon and Cornwall	30	40	20	1.50	30	48	10	3.00
Wessex	40	39	16	2.50	24	43	14	1.71
Inner London	36	32	22	1.64	36	38	16	2.25
Outer London	25	46	16	1.56	33	41	10	3.30
Outer Metropolitan	41	39	13	3.15	43	42	7	6.14
Outer Southeast	41	44	8	5.13	40	36	9	4.44
National	33	40	16	2.06	34	41	11	3.09

* The data are percentages of the respondents reporting – B, better; S, the same; W, worse. The ratio is B/W

ing the situation in the twelve months prior to each election, Table 6.4 shows people's perceptions of the national situation in 1983 and 1987. Again, there was an improvement over time; whereas nationally only 36 per cent thought things had improved in the twelve months prior to the 1983 election, compared to 43 per cent who thought there had been a deterioration, four years later the respective percentages were 42 and 30. Further, the north:south divide was clearly present in the regional perceptions, especially in 1987 when the southern regions of Rest of West Midlands, East Anglia, Devon and Cornwall, Wessex, Outer Metropolitan and Outer Southeast recorded better:worse ratios in excess of the national figure of 1.40, and some very substantially so. Elsewhere in Great Britain, most regions recorded ratios below that level; the only exceptions were the three rural regions (Scotland, North, and Wales) plus, somewhat surprisingly, Industrial South Wales.

People were generally much more optimistic about the next twelve months than they were satisfied with the national performance over the previous twelve

Table 6.4 Perceptions of Changes in the National Economic Situation over the last Twelve Months, by Geographical Region*

	1983				1987			
	B	S	W	Ratio	B	S	W	Ratio
Strathclyde	23	14	60	0.38	21	19	58	0.36
E. Scotland	27	18	53	0.50	40	22	34	1.18
Rural Scotland	37	19	41	0.90	40	29	28	1.43
Rural North	33	21	42	0.79	49	27	22	2.22
Industrial								
*Northeast	33	19	46	0.72	38	26	32	1.19
Merseyside	28	21	50	0.56	38	27	29	1.31
Greater Manchester	33	16	49	0.67	33	25	42	0.79
Rest of Northwest	38	21	40	0.95	43	19	32	1.34
West Yorks.	40	18	38	1.05	37	26	30	1.23
South Yorks.	21	29	46	0.46	43	16	42	1.02
Rural Wales	34	24	37	0.92	43	32	25	1.72
Industrial								
South Wales	29	21	45	0.64	41	26	25	1.64
W. Midlands								
Conurbation	33	20	46	0.72	31	35	25	1.24
Rest of West								
Midlands	42	15	42	1.00	47	29	18	2.61
East Midlands	40	17	41	0.98	48	25	24	2.00
East Anglia	44	17	35	1.26	66	16	16	4.13
Devon and Cornwall	39	17	42	0.93	50	28	23	2.17
Wessex	45	20	33	1.36	43	27	26	1.65
Inner London	33	23	43	0.77	36	21	41	0.88
Outer London	36	20	42	0.86	43	20	31	1.39
Outer Metropolitan	46	19	32	1.44	51	24	21	2.43
Outer Southeast	54	20	22	2.45	52	26	20	2.60
National	36	19	43	0.84	42	24	30	1.40

* The data are percentages of the respondents reporting -B, better; S, the same; W, worse. The ratio is B/W

(compare Tables 6.4 and 6.5). This was especially so in 1983, when 43 per cent thought things had got worse over the year preceding the June election but only 20 per cent thought they would get worse in the next year; the better:worse ratio of 0.84 for the immediate past was replaced by one of 2.10 for the immediate future, an increase of exactly 150 per cent. The increase in 1987 was only slightly lower, at 109 per cent. This optimism was regionally variable, though not clearly indicating a north:south demarcation. Thus in 1983, for example, respondents in Merseyside, Greater Manchester, Rest of Northwest and West Yorkshire were on average more optimistic than the population at large, whereas residents of East Anglia and London were relatively gloomy. Four years later, people in the far north of England (Rural North and Industrial Northeast) remained optimistic whereas those in the urban regions immediately to the south were relatively pessimistic, along with the lowland Scots who were pessimistic in both years. Further south, optimism was widespread, though again relatively less so in London and also in Wessex.

Table 6.5　Perceptions of changes in the National Economic Situation over the Next Twelve Months, by Geographical Region*

	1983				1987			
	B	S	W	Ratio	B	S	W	Ratio
Strathclyde	35	18	26	1.35	27	22	18	1.50
E. Scotland	33	21	29	1.14	37	23	22	1.68
Rural Scotland	38	24	21	1.81	37	21	11	3.36
Rural North	38	24	24	1.58	48	16	9	5.33
Industrial								
Northeast	42	23	21	2.00	39	29	11	3.54
Merseyside	39	21	14	2.79	32	16	14	2.29
Greater Manchester	44	23	19	2.32	32	34	19	1.68
Rest of Northwest	46	26	16	2.88	42	14	20	2.10
West Yorks.	40	25	17	2.35	34	23	15	2.27
South Yorks.	37	17	31	1.19	20	37	16	1.25
Rural Wales	39	27	17	2.29	46	17	17	2.71
Industrial								
South Wales	38	24	15	2.53	35	28	18	1.94
W. Midlands								
Conurbation	37	23	14	2.64	31	23	9	3.44
Rest of West								
Midlands	49	19	14	3.50	47	20	6	7.83
East Midlands	43	20	18	2.39	42	28	8	5.25
East Anglia	34	23	22	1.55	50	15	9	5.56
Devon and Cornwall	43	24	23	1.87	41	25	9	4.56
Wessex	48	24	18	2.67	32	28	12	2.67
Inner London	44	15	24	1.83	31	26	16	1.94
Outer London	44	14	24	1.83	36	22	16	2.25
Outer Metropolitan	48	23	13	3.69	43	24	11	3.91
Outer Southeast	58	18	12	4.83	45	16	8	5.63
National	42	22	20	2.10	38	23	13	2.92

* The data are percentages of the respondents reporting – B, better; S, the same; W, worse. The ratio is B/W

As already stressed above, too much cannot be read in to the regional variations portrayed in Tables 6.2–6.5, because of the small samples in some regions and the fact that some of them may not be representative of the regional population as a whole. (The samples in each region were taken as part of a national picture, not as a series of local pictures.) Nevertheless, we can conclude from them that there were undoubtedly regional variations in both perceptions of recent economic trends and expectations for the immediate future. Those variations, in general terms, fit the patterns of voting that we have already described here and suggest, though no more, that the growing regional variation in party performance over the period was linked to regional variations in perceived economic and social well-being. We can be no firmer than that in our conclusion at present, but it is a topic we return to below.

Turning to patterns of *party evaluation*, a number of relevant questions in each of the surveys allows us to explore regional variations in people's evaluations of party policies and abilities. The first two tables related to this

Table 6.6 Opinion on which Party offered the Best Policies, by Geographical Region*

	1979			1983			1987		
	C	L	A	C	L	A	C	L	A
Strathclyde	19	45	11	27	34	19	19	44	15
E. Scotland	29	39	11	27	30	23	27	36	19
Rural Scotland	27	30	21	38	17	16	26	24	21
Rural North	36	32	14	42	23	18	43	26	16
Industrial									
Northeast	25	49	13	40	31	14	32	36	19
Merseyside	39	44	5	35	25	25	33	36	16
Greater Manchester	31	22	28	41	24	22	35	34	10
Rest of Northwest	30	32	16	42	22	22	39	29	15
West Yorks.	25	60	10	42	29	15	30	34	17
South Yorks.	16	53	9	43	20	29	21	43	21
Rural Wales	11	11	5	47	23	13	32	26	16
Industrial									
South Wales	32	47	5	34	27	22	32	40	16
W. Midlands									
Conurbation	47	26	5	38	27	15	36	35	11
Rest of West									
Midlands	47	25	17	43	25	17	48	21	18
East Midlands	42	34	10	40	24	20	42	28	18
East Anglia	41	32	16	44	15	28	47	16	21
Devon and Cornwall	30	28	17	42	6	39	48	18	23
Wessex	43	23	22	47	12	25	37	21	22
Inner London	30	34	14	38	28	11	24	43	19
Outer London	46	26	17	47	20	18	36	32	16
Outer Metropolitan	47	24	19	52	12	21	45	17	23
Outer Southeast	50	19	15	57	9	23	47	18	18
National	32	34	14	41	22	21	36	29	18

* The percentage are of the respondents reporting: C – Conservative; L – Labour; A – Alliance

(Tables 6.6 and 6.7) look at general evaluations. One tabulates responses to questions regarding the parties with the best policies overall: the questions were

1979/1983/1987 "Taking everything into account, which party has the best policies?"

The other presents the answers to questions on the parties which respondents perceived as best for them: the questions were

1979 –"And leaving on one side the question of which party you support, which party is best for people like you?"

1983 –"And leaving on one side the question of which party you vote for, which party is best for people like you?"

1987 –"And leaving on one side the question of which party you vote for, which party best serves the interests of people like you and your family?"

In 1979, as Table 6.6 shows, slightly more people thought Labour had a better package of policies than thought the Conservative party did; four years

Table 6.7 Opinion on which Party was Best for the Individual Respondent, by Geographical Region*

	1979			1983			1987		
	C	L	A	C	L	A	C	L	A
Strathclyde	20	54	8	24	43	18	23	50	12
E. Scotland	30	40	11	26	42	22	31	43	13
Rural Scotland	31	33	16	33	28	19	29	29	14
Rural North	40	13	17	41	34	15	46	33	13
Industrial Northeast	25	55	9	29	44	19	32	41	18
Merseyside	33	44	15	33	34	21	31	40	19
Greater Manchester	44	25	13	37	33	19	31	44	12
Rest of Northwest	35	36	13	43	29	21	41	33	12
West Yorks.	25	50	15	36	36	14	32	42	17
South Yorks.	16	60	11	34	40	20	25	54	13
Rural Wales	21	11	0	49	27	11	34	34	14
Industrial South Wales	35	49	7	29	35	21	33	45	16
W. Midlands Conurbation	48	31	7	37	30	14	38	40	10
Rest of West Midlands	51	26	12	39	31	17	44	28	17
East Midlands	43	36	10	31	34	22	42	32	17
East Anglia	40	33	16	38	22	28	49	23	14
Devon and Cornwall	30	35	23	38	11	39	45	24	19
Wessex	43	23	20	44	19	23	40	25	19
Inner London	30	40	13	31	44	11	20	51	16
Outer London	45	32	14	38	28	22	38	36	12
Outer Metropolitan	43	29	18	49	19	21	42	24	21
Outer Southeast	50	25	12	54	12	22	53	23	16
National	34	39	12	37	30	20	37	35	15

* The percentages are of the respondents reporting: C – Conservative; L – Labour; A – Alliance

later, nearly twice as many favoured the Conservative package, and almost exactly the same percentage preferred the Alliance's as they did Labour's. The Labour party regained ground on both in 1987, and the Conservative:Labour gap was substantially narrowed. Indeed, in 1987 that gap was narrower than the distribution of votes suggested, implying that some people who preferred the Labour package nevertheless voted either Conservative or Alliance. This difference between evaluation and voting was clearly much greater in 1979, when many more people who preferred the Labour package must nevertheless have voted against it. (In part, though only in part, this may be a function of the weighting of the sample in favour of Scotland and Wales.)

The regional variations provide some clue as to the reasons for that apparent paradox. In 1979, the percentage thinking that Labour had the best package did not exceed the national figure of 34 in any of the regions of southern England – although in Devon and Cornwall the large pro-Alliance percentage meant a below-average pro-Conservative figure and a large percentage in

Inner London expressed no preference. Further north (excluding Rural Wales, where the data were clearly non-representative and a large percentage expressed no opinion), the picture was that Labour was especially preferred in Strathclyde, the Industrial Northeast, Merseyside, urban Yorkshire, and Industrial South Wales (though the Conservative percentage was high on Merseyside too, with a very low Alliance figure) and the Conservative package was generally not favoured, even in the rural areas.

Four years later, there was relatively little regional variation in party evaluation. The difference between the national and the regional figure preferring the Conservative package exceeded five percentage points in only eight regions, for example, and was in excess of ten percentage points in only four: the Conservative package was particularly unpopular in Strathclyde and East Scotland, but popular in the Outer Metropolitan and Outer Southeast regions. Support for the Labour package was a little more variable, though not much, and the same was true (with a few exceptions, such as Inner London and Devon and Cornwall) for the Alliance. Thus in 1983, it seems, the pattern of party evaluation was virtually the same everywhere.

Four years later, the regional variations reappeared. In only two of the northern regions (Rural North and Rest of Northwest) do the percentages preferring the package presented by the Conservative party exceed the national figure of 36, and only in one (Rural North) was the Labour figure below the national percentage of 29. From the West Midlands southwards (excluding Wales) there was a clear preference for Conservative policies except in London, and in four southern regions the Alliance offering was preferred to Labour's. Thus, whereas in 1983, it seems that the Conservative party had been able to convince most British voters, wherever they lived, of the superiority of its policies, by 1987 the recovery of the Labour party meant that once again the Conservatives were much less preferred in the north than in the south.

When we turn to opinions on which party offered policies that were perceived to be best for the individual respondents (Table 6.7), the Labour lead over Conservative was larger in 1979 than reported in Table 6.6, and the Conservative lead over Labour smaller in both 1983 and 1987. Over all three elections, more people thought Labour was better for them personally than thought Labour had the best package of policies. And there were clear regional variations in all three years. In 1979, for example, over 50 per cent of the respondents in some northern regions (though not the rural ones) indicated that Labour was best for them personally, compared to the national figure of 39; in 1983, several of the same regions (plus Inner London) recorded percentages of 40 or more when the national figure was 30; and in 1987 again there were some percentages of 50 or more (including Inner London again) compared to 35 nationally. Countering this, above-average percentages of voters in southern regions, especially Outer Metropolitan and Outer Southeast, thought the Conservative party best for them.

When we turn to particular policies, in general the same regional pattern shows through. Unemployment was a major issue in all three campaigns, and

Table 6.8 Opinions on which Party's Policies were best for Reducing Unemployment, by Geographical Region*

	1979			1983			1987		
	C	L	A	C	L	A	C	L	A
Strathclyde	19	52	5	17	45	15	13	60	10
E. Scotland	31	38	4	20	45	16	17	50	11
Rural Scotland	31	33	13	24	29	19	18	39	14
Rural North	32	38	9	33	32	10	36	39	9
Industrial									
Northeast	24	53	8	31	45	13	19	50	11
Merseyside	28	44	8	25	31	20	28	49	9
Greater Manchester	38	38	9	30	37	15	27	50	11
Rest of Northwest	32	46	2	21	37	15	28	38	9
West Yorks.	15	55	5	29	35	11	26	49	9
South Yorks.	22	47	7	23	37	14	15	61	10
Rural Wales	16	26	0	30	40	11	27	41	9
Industrial									
South Wales	31	40	5	19	40	17	24	51	15
W. Midlands									
Conurbation	53	28	2	28	37	15	31	47	6
Rest of West									
Midlands	36	31	6	34	31	16	37	34	13
East Midlands	39	36	6	23	40	18	32	42	8
East Anglia	32	37	8	28	31	25	36	29	17
Devon and Cornwall	30	30	10	29	16	32	36	29	19
Wessex	39	29	11	33	27	15	27	34	17
Inner London	29	41	5	27	43	6	13	63	11
Outer London	34	31	5	31	31	15	26	46	9
Outer Metropolitan	40	38	9	34	26	19	35	36	13
Outer Southeast	45	23	5	44	19	18	37	32	11
National	31	39	6	28	34	16	27	44	11

* The percentages of the respondents reporting: C – Conservative; L – Labour; A – Alliance

questions regarding which party could best reduce it were asked in each survey, viz:

> 1979/1983/1987 – "Would you tell me which party you think would be best at reducing unemployment?"

Table 6.8 shows that, in each year, more people thought Labour better able to reduce unemployment than either Conservative or Alliance. In 1979, the Conservative slogan was 'Labour isn't working', alongside a picture of a dole queue, but only 31 per cent of the respondents thought that the Conservatives could do better than Labour at reducing unemployment, compared to 39 per cent whose trust was in Labour. In general, the Conservative campaign on this issue was more successful in southern England, whereas further north – where unemployment was highest – respondents were more likely to prefer Labour's policies. Four years later, that faith in Labour had fallen somewhat nationally, but especially so in many of the northern regions; only in urban Scotland and the Industrial Northeast, plus Inner London, was confidence in Labour's ability to reduce unemployment as high as 40 per cent. In general, support for

Table 6.9 Opinions on which Party's Policies were best for the Control of Strikes, by Geographical Region*

	1979			1983			1987		
	C	L	A	C	L	A	C	L	A
Strathclyde	24	43	4	39	29	9	45	31	8
E. Scotland	31	33	5	44	29	9	54	23	8
Rural Scotland	31	33	11	48	21	9	52	16	12
Rural North	31	36	7	51	20	9	64	15	7
Industrial Northeast	31	46	3	52	28	7	61	18	7
Merseyside	26	44	10	41	24	17	60	20	10
Greater Manchester	41	31	3	48	21	12	47	31	8
Rest of Northwest	30	37	5	52	18	10	61	18	7
West Yorks.	25	40	5	44	29	5	52	25	7
South Yorks.	22	47	4	51	17	14	51	31	6
Rural Wales	26	5	0	57	24	6	57	23	3
Industrial South Wales	40	37	3	56	24	12	53	30	8
W. Midlands Conurbation	43	24	0	46	23	9	55	26	3
Rest of West Midlands	36	26	4	53	22	12	64	12	10
East Midlands	42	25	9	51	20	11	64	17	7
East Anglia	35	35	8	50	20	14	63	11	11
Devon and Cornwall	23	40	8	48	8	27	67	7	14
Wessex	30	33	8	59	11	15	57	15	12
Inner London	35	36	4	50	24	5	53	21	9
Outer London	41	39	8	48	24	10	60	20	6
Outer Metropolitan	42	36	7	60	12	12	60	13	10
Outer Southeast	44	20	6	63	15	13	68	12	8
National	33	35	6	50	21	11	58	19	8

* The percentages are of the respondents reporting: C – Conservative; L – Labour; A – Alliance

the Conservative policies, though lower than in 1979, was more evenly distributed, though the Scots had little faith and London's exurbanites had a great deal. The new Alliance drew particular strength on this issue in southern rural areas, but much less in the Rural North and Rural Wales, and very little in Inner London.

Between 1983 and 1987 there was no change overall in the percentage who believed that the Conservative party could best solve the problem of unemployment, but support for Labour's policies soared by ten percentage points. The increase in preference for Labour was widespread, even in the 'deep south'; only East Anglia, the East Midlands, the Rest of West Midlands, Rural Wales, and Rest of Northwest recorded increases in support for Labour's policies of less than five points. Not all of the regions recording upsurges in support for Labour similarly had falls in Conservative preferences, however; in Merseyside, the West Midlands Conurbation and in Devon and Cornwall for example, the growth in support for Labour was largely at the Alliance's cost. Overall, however, the major regional differences remained.

Table 6.10 Opinions on which Party's Policies were best for Britain's Prosperity, by Geographical Region*

	1979			1983			1987		
	C	L	A	C	L	A	C	L	A
Strathclyde	27	45	4	32	33	16	33	41	9
E. Scotland	34	33	5	38	27	17	44	28	12
Rural Scotland	38	28	13	45	19	15	38	23	17
Rural North	49	31	10	53	20	8	56	22	11
Industrial Northeast	35	44	4	44	27	12	46	27	11
Merseyside	39	33	5	47	18	23	52	30	9
Greater Manchester	41	25	16	45	21	15	42	34	11
Rest of Northwest	42	33	6	44	27	19	52	27	9
West Yorks.	35	40	10	51	25	7	47	29	14
South Yorks.	29	51	7	46	23	14	39	34	10
Rural Wales	47	11	0	50	17	13	46	27	10
Industrial South Wales	32	40	5	41	25	18	43	37	14
W. Midlands Conurbation	52	26	3	44	28	12	47	32	6
Rest of West Midlands	58	24	4	50	19	14	57	19	12
East Midlands	51	29	9	47	20	14	53	24	12
East Anglia	48	29	10	49	14	19	59	12	15
Devon and Cornwall	28	28	8	48	6	33	56	14	19
Wessex	46	20	11	56	12	17	50	15	15
Inner London	39	27	10	49	24	7	42	31	10
Outer London	49	25	6	53	21	13	50	25	9
Outer Metropolitan	57	21	10	62	11	15	56	16	15
Outer Southeast	65	15	7	67	7	16	63	18	12
National	41	32	7	48	20	15	49	25	12

* The percentages are of the respondents reporting: C – Conservative; L – Labour; A – Alliance

Turning to other policy issues, control of the trade unions was a major aspect of the Conservative manifesto and rhetoric in each of the three campaigns, and Table 6.9 looks at the degree to which voters believed that it was the best party to handle the most contentious aspect of that issue – strikes: the questions were

1979/1983/1987 – "Would you tell me which party you think would be best at cutting down strikes?"

Clearly in 1979 a small plurality of the electorate nationally thought Labour was best able to handle the issue: the Conservative party received the support of one-third of the respondents, but over forty per cent in three of the south-eastern regions, as well as in the East Midlands and also in Greater Manchester, the West Midlands Conurbation and Industrial South Wales. (In the last three, very small percentages believed that the Alliance offered the best policies on this issue.) Four years later, half of the respondents favoured Conservative policies; only in Merseyside and Strathclyde was support for that party substantially below the national level (though in neither was the support for Labour significantly greater than the national figure for this issue), whereas in the two zones around London over 60 per cent were pro-Conservative. Finally, in 1987 support for the Conservative policy was even stronger, again with very little regional variation; the highest expressions of support for Labour were in the three regions (Strathclyde, South Yorkshire, and Industrial South Wales) where there were large mining populations and support for the 1984–1985 strikes was strongest within the National Union of Mineworkers.

Each of the surveys asked a range of other questions inviting respondents their opinions on the parties' policies for issues such as defence, race relations, the national health service and income tax. The results all show very similar patterns of variations by region, so the tabulations have not been included here. One other is given to exemplify the general pattern. It refers to policies which are designed to make Britain prosperous, with the questions:

1979/1983/1987 – "Would you tell me which party you think would be best at making Britain more prosperous?"

Table 6.10 gives the tabulated results. In 1979, the Conservative party had a small lead over Labour. This was tripled in 1983, and only reduced very slightly in 1987, mainly, it seems, through Labour regaining support that in 1983 went to the Alliance. Many of the regions report percentage support for the parties close to the national distribution, in each of the three years. There are notable exceptions, however. Strathclyde records support for Conservative policies well below the national level at each election, matched by substantially above-average support for Labour; the Outer Metropolitan and Outer South-east zones show above-average support for Labour. (Interestingly, despite the voting patterns reported earlier, Merseyside does not also show strong support for Labour.) Thus on this, as with other issues, most regions show patterns of support not substantially different from the national.

On a range of policy issues, therefore, regional variations in support for the different parties were not pronounced, so it is unclear whether spatial variations in party evaluation were responsible for the voting patterns that we have described earlier. In part this is not surprising, since certain policies – on defence, for example – are not regionally selective in their impact. For those that are, such as unemployment, strikes and, to a lesser extent, general prosperity, there is evidence (largely consistent with the north:south divide) that people were more pro-Conservative in some areas, more pro-Labour in others, and more pro-Alliance in a third, usually small, group (and usually, though not invariably, rural).

Regarding the *evaluation of party leaders* we use responses to the questions:

1979 – "Who would make the best Prime Minister – Mr. Callaghan, Mrs. Thatcher or Mr. Steel?"
1983 – "Leaving aside your general party preference, who would make the best Prime Minister: Margaret Thatcher, Michael Foot, David Steel or Roy Jenkins?"
1987 – " . . . Margaret Thatcher, Neil Kinnock, David Steel or David Owen?"

Table 6.11 Opinions on which Party Leader would make the best Prime Minister, by Geographical Region*

	1979			1983				1987			
	Th	Ca	St	Th	F	St	J	Th	K	St	O
Strathclyde	13	51	26	24	19	43	5	22	45	13	13
E. Scotland	22	43	22	27	15	44	5	30	29	16	13
Rural Scotland	20	33	37	33	11	44	6	29	25	22	16
Rural North	35	30	27	45	12	34	6	43	27	8	15
Industrial Northeast	21	54	15	44	9	40	6	31	35	10	17
Merseyside	23	56	18	41	11	35	7	35	33	9	16
Greater Manchester	22	41	28	46	14	27	7	40	28	7	16
Rest of Northwest	25	45	19	43	15	24	13	40	32	7	13
West Yorks.	30	50	15	44	13	27	6	34	34	12	13
South Yorks.	13	56	24	46	11	31	6	32	43	7	15
Rural Wales	26	32	21	44	13	30	7	39	25	17	10
Industrial South Wales	24	53	13	36	18	37	3	31	38	11	16
W. Midlands Conurbation	41	31	12	41	16	30	4	42	35	2	10
Rest of West Midlands	39	31	19	49	14	22	5	49	24	8	15
East Midlands	33	31	22	39	10	41	4	42	28	10	16
East Anglia	22	38	25	44	4	40	4	45	22	9	18
Devon and Cornwall	20	40	28	43	5	37	6	43	19	13	19
Wessex	29	36	20	46	8	36	5	45	20	13	19
Inner London	28	41	18	45	20	20	5	32	40	6	13
Outer London	32	40	16	46	13	28	8	35	33	6	18
Outer Metropolitan	29	31	30	50	7	32	7	42	21	11	20
Outer Southeast	41	31	14	59	4	26	7	50	20	9	16
National	25	41	23	41	12	34	6	37	29	11	16

* The percentages are for respondents reporting support for: Th – Thatcher; Ca – Callaghan; St – Steel; F – Foot; J – Jenkins; K – Kinnock; O – Owen

Table 6.11 gives these data. They show that in 1979 the Labour leader, James Callaghan, was thought by over 40 per cent of the respondents to be the best of the three leaders, while Margaret Thatcher and David Steel were very close in second and third place, with the support of one-quarter of the electorate each. Four years later, Margaret Thatcher remained only a short distance ahead of David Steel, but had a lead of nearly thirty points over Michael Foot, the Labour leader; the leader of the SDP, Roy Jenkins, came a poor fourth. Mrs. Thatcher's popularity dropped slightly between 1983 and 1987. Below her, there was a substantial shift, as Neil Kinnock increased support for the Labour leader to more than twice that achieved by Michael Foot and David Steel suffered a major drop in support, to a considerable extent because of the preferences expressed for the SDP leader, David Owen, it seems.

Regionally, there are considerable variations in the popularity of the leaders. Each of the three Labour leaders (Callaghan, Foot, Kinnock) represented a South Wales constituency at the time, and each got well-above-average support

Table 6.12 Switches in Voting by Geographical Region, 1979–1983*

Vote in 1979	C			L			A		
1983	C	L	A	C	L	A	C	L	A
Strathclyde	74	8	17	4	80	16	10	5	85
E. Scotland	80	2	18	2	76	22	25	5	70
Rural Scotland	84	0	16	3	73	24	19	10	71
Rural North	89	0	11	5	86	9	–	–	–
Industrial Northeast	76	13	11	10	74	16	–	–	–
Merseyside	65	0	35	6	64	30	–	–	–
Greater Manchester	87	0	13	6	73	21	–	–	–
Rest of Northwest	82	5	13	0	72	28	–	–	–
West Yorks.	92	0	8	12	68	20	–	–	–
South Yorks.	92	8	0	–	–	–	–	–	–
Rural Wales	81	5	14	–	–	–	–	–	–
Industrial South Wales	78	9	13	5	69	26	–	–	–
W. Midlands Conurbation	89	4	7	9	72	19	–	–	–
Rest of West Midlands	84	5	11	0	89	11	–	–	–
East Midlands	79	4	17	12	67	21	–	–	–
East Anglia	85	0	15	9	60	31	–	–	–
Devon and Cornwall	78	2	20	–	–	–	9	2	89
Wessex	84	1	15	9	55	36	–	–	–
Inner London	94	3	3	7	83	10	–	–	–
Outer London	86	8	6	8	74	18	20	5	75
Outer Metropolitan	89	1	10	11	59	30	9	3	88
Outer Southeast	88	3	9	12	50	38	–	–	–
National	84	3	13	6	71	23	12	8	80

* The data are the percentages of those voting for a party in 1979 who voted for each party in 1983

in Industrial South Wales. This example of the 'friends and neighbours' effect (Taylor and Johnston, 1979) extends to two of the three Alliance leaders, as well. David Steel was from Rural Scotland, and got the support of at least ten percentage points more of the voters there than he did nationally; David Owen represented a Plymouth seat, and did better in Devon and Cornwall and in Wessex than almost anywhere else. Roy Jenkins represented a Glasgow constituency at the time of the 1983 election, but had only been its MP since 1981. Finally, Margaret Thatcher represented an outer London constituency (Finchley) but there is no clear evidence that she did better in that region than elsewhere in the south.

Apart from the 'friends and neighbours' effect, Table 6.11 provides evidence of considerable regional variation in support for the leaders, which largely follows what we have already described with regard to support for the parties. Among the Labour candidates for the Prime Minister's job, for example, both James Callaghan and Michael Foot did much better in the northern urban regions than they did in the south where, for example, Michael Foot received almost no support at all from the respondents in East Anglia. Support for Neil Kinnock was not notably strong in many of those northern regions, however, though he did perform well in Strathclyde and South Yorkshire, plus Inner London. David Steel's support has always been strongest in the rural areas – where support for the Liberals has been greatest and where, as we showed in Chapter 5, Alliance support strengthened in 1987 – and also in his native Scotland. Margaret Thatcher has always polled well in the West Midlands, as well as in London's exurbia.

Finally, we turn to the flow-of-the-vote in the various geographical regions. Tables 6.12 and 6.13 show the percentages of those who voted for one of the three parties at the first election in a pair who also voted for one of the three at the second, so that non-voters are excluded. (Data are not provided for any region where a party won less than twenty votes at the first election.) In general, and as would be expected, the north:south divide is clear, especially with regard to Labour loyalists, who were relatively more numerous in the northern than in the southern regions. (There were exceptions, however, with Merseyside recording below-average Labour loyalty between 1979 and 1983.) There was less spatial pattern to the distribution of Conservative loyalists, with little variation around the national figure.

These discussions of regional variations in party identification, economic optimism, party evaluation, leader evaluation and vote-switching have, despite the drawbacks in the data, provided valuable insights to possible reasons for the changing electoral geography described earlier in the book. They suggest that all of the four factors outlined in the model in Figure 6.2 to some extent account for both the patterns outlined in Chapter 5 and the switches between parties. The next sections follow up the hints that they provide.

OPINIONS AND VOTES

The tabulations discussed in the previous section have indicated regional differences on a range of opinions, many of which appear to be linked to the regional differences in voting reported in Chapter 5. Because of the small number of respondents in several of the regions, however, it is difficult to make a direct link between the two sets of differences. For that, we need further explorations of the opinion data. In the present section we do this by looking at the links between opinions and voting, at the national level.

As would be expected, the majority of people who identify with a party vote for it. A substantial number did not at the elections reviewed here, however, as Table 6.14 indicates; indeed, the largest percentage there indicates that 86 per cent of Conservative identifiers voted Conservative in 1983. The Alliance failed to get majority support from those who identified with it (i.e. with the

Table 6.13 Switches in Voting by Geographical Region, 1983–1987*

Vote in 1983	C			L			A		
1987	C	L	A	C	L	A	C	L	A
Strathclyde	60	17	23	1	97	2	10	16	74
E. Scotland	91	5	4	0	97	3	7	15	78
Rural Scotland	78	9	13	4	85	11	0	4	96
Rural North	90	2	8	8	84	8	–	–	–
Industrial Northeast	64	9	27	5	85	10	5	17	78
Merseyside	84	3	13	3	86	11	–	–	–
Greater Manchester	79	8	13	6	83	11	–	–	–
Rest of Northwest	80	7	13	10	80	10	–	–	–
West Yorks.	79	8	13	2	91	7	9	22	69
South Yorks.	71	4	25	3	83	14	–	–	–
Rural Wales	82	3	15	9	88	3	–	–	–
Industrial South Wales	80	12	8	5	82	13	–	–	–
W. Midlands Conurbation	88	3	9	6	88	6	–	–	–
Rest of West Midlands	84	3	13	3	72	25	20	15	65
East Midlands	91	2	7	3	86	11	10	10	80
East Anglia	89	0	11	0	83	17	–	–	–
Devon and Cornwall	75	5	20	0	68	32	0	11	89
Wessex	72	7	21	13	65	22	8	2	90
Inner London	83	4	13	0	90	10	–	–	–
Outer London	81	7	12	4	83	13	15	15	70
Outer Metropolitan	87	5	8	5	67	28	14	12	74
Outer Southeast	83	3	14	10	74	16	18	8	74
National	81	6	13	5	84	11	10	12	78

* The data are the percentages of those voting for a party in 1983 who voted for each party in 1987

Liberal party) in 1979, presumably because many felt that it had no chance of winning, either in their individual constituencies or in the country as a whole. In 1983 and 1987 it did as well as Labour and almost as well as the Conservative party in winning the votes of those who identified with it, however.

Just as people who identify with a party are likely to vote for it, so are people who think that a party has the best policies, whether for the country as a whole or just for themselves. Tables 6.15 and 6.16 show this to have been the case at the 1979, 1983 and 1987 elections, again with the exception of Alliance voting in 1979. On specific policies too, voting followed the expected lines; as Table 6.17 shows, the party that people thought was best for Britain's prosperity was the most likely to get their vote – although only two-thirds of those who thought the Conservatives best in 1987 actually voted for them and one-seventh voted Alliance. (Presumably, given our earlier findings, those Alliance voters were mainly in the Agricultural regions.) Substantial numbers of those who thought that Labour was best for reducing unemployment preferred to vote for another party, however (Table 6.18), especially the Alliance in 1983 and 1987; presumably they feared the possible consequences of Labour's poli-

Table 6.14 Party Identification by Vote*

Vote	Party Identification		
	Conservative	Labour	Alliance
1979			
C	81	4	21
L	3	74	11
A	4	6	46
1983			
C	86	5	9
L	1	71	5
A	7	15	78
1987			
C	82	3	10
L	3	79	6
A	8	10	76

* The data are the percentages of the respondents identifying with a party who voted for it at the relevant election

Table 6.15 Opinion of Which Party had the Best Policies, by Vote*

Vote	Party With Best Policies		
	Conservative	Labour	Alliance
1979			
C	84	1	13
L	2	81	12
A	2	3	51
1983			
C	86	1	5
L	3	90	5
A	5	5	80
1987			
C	86	1	5
L	3	88	6
A	6	6	79

* The data are the percentages of the respondents identifying which party had the best policies who voted for the relevant party

cies on that issue, could not accept other policies on salient issues (such as defence, perhaps), or voted tactically for another party.

Regarding the party leaders, about three-quarters of those who thought Mrs. Thatcher would make the best Prime Minister voted for her at each of the three elections (Table 6.19). James Callaghan only got the votes of two-thirds

Table 6.16 Opinion of which Party is Best for the Individual Voter by Vote*

Vote	Party Best for Individual Voter		
	Conservative	Labour	Alliance
1979			
C	79	3	18
L	3	73	15
A	4	5	46
1983			
C	85	5	12
L	2	74	7
A	6	11	71
1987			
C	79	2	10
L	4	79	6
A	11	9	76

* The data are the percentages of the respondents identifying which party was best for them who voted for the relevant party

Table 6.17 Opinion of Which Party was Best for British Prosperity, by Vote*

Vote	Best Party for Prosperity		
	Conservative	Labour	Alliance
1979			
C	71	1	6
L	5	80	10
A	6	4	60
1983			
C	75	1	1
L	6	88	5
A	10	4	84
1987			
C	65	1	2
L	9	87	7
A	14	5	81

* The data are the percentages of the respondents identifying which party was best for prosperity who voted for the relevant party

of those who thought him best for the job in 1979; his Labour successors, Michael Foot and Neil Kinnock, did much better, but clearly not enough thought them the best candidates. The Alliance candidates (Steel, Jenkins and Owen) saw an increasing percentage of their supporters actually voting Alliance, but clearly many more were impressed by their leadership credentials

Table 6.18 Opinion of Which Party was Best for Cutting Unemployment, by Vote*

Vote	Best Party Cut Unemployment		
	Conservative	Labour	Alliance
1979			
C	76	7	6
L	4	68	9
A	5	7	58
1983			
C	89	9	7
L	2	65	5
A	3	15	78
1987			
C	85	8	7
L	2	66	3
A	5	15	79

* The data are the percentages of the respondents identifying which party was best for cutting unemployment who voted for the relevant party

Table 6.19 Opinion of Which Party's Leader would make the Best Prime Minister, by Vote*

Vote	Best Prime Minister		
	Conservative	Labour	Alliance
1979			
C	79	8	24
L	2	68	16
A	3	4	31
1983			
C	78	4	13
L	6	84	26
A	8	5	47
1987			
C	75	3	15
L	6	80	15
A	9	8	54

* The data are the percentages of the respondents identifying each party's leader as best potential Prime Minister who voted for the relevant party

than they were by either or both of their parties' policies and their chances of becoming Prime Minister.

    Turning now to respondents' views of the economic situation, Table 6.20 looks at the voting reported by people according to their assessments of their personal financial situation in the twelve months prior to each election. In

Table 6.20 Perceptions of Personal Economic Situation over the last Twelve Months, by Vote*

Vote	Personal Economic Situation last Twelve Months				
	Lot Better	Little Better	Same	Little Worse	Lot Worse
1979					
C	22	24	30	39	45
L	50	45	35	23	18
A	10	10	10	12	9
1983					
C	72	60	45	23	10
L	9	12	21	37	48
A	9	20	22	28	30
1987					
C	63	51	35	15	8
L	9	18	31	50	55
A	22	20	20	20	19

* The data are the percentages of people reporting their economic situation in each category who voted for the relevant party

1979, there was a clear trend that the better things are thought to have been the more likely people were to have voted Labour; the worse they had apparently become, the more likely the respondent was to have voted Conservative. As anticipated, those who thought they had done well out of the last year of the Labour government voted for it; those who perceived they had done badly voted against the government. The same was generally true in both 1983 and 1987, elections held after a period of Conservative government. At both dates, however, voting for the incumbent government was much greater among those who thought they had done well than was the case with Labour in 1979. In 1983, the ratio of Labour:Alliance voters among those who thought things had got much worse for themselves over the previous twelve months was 1.6:1.0. In 1987 it was 2.9:1.0, suggesting that whereas in 1983 people who thought the Conservatives had not served them well were quite likely to vote Alliance rather than Labour, four years later similar people were much more likely to vote Labour. In 1987, as in 1979, people voting Alliance came from across the economic satisfaction spectrum; in 1983, at the nadir of Labour's vote-winning powers, the Alliance was a recipient of many votes against a 'failed' government's policies.

For other aspects of economic satisfaction and optimism we have data for 1983 and 1987 only; the patterns they show are similar to those in Table 6.20. With regard to the national economic situation, both retrospective and prospective, the most striking feature is the range in the voting percentages (Tables 6.21–6.23). Between 75 and 80 per cent of the 'extreme optimists' (those who thought things had got a lot better and those who thought things

Table 6.21 Perceptions of the National Economic Situation over the last Twelve Month's, by Vote*

Vote	National Economy last Twelve Months				
	Lot Better	Little Better	Same	Little Worse	Lot Worse
1983					
C	83	67	43	17	4
L	4	8	16	37	57
A	8	17	27	33	26
1987					
C	78	55	24	7	1
L	4	14	34	57	68
A	13	19	27	21	14

* The data are the percentages of people reporting the national economic situation in each category who voted for the relevant party

Table 6.22 Perceptions of the National Economic Situation over the next Twelve Months, by Vote*

Vote	National Economic Situation next Twelve Months				
	Lot Better	Little Better	Same	Little Worse	Lot Worse
1983					
C	79	63	34	12	3
L	9	14	24	41	55
A	7	16	30	34	26
1987					
C	75	55	22	7	2
L	11	20	34	55	64
A	8	14	29	27	17

* The data are the percentages of people reporting the national economic situation in each category who voted for the relevant party

were going to get a lot better) voted Conservative; less than five per cent of the 'extreme pessimists' (perceived things as a lot worse) did so. Labour did better among the pessimists than the optimists, not surprisingly: those who thought the government's economic policies had failed/were likely to fail were more likely to vote for the opposition. The Alliance's main support came from people in the middle – they thought things had stayed about the same, and were likely to remain that way.

Finally, what of people's perceptions of the likely changes in their personal financial situations over the next twelve months? In both 1983 and 1987, the

Table 6.23 Perceptions of Personal Economic Situations over the next 12 Months, by Vote*

Vote	Personal Economic Situation next Twelve Months				
	Lot Better	Little Better	Same	Little Worse	Lot Worse
1983					
C	70	56	40	15	7
L	16	19	23	36	53
A	10	18	26	35	25
1987					
C	60	46	34	11	7
L	18	26	32	52	56
A	15	17	23	23	18

* The data are the percentages of people reporting their economic situation in each category who voted for the relevant party

better the perceived prospects the greater the probability of a Conservative vote; the worse that the situation was perceived as, the greater the probability of voting Labour (Table 6.23). But the Conservatives didn't do as well among people who thought their own situation would get a lot better as they did among those who thought the national situation would improve (Table 6.21); the votes to return the Conservatives to power were more a function of people's perceptions of the national situation than of their own self-interest, it seems. For the Alliance, most votes came from people who thought things would either stay the same or get a little worse; the extreme optimists and pessimists were more likely to vote either Conservative or Labour.

Interrelationships among the Independent Variables

The relationships between opinions, evaluations and voting discussed above show that people tend to vote for the party that they think has the best policies, the best candidate for Prime Minister, the best economic record, and the greatest potential for improving the national economic situation. Those factors are undoubtedly inter-related, however, and linked to people's party identification.

Table 6.24 shows that the great majority of people who thought that either the Conservative or the Labour party had the best policies identified with that party, in each of the three election years. Many fewer identified with the Alliance among those who thought it had the best policies, however. Similarly, Table 6.25 shows that, in general, the people who identified with a party thought its leader(s) the best candidate(s) for Prime Minister. The main exception was with the Labour party in 1983; only 31 per cent of Labour identifiers thought Michael Foot the best candidate for Prime Minister and nearly half

Table 6.24 Opinions of which Party had the Best Policies, by Party Identification*

Party Identification	Party with Best Policies		
	Conservative	Labour	Alliance
1979			
C	80	2	15
L	4	86	18
A	5	3	51
1983			
C	80	2	9
L	7	90	19
A	5	2	55
1987			
C	78	3	12
L	5	87	15
A	6	3	60

* The data are the percentages who reported that each party had the best policies who identified with the relevant party

Table 6.25 Opinion of Which Party had the Best Leader, by Party Identification*

Party with Best Leader	Party Identification		
	Conservative	Labour	Alliance
1979			
C	61	3	14
L	10	79	18
A	19	13	59
1983			
C	79	14	17
L	1	31	2
A	18	46	78
1987			
C	70	5	19
L	9	80	22
A	7	5	41

* The data are the percentages who identified with each party who thought the relevant party leader(s) would make the best Prime Minister

preferred one of the Alliance leaders (David Steel and Roy Jenkins). Four years later, the Alliance was in a somewhat similar situation: only 41 per cent of its identifiers preferred one of the Alliance leaders (David Steel and David Owen) to either Margaret Thatcher or Neil Kinnock.

Turning to economic and party evaluations, Table 6.26 shows that people who thought their personal financial situations had improved over the last

Table 6.26 Perceptions of Personal Economic Situation over the last Twelve Months, by Opinions of which party had the Best Policies*

Party with Best Policies	Lot Better	Little Better	Same	Little Worse	Lot Worse
1979					
C	22	25	30	41	42
L	49	48	36	23	19
A	13	12	14	17	15
1983					
C	70	63	46	24	13
L	8	10	17	32	39
A	12	17	20	24	25
1987					
C	65	53	35	19	12
L	7	16	28	49	51
A	19	18	18	17	14

* The data are the percentages of people reporting in each category who thought that the relevant party had the best policies

twelve months were most likely to think the party of the incumbent government had the best policies. Support for Labour in 1979 among the 'extremely satisfied' was much less than was the case for the Conservative party in 1983 and 1987, however. With regard to the national economic situation, in both 1983 and 1987 the Conservative policies get resounding approval from those who thought things had got a lot better and those who thought things would get a lot better (Table 6.27). Similarly, people who were optimists about their own financial situation over the next twelve months were more favourably inclined to the Conservative policies than were the pessimists, but, as with voting, optimism about the national situation was more closely linked to favouring Conservative policies than was optimism about personal financial futures.

Party evaluation was a product of economic optimism during the period under review, it seems; people who thought the economy had improved and was likely to improve were much more likely to think that the party in power had the best policies than were people who thought things had become worse and/or were going to get worse. Party evaluation was also closely linked to party identification; those who thought a party had the best policies were very likely indeed to identify themselves politically with that party and also (with two notable exceptions) to think that the party's leader was the best candidate for Prime Minister. Overall, therefore, we can argue that the changing pattern of voting in Britain over the period 1979–1987 should be closely linked to the geography of economic optimism, and it is to testing that hypothesis that we now turn.

Table 6.27 Evaluation of the Economic Situation, by Opinion of which Party has the Best Policies*

Party with Best Policies	Lot Better	Little Better	Same	Little Worse	Lot Worse
National Economic Situation last Twelve Months					
1983					
C	85	69	45	18	7
L	5	6	13	31	48
A	9	15	23	30	23
1987					
C	80	56	28	8	3
L	4	13	31	52	61
A	12	17	22	18	13
National Economic Situation next Twelve Months					
1983					
C	80	65	36	14	4
L	8	11	18	34	50
A	7	15	25	30	22
1987					
C	77	57	26	9	4
L	9	19	33	47	55
A	9	12	21	23	21
Personal Economic Situation next Twelve Months					
1983					
C	68	57	42	17	8
L	14	15	19	31	48
A	9	16	22	33	21
1987					
C	60	48	35	14	15
L	18	24	28	48	51
A	10	15	20	21	13

* The data are the percentages of people reporting in each category who thought that the relevant party had the best policies

ECONOMIC OPTIMISM, REGION AND VOTING

As noted previously, there are insufficient respondents in each of the 22 geographical regions to allow detailed cross-tabulations of characteristics, such as economic optimism and voting. Thus to link the geography of voting to the geography of economic evaluation we have had to reduce the number of regions. Seven amalgamated regions were defined:

London – Inner London; Outer London;
South – East Anglia; Wessex; Outer Metropolitan Area; Outer Southeast;
Devon and Cornwall – Devon and Cornwall;

Midlands – Rest of West Midlands; East Midlands;

North Urban – Industrial Northeast; Merseyside; Greater Manchester; Rest of
    Northwest; West Yorkshire; South Yorkshire; West Midlands Conurbation;

North Rural – Rural North;

Scotland/Wales – Strathclyde; E. Scotland; Rural Scotland; Rural Wales; Industrial
    South Wales.

For two of these – Devon and Cornwall; North Rural – the number of respondents in each was still too small to provide reliable cross-classifications. Rather than include them with other adjacent regions, from which they differed substantially in many of the tabulations in Tables 6.1–6.11, we decided to omit them entirely. Thus our discussion here is of five regions only. (For a map of the five regions, see the Appendix, Figure A.6.)

Looking first at the evaluation of the national financial situation, Tables 6.28 and 6.29 present data for 1983 and 1987 which are very much consistent with the general hypothesis, and which also provide further insights to the geography of voting. Regarding the twelve months prior to each election, Table 6.28 shows that at each the percentage voting Conservative was very much larger among those who thought the national situation had improved (whether by a lot or by a little is not shown, since the number of observations suggested that the two categories should be amalgamated) than among those who thought it had got worse (again, the two categories have been amalgamated, as is the case throughout this discussion). Between 1983 and 1987 there was a major shift, however. At the first of those dates, in London the percentage voting Conservative among those who thought things got better was six times greater than it was among those who thought the situation had deteriorated, whereas in Scotland and Wales the percentage was nine times greater; in 1987, the London percentage was just under six times greater in the former than in the latter category, whereas in Scotland it was 26 times greater. In 1987, people who thought the situation had deteriorated over the previous twelve months were much less likely to vote for a return of the government, especially in the north regions, than was the case in 1983, presumably because in 1987 they had much more confidence in the Labour party's policies and, especially, leadership.

In both years, there were clear differences between regions in the propensity of people to vote Labour, even when their evaluations of the recent economic performance are held constant. The region that stands out is the South, where Labour voting was much lower, whatever the economic evaluation, whereas Alliance voting was much greater than it was elsewhere, especially among people who thought things had either stayed the same or deteriorated. Thus in 1987, for example, the percentage voting Labour among those who thought things had remained about the same was only 20 in the South, approximately half the value recorded in every other region, whereas of those who thought the situation had got worse the percentage voting Alliance was 34, nearly twice the figure for the Midlands and four times that for London.

Across the five regions there were also substantial variations in the degree of economic satisfaction, as shown by the B:W ratio, the ratio of the number

Table 6.28   Vote by Perceptions of National Economic Situation over the last Twelve Months and Aggregated Region*

	Got Better			The Same			Got Worse			B:W Ratio
	C	L	A	C	L	A	C	L	A	
1983										
London	77	8	11	49	23	15	12	54	25	1.01
South	77	3	15	48	11	33	14	32	45	1.65
Midlands	56	14	18	52	14	18	13	49	24	1.03
North Urban	67	10	16	48	19	21	11	55	25	0.80
Scotland/Wales	65	8	15	32	19	30	7	52	24	0.57
1987										
London	51	22	16	29	40	23	9	74	9	1.29
South	72	5	17	30	20	36	3	45	34	2.66
Midlands	68	10	14	21	39	30	9	52	18	2.27
North Urban	63	16	22	23	37	26	3	69	15	1.17
Scotland/Wales	52	15	17	17	42	17	2	63	13	0.93

* The data in the first nine columns are the percentages reporting the perceptions at the head of the columns voting for the relevant parties. The final column shows the ratio of the number who thought things had got better to those who thought they had got worse

Table 6.29   Vote by Perceptions of National Economic Situation over the Next Twelve Months and Aggregated Region*

	Get Better			The Same			Get Worse			B:W Ratio
	C	L	A	C	L	A	C	L	A	
1983										
London	71	12	11	51	22	22	10	50	27	2.28
South	74	5	15	46	15	34	10	28	50	3.22
Midlands	61	17	14	36	21	29	5	57	27	2.82
North Urban	61	16	16	31	31	25	10	53	28	2.67
Scotland/Wales	56	20	16	24	27	30	7	51	23	1.51
1987										
London	50	29	13	23	45	21	11	64	17	2.39
South	74	8	12	29	17	44	8	46	40	4.32
Midlands	61	17	12	21	40	23	8	38	38	6.92
North Urban	54	24	14	23	37	26	4	62	21	2.31
Scotland/Wales	44	25	13	16	40	23	4	60	14	2.02

* The data in the first nine columns are the percentages reporting the perceptions at the head of the columns voting for the relevant parties. The final column shows the ratio of the number who thought things would get better to those who thought things would get worse

thinking things had improved to the number who thought they had got worse. In 1983, more people in the South, the Midlands and London thought things had improved than thought they had got worse; the reverse was the case in North Urban and Scotland/Wales regions. Four years later, more people in every region except Scotland/Wales thought things had improved; in the South

2.66 times more than thought they had deteriorated. Since voting propensity is linked to this evaluation (Table 6.21), then clearly if there were more people in some regions than others with such negative evaluations this would lead to inter-regional variations in voting.

In brief, we can summarise Table 6.28 as showing:

1   That there were substantial inter-regional variations in people's evaluations of recent national economic performance; and

2.   That people who thought things had improved were more likely to vote Conservative whereas those who thought things had deterioriated were more likely to vote Labour; so that

3.   Conservative voting was likely to be greater in the regions where more people thought things had got better, whereas it would be less in the regions where more people thought they had got worse.

Together, these can account for a great deal of the regional pattern of voting in Britain. In addition, however:

4.   People in some regions (notably London, North Urban, and Scotland/Wales) were more likely to vote Labour, whatever their evaluation of recent economic performance (no doubt because of the occupational class structure of those regions), whereas people in the South were more likely to vote Conservative;

5.   People in the South were much more likely to vote for the Alliance than for Labour if they thought the country's economic performance was unsatisfactory than were people elsewhere; and

6.   In 1987, people dissatisfied with the national economic performance were much less likely to vote Conservative than was the case in 1983.

Together, these three additional points provide an account of the changing pattern of voting. The Conservative loss of votes in the north can be associated with the relatively poor perceptions of the economic situation there, together with the greater propensity of the residents of those regions to vote Labour. The growth of the Alliance vote in the South, and the decline of Labour, is apparently because dissatisfied people there are more likely to vote for the former than for the latter.

Turning to people's perceptions of the national economic situation over the next twelve months after the 1983 and 1987 elections, Table 6.29 provides information consistent with our thesis. In all regions, more people thought things were going to get better than thought they would get worse, with the greatest optimism in the South and the Midlands in both years. In both 1983 and 1987, optimism was associated with Conservative voting in every region, but in 1987 the level of support for that party was much less among the optimistic in London, North Urban and Scotland/Wales than it was in 1983, whereas there was no difference between the two dates in the percentages voting Conservative in South and Midlands. (Again, in part this will reflect different class structures.) In the former group of regions, the relatively optimistic were more prepared to vote Labour in 1987 than in 1983; presumably they had more faith in Labour policies and leadership at the later election, and were prepared to vote for it to run the reviving/expanding economy. This suggests (as the Conservative voting data in London and Scotland/Wales in Table 6.28 also imply) that in regions where Labour has traditionally been strong, more people were prepared to support it in 1987 than was the case in 1983, irrespective of the likely economic future. This is consistent with the existence of a regional effect in voting patterns that is independent of economic optimism; the north remains more pro-Labour.

One other salient feature of Table 6.29, distinguishing it from Table 6.28, refers to Alliance voting among the economic pessimists. In 1983, the percentage of those who thought things would get worse and who voted Alliance was about the same in four of the regions, but double that value in the South. Four years later, there was much greater variability. The Alliance was relatively favoured by the pessimists in the South and the Midlands, and much less so in the other three regions. As a consequence, whereas Labour picked up 60 per cent or more of the votes of the pessimists in London, North Urban, and Scotland/Wales, it obtained only 38–46 per cent in the other two. The Alliance was not similarly favoured by people in the Midlands who thought things would stay about the same, however; they gave their votes to Labour in almost equal proportions to similar people in all other regions except the South.

When we look at people's evaluations of their personal (household) financial circumstances over the twelve months previous to each election (including 1979 in this case) we find that many more thought things had got worse than thought they had improved (Table 6.30). In 1979, no region had more optimists than pessimists; in 1983, only people in the South had more; and in 1987 people in the South and the Midlands both reported a plurality of optimists. The middle year – 1983 – was the gloomiest yet it was the election which saw the incumbent government win by a Parliamentary landslide; it lost votes, but so did Labour, to the Alliance.

In 1979, people were evaluating an incumbent Labour government. Nevertheless, relatively few (compared with 1983 and 1987) of those who thought that their personal situations had improved over the previous year were prepared to vote Labour; it won majority support in the North Urban and Scotland/Wales regions only, and in the South the Conservative party won more votes than Labour from such people. Among those who thought their situation had stayed about the same, Labour got most votes in three regions but the Conservative party won most support in the South and the Midlands. The Conservative party was by far the most popular among those who thought their situations had worsened in four of the regions, but achieved only a small margin of victory among such people in Scotland/Wales. Even when economic evaluations were held constant, therefore, substantial regional variations in voting patterns remained.

The same was true in 1983, when people were passing judgement on four years of Conservative government. More than half of those who thought things had improved voted Conservative in every region, but the party did much better in the South and London than it did elsewhere; support for the Alliance was fairly uniform. Among those whose situations had remained about the

Table 6.30 Vote by Perceptions of Personal Economic Situation over the Last Twelve Months and Aggregated Region*

	Got Better			The Same			Got Worse			B:W Ratio
	C	L	A	C	L	A	C	L	A	
1979										
London	33	39	12	28	42	10	40	13	15	0.55
South	37	32	17	41	28	12	58	15	13	0.73
Midlands	31	48	9	41	26	8	60	13	7	0.85
North Urban	20	50	8	29	39	6	40	21	13	0.99
Scotland/Wales	14	51	7	24	38	10	30	28	8	0.75
1983										
London	74	4	17	53	26	14	19	51	22	0.77
South	71	5	18	56	11	25	21	28	43	1.15
Midlands	54	16	15	41	26	17	21	39	26	0.61
North Urban	60	15	20	47	23	18	16	49	26	0.61
Scotland/Wales	53	15	18	34	28	25	13	46	21	0.49
1987										
London	45	33	13	34	40	17	12	60	15	0.98
South	67	8	18	48	14	26	18	35	34	1.55
Midlands	59	17	17	44	27	19	17	42	22	1.29
North Urban	43	22	25	33	34	20	10	58	17	0.75
Scotland/Wales	43	17	20	22	43	16	10	57	11	0.88

* See Table 6.28

same, also, the Conservative party was much more popular in London and the South than it was elsewhere, but it got more support than either of the other parties in every region. Among those who thought things had got worse, the Alliance was the favoured party in the South, whereas Labour got most support elsewhere.

In 1987, there was a substantial shift away from the Conservative party in most regions, whatever people's perceptions of their changing circumstances over the preceding twelve months. The South and Midlands now stand out as the two major regions of Conservative support among those who thought things had either improved or stayed the same. Less than half of the optimists voted Conservative in the other three regions, and in all three of them Labour out-polled the incumbent party of government among those whose situations had remained unaltered. Where substantial numbers of people believed things had improved for themselves (in the South, the Midlands and, to a much lesser extent, London) the Conservative party did relatively well. In other regions, where relatively few experienced improvement, support for the incumbent government was much less, even among those whose own positions had improved/stayed the same. And finally, among those whose individual positions had deteriorated, Labour improved its performance substantially (over 1983) in London, North Urban and Scotland/Wales, but achieved much less in the South and Midlands because of the relative success of the Alliance.

Table 6.31 Vote by Perceptions of Personal Economic Situation over the Next Twelve Months and Aggregated Region*

	Get Better			The Same			Get Worse			B:W Ratio
	C	L	A	C	L	A	C	L	A	
1983										
London	71	15	10	46	24	24	20	48	14	1.95
South	67	8	19	49	15	28	19	16	55	3.47
Midlands	52	24	12	41	25	23	9	46	30	2.44
North Urban	56	22	16	40	24	25	15	57	22	2.19
Scotland/Wales	47	25	18	30	30	24	8	45	26	1.60
1987										
London	29	42	12	31	40	17	13	63	13	3.38
South	67	8	17	42	18	33	18	41	32	4.14
Midlands	52	24	15	38	25	25	15	40	30	4.35
North Urban	41	30	21	32	37	19	6	59	21	2.42
Scotland/Wales	31	33	14	26	41	17	5	58	14	2.69

* See Table 6.29

Table 6.32 Vote-Switching by Perceptions of the Economic Situation, 1979–1983*

1979	C			L			A		
1983	C	L	A	C	L	A	C	L	A
National Economic Situation over Last Twelve Months									
Got Better	68	17	36	60	9	20	62	17	24
The Same	20	24	24	22	10	18	28	17	22
Got Worse	11	59	39	14	79	61	8	67	52
Personal Economic Situation over Last Twelve Months									
Got Better	39	19	22	25	10	17	28	17	18
The Same	44	45	40	52	31	33	49	17	37
Got Worse	15	33	38	19	59	50	23	66	43
National Economic Situation over Next Twelve Months									
Get Better	73	22	36	59	21	25	51	17	26
The Same	17	24	28	21	18	26	26	29	29
Get Worse	3	27	19	14	36	31	8	29	24
Personal Economic Situation over Next Twelve Months									
Get Better	49	21	23	44	21	22	36	33	22
The Same	41	45	49	38	36	40	54	21	47
Get Worse	5	24	18	11	27	27	5	21	20

* The data are the percentages of voters in each pair (e.g. voted C at both dates) drawn from the three evaluation categories

Finally, people's perceptions of their likely individual circumstances over the next twelve months provide a very similar picture (Table 6.31). Support for the Conservative party fell among the optimists in London, North Urban and Scotland/Wales, but not in the South and the Midlands, with Labour doing very much better in the former regions in 1987 than in 1983. Labour also increased its votes among those in the same regions who thought things would stay the same, as it did among the pessimists in London, the South, and Scotland/Wales. The overall general improvement of Labour's performance in the three northern regions in particular suggests the existence of a much greater willingness to support it there, whatever the economic situation; the low levels in 1983 are presumably associated with the party's poor image generally (including that of its leader).

Overall, then, we find that although the propensity of people to vote for one of the three parties was very much influenced by their levels of economic satisfaction concerning the recent past and optimism for the immediate future, this is insufficient to account for all of the variation in voting patterns. Because regions differed in the relative importance of optimistic and pessimistic people within their populations, in part the changing electoral geography of Britain is a function of the changing geography of optimism and pessimism. But this is not all; in some regions optimistic people were more likely to vote Conservative in 1987 than were those in others. There are clear regional differences (at the macro-scale of five regions we have been obliged to use here because of data constraints) that are not linked to optimism/pessimism directly. Basically, people in the Scotland/Wales, North Urban and London regions were much more prepared to vote Labour, especially in 1987, than were their contemporaries in the South and the Midlands, which was undoubtedly in part at least a class effect. In the latter two regions, not only were people unprepared to vote Labour; if they were pessimists they were much more ready to vote Alliance.

Economic Optimism and Vote-Switching

Finally, what of the vote-switchers? The national patterns are shown in Tables 6.32 and 6.33, where the voters in each situation are divided into the percentages who thought things had got/would get better, had stayed/would stay the same, and had got/would get worse. In the top panel of Table 6.32, therefore, of those who voted Conservative in both 1979 and 1983, 68 per cent thought things got better nationally over the previous twelve months, 20 per cent thought things had remained about the same, and 11 per cent thought things had got worse. This contrasts strongly with Labour loyalists (those who voted Labour in both years) of whom only 9 per cent thought things had got better and 79 per cent thought they had got worse.

The switching patterns between 1979 and 1983 were in general as would be expected. Regarding the national economic situation, both retrospectively and prospectively, the Conservative loyalists were mainly optimists whereas the Labour loyalists were mainly pessimists. (There were a lot of 'don't knows' among the latter regarding likely developments in the next twelve months.) Alliance loyalists were predominantly people who thought things had got worse (both nationally and personally) over the preceding twelve months, but thought they would stay the same over the next. Conservative loyalists were more likely to have done better personally over the last twelve months than were Labour

Table 6.33 Vote-Switching by Perceptions of the Economic Situation, 1983–1987*

1983 1987	C			L			A		
	C	L	A	C	L	A	C	L	A
National Economic Situation over Last Twelve Months									
Got Better	79	21	52	67	15	30	84	16	34
The Same	15	21	29	29	24	29	13	24	36
Got Worse	3	58	16	4	58	41	3	56	26
Personal Economic Situation over Last Twelve Months									
Got Better	45	16	31	50	12	29	42	16	27
The Same	47	40	51	38	41	30	32	40	49
Got Worse	8	44	18	13	45	41	23	44	24
National Economic Situation over Next Twelve Months									
Get Better	67	23	31	71	23	22	68	20	23
The Same	14	23	31	4	22	40	19	20	28
Get Worse	2	14	13	4	25	17	3	36	19
Personal Economic Situation over Next Twelve Months									
Get Better	48	40	22	50	23	26	39	28	30
The Same	41	33	51	21	41	49	52	44	46
Get Worse	2	14	13	17	19	14	3	16	11

* See Table 6.32

loyalists, and also were much more optimistic about their personal futures.

People who moved away from the Conservative party between 1979 and 1983 were less optimistic than those who remained loyal; in general, those who shifted to Labour were more likely to think things had got worse/would get worse than those who shifted to the Alliance. Labour converts to the Conservative cause in 1983 were generally those who thought the national situation had improved and would go on doing so; they were less hopeful about their own situations, though much more optimistic in general than those who remained loyal to Labour. People who shifted from Labour to the Alliance were generally pessimists, as were those who shifted from the Alliance to Labour with regard to their previous year's experience; they were more optimistic about their future, however, perhaps linked to their switch to Labour. People who voted for the Alliance in 1979 but the Conservatives in 1983 were optimistic about the country's future but thought their own situation would stay about the same.

Between 1983 and 1987 (Table 6.33) Conservative loyalists were again overwhelmingly optimistic about the national situation, but less so about their own positions; few were pessimistic about their personal situation, however, in marked contrast to both Labour loyalists and those who switched to Labour from another party. Alliance loyalists were relatively 'middle-of-the-road', with 'the same' category obtaining the largest percentage in each of the four analyses. Those who switched from either Labour or the Alliance to Conservative were optimists – those who thought the government's policies were working were likely to change their allegiance to vote for it – whereas Alliance switchers to Labour were generally much more pessimistic (and believed, presumably, that Labour was better able to introduce policies to counter their pessimism than was the Alliance). As in the previous period, Labour switchers to the Alliance were people who thought that the previous year had not been very good for the country and for themselves, but were more optimistic about the future.

Turning to the differences between regions, Tables 6.34–6.41 show percentages of people either remaining loyal or switching according to their level of economic optimism. (In these tables, there are no entries where the number of respondents involved was too small – less than one per cent of the sample – to provide reliable data.)

In general the differences shown for the 1979–1983 period are slight. In Table 6.34, for example, there are no substantial inter-regional differences within any of the levels of economic satisfaction in the levels of Conservative

Table 6.34 The Flow-of-the-Vote by Perceptions of the National Economic Situation over the Last Twelve Months and Aggregated Region, 1979–1983

1979* 1983	C			L			A		
	C	L	A	C	L	A	C	L	A
Better									
London	96	2	2	–	–	–	–	–	–
South	92	1	7	34	24	42	17	4	79
Midlands	88	1	11	16	64	20	–	–	–
North Urban	89	1	10	25	44	31	–	–	–
Scotland/Wales	91	1	8	29	42	29	–	–	–
NATIONAL	91	1	8	26	44	30	27	5	68
Same									
London	85	12	3	–	–	–	–	–	–
South	84	2	14	8	46	46	20	4	76
Midlands	87	–	13	–	–	–	–	–	–
North Urban	86	3	11	19	53	28	–	–	–
Scotland/Wales	70	7	23	5	60	35	–	–	–
NATIONAL	81	4	15	11	56	33	16	6	78
Worse									
London	–	–	–	2	84	14	–	–	–
South	58	2	40	2	68	30	2	4	94
Midlands	56	20	24	3	79	18	–	–	–
North Urban	57	17	26	2	79	19	4	17	79
Scotland/Wales	53	12	35	0	83	17	3	16	81
NATIONAL	56	12	32	1	80	19	2	11	87

* The data are the percentages who voted for the party indicated in 1979 and for the party indicated in 1983

Table 6.35 The Flow-of-the-Vote by Perception of Personal Economic Situation over the Last Twelve Months and Aggregated Region, 1979–1983

1979* 1983	C C	L	A	L C	L	A	A C	L	A
Better									
London	100	0	0	–	–	–	–	–	–
South	89	3	8	–	–	–	14	5	81
Midlands	85	4	11	–	–	–	–	–	–
North Urban	88	2	10	11	53	36	–	–	–
Scotland/Wales	90	0	10	9	60	31	–	–	–
NATIONAL	90	2	8	13	56	31	18	7	75
Same									
London	86	10	4	8	81	11	–	–	–
South	89	1	10	16	53	31	19	0	81
Midlands	83	6	11	14	70	16	–	–	–
North Urban	89	2	9	12	68	20	–	–	–
Scotland/Wales	79	5	16	6	69	25	16	4	80
NATIONAL	85	3	12	10	67	23	16	3	81
Worse									
London	–	–	–	4	83	13	–	–	–
South	74	0	26	0	64	36	0	9	91
Midlands	74	3	23	4	76	20	–	–	–
North Urban	60	10	30	3	76	21	14	23	63
Scotland/Wales	64	9	27	1	84	15	10	13	77
NATIONAL	68	6	26	2	78	20	7	12	81

* See Table 6.34

and Labour loyalty, except in the South for the latter; people were more likely to switch from Labour to the Alliance in the South than was the case else-where, also. The same is true with regard to people's evaluation of their own financial circumstances over the previous year (Table 6.35), except for the slight evidence of greater Labour loyalty and lesser Conservative loyalty in Scotland/Wales and lower than average Labour loyalty in the South (where the Alliance was the major beneficiary) was also the case with regard to respondents' optimism regarding the next year (both for the country and for themselves). Otherwise, there are few salient differences between regions in those tables (6.36, 6.37).

For the 1983–1987 period, the picture is very much the same. With regard to their evaluations of the previous year, residents of the South were much less likely to be loyal to Labour in both elections, whatever their evaluation, than was the case in the other regions, and they were much more likely to switch to the Alliance (Tables 6.38, 6.39). In addition, among those who voted Conservative in 1983 and thought economic circumstances had got worse in the

Table 6.36 The Flow-of-the-Vote by Perceptions of the National Economic Situation over the Next Twelve Months and Aggregated Region, 1979–1983

1979* 1983	C			L			A		
	C	L	A	C	L	A	C	L	A
Better									
London	96	0	4	19	67	14	–	–	–
South	92	1	7	29	42	29	13	4	83
Midlands	90	1	9	18	67	15	–	–	–
North Urban	92	1	7	13	62	25	–	–	–
Scotland/Wales	90	2	8	10	65	25	40	5	55
NATIONAL	92	1	7	15	62	23	22	4	74
Same									
London	–	–	–	–	–	–	–	–	–
South	85	1	14	6	54	40	21	0	79
Midlands	73	8	19	–	–	–	–	–	–
North Urban	73	7	20	12	61	27	–	–	–
Scotland/Wales	72	2	26	3	70	27	4	13	83
NATIONAL	76	4	20	7	65	28	11	8	81
Worse									
London	–	–	–	6	75	19	–	–	–
South	35	5	60	4	60	36	0	9	91
Midlands	–	–	–	3	82	15	–	–	–
North Urban	–	–	–	3	74	23	–	–	–
Scotland/Wales	42	21	37	1	84	15	–	–	–
NATIONAL	45	14	41	3	77	20	5	12	83

* See Table 6.34

twelve months prior to the 1987 election, more were likely to switch to the Alliance in the South than elsewhere, and more to Labour in Scotland/Wales. Finally, of those who voted Labour in 1983, more were likely to switch away from Labour in 1987 – usually to the Alliance – in the South than elsewhere, whatever their evaluations of the future (Tables 6.40, 6.41).

This last set of tables suggests that the pattern of vote-switching varied only slightly between regions over both electoral periods, within each economic optimism category. This is not necessarily running counter to the general thesis developed here, however. Because the relative flows are the same in each region does not mean the relative standing of the parties in each is unaffected, since that depends on the interaction of three factors: the number of voters for each party at the first election; the proportion of those voters who were optimistic or pessimistic about the future; and the inter-party flows. We know, for example, that in 1983 there were more Conservative voters in the South than elsewhere, and also more people who were optimistic in 1987. Thus, compared with Scotland/Wales, where there were fewer Conservative voters

Table 6.37 The Flow-of-the-Vote by Perception of Personal Economic Situations over the Next Twelve Months and Aggregated Region, 1979–1983

1979* 1983	C			L			A		
	C	L	A	C	L	A	C	L	A
Better									
London	100	0	0	17	66	17	–	–	–
South	92	1	7	19	45	36	17	4	79
Midlands	85	6	9	18	78	4	–	–	–
North Urban	92	2	6	9	49	42	–	–	–
Scotland/Wales	88	1	11	8	70	22	–	–	–
NATIONAL	92	2	6	12	67	21	18	10	72
Same									
London	89	4	7	0	85	15	–	–	–
South	82	2	16	9	64	27	10	0	90
Midlands	79	14	17	6	75	19	–	–	–
North Urban	82	3	15	12	62	26	–	–	–
Scotland/Wales	76	6	18	3	72	25	–	–	–
NATIONAL	81	4	15	7	67	24	14	3	83
Worse									
London	–	–	–	10	76	14	–	–	–
South	70	0	30	0	48	52	4	8	88
Midlands	–	–	–	3	72	25	–	–	–
North Urban	57	19	24	4	75	21	–	–	–
Scotland/Wales	55	14	31	1	82	17	–	–	–
NATIONAL	57	11	32	3	74	23	3	9	88

* See Table 6.34

and optimists, there will have been a swing to the Conservatives in the South, even if the percentage of loyalists was the same in the two regions in each of the three categories. (Tables 6.40 and 6.41 back this up; there were too few pessimists in any region who voted Conservative in 1983 to give reliable flow estimates. The great majority of Conservative voters thought things would either improve or stay the same.)

In general, then, we find that the national pattern of flows was reproduced in most regions. Briefly stated, the main components of that pattern are:

1. The greater the degree of satisfaction with the past and optimism about the future, the greater the percentage of Conservative voters who remained loyal to the party.

2. The greater the degree of dissatisfaction with the past and pessimism about the future, the greater the percentage of Labour voters who remained loyal to the party.

Table 6.38 The Flow-of-the-Vote by Perceptions of the National Economic Situation over the Last Twelve Months and Aggregated Region, 1983–1987

1983*	C			L			A		
1987	C	L	A	C	L	A	C	L	A
Better									
London	85	2	13	0	87	13	–	–	–
South	89	2	9	30	55	15	44	0	56
Midlands	94	3	3	–	–	–	36	9	55
North Urban	86	1	13	11	58	31	26	11	63
Scotland/Wales	94	1	5	16	72	12	6	0	94
NATIONAL	89	2	9	14	66	20	27	4	69
Same									
London	74	13	13	0	91	9	–	–	–
South	75	9	16	6	61	33	4	0	96
Midlands	79	0	21	0	83	17	–	–	–
Northern	67	10	23	9	77	14	0	18	82
Scotland/Wales	86	7	7	3	94	3	7	7	86
NATIONAL	72	8	20	5	81	14	5	8	87
Worse									
London	50	50	0	0	95	5	–	–	–
South	18	45	37	0	77	23	0	8	92
Midlands	–	–	–	0	85	15	–	–	–
North Urban	29	43	28	0	95	5	0	30	70
Scotland/Wales	21	64	15	1	94	5	0	19	81
NATIONAL	33	44	23	1	90	9	2	21	77

* The data are the percentages who voted for the party indicated in 1983 and the party indicated in 1987

3. Conservative voters who were satisfied/optimistic but switched away were more likely to move to the Alliance than to Labour; those who were dissatisfied/pessimistic were more likely to shift to Labour.

4. Labour voters who changed their allegiance were more likely to switch to the Conservative party if they were satisfied/optimistic, but to the Alliance if they were dissatisfied/pessimistic.

5. Alliance voters who changed their allegiance were more likely to switch to the Conservative party if they were satisfied/optimistic and to the Labour party if they were dissatisfied/pessimistic.

These features are largely unremarkable. They helped to accentuate the inter-regional differences in voting patterns over the period because of the spatial concentration of satisfied/optimistic people into certain regions. In addition, there were two important differential shifts which saw above-average levels of Labour loyalty in Scotland and greater-than-expected shifts from Labour to the Alliance in the South.

Table 6.39 The Flow-of-the-Vote by Perceptions of Personal Economic Situation over the Last Twelve Months and Aggregated Regions, 1983–1987

1983* 1987	C C	L	A	L C	L	A	A C	L	A
Better									
London	91	9	0	–	–	–	–	–	–
South	87	3	10	20	60	20	42	5	53
Midlands	96	2	2	0	75	25	–	–	–
North Urban	82	2	16	13	55	32	9	9	82
Scotland/Wales	96	0	4	17	66	17	8	0	92
NATIONAL	89	2	9	13	67	20	19	6	75
Same									
London	78	7	15	0	93	7	9	18	73
South	82	5	13	13	69	18	16	0	84
Midlands	88	3	9	0	88	12	20	10	70
North Urban	77	5	18	6	84	10	7	18	75
Scotland/Wales	82	9	9	1	96	3	0	5	95
NATIONAL	82	5	13	4	87	9	9	9	82
Worse									
London	–	–	–	0	90	10	–	–	–
South	64	18	18	2	67	31	5	5	90
Midlands	64	0	36	4	83	13	–	–	–
North Urban	61	28	11	0	92	8	11	28	61
Scotland/Wales	53	41	6	1	95	4	8	23	69
NATIONAL	58	23	19	1	87	12	11	17	72

* See Table 6.38

IN SUMMARY

This chapter has analysed individual opinion poll data to explore the reasons for the changing geographical patterns of voting outlined earlier in the book. As with all such analyses, it has been constrained by the available data, which in particular have limited the number of regions we could analyse in detail to only five. Nevertheless, the findings have provided very substantial evidence that links the changing geography of voting to the country's economic and social geography.

We began the chapter with a model of the voting choice process. The analyses we have presented since are in no sense an exhaustive evaluation of that model, but they provide us with grounds for suggesting modifications. These are incorporated in the revised format presented in Figure 6.3

Compared to Figure 6.2, the salient features of the model in Figure 6.3 are the links that it includes that were not incorporated in the original formulation.

Table 6.40   The Flow-of-the-Vote by Perceptions of the National Economic Situation over the Next Twelve Months and Aggregated Region, 1983–1987

1983* 1987	C			L			A		
	C	L	A	C	L	A	C	L	A
Better									
London	82	9	9	0	93	7	–	–	–
South	94	2	4	14	67	19	59	0	41
Midlands	94	2	4	7	79	14	–	–	–
North Urban	90	3	7	16	75	9	26	16	58
Scotland/Wales	93	2	5	11	80	9	8	8	84
NATIONAL	92	2	6	11	77	12	30	7	63
Same									
London	75	8	17	0	88	12	–	–	–
South	61	12	27	5	53	42	15	0	85
Midlands	73	0	27	0	84	16	–	–	–
North Urban	71	6	23	0	77	23	0	36	64
Scotland/Wales	80	13	7	0	84	16	7	0	93
NATIONAL	69	9	22	1	78	21	9	8	83
Worse									
London	–	–	–	0	94	6	–	–	–
South	–	–	–	0	87	13	8	8	84
Midlands	–	–	–	–	–	–	–	–	–
North Urban	–	–	–	0	86	14	0	25	75
Scotland/Wales	–	–	–	2	98	0	0	17	83
NATIONAL	41	14	45	1	90	9	2	20	78

* See Table 6.38

The most important of these are the link from party identification to economic optimism – there was clear evidence that people who identified with the party in power prior to an election were more likely to be economically satisfied/optimistic than were people who identified with the opposition; the two-way link between party identification and party evaluation; the two-way link between leader evaluation and party evaluation; and the clear link between locational influences and leader evaluation. All of these are relatively tentative, and are hypotheses deserving of further testing rather than definitive statements about voting behaviour in the period analysed.

For our purposes, the most important elements of the model in Figure 6.3 are the retention of the links between locational influences and both party evaluation and economic optimism. Regarding the former, we have provided clear evidence of regional variations in the propensity of British voters to prefer one party's policies over those of others, both generally and on specific issues.

Table 6.41 The Flow-of-the-Vote by Perceptions of Personal Economic Situation over the Next Twelve Months and Aggregated Region, 1983–1987

1983* 1987	C			L			A		
	C	L	A	C	L	A	C	L	A
Better									
London	81	13	6	0	100	0	–	–	–
South	91	3	6	11	73	26	44	0	56
Midlands	96	2	2	4	82	14	–	–	–
North Urban	85	4	11	10	73	17	4	21	75
Scotland/Wales	84	14	2	10	80	10	–	7	93
NATIONAL	89	6	5	8	79	13	16	9	75
Same									
London	76	7	17	0	92	8	25	17	58
South	78	5	17	7	63	30	19	3	78
Midlands	81	3	16	0	81	19	10	10	80
North Urban	81	6	13	3	84	13	12	24	64
Scotland/Wales	89	4	7	0	93	7	9	4	87
NATIONAL	80	5	15	2	83	15	14	10	76
Worse									
London	–	–	–	0	92	8	–	–	–
South	46	15	39	6	82	12	–	–	–
Midlands	–	–	–	–	–	–	–	–	–
North Urban	–	–	–	3	88	9	–	–	–
Scotland/Wales	–	–	–	7	93	0	–	–	–
NATIONAL	43	20	37	4	88	8	4	15	81

* See Table 6.38

To a large degree, these are probably closely allied to the locational influences on the processes of political socialisation that stimulate party identification, but whereas those are long-term processes the ones we identify here are closely allied to contemporary conditions. Regarding the link to economic optimism, again we have provided firm evidence of regional variations in 1979, 1983 and 1987 in levels of voter satisfaction and economic optimism.

Those links are crucial because they are major influences on voter choice and, in particular, voters' decisions to switch their affiliation between elections. The data that we have suggested indicate that voter satisfaction/optimism was a major (probably *the* major) influence on changing patterns of voting over the period considered. Because there was a clear geography to satisfaction/optimism – linked to the country's contemporary economic geography – then the changing geography of voting can be identified as a product of the country's changing geography of economic and social well-being.

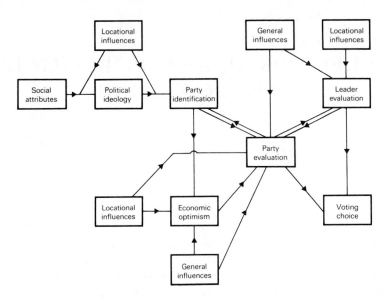

Figure 6.3 A revised model of British voting behaviour, 1979–1987.

In many ways, this is the crucial research finding of the present book since we have been able to provide a firm link between aggregate studies of voting patterns on the one hand and individual studies of voting decisions on the other. In doing that we have not only countered the arguments of McAllister and others regarding the need for spatial analysis of voting and the presence of important locational influences, but have provided a convincing argument for the causes of the changing electoral geography which, as we noted in the Introduction, concern so many contemporary commentators. Research into this field has been set in new and, we believe, fertile directions by these analyses, for they provide a first important means of linking the study of behaviour to the study of its outcome.

7

ELECTORAL AND POLITICAL IMPLICATIONS

Our analyses here have shown, unequivocally, that there were marked shifts in the geography of voting in Great Britain over the period 1979–1987. At the simplest and grossest level of generalisation, those shifts can be characterised by the dichotomy represented by the north:south divide, but there has been much more to the changing electoral geography of Britain than a straight-forward widening of the gap along the Plymouth-Hull line. We have shown, for example, that within the south there has been a substantial change in voting behaviour in the more rural areas (away from Conservative and towards the Alliance), whereas within the north the fortunes of the Labour party have been rosier in some areas (Merseyside, South Yorkshire, Strathclyde, and South Wales, for example) than others (such as the Textile Towns).

As well as describing the changing geography of voting in substantial detail we have also provided major insights to the reasons for the changes. Those insights stress the role of the local context as an influence on voting behaviour. In the past, studies of local context have emphasised the role of the social milieu as the environment within which people discuss politics and influence each other – discussions involving 'families, neighbours, friends and work-mates' (Harrop and Miller, 1987, p. 207). We do not doubt the important role of such conversations in the processes of political socialisation, by which people learn their political ideologies and attitudes, though the role of political parties and other agents in those local socialisation processes is often understated (Johnston, 1986c, 1986d). What we focus on here, however, is a set of local influences that may be mediated and enhanced by social interaction, but not necessarily so. Those influences are concerned with the local material environment. People learn about that through observation and messages delivered via the mass media (both local and national). Their understanding of the local environment influences their evaluation of political parties – their records when (and if) they are in power (nationally and, importantly to many people, locally) and the plausibility of the policies offered in their election manifestos. Talking to other locals may influence their evaluations, but such interaction is not necessary to a model of voting behaviour (as presented in Chapter 6) which sees people making their voting decision on local as well as national criteria.

The analyses reported in Chapters 4–6 contain a great deal of detail. In summary, however, they suggest the following sequence of points as a general description of changes in the geography of voting in Great Britain over the period 1979–1987.

1.   People are socialised into particular sets of political attitudes that reflect their occupational class origins and the local contexts within which they learn the political meanings of their class positions. This produces the general pattern of voting by occupational class that is known as the class cleavage. That cleavage is far from complete, because of a variety of other influences, but it remains the single most important influence on the development of political attitudes and the identification of voters with particular political parties that follows.

2.   Because the milieux in which people are socialised vary considerably, the processes do not produce the same outcome in every place, thereby resulting in a geography of the class cleavage. The major geographical variation is reflected in a general emphasis on the dominant local ideology so that, for example, in areas where an ideology closely linked to the Labour party dominates, people are more likely to be Labour identifiers than in areas where that ideology is relatively weaker. Areas with strong Labour ideologies, and thus large percentages of their populations politically (though not necessarily formally) affiliated to Labour, are mostly areas where the occupational class which favours Labour is most numerous, but this is not always the case. Certain areas (e.g. most of the coalfields) are even more pro-Labour than one would expect; others are less.

3.   Although they are able to identify themselves as closer to one party than another ideologically, an increasingly large proportion of the British electorate is not willing to give that party its support habitually. Instead they evaluate its record, its policies, and its leaders (relative to those on offer from the other parties) before deciding whether to vote for it at any particular election. The major reason for shifts in voting – if not in long-term allegiance – appears to have been people's economic optimism in recent years; the more satisfied people have been with both the national economic performance and their own circumstances in recent months, and the more optimistic they are about national and personal trends in the immediate future, the more likely they are to vote for the party of the incumbent government. Other factors, such as evaluation of the party leaders, influence the degree to which people are prepared to vote for one party or another in the context of these evaluations, but overall voting appears to be predicated on a combination of both long-term partisan identification and short-term political evaluation.

4.   Over the period 1979–1987 there have been major changes, identified in analyses of both geographical and functional regions, to Britain's electoral geography. A major reason for these changes appears to be the growing socio-economic polarisation of Britain; the divide between the relatively prosperous and the relatively deprived areas, on a range of indicators of social and economic well-being, is widening, and people are reacting to this. In the regions

of relative affluence, they are more prepared to vote for the party in power, as a reward for policies that have helped to produce that affluence which they and their neighbours are enjoying, and as a statement of faith that continuation of those policies is the best of the available courses for sustaining and enhancing the affluence. For the residents of the regions of relative deprivation, on the other hand, a vote against the government is more likely, because its policies can be blamed for either or both of the origins of the deprivation and the failure to remove it. People who themselves are not suffering, or are suffering less than others, may nevertheless identify the problems they see around them with that policy failure, and be prepared to vote, along with those who clearly are suffering, for the policies offered by an opposition party.

5.   The changing geography of voting in Britain is thus a reflection of the geography of economic and social well-being. At its simplest, it is represented by growing support for the Conservative party in 1983 and 1987 in the more affluent regions and for Labour in the more deprived. But there are variations around that theme. Within the deprived regions, for example, there are areas where the willingness to vote Labour is greater than it is in others, in part it seems because of the long tradition of Labour support and organisation there. And in the affluent regions, those less satisfied with the Conservative governments have been more prepared to vote for the Alliance than for Labour.

This brief sketch of our findings provides the context for this final chapter, in which we look at the electoral and political implications of the changes that we have described. This is done in two main sections. The first looks at the electoral implications and the second at the political; the two are, of course, linked but by separating them we are able to focus separately in the short- and the long-term.

THE CHANGING GEOGRAPHY OF PARTY COMPETITION

In a major article, following up their seminal contribution to the understanding of the changing electoral geography of Britain, Curtice and Steed (1986) have explained the implications of the growing spatial polarisation of support for at least two of the main political parties – Conservative and Labour. Their thesis is that in the past, when British politics were dominated by those two parties, what they call the 'exaggerative qualities' of the British electoral system (as represented mathematically by the cube law: Gudgin and Taylor, 1979) led to two main consequences: the inability of small parties to win seats commensurate with the votes that they got, as a percentage of the national total; and the benefits that one of the largest parties (usually the largest in terms of votes won) received relative to the others. The result was that one of the two largest parties almost always won a majority of the seats in Parliament despite not getting a majority of the votes cast; this did not lead to permanent power for that party, however, because a relatively small swing in voters from one of the two largest parties to the other was exaggerated in the distribution of seats, so that with two parties fairly close in the number of votes won power was likely to change hands to reflect changing voter preferences. (See Gudgin and Taylor, 1979, for amplification of this point, and Taylor, 1984b, for an analysis of recent British results in this context.)

Curtice and Steed conclude, from analysis of the 1983 results and the trends to that date, that

> the single member plurality electoral system has now almost lost its ability to exaggerate the relative electoral strength of the Conservative and Labour parties in terms of the seats that they win (p. 218)

But, at the same time, the changing geography of voting has resulted in

> substantial exaggeration of the lead of one party over another in any particular region (p. 218)

(See also Johnston, 1985b.) This point is similarly made and reinforced by the 1987 results presented in Tables 1.3 and 1.4. Increasingly, the southern regions of Britain return only Conservative MPs whereas the northern regions return Labour MPs in greater proportions.

If the exaggerative processes typical of the cube law were to operate in each region of Britain, this recent polarisation trend would be of little long-term importance (though it may be a short-term issue, since any government is likely to be dominated by members representing one part of Britain only; currently the Conservative party has virtually a majority in the House of Commons from the regions south and east of the Plymouth-Hull line). But the cube law does not apply in the regions, for two reasons. First, as Johnston and Rossiter (1982) have shown, the way in which British parliamentary constituencies are defined, and the social geography on which they are imposed, determines that the largest party will have an almost certain majority of the seats in each place, whatever the swing against it, whilst it remains the largest. Secondly, the voting trends in recent years have exaggerated this in two ways: first, the smaller of the two largest parties (Conservative and Labour) in each area has tended to lose its relative share of the votes there; and secondly, the growth of third parties (especially the Alliance) has tended to split the opposition vote to the largest party, thereby protecting its hold on most seats.

Curtice and Steed have examined the trend in the number of marginal seats, constituencies where the gap between the two leading parties is small and where a relatively small shift in voting preferences between the two could result in the seat changing hands. They show that the number has declined, and is likely to continue to do so, suggesting that there are only

> about 20–30 seats (4 per cent of all seats) which are likely to remain marginal in the foreseeable future even if there is a strong continuation of the North/South urban/rural variation in swing. (p. 217)

Most of those seats are in three areas: the region that we term Rest of the Northwest here; the borders between Inner and Outer London; and medium-sized cities (such as Nottingham and Southampton) in southern England.

The Changing Geography of Inter-Party Competition

Our analyses here extend Curtice and Steed's work, and incorporate the 1987 results. We start by looking at the geography of inter-party competition by focusing on which are the two main parties in each constituency, and on the situation of the third.

Figures 7.1–7.6 show for each of the three elections the geography of the seats won by Conservative and Labour and of the parties that came second in those seats. Regarding the seats won by the Conservatives, we see a major change. In 1979, the Labour party was the main challenger to the Conservatives in most parts of Britain. (Recall that the 1979 results are the national ones for the 1983 constituencies: p. 1.) The Alliance (i.e. the Liberal party) provided the second-placed candidate in much of Devon and Cornwall, Wessex and Hampshire, but in Kent, the northern Home Counties, London and most of northern Britain (with the exception of the far north of Scotland), Labour candidates occupied the runner-up positions. Four years later the situation had changed quite dramatically, with the Alliance parties providing the runner-up in most of the southern constituencies won by the Conservatives, including Greater London (Figure 7.2); only in Lancashire and parts of the Midlands was a Labour candidate likely to come second. In 1987, the Labour party regained ground in some northern and midland constituencies, plus a few in the south, and once more provided a majority of the second-place getters in Greater London (Figure 7.3). Overall, however, there is a clear trend over the period of the Alliance providing the main challenger to the Conservative party, especially in its southern Britain strongholds.

The problem faced by the Labour party in those southern constituencies is made even clearer by Figures 7.4–7.6, which show the constituencies where that party's candidates lost deposits at each election (notionally in 1979). According to the electoral law, each candidate had to pay a deposit when filing nomination papers, of £150 in 1979 and 1983, and £500 in 1987; this deposit was returned if the candidate obtained at least 12.5 per cent of the votes cast. Labour lost only 20 deposits at the (notional) 1979 election (at the 'real' election, it lost 21), mainly in rural areas and with a substantial block in southwest England (Figure 7.4). Four years later it lost 119, an unprecedented number (the previous maximum was 35, in 1925; Butler and Kavanagh, 1984, p. 119). The great majority of these were in southern England, especially in Cornwall, Devon, Dorset, Hampshire and Surrey (Figure 7.5). That was the nadir, but in 1987 it still lost 94, with the great majority even more concentrated in the south (Figure 7.6).

Labour's decline in the south of Britain was clearly very substantial. A major beneficiary was the Alliance. In 1979, the Liberal party lost a large number of deposits (Figure 7.7). The seats where this occurred were mainly in the northern regions, but there was a not insignificant number of constituencies in southern England, including a substantial majority of those in Greater London, where it failed to win one-eighth of the votes cast. Four years later it lost just ten, only two of them in either southern England or the

Alliance second

Labour second

Figure 7.1 The runner-up in seats won by the Conservative party, 1979.

Figure 7.2 The runner-up in seats won by the Conservative party, 1983.

Alliance second

Labour second

Figure 7.3 The runner-up in seats won by the Conservative party, 1987.

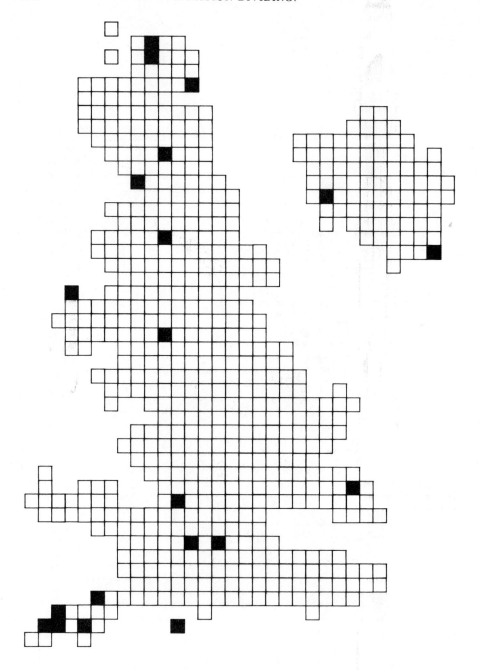

Figure 7.4 Seats where the Labour party lost its deposit, 1979.

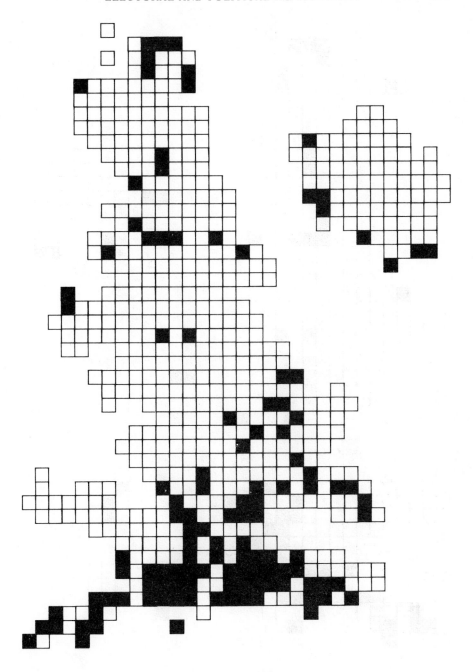

Figure 7.5 Seats where the Labour party lost its deposit, 1983.

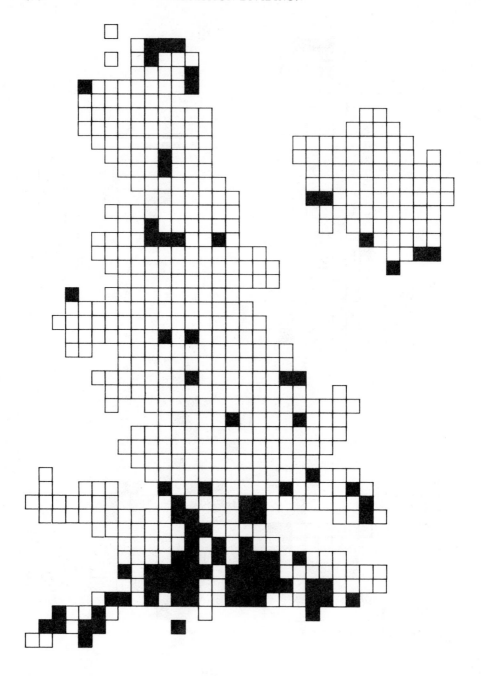

Figure 7.6 Seats where the Labour party lost its deposit, 1987.

Figure 7.7 Seats where the Alliance lost its deposit, 1979.

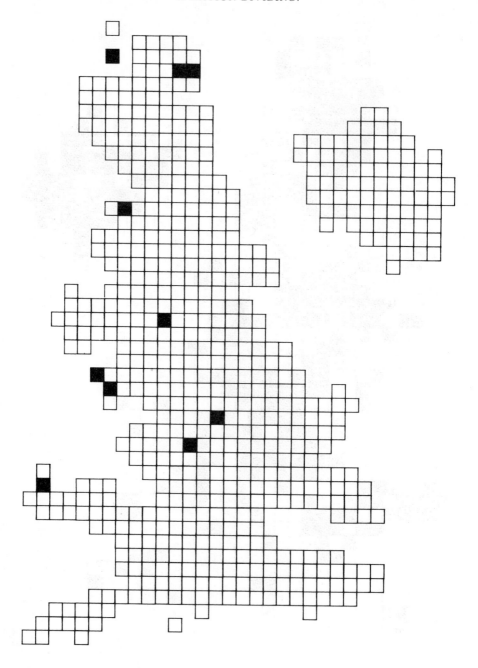

Figure 7.8 Seats where the Alliance lost its deposit, 1983.

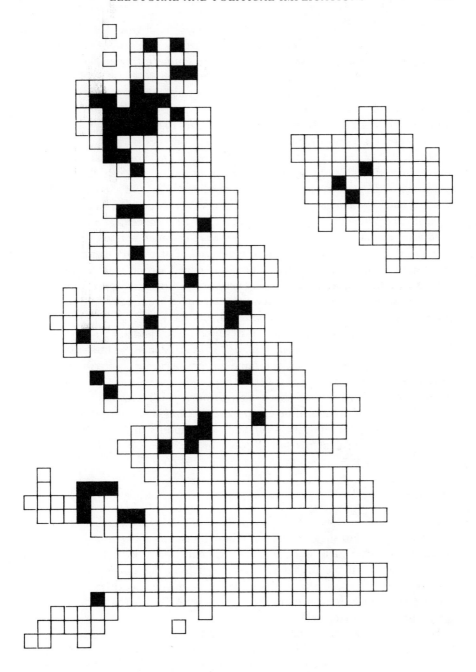

Figure 7.9 Seats where the Alliance lost its deposit, 1987.

midlands (one each in Walsall and West Bromwich: Figure 7.8). In 1987, it lost 54, including a very large block in Strathclyde. Apart from three inner London seats, it had all its deposits returned in southern England (Figure 7.9).

The patterns outlined so far suggest that in much of southern England the main electoral competition has become a contest between the Conservative and Alliance parties, with the Labour party a very poor third in many cases. But what of the position further north, where the Labour party has won the majority of seats in most regions? In 1979, the Conservative party came second in all but one of the Labour-won seats (Greenock and Port Glasgow, where it was estimated – BBC/ITN, 1983 – to win only 10 per cent of the votes, compared to 27 per cent for the Liberal candidate). By 1983, however (Figure 7.10), it had been relegated to third place in 45 constituencies, most of them in Scotland and Wales; the main (albeit minor) English concentrations of Alliance candidates coming second to Labour then were in Inner London, South York-shire, and parts of Tyneside (where several of the SDP candidates were ex-Labour MPs). Conservative candidates regained second place in 13 constit-uencies in 1987 (Figure 7.11), leaving very few in England (apart from a small concentration in Merseyside where Conservative candidates did especially badly) where the Alliance ran second to Labour.

Whereas the Labour party has lost support substantially in the areas of Conservative dominance, being replaced by the Alliance as the main chal-lenger in many constituencies, the same has not occurred to anything like the same extent in the Labour-held seats. There the Conservatives have remained the main contestants in most cases. Furthermore, the Tories have not suffered the widespread substantial drop in support that has characterised the Labour party. Only two Conservative candidates lost deposits in 1979, five in 1983, and 14 in 1987. (All of the lost deposits in 1987 were in either Scotland – mainly Strathclyde – or South Wales: Figure 7.12.)

Marginality

The descriptions in the above section show the changing pattern of winners and challengers, and suggest that, on a broad scale, elections in the south have become a Conservative:Alliance affair in many seats, with Labour a poor third, whereas in the north they are more likely to be dominated by the Labour and Conservative contestants, with Alliance candidates occupying respectable third places. But how secure are the seat-holders? To answer this, we look at the geography of marginality.

Figures 7.13 and 7.14 provide a general picture that suggests that, as Curtice and Steed argued, incumbent parties are becoming increasingly secure in their tenure. The histograms refer, respectively, to all of the seats won by Conservative and by Labour.

In the Conservative-won seats (Figure 7.13) the situation with regard to Labour challengers is that although the number of very marginal seats (a Conservative:Labour gap of less than five percentage points) increased slightly between 1979 and 1987 (with a peak in 1983), for the remainder the gap

Alliance second

Conservative second

Figure 7.10 The runner-up in seats won by the Labour party, 1983.

Figure 7.11 The runner-up in seats won by the Labour party, 1987.

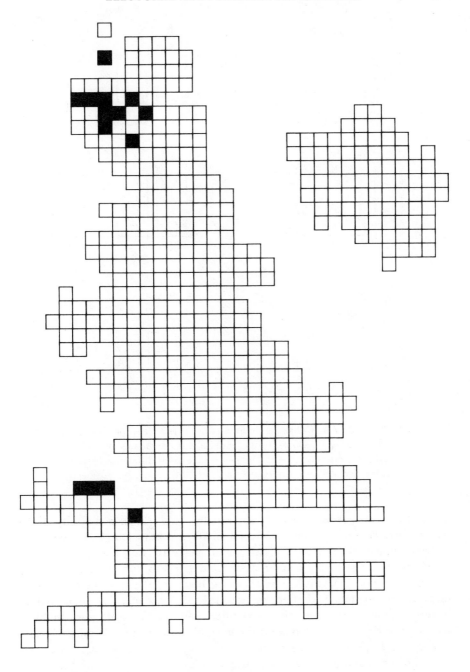

Figure 7.12 Seats where the Conservative party lost its deposit, 1987.

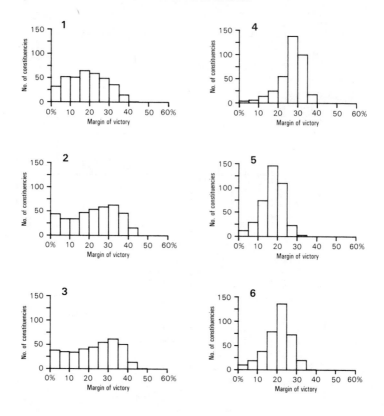

Figure 7.13 Marginality in Conservative-held seats. (1)-(3) The percentage point difference between Conservative and Labour candidates in 1979, 1983 and
1987, respectively; (4)-(6) The percentage point difference between Conservative and Alliance candidates in 1979, 1983 and 1987, respectively.

between the two parties widened substantially. In 1979, in a majority of the
seats the gap between the two was less than 20 percentage points; by 1987, the
gap was greater than that in a substantial majority. For Labour, it seems,
unless its challenge to the Conservative candidate was very credible, and the
chances of victory with only a small swing high, its ability to pose a serious
threat to the incumbent declined substantially. In part that was countered by
increased Conservative:Alliance competition; but only in small part. In 1979,
the distance between the Conservative incumbent and the Liberal challenger
was at least 25 percentage points in the great majority of seats. Four years later
the majority of Alliance candidates came within 20 points of the Tory. The
same was true in 1987, but the majority was smaller. Most Conservative
candidates were under little threat from the Alliance, however: in 1983, the
gap between the two was less than 10 points in only about 75 constituencies,
and less than 5 in fewer than 25; in 1987, the Conservative lead over the
Alliance exceeded ten points in all but some 60 constituencies.

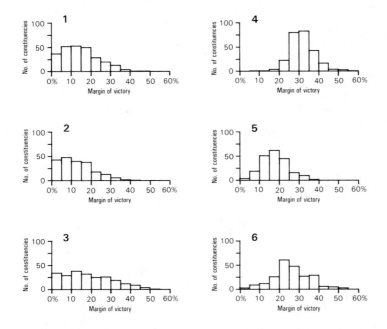

Figure 7.14 Marginality in Labour-held seats. (1)-(3) The percentage point difference between Labour and Conservative candidates in 1979, 1983 and 1987 respectively; (4)-(6) The percentage point difference between Labour and Alliance candidates in 1979, 1983 and 1987, respectively.

Turning to the Labour-held seats (Figure 7.14) the same general trends can be seen over the period as a whole. The number of constituencies in which the Conservative candidate came within ten percentage points of the Labour share of the vote fell very sharply between 1979 and 1987, with an increasing number showing a separation between the two of 30 percentage points or more. Between those dates, Conservative candidates closed the gap on the Labour incumbents in a considerable number of seats in 1983, but the general Labour recovery in 1987 clearly saw many of those Tory challenges wither. Between 1979 and 1983 the Alliance challenge to Labour also closed the gap substantially; at the former date the average gap between Labour and Alliance was some 35 percentage points, whereas four years later it was about 18. But the gap did not continue to close; in 1987, the average was about 25 points and Alliance candidates were within five points of the Labour incumbents in only a small handful of seats.

We can illustrate three-party competition using the triangular graph, as shown in Figure 7.15. On this, if the horizontal axis of the isosceles triangle is the percentage of those voting for one of the three parties who voted Conservative and the vertical axis is the percentage who voted Labour, then the third

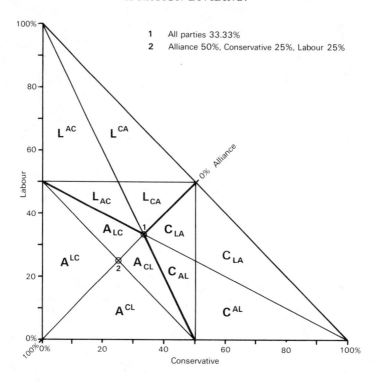

Figure 7.15 The electoral triangle. (For a description of the terms, see text.).

axis, the hypotenuse of the triangle, is the percentage who voted Alliance. The triangle can then be divided into three 'regions', the boundaries of which (shown by the solid lines in Figure 7.15) converge on the point where each party has one-third of the votes and each of which meets one of the three axes at the 50 per cent mark. These are the three regions where one party is the victor. Those marked by the capital letter C in the figure are where the Conservative party wins. Where the other parties (A and L) are given as superscripts – e.g. C^{AL} – the Conservative party wins with an absolute major-ity (over 50 per cent) of the votes cast; where they are marked by subscripts – e.g. C_{AL} – the Conservative party wins with a plurality of the votes (i.e. the largest percentage) but not a majority. The order of the subscripts/superscripts indicates which party came second and which third. (Thus L^{AC} is the region in which Labour wins with an absolute majority, with Alliance second and Conservative third.)

Our interest here is clearly in the relative density of constituencies in the various regions of the electoral triangle and in their proximity to the solid lines demarcating regional boundaries; the closer a constituency is to one of those lines, the more marginal it is. Figures 7.16–7.18 are the electoral triangles for the three elections, and provide further evidence of the changing pattern of party competition. Thus in 1979 most constituencies were a long way from the

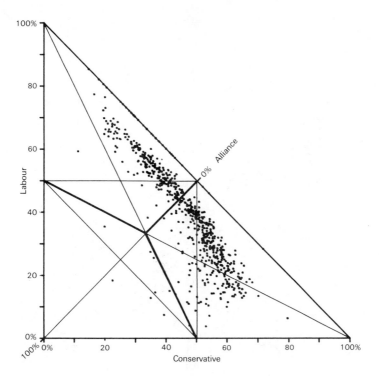

Figure 7.16 The electoral triangle for 1979.

boundaries of the A region, indicating that the Alliance needed a major swing
to win many seats. There were also relatively few close to the CL border,
although there were more on the L side close to it than on the C side,
indicating a larger number of easily lost Labour seats. Within the L region,
few were close to the region dividing CA constituencies from AC, indicating
that the Alliance was weak in most; there were many more on the Alliance side
of the AL:LA line in the Conservative region, and a large number close to it
on the LA side, indicating the vulnerability of Labour's second place in many
cases.

The situation in 1983 (Figure 7.17) saw a general shift in the distribution of
constituencies towards the AC and AL regional borders as a consequence of
the growth in the Alliance vote, though relatively few came very close to those
borders: the Alliance's success across a wide spectrum of constituencies in
winning about one-quarter of all votes cast meant that it still needed a major
shift in a large number in order to win seats. The border between the C and L
regions had fewer constituencies close to it than was the case in 1979, indicating the growing safety of the Labour and Conservative incumbents from the
others' challengers.

There is a major distinction to be drawn between the C and L regions,
however. In the former, a majority of the constituencies are in the AL rather

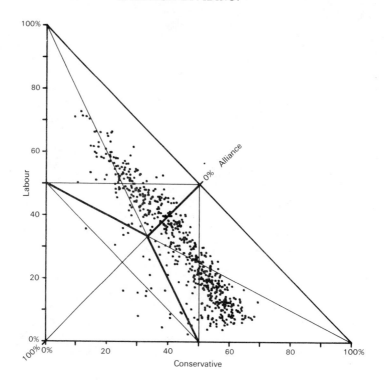

Figure 7.17 The electoral triangle for 1983.

than the LA subregion, whereas in the L region, many more are in the CA than the AC. In the Conservative-held seats there was a major shift away from Labour and towards the Alliance between 1979 and 1983, therefore, whereas the Conservative party remained in second place in most Labour-held constituencies, albeit only just in many.

Figure 7.18 shows that in 1987 there was a shift away from the major regional boundaries involving the Alliance, though the CL frontier area became slightly more populated than it was in 1983. As in 1983, however, the Alliance remained more successful in 1987 in the Conservative-held than in the Labour-held seats.

This sequence of electoral triangles further illuminates the basic argument of Curtice and Steed that overall marginality is declining as a characteristic of the British electoral system. The Conservative and Labour parties are relatively safe in the great majority of constituencies that they hold now, and it will take a major shift in voting patterns for a large number of seats to change hands, especially if the Alliance is to be more successful than it has been at the last three elections. Very few constituencies indeed are truly competitive for all three parties – i.e. are close to the point where the boundaries of all three regions meet. The competition between the parties at the national scale, as

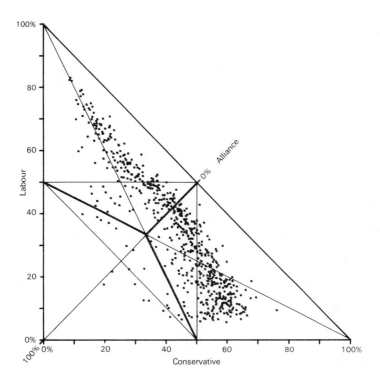

Figure 7.18 The electoral triangle for 1987.

reflected in their standing in national opinion polls and voting returns, is not mimicked in most constituencies, therefore. Instead, we have a large number of very different competitive situations.

The Geography of Marginality

Are those different types of contest found in different parts of the country? Table 7.1 shows the number of constituencies after each election according to the distance between the winning and second-placed parties, and indicates that: the Alliance rarely did well in Labour-held seats; and Labour's hold in second place has declined in Conservative-held seats. These suggest a geography of marginality, which is mapped out in Figures 7.19–7.26. (In these maps – which show 1979 and 1987 only – the differences between the winning party and one other are shown, irrespective of which came second; non-voters are included.)

The decline in the Labour challenge to the Conservatives in the south is clearly shown by Figures 7.19–7.20, with an increasing number of constituencies where the distance between the two is 40 percentage points or more. Further north, the Conservative hold is less secure, except in the block of seats

Table 7.1 Marginality after Each Election

Conservative-Won Seats

Percentage Difference First:Second	Alliance Second			Labour Second		
	1979	1983	1987	1979	1983	1987
0 – 5	4	12	10	31	42	37
6 – 10	6	20	18	53	30	33
11 – 15	9	36	32	45	23	29
16 – 20	11	90	44	59	24	25
21 – 25	20	83	71	46	7	19
26 – 30	18	20	40	26	0	1
31 or greater	12	3	14	12	0	0
TOTAL	80	264	229	268	126	144

Labour-Won Seats

Percentage Difference First:Second	Alliance Second			Conservative Second		
	1979	1983	1987	1979	1983	1987
0 – 5	0	3	3	37	40	34
6 – 10	0	5	9	51	41	27
11 – 15	0	12	1	46	38	35
16 – 20	0	5	2	47	20	25
21 – 25	1	9	3	27	15	20
26 – 30	0	7	4	22	5	18
31 or greater	0	6	8	21	2	29
TOTAL	1	47	30	251	161	188

in the Blackpool-Scarborough belt. This is countered by the closing gap between Conservative and Alliance candidates in most parts of the south (Figures 7.21, 7.22). In the north, over the same period, the Labour-Conservative gap generally widened (Figure 7.23, 7.24), with relatively little change in its advantage over the Alliance (Figures 7.25, 7.26).

Analyses of variance have been conducted on the inter-regional variability in marginality levels, according to which party won each seat and which came second. Looking first at the seats won by the Conservative party, the major change (especially between 1979 and 1983) is in the number of constituencies where the Alliance displaced the Labour party from second position (Tables 7.2, 7.3). Only four geographical regions (Industrial Northeast, West Yorkshire, Industrial South Wales, and Inner London) had no decline in the number of Conservative-won seats with Labour in second place; all of the others saw substantial Alliance gains (except in the West Midlands conurbation where the shift was relatively slight: Table 7.2). The same was true in many of the functional regions where the Conservatives won seats; it was only in some of the urban types (City Service; Recent Growth; Stable Industrial; Metropolitan

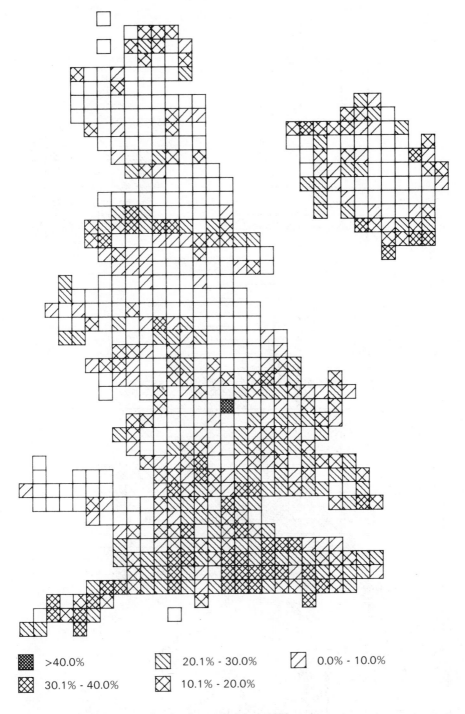

Figure 7.19 The Conservative lead over Labour, 1979.

Figure 7.20 The Conservative lead over Labour, 1987.

Figure 7.21 The Conservative lead over Alliance, 1979.

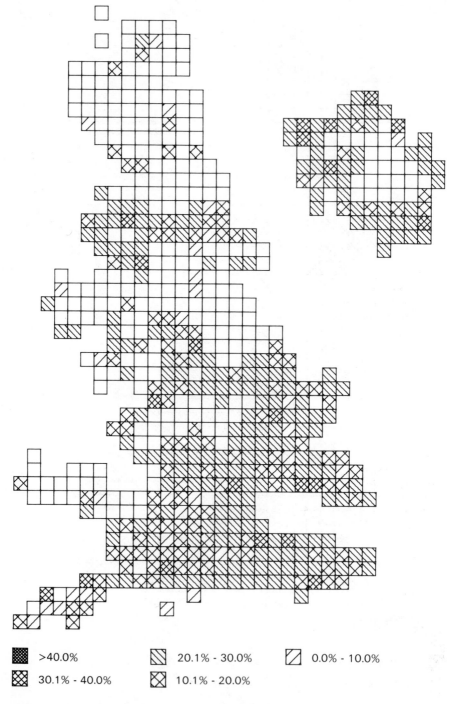

▓	>40.0%	▧	20.1% - 30.0%	▨	0.0% - 10.0%
▩	30.1% - 40.0%	▧	10.1% - 20.0%		

Figure 7.22 The Conservative lead over Alliance, 1987.

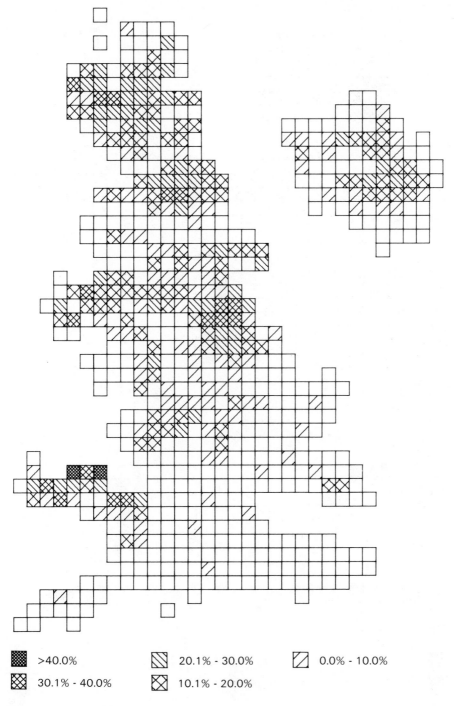

Figure 7.23 The Labour lead over Conservative, 1979.

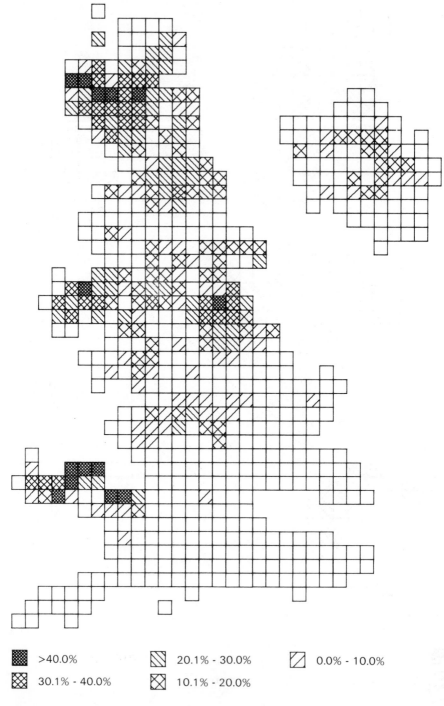

Figure 7.24 The Labour lead over Conservative, 1987.

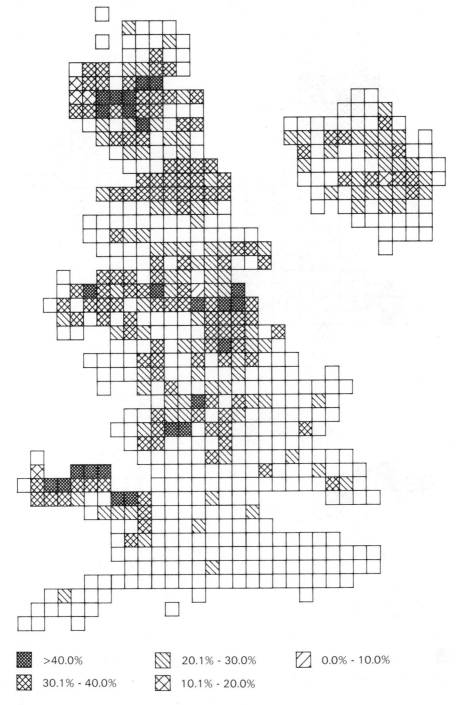

▓ >40.0%	◩ 20.1% - 30.0%	◪ 0.0% - 10.0%
▨ 30.1% - 40.0%	▧ 10.1% - 20.0%	

Figure 7.25 The Labour lead over the Alliance, 1979.

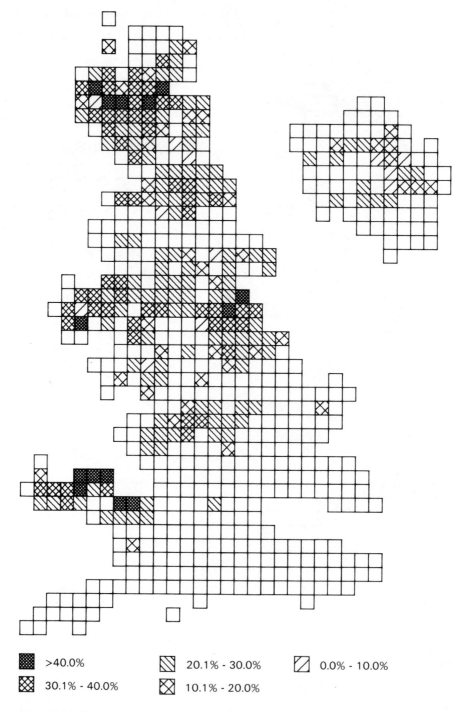

▓	>40.0%	▨ 20.1% - 30.0%	◩ 0.0% - 10.0%
⊠	30.1% - 40.0%	⊠ 10.1% - 20.0%	

Figure 7.26 The Labour lead over the Alliance, 1987.

Table 7.2 Average Marginality by Party in Second Place and Geographical Region: Conservative-Held Seats*

Election	1979		1983		1987	
Second Party	Labour	Alliance	Labour	Alliance	Labour	Alliance
Strathclyde	10.7(4)	–	7.8(2)	7.9(3)	0.3(1)	9.7(1)
E. Scotland	6.5(5)	0.4(1)	7.0(2)	4.9(3)	4.0(2)	2.0(1)
Rural Scotland	10.2(3)	12.6(2)	6.3(1)	10.4(4)	12.6(1)	3.2(1)
Rural North	18.5(10)	24.7(5)	4.1(3)	21.8(14)	8.4(3)	20.3(13)
Industrial Northeast	8.5(3)	–	7.4(4)	–	3.4(3)	1.0(1)
Merseyside	15.7(6)	9.3(1)	9.8(1)	14.7(4)	12.7(3)	8.2(1)
Greater Manchester	9.4(9)	22.1(2)	6.4(6)	11.3(5)	6.6(6)	12.2(4)
Rest of Northwest	14.8(19)	–	12.0(11)	20.9(9)	7.8(13)	21.9(7)
West Yorks.	10.6(6)	13.6(1)	4.2(6)	12.4(5)	6.6(4)	10.1(5)
South Yorks.	25.4(1)	–	–	16.2(1)	–	10.3(1)
Rural Wales	9.1(7)	4.3(1)	14.1(3)	9.1(3)	9.3(3)	5.7(1)
Industrial South Wales	8.8(4)	–	5.9(4)	11.9(3)	11.1(4)	–
W. Midlands Conurbation	11.9(13)	38.6(1)	11.4(10)	22.5(4)	10.5(13)	28.6(2)
Rest of West Midlands	13.8(13)	18.2(6)	12.6(7)	17.6(15)	16.1(9)	17.7(12)
East Midlands	17.3(21)	13.7(2)	9.0(17)	20.5(16)	13.5(17)	22.6(13)
East Anglia	14.5(16)	22.8(1)	12.3(5)	18.3(13)	11.0(8)	20.0(14)
Devon and Cornwall	17.9(5)	18.1(9)	–	14.4(14)	6.6(14)	13.2(13)
Wessex	18.1(15)	18.8(13)	6.5(5)	16.0(25)	9.7(25)	16.1(24)
Inner London	9.4(10)	–	6.9(10)	21.0(2)	6.6(11)	23.9(2)
Outer London	16.4(32)	22.7(6)	12.4(15)	17.6(29)	15.3(23)	23.0(22)
Outer Metropolitan	19.6(40)	24.7(15)	11.6(10)	19.3(50)	11.6(11)	22.9(50)
Outer Southeast	18.1(30)	28.3(14)	10.9(4)	19.6(42)	11.8(5)	20.1(41)
R^2	0.19	0.47	0.19	0.28	0.26	0.33

* The figures in parentheses refer to the number of constituencies

Industrial) that the Labour party retained second place in a majority of the Tory-held seats (Table 7.3), suggesting that the Alliance was least able to outflank Labour in the more industrial areas.

Tables 7.2 and 7.3 also show that the Alliance was more likely to displace Labour from the runner-up position in constituencies where the Conservative majority over Labour was a large one. Labour held on to second place in the more marginal seats, but lost in those where its cause was much less hopeful. Thus in the East Midlands, for example, the average Conservative majority in 1979 was 17.3 percentage points in the 21 seats where Labour came second; in 1983, when Labour came second in 17, the average distance was only 9.0 points, whereas in those where the Alliance came second the average increased from 13.7 in 1979 to 20.5 in 1983. In general, then, the Alliance has displaced Labour from second spot in many seats in southern England and the more prosperous functional regions, but has not made substantial inroads to Conser-

Table 7.3 Average Marginality by Party in Second Place and Functional Region: in Conservative-Held Seats*

Election Second Place	1979		1983		1987	
	Labour	Alliance	Labour	Alliance	Labour	Alliance
I.C./Immig.	2.4(1)	–	0.1(1)	7.0(1)	7.0(1)	–
Ind./Immig.	1.3(1)	–	3.7(4)	–	5.3(3)	–
Poorest Immig.	–	–	–	. –	–	–
Intermed. Ind.	7.7(4)	–	7.2(9)	–	7.0(11)	–
Old Indust./Mining	3.6(1)	–	8.0(4)	–	8.8(4)	–
Textile	3.9(1)	–	4.6(7)	11.2(1)	5.5(6)	2.4(1)
Poorest Domestic	–	–	–	–	–	–
Conurb. L.A.	5.2(5)	–	3.7(5)	–	3.3(4)	–
Black Co.	–	–	–	–	0.3(1)	–
Maritime Ind.	1.1(1)	–	0.9(1)	–	–	–
Poor I.C.	–	–	2.1(1)	–	0.7(1)	–
Clydeside	3.3(1)	–	–	–	–	–
Scott. Ind.	–	–	3.1(1)	–	–	–
Scott. Rural	14.8(2)	8.7(2)	–	10.4(4)	12.6(1)	3.2(1)
High Status I.M.	12.6(9)	–	7.3(6)	18.7(3)	7.8(5)	19.6(3)
I.M.	5.5(2)	–	9.5(2)	–	5.6(3)	–
Outer London	18.9(20)	27.7(4)	16.2(2)	19.1(22)	17.9(5)	24.7(19)
Very High Status	26.0(18)	28.2(13)	15.6(2)	21.5(29)	18.6(3)	23.7(28)
Conurb. W. Collar	14.1(22)	12.3(2)	7.9(6)	14.0(18)	11.7(7)	13.9(13)
City Service	11.0(13)	–	7.8(13)	14.6(5)	6.2(11)	14.1(4)
Resort/Retirement	21.6(13)	25.8(15)	17.6(1)	19.3(27)	14.0(3)	19.7(25)
Recent Growth	9.6(12)	7.9(1)	11.8(12)	17.5(3)	10.2(10)	16.6(5)
Stable Ind.	11.2(14)	–	12.3(13)	15.3(6)	13.2(14)	14.1(5)
Small Towns	14.0(23)	12.5(3)	14.7(8)	17.1(16)	12.7(11)	17.1(13)
Southern Urban	19.2(22)	16.1(2)	16.7(3)	18.8(21)	14.2(2)	21.3(22)
Modest Aff.	16.2(22)	16.1(2)	10.8(4)	19.2(21)	17.3(11)	18.9(13)
Met. Ind.	10.7(18)	–	10.4(16)	14.4(13)	14.9(21)	19.6(6)
Modest Aff. Scot.	10.4(5)	–	11.0(2)	9.6(3)	2.8(3)	9.7(1)
Rapid Growth	20.6(12)	16.9(4)	16.8(1)	18.6(15)	9.6(1)	22.8(15)
Prosperous/No Ind.	22.9(8)	20.9(11)	–	17.4(19)	6.6(1)	16.2(18)
Agricultural	17.6(19)	19.7(21)	16.4(2)	17.4(37)	8.1(1)	18.9(37)
R^2	0.42	0.39	0.36	0.17	0.43	0.23

* The figures in parentheses refer to the number of constituencies

vative support in many of them. The average distance between a Conservative victor and an Alliance runner-up increased in all of the southern regions except Devon and Cornwall between 1983 and 1987 (Table 7.2) but declined in most of the northern regions – where the Alliance came second in a few seats only. Of the functional regions, ten of those with Alliance candidates in second place saw an increase in the Conservative:Alliance gap between 1983 and 1987, whereas eight saw a decrease (Table 7.3); in some of those regions, then, the Alliance was making inroads to the Conservative hold, whereas in others it was not. Further, the amount of intra-regional variability in

Table 7.4 Average Marginality by Party in Second Place and Geographical Region: Labour-Held Seats*

Selection Second Party	1979		1983		1987	
	Con	Alliance	Con	Alliance	Con	Alliance
Strathclyde	20.4(26)	20.1(1)	19.3(14)	19.0(12)	24.9(17)	27.3(7)
E. Scotland	18.3(8)	–	13.7(7)	13.1(5)	20.0(11)	19.9(2)
Rural Scotland	17.9(2)	–	15.9(1)	14.5(1)	14.3(2)	25.8(1)
Rural North	11.4(10)	–	6.5(8)	–	10.4(9)	–
Industrial Northeast	18.0(24)	–	11.1(16)	13.4(6)	20.8(17)	14.9(6)
Merseyside	18.1(10)	–	17.1(11)	–	28.1(8)	27.1(3)
Greater Manchester	14.2(15)	–	11.0(15)	–	15.2(16)	–
Rest of Northwest	9.7(10)	–	8.4(8)	23.9(1)	15.7(9)	–
West Yorks.	13.6(16)	–	7.3(8)	19.6(2)	12.3(13)	7.1(1)
South Yorks.	22.7(14)	–	14.5(10)	20.6(4)	27.0(13)	4.3(1)
Rural Wales	19.0(3)	–	6.5(4)	–	11.8(5)	–
Industrial South Wales	25.2(19)	–	3.7(4)	27.0(12)	25.2(15)	37.4(3)
W. Midlands Conurbation	11.5(18)	–	8.5(18)	–	10.6(17)	–
Rest of West Midlands	11.2(7)	–	9.4(4)	–	8.8(4)	7.8(1)
East Midlands	8.5(18)	–	7.1(8)	–	5.3(10)	12.2(1)
East Anglia	4.6(2)	–	1.6(1)	–	0.5(1)	–
Devon and Cornwall	4.6(1)	–	–	–	–	–
Wessex	8.7(4)	–	6.1(1)	–	2.0(1)	–
Inner London	13.6(22)	–	9.2(4)	9.2(4)	11.1(13)	6.2(3)
Outer London	9.5(14)	–	9.6(8)	–	7.0(6)	8.1(1)
Outer Metropolitan	5.1(6)	–	2.6(1)	–	–	–
Outer Southeast	0.7(2)	–	–	–	2.1(1)	–
R^2	0.32	–	0.32	0.37	0.38	0.60

* The figures in parentheses refer to the number of constituencies

Conservative:Alliance margins increased, as shown by the R^2 values for both types of regions. With Labour the opposite was true, with increases in R^2 indicating greater inter-regional variability.

Turning to the seats won by Labour, the main differences clearly refer to 1983 and 1987 since the Alliance came second in only one such constituency in 1979 (Tables 7.4, 7.5). In terms of geographical regions the Alliance's main advances from 1979 to 1983 were in Scotland, the Industrial Northeast, South Yorkshire, Industrial South Wales, and Inner London; much of that ground was lost over the next four years in all but the Industrial Northeast (where the Alliance candidates included such prominent SDP members – and former Labour MPs – as Bill Rodgers, Mike Thomas, and Ian Wrigglesworth) and Inner London (where there were several Alliance successes in terms of winning seats as well as coming second). There is little evidence that the Alliance was

Table 7.5 Average Marginality by Party in Second Place and Functional Region:
Labour-Held Seats*

Election Second Place	1979		1983		1987	
	Con	Alliance	Con	Alliance	Con	Alliance
I.C./Immig.	14.6(7)	–	13.6(6)	–	10.5(6)	8.1(1)
Ind./Immig.	9.6(16)	–	7.4(13)	–	10.7(14)	–
Poorest Immig.	17.4(4)	–	16.3(4)	–	19.4(4)	–
Intermed. Ind.	11.5(26)	–	5.5(18)	11.1(3)	10.6(12)	14.7(7)
Old Indust./Mining	22.4(33)	–	12.8(19)	27.2(11)	24.6(28)	34.4(2)
Textile	7.7(13)	–	7.0(8)	–	9.4(10)	–
Poorest Domestic	32.4(6)	–	12.8(2)	28.0(4)	22.8(3)	37.6(4)
Conurb. L.A.	18.3(21)	–	11.9(19)	22.6(1)	19.4(21)	7.1(1)
Black Co.	10.1(9)	–	5.8(9)	–	6.1(8)	–
Maritime Ind.	15.6(14)	–	11.5(13)	–	17.1(13)	39.8(1)
Poor I.C.	21.5(12)	–	19.1(6)	14.9(4)	24.5(8)	8.7(2)
Clydeside	24.5(13)	20.1(1)	17.9(7)	18.7(9)	27.6(8)	32.1(5)
Scott. Ind.	19.1(19)	–	17.6(14)	15.6(9)	26.0(16)	22.7(4)
Scott. Rural	11.9(2)	–	10.3(1)	–	15.5(1)	–
High Status I.M.	–	–	–	–	3.8(1)	–
I.M.	9.8(12)	–	8.1(10)	0.6(1)	9.3(9)	3.5(2)
Outer London	–	–	–	–	–	–
Very High Status	–	–	–	–	–	–
Conurb. W. Collar	–	–	–	–	3.5(4)	–
City Service	6.1(11)	–	4.0(1)	5.9(3)	9.6(1)	
Resort/Retirement	–	–	–	–	–	–
Recent Growth	10.1(6)	–	–	11.9(2)	13.8(2)	1.4(1)
Stable Ind.	11.2(12)	–	9.5(5)	16.3(2)	20.0(7)	–
Small Towns	9.1(1)	–	0.4(1)	–	1.5(1)	–
Southern Urban	–	–	–	–	–	–
Modest Aff.	10.0(2)	–	2.2(1)	–	8.7(2)	–
Met. Ind.	4.1(12)	–	–	2.9(1)	6.1(2)	9.2(1)
Modest Aff. Scot.	–	–	–	–	3.9(1)	–
Rapid Growth	–	–	–	–	–	–
Prosperous/No Ind.	–	–	–	–	–	–
Agricultural	–	–	18.1(1)	–	4.2(2)	–
R^2	0.46	–	0.39	0.50	0.42	0.82

* The figures in parentheses refer to the number of constituencies

more likely to displace Conservative candidates in the less winnable seats,
however. Of the functional regions (Table 7.5) the Alliance advance was
particularly concentrated in: the Intermediate Industrial areas, especially in
1987, when the Conservatives yielded second place in less winnable constituencies; the Poorest Domestic Conditions areas, where again it was the least
marginal seats in which the Alliance did relatively well; in the Poor Inner City
areas, where the Alliance was more successful in the more winnable seats; and
in the two Scottish regions of Clydeside and Industrial, where the Conservatives regained some of the ground lost in 1983 four years later, but where the
margins were overall very wide in any case.

Overall, therefore, we see quite significant regional variations in several
aspects of the marginality of seats, including the switch from one party to

another in the occupancy of second place. These trends have considerable significance for the parties' future strategies, which is the topic of our next, and final, discussion.

THE PARTIES IN THE FUTURE

Our analyses so far in this chapter have shown that the regional shifts in voting patterns over the period 1979–1987 have substantially altered the framework within which the parties will compete at the next election(s). The relatively small number of marginal seats means that the two challenging parties face a daunting task in seeking to demolish the Conservative party's majority in the House of Commons. In the 1960s, Harold Wilson claimed that Labour was 'the natural party of government'; could Margaret Thatcher claim the same for the Conservative party in the late 1980s, because its electoral hold looks unassailable?

We showed in the previous chapter that the main short-term influences on people's voting choices are their levels of satisfaction and optimism with the country's economic performance and their personal and household financial situations, their evaluations of the party leaders, and their opinions of the efficacy of the parties' policy manifestos. For the challengers to the incumbent government, therefore, their greatest hope must lie in either or both of a widespread economic recession and a lack of confidence in the Conservative leader at the time of the next election. These may create sufficient disenchantment for a major switch of votes away from the government (though the distribution of those votes between the competing beneficiaries could have an important influence on the result; after all, the Conservative party lost votes both between 1979 and 1983 and between 1983 and 1987). If those don't occur, then the opposition parties must create a situation where they win votes from Conservative supporters in 1987, not so much because of disenchantment with the government as because they have been convinced that things could be even better under either or both of Labour and the Alliance.

The findings about the geography of voting provide us with some insights into the issues that the Labour and Alliance parties have to face, and also to those confronting the Conservative party as it seeks to repulse those challenges. In discussing those issues, we assume that the party system remains unchanged, with two main challenges only – Labour and Alliance – to the apparent Conservative hegemony.

The Problems for Labour

Among the challengers, the major problem for Labour is not just winning more votes but winning them in sufficient numbers in enough places. As Table 7.1 shows, there were 70 seats where Labour came within ten percentage points of the Conservative winning total in 1987; if it won all of those, it would still trail the Conservatives by 15 seats in the House of Commons. If the

Alliance were also to win all 28 seats in which it came second to the Conservatives in 1987 by ten percentage points or less, then the Labour party would be the largest in Parliament, but without an absolute majority of MPs. To win such a majority, therefore, Labour must win a large number of seats where it currently comes a fairly poor second.

How can it do that? In the last few decades there has been much debate over Labour's long-term electoral future. After its third defeat in a row in 1959, the question being asked was 'Must Labour lose?' (see Abrams, Rose and Hinden, 1960). Victories in 1964 and 1966, and then two in 1974, provided the answer, but a further sequence of three defeats has raised the question again.

The basis of many arguments that Labour's electoral future is bleak is the change in Britain's social structure in recent decades. The party's enduring support has come from the manual (or working) classes, especially those in trades unions, and from the tenants of council houses. That support base has been shrinking, with the relative growth of the non-manual occupational classes (especially the professional and managerial groups, which expanded from 11 per cent of the workforce in 1951 to 25 per cent in 1981) and consequent decline of the manual classes, plus the expansion of home-ownership (from 30 per cent of all households in 1951 to 62 per cent in 1985: see Heath and McDonald, 1987). Non-manual workers and home-owners are much less likely to vote Labour than are manual workers and council tenants, so social change is leading to an erosion of Labour's support base.

The component of Labour's electoral foundation that has not substantially altered over recent decades is the number of trade unionists; Heath and McDonald (1987) show that the percentage of potential unionists (i.e. the employed workforce, excluding the self-employed and employers) was almost exactly the same in 1984 (at 45.8 per cent) as it was in 1951 (at 45.0 per cent). But the composition of the unionised workforce has changed very substantially, with the growth of 'white-collar unionism', notably in the public sector (such as the civil service and the health service).

Dunleavy (1980a) shows very high levels of unionisation in the public services (education, health, national and local government; almost entirely white-collar) as well as in the public corporations (coal, gas, railways, etc.) in 1974, sustaining his argument that

> there is *no* simple, unmediated relationship between unionization and occupational class. There are very large groups of manual workers who are barely unionized, and there are similarly a substantial minority of non-manual employees working in industries which are amongst the most unionized of any (p. 371)

The result is a substantial variety of production sectors, in which at least seven characteristics interact that produce a milieu that favours certain political attitudes: occupational class; work context; industry; level of technology; image of society; level of unionization; and unionateness (or union militancy).

Dunleavy's (1980b) analyses of 1974 survey data provide important explorations of the link between occupational class, sectoral location (he identifies five sectors: public corporations; public services; market sector manufacturing; corporate sector manufacturing; private sector industries), unionisation and political alignment. Importantly for the present analysis, his findings include: the absence of any significant relationship, within the wage-earning labour force, between occupational class and unionisation; greater unionisation in the public sector than in the market sector manufacturing and private sector services; and 'a significant and moderately strong association between union membership and an anti-Conservative/pro-Labour alignment' (p. 546). This leads him to conclude that

> The objective effect of the growth of the union/non-union cleavage . . . is apparently to strengthen support for Labour amongst the unionized minority of the electorate, while constituting a basis for anti-Labour voting amongst the non-unionized majority, including a minority of manual workers (p. 548)

Analyses of a survey of the electorate taken at the time of the 1983 general election led Dunleavy and Husbands (1985) to two conclusions: (1) that Labour had a substantial lead over Conservatives among unionised and non-working members of the manual class, but not among the non-unionised; and (2) that unionised non-manual workers in the public sector were markedly anti-Conservative, whereas the non-unionised were strongly pro-Conservative (among the unionised, however, the Alliance won more votes than the Labour party). Throughout the analysis, however, only three categories were shown as having a majority who voted Labour: women manual workers who were trade union members (52 per cent); public sector, not-working, manual workers (57 per cent); and not-working manual workers (50 per cent). There is little evidence, therefore, that the unions have delivered large blocks of votes to Labour in recent elections. (See also Webb, 1987, who shows that the link between union membership and voting weakened considerably between 1964 and 1983.)

Unfortunately, we know little of the geography of trade union membership and its link to voting, but it is likely that the highest degrees of unionisation in the public corporations and in the market sector are in the traditional heavy industrial areas of the north; these are likely to be the contexts in which most manual workers vote Labour also. It is strongly argued by many that the changing geography of manufacturing industry in Britain reflects a desire by employers and investors to move away from those areas of industrial militancy into contexts (such as small towns) where union traditions are weak and to create conditions – small factories etc. – where unionisation will not develop very fast, if at all (see Massey, 1984a). It could be, therefore, that part of the geography of voting by class that we have reported here reflects spatial variations in the levels of both unionisation and unionateness and the creation of milieux in which the traditional strong links between occupational class, trade unionism and Labour voting will not be normal. This suggests that Labour's ability to mobilise substantial support in the south will be hampered by the absence of that organisational focus. But in any case, it must not be assumed that unions necessarily will deliver votes to Labour from manual workers. In 1979, the heavily unionised car-manufacturing areas of the West Midlands delivered large blocks of votes to the Conservative party, reflecting the local context of the time. And just as Labour doesn't always get the votes of the unionised, so it might be able to develop strategies to win them from the non-unionised.

Not all commentators argue that Labour's chances of electoral success are small, however. Indeed, some claim that although social change has worked against Labour, the amount of movement has not been so great as either to produce the major vote loss that the party has suffered in recent years or to mean that Labour could never rebuild a Parliamentary majority on its traditional foundations. Thus, for example, Heath, Jowell and Curtice (1985, p. 174) concluded their book on the 1983 general election by arguing that

> the working class is still the largest single class and, although not perhaps so disadvantaged as it once was, is still relatively disadvantaged not only in income terms but perhaps even more importantly in terms of job security, pension schemes, working conditions, and of course unemployment . . . these class inequalities provide a potential for class ideology.

Similarly, Heath and McDonald (1987) claim that social change can only account for a drop of five percentage points in Labour's vote – which fell from 48 per cent of the electorate in 1966 to 28 per cent in 1983. Their argument is that

> more votes are won and lost through political fluctuations than through social changes . . . social change may be on balance adverse for Labour, but even now it does not rule out a Labour victory (p. 374)

In this argument, a lot depends on the definition of class (as Kavanagh, 1986, makes clear) and on analyses which some (e.g. Dunleavy, 1987) find misleading. Thus others are not so sanguine, and argue that Labour's chances are much less rosy. Crewe (1982), for example, argues that in the 1980s Labour has an

> ever-present problem: the lack of appeal that socialist *policies* (although not ultimate goals), of almost any variety, hold for a large – and growing – portion of the working class (p. 38).

Many of Labour's core policies, around which the party was united in its resolve, were unpopular with the working-class (on law and order, public morality, and education issues, for example), and he concludes that

> It is . . . especially difficult for the party to construct a package of *policies* with broad electoral appeal, because so many of the policies favoured by the party promote some working-class interests at the expense of others (p. 46)

The erosion of its electoral base by social change, the embourgeoisement of parts of the working class (especially the skilled manual workers) which has made them open to Conservative blandishments, and divisions within the Labour party over policy directions all go to make up the crisis of the Labour party about which Whiteley (1983) and others have written. Labour added to this in the early 1980s through its internal divisions, which led to the establishment of the SDP, very largely by disaffected Labour members, and through the inept leadership at the time of the 1983 general election (Cozens and Swaddle, 1987, refer to 'Michael Foot's quixotic and sadly improbable leadership', p. 263). Not only has Labour lost votes, however, it has also lost members, and thus an organisational base on which to rebuild. Whiteley (1982) has illustrated this with an analysis of Labour's declining membership, a major cause of which appears to have been negative reactions to the party's performance when in office in the 1960s and 1970s. (One problem with analyses of Labour membership has been the inflated figures prior to the 1980s because of the high threshold for each constituency party to affiliate with; many local parties thus paid affiliation fees for more members than they had. The decline of the late 1970s/early 1980s was thus in part more apparent than real.)

All of these commentators, whether believing that Labour has a solid and substantial-enough electoral base on which to build or not, argue that the party's future lies in extending its electoral appeal. Heath, Jowell, and Curtice (1985, p. 514), for example, argue that

> Labour must shift its ground towards the affluent centre

and must reduce the class ideology aspect of its rhetoric:

> the language of class struggle is unlikely to be successful in securing an ideological move back to the left. Class inequalities persist but the classes have not been polarised in their values at any time in the postwar period. We doubt if they will become so. An appeal to social justice rather than to class struggle has more hope of success.

Likewise, Heath and McDonald (1987) argue that Labour must not only do better in its traditional electoral heartland (what they call the 'integrated working class') but must also expand its appeal. In terminology reminiscent of Miller's (1977) core classes, they identify as potential Labour vote-winning sections of society both the 'intermediate class' (the routine non-manual occupational grouping in our analysis) and

> the two marginal sections of the salariat and the working class – unionized members of the salariat and nonunionized owner-occupiers in the working class respectively (p. 375)

This requires organisation, a revival of the party machine, as Whiteley (1982) acknowledges.

It also requires policies that will appeal to those groups. Heath and Mc-Donald (1987) believe that this can be done through the unions, so that voters get involved in the Labour movement through workplace organisation and, through social interaction, come to accept its values. (One problem in that is that contemporary developments in workplace organisation focus on small units, breaking up the working class and thereby preventing large-scale solidarity developing: see p. 327.) But what values will be imparted through the unions? The Labour party is clearly divided on this, between those who believe that radical socialist policies are needed and those who want to distance the party from its roots and adopt policies that are 'centrist' in their orientation. For the former, the failure of the centrist policies that Labour enacted when in office in the 1960s and 1970s is proof that radical approaches are needed; for the latter group, there is a strong belief that a majority of the British electorate will never again vote for a major deviation from the centre-ground of British politics, so that the party must refashion its policies to meet the aspirations of late 1980s' Britons. This, for example, is the argument advanced by Austin Mitchell (1987, p. 403), who sees that Labour's only hope is to focus attention on

> improvement in the lot of the mass of the British people . . . To do anything at all we have had to win power and to do that we have to move with the tide. Socialising individuals helps both ends . . . Labour has to slim down, smarten up and abandon much of its baggage, if it is to pass through the narrow gateway to power.

What most of these analyses ignore, or virtually so, is the geography of the Labour party's present condition, so clearly displayed throughout this book. Heath and McDonald (1987, p. 375) do note that

> Labour may have a handsome lead within the "integrated working class", but this part of the working class now amounts to only 23 per cent of the electorate (although it is a geographically concentrated section of the electorate that brings a substantial bonus of parliamentary seats)

and Crick (1987, p. 434) recognises that

> To win next time Labour will need to claw back a hundred seats, nearly all of which must be in the South since in the North Labour's cup is already full to overflowing.

But neither develops this important issue.

As we have shown here, Labour's strength in the northern regions of Britain (especially the northern urban regions) stems from a combination of factors. First, the party had traditionally been strong there, so that a large proportion of the working-class (and probably a substantial proportion of the middle class too, especially those who have been upwardly mobile socially, relative to their parents' position) have been very deeply socialised in pro-Labour milieux sustained by strong trades unions and, in many places, strong local party organisations; they will also have been encouraged by Labour victories in local government elections and the anti-government stance that many Labour councils have taken in recent years. Northerners are more likely to identify with Labour, to support its policies, and believe in its leaders. Secondly, the geography of economic and social well-being that has emerged over recent decades has involved a growing north:south divide which means that northerners are more likely to feel relatively deprived than southerners, and certainly to feel (based on their local experience) that their fellows are so deprived. These feelings of relative deprivation are likely to generate pro-Labour voting, not because Labour has a particularly distinguished record of promoting the interests of those deprived regions (as Sharpe, 1982, argues) but because a vote for Labour (in 1983 and 1987) can be used as a vote against a Conservative government whose policies have been widely criticised as the source of the opening-up of the north:south divide. Thirdly, since it was elected in 1979, a number of the Conservative government's policies appear to have been directed against the north in general and specific places in particular. We have already noted the Scottish resentment in Chapter 3 (see also Denver, 1987); the policies against Liverpool's City Council, against the cheap fares policy of South Yorkshire County Council, and against the National Union of Mineworkers, to take just three other examples, also helped to crystallise anti-Conservative opinion in those areas.

Labour has an electoral base on which to build in the north, therefore; it already has, and does. Success there may not, as yet, mean that 'its cup is already overflowing', to use Crick's words, but the electoral benefits of further vote-winning in the north will be slight, and certainly insufficient alone to bring a parliamentary majority. So what about the foundations for an electoral revival in the south? Here, the advantages of the north are largely absent. The proportion of the electorate socialised in strongly pro-Labour milieux is much smaller, population change (both unplanned and planned – e.g. gentrification and urban redevelopment) is 'watering down' many Labour strongholds and moving pro-Labour voters into ghettos within Conservative heartlands, and Labour organisation is in general weak. Labour did do well in much of the south in 1945, but since then its stock has gradually declined there. Before 1939, there were few pockets of Labour strength in the south outside London and a number of industrial towns (such as Swindon), so there was no deep-rooted Labour tradition to build on after the Second World War. Labour's success in 1945 was part of a national shift reflecting a reaction to the economic and social consequences of Conservative rule in the 1930s, and it was not followed-up by the development of strong Labour organisation and pro-Labour milieux. Major disenchantment with the Conservative 1980s could produce another such wholesale shift again – if Labour were ready with both policies and leaders acceptable to the disenchanted – but it seems a slender thread on which to hang hopes of another electoral success.

Alongside Labour's deepseated weaknesses in the south is the fact that, in general, people in the south are more affluent, have benefited more from Conservative rule in the 1980s, and are more optimistic about the future. There are pockets of deprivation in the south, of course (SEEDS, 1987), just as there are of affluence in the north, but at present they are insufficient to form any basis for a surge in Labour support and, more importantly, seats. The south is an area where economic and social circumstances do not favour Labour, certainly not a Labour party whose policies are in any way seen as threatening to the burgeoning prosperity.

So what does Labour do? According to some of its strategists it reworks its policies (just like the Labour party in New Zealand did; Johnston and Honey, 1988) to appeal to the affluent working class of the south, plus the middle classes there. It must, according to Pulzer (1987), become more adaptable

in policy, in organisational structure, in social appeal. Without it there can be no survival. It will, in the end, determine whether a party founded to further social and

political emancipation of the proletariat can survive in a progressively post-industrial
climate (p. 379)

That adaptability must involve, Pulzer argues, a commitment to reducing the
power of the centralized, bureaucratic state, a change from the traditional,
hierarchical organisation of collective action via the unions and the party, and
the development of a new political agenda more in tune with a

more educated, less traditionally-minded middle-class work-force and of a greatly
expanded intelligentsia (p. 393).

To Austin Mitchell (1987) that means moving 'beyond socialism', to be
pragmatic, because

Pragmatic parties learn from defeats. Parties of principle pick themselves up and
carry on as if nothing happened (p. 389)

Labour's traditional principles will not bring electoral success, he notes,
because of the geography

we face a difficult struggle in those huge southern areas we need to win in: the
Worcesters, Plymouths, Readings, Harlows and Basildons, because we have already
squeezed most of what is possible from Scotland, the North and everywhere in fact
except the West and East Midlands (p. 389)

But at present, he argues, Labour is 'relegated to the peripheries of British life.
We represent a world that is going. Our structure, attitudes, and policies are
products of the past' (p. 390).

Those peripheries that Mitchell sees Labour as occupying, including the
geographical peripheries, must be broken out of: the only alternative is to wait
and hope for economic failure and/or war, when the state might once again be
called upon to act as 'a machinery for protecting a community in difficulties'
(p. 391). But Mitchell is not prepared to wait, in part because he fears that
economic failure will lead to fascism not socialism. To him, the language of
socialism is the language of a ghetto; 'the more we talk about Socialism the
more we talk to ourselves' (p. 397). He wants it replaced by 'reconciliation
with reality', by a pragmatic set of policies built on individualism within a
community context. Thus

Our base conditions us, as do our responsibilities, to the poor, the disadvantaged,
the deprived, the unions, the wage earners, those who do not have capital, class or
education to allow them to control their own destinies. That defines our purposes: to
serve their interests. So we will. Yet we need not prate about them, or to them, quite
so obsessively and exclusively. A grown up party requires two buttocks not just one.
Our old base is now insufficient for power. We do not help the have nots without
winning support, a lot of it, from the haves. So take our base for granted, and talk
to those we have to win by making them offers they can't refuse. That shouldn't be
too difficult in a society which keeps interest rates high, refuses to intervene against
monopoly, lavishes benefits on the strong, rejects the weak, looks to the real interests
of a tiny minority with real wealth and which is limping along wasting time, growth,
and opportunity (pp. 399–400)

But will a new package of policies designed to attract the votes of the affluent southerners at the same time retain the support of the relatively deprived and traditional northerners? Will Labour have to form a coalition of the two groups in order to gain power, just as the Democratic party did in the United States in the decades after 1932? Labour is already a coalition of left and right, of course, but the arguments that it should shift its policies into the centre ground, downplay if not jettison traditional policies on, for example, nationalisation, and embrace changes introduced by the Conservatives such as widespread share ownership suggest the need for a very different form of coalition. Just as such policy shifts might be necessary to attract votes from the affluent working and middle classes of the south, in a new campaign to mobilise support there, so there may be a need to sell such shifts to traditional Labour supporters in the party's heartland. It may be possible both to retain the support of the latter and to win over the former with a package of policies that is differently interpreted in the two areas. Evidence of changes in New Zealand in recent years suggests that would be difficult, however (Johnston and Honey, 1988). There the Labour party won substantial support at the 1987 general election from the professional middle classes who were benefiting from a new set of economic policies similar to those promoted by the British Conservative government, but it obtained only grudging support from its traditional voters (and the Prime Minister suffered a major reduction in his majority in a safe Labour seat). Of course, the New Zealand Labour party was already in office, and could claim that its attention to social policies in the next Parliament would show its commitment to its long-term supporters. Labour in Britain is not in that fortunate position!

Labour faces major problems in deciding how to go forward and promote policies that will win it Parliamentary power again. Those problems are the product of three main interacting factors: the decline of its traditional social base in the proletariat as a result of social change and mobility; the declining support for Labour in particular parts of the proletariat, especially the more affluent and the more authoritarian in their views; and the growing concentration of Labour voters in a minority of seats in certain parts of the country only, thereby eroding its organisational strength and ability to mount substantial campaign challenges in sufficient constituencies. Most analysts of Labour's problems focus on the first and second of these factors: Crewe (1986a, p. 638), for example, arguing that

> Retaining the proletarian vote is almost certainly a necessary condition for Labour's survival. But it is self-evidently not a sufficient condition for Labour's recovery. If Labour is ever again to form a secure majority government it must pitch camp on the 'affluent centre ground' . . . This does not necessarily require the Labour Party to abandon the old true faith. Its traditional gospel of egalitarianism, social justice and the collectivist trinity of nationalization, trade unionism and welfare *might* make enough conversions among the heathen and apostates.

To do this, Crewe notes that Labour has to develop both a social strategy and a political strategy. Socially, it must decide how to retrieve working-class support and how to appeal to other classes; politically it must decide whether to appeal on traditional or new grounds. Together, this gives four strategy options:

1) Appealing on traditional grounds in order to retrieve working-class support, by, for example, either escalating the class war or 'worker economism';
2) Appealing on traditional grounds and to other classes, by promoting policies based on social justice and a strong welfare state;
3) Appealing on new grounds in order to retrieve working-class support as, for example, in calls for 'populist authoritarianism'; and
4) Appealing on new grounds and to other classes, producing, perhaps, a coalition of minorities.

It is unclear whether any one of them would produce a majority in Parliament. Crewe (p. 637) suggests that only the second does, since it involves

> a 'shift to the affluent centre' in the sense of appealing to groups outside the working class (the affluent) on the basis of newly minted values (centrist values).

All others would see Labour winning, at best, only minority electoral support. But even the second poses great problems, because not only might it divide the working class (affluent against the rest) but it would also suggest playing-down class differences: in both cases, these would be geographical as well as social divisions, with Labour's shift into the centre ground potentially damaging its hold in its northern heartland. Some interesting work on this topic in seven European countries, but excluding Great Britain, has been done by Przeworski and Sprague (1986). They look at the price a working class party has to pay when it extends its activities to win the votes of office-workers, a process which 'generates ideological and organizational transformations which contrive to weaken the salience of class identification among workers' (p. 67). In Sweden, for example, they suggest that for each 100 office employees whose votes were won in 1956, 12 working class votes were lost three elections later (in 1964). In France, the loss was 124 over the same period, and in Germany 219 (p. 68). This is clearly a major problem.

> Faced with a working class which is a numerical minority, class-based parties seek electoral support from other groups. They often win this support, but in the process they dilute the salience of class as a cause of the workers' political behaviour, and they erode their strengths among workers (p. 79).

Thus their ability to extend into the middle classes, and so enhance their vote-winning overall, depends on the degree to which the working class support is guaranteed. This is clearly the problem that Labour faces in Britain, accentuated by the geographical issue we have identified here, for, as Cozens and Swaddle (1987, p. 266) express it

> The new political geography of Britain holds . . . [little] comfort for Labour in the light of the likely demographic changes of the next few years. The regions which are growing, and which will benefit from future changes in parliamentary boundaries,

are those in which the Tories are strong and Labour is weak; just like Labour's class basis, it would seem that Labour's geographical basis is a dwindling inheritance.

The Advance of the Alliance?

The Alliance was formed in the early 1980s as a coalition of traditional Liberals with the Social Democratic Party, a group of, largely, ex-Labour members who had failed to see that party shift into the centre ground and throw off the links to militant trade unionism and policies such as nationalisation. It achieved rapid success electorally in terms of winning votes in 1983, but gained very few seats; its performance declined in 1987, with the vote count dropping and several seats being lost.

The Alliance has faced a number of problems in projecting itself over the small number of years that it has been in being, and especially at the two general elections of 1983 and 1987. Four main difficulties can be identified.

1) First, it had to develop a positive image, as a party with policies deserving of support for what it promises to do in power rather than as a party of protest. For decades, a vote for the Liberal party had usually been a vote *against* both Conservative and Labour rather than a vote *for* Liberal policies, as Himmelweit et al. (1985) have shown. Similarly, the SDP's initial image was as an anti-Labour group (organisationally in particular). These negative elements could be developed by Conservative and Labour as reasons for not voting Alliance: you should make the choice between parties with policies, was their claim, rather than parties who promise something new but fail to tell us what it is. The Alliance has policies, but has found it difficult to project them.

2) Secondly, and following on from the first problem, the Alliance has had to establish a firm electoral foundation among sections of the population, a 'heartland' of support similar to the cores of support for Conservative and Labour which would give it organizational strength for its mobilisation efforts and a context for socialisation of new generations of supporters.

3) Thirdly, the Alliance has had to face leadership problems. These were particularly severe in 1987, when the decision to promote the two leaders (Steel and Owen) jointly clearly backfired with the electorate: British voters want to know who they will get as Prime Minister if they vote in a particular way, it seems, as well as what policies will be enacted.

4) Finally, the Alliance has suffered because not enough people have believed that it can win. As a consequence, though they may have preferred either or both of Alliance policies and leaders they have decided not to vote Alliance because the chances of victory (at the constituency level and, even more, nationally) are so slim. In this, they may well have been influenced by Conservative and Labour claims that 'an Alliance vote is a wasted vote', and that by voting Alliance people might produce a result even worse than they feared: the Conservative party would tell people that to vote Alliance rather than Conservative could produce a Labour victory, and the Labour party would argue similarly about a possible Tory success.

Together, these four main difficulties have presented the Alliance with major strategical problems. The third was tackled immediately after the 1987 general election, with David Steel's recognition of a need for the two parties to merge under a single leader – though this immediately led to a split within the SDP. The second is also being tackled. Heath, Jowell and Curtice's (1985) analyses suggest that the Alliance now has a clear ideological base within the attitudinal map of the British electorate (see p. 58 and Johnston and Pattie, 1988a), and our analyses here suggest that it has been particularly successful in mobilising the professional occupational class and the residents of the more rural parts of Britain.

The Alliance's electoral base is still too narrow for it to hope for electoral victory without a major expansion of support, however, because the centre ground that it occupies ideologically is also the arena of major Conservative and Labour incursions and its social base in the Professional occupational class, though substantial, is insufficient. It must expand its appeal, just as Labour must. But geography works against the Alliance, too, though in very different ways. As we have shown here, the Alliance, unlike Labour, does not have a clearly-defined geographical heartland. It has gained ground substantially in the constituencies with Professional concentrations and in the rural areas, especially of southern England, but in neither is its support sufficient that it is 'guaranteed' even a few Parliamentary seats; those that it wins are in most cases the product of particular local issues – such as a by-election victory on which it has continued to capitalise through a great deal of local organisational hard work.

Whereas for Labour the problem is one of breaking out of its geographical heartland, the problem for the Alliance is that it lacks one. Such a lack is not important for a party winning a substantial percentage of the votes nationally (35 or more) since this will probably bring seats in its wake. But for one winning 20–25 per cent it means very few seats are won with consequences in the lack of sustained public visibility through the performance of its MPs inside and outside Parliament. Such geographical heartlands are not rapidly created, however, especially in a situation where each of the other two parties has 'colonised' a substantial part of the country and the Alliance's policies have no particular appeal to certain geographical sections of the electorate.

A Labour:Alliance Pact?

The problems of the Labour and Alliance parties are to a considerable extent complementary: Labour has a geographical heartland which delivers a minority of the Parliamentary seats and the Alliance has not insubstantial voter support but very few seats. Would it not be in their interests to combine in some way, especially if their major goal is to remove the Conservative government and each realises that it is unlikely to succeed in that alone?

For the Alliance, of course, there has long been realisation that winning a Parliamentary victory outright is unlikely and that its major route to power would be through a coalition formed after an election. The likelihood of the necessity of such a coalition was high according to some observers in the early 1980s, producing a spate of analyses of the processes of coalition-formation and their likely consequences (see Bogdanor, 1983; Butler, 1983). But the Alliance didn't get as many votes in 1983 as anticipated, the Labour vote slumped in all but its heartland, and instead the Conservatives were returned with a landslide majority – as happened again in 1987. A decline in the Conservative vote in southern England matched by Alliance growth could result in a 'hung parliament' after the next election but, as Table 7.2 shows, the Alliance is a long way from winning many Tory seats there.

The other strand of Alliance thinking regarding coalition is in its very strong belief in electoral reform and commitment to the introduction of a system of proportional representation. This is promoted not so much because it would necessarily give the Alliance access to power – which it undoubtedly would – but also because it is fair (there is a strong moral component to the arguments of the electoral reformers: Taylor, 1984b) and sensible: electoral reform is likely to lead to the end of adversary politics (Finer, 1975) and bring about stable centrist government (Johnston, 1984). Although there are supporters of electoral reform within both the Conservative and Labour parties, these are small minorities only; the majority view there is that electoral reform produces coalition government which is weak government (an argument challenged in the essays in Bogdanor and Butler, 1983) whereas the present British system leads to strong governments with Parliamentary majorities to enable them to enact the people's mandate. (See also Taylor's, 1984b, argument regarding proportional tenure.)

Electoral reform is unlikely to be introduced under a Conservative administration, so how do the Alliance and Labour parties ensure that the Conservatives don't win the next election(s)? To some, the best way forward is some type of electoral pact. According to Crick (1987, p. 433)

> The alternatives before Labour if it wishes to be a governing party ever again are not between *either* modernisation *or* electoral alliances. The only realistic inference from the figures, the results, the record, the public mind and the sociology of contemporary Britain is that *both* would be needed.

He sees the trend as towards 'an egalitarian or classless society through the people and the society already here' and argues for a pact with the Alliance because

> We [i.e. Labour] might never form a majority government but the people are not likely to vote for one anyway. Yet we could be the dominant partner in a Lab-Lib coalition for a very long time. And would the electorate ever forgive us if the Conservatives got in again with a minority vote because we refused such an electoral arrangement? (p. 439)

Thus the rationale for the pact is the defeat of the Conservative government, and the presentation of it to the Labour party involves a belief that it would be the dominant partner in any government formed as a consequence of the pact.

Others are not so certain about either the desirability or the benefits of a pact for Labour. Pimlott (1987a, pp. 442–443) notes that if Labour hopes to win merely by default it may have to wait a long time. There are several democratic countries in which the pendulum is stuck or seldom swings; this is one possible future for Britain. Another possibility is that if and when the Tory collapse takes place, Labour appears insufficiently attractive to disillusioned Conservative voters . . . [and] the new, Liberal-based formation will contrive to offer a strong challenge . . . At this point it may seem that the obvious solution is an electoral pact between left and centre, in order to maximise the representation of non-Conservative parties and reduce the danger that a divided Opposition vote will enable the Tories to stay in power.

But he concludes that such a pact would be 'a dangerous and profitless folly' (p. 443). His reasoning is based on the relative equality of Labour and Alliance as vote-winners, if not seat-winners, in 1987. If either had done very badly and the other had come fairly close to the Conservatives, then a pact could be important to swing the next election against the government. But in the current situation, the pact may well not work, for several reasons. First, although many Labour voters might be prepared to switch to the Alliance to defeat the Conservative candidate in seats where Labour withdrew, the same would not occur, he feels, where the Alliance withdrew in favour of the Labour candidate; 1987 Alliance voters may switch about equally between Labour and Conservative, and thus not benefit Labour, whereas if the Alliance candidate remained she/he may hold on to the 'Tory second' vote and lose the 'Labour second' vote, thereby advantaging Labour by being present. Secondly, by boosting the Alliance's votes and seats, Labour may increase the Alliance's credibility as a party that can responsibly exercise power, thereby damaging Labour's long-term prospects, including those of dominating a Lab-Lib coalition. Further, by withdrawing in some seats, Labour would be admitting that it couldn't win power alone, and could thereby substantially alienate its traditional supporters. Finally, could a pact successfully be sold to the electorate? The experience of the Liberal-SDP Alliance in 1987 suggests not. Overall, the benefits could be substantial for the Alliance but the whole strategy would be very much a gamble for Labour.

For Pimlott, then, a pact is undesirable. Instead, he suggests that Labour should indicate its intention of ousting the Conservative government and its preparedness to come to terms with the Alliance on what policy areas they would not disagree over in the campaign and how they would work together in the next Parliament. Given the result of the 1987 election, and the subsequent 'implosion' of the SDP, the Alliance could demand no more. Talk of a pact is premature, he believes. Instead (Pimlott, 1987b, p. 5)

A time may come when Labour's continued impotence forces it into the kind of self-sacrifice a pact would entail, with agreements to stand down in some seats in order to give Liberals a free run, as the only means of depriving the Conservatives of their majority. But in 1992, at least, it may be taken for granted that there will be no pooling of votes by opposition parties.

Steed (1987) disagrees, however, arguing that only the Conservative party has more than a slim chance of an absolute majority after the next election, and that a limited pact to prevent that could involve Labour and the Alliance each agreeing not to nominate a candidate in no more than thirty seats each. His arithmetic suggests that through such a limited pact the Labour party could gain 32 more seats and the Alliance 29; this is unlikely, however, unless the Conservative vote falls too, in which case, should the Tory vote fall to 40 per cent nationally, a pact 'would decide whether or not we had a Conservative government into the mid-1990s' (p. 16). (Note that Mitchell, 1987, would be prepared for such a pact with the Liberals alone, while fighting to win back the SDP supporters: 'There can be no question of leaving the South to the housetrained Alliance and keeping the North for the rough but honest' – p. 395. Rodgers, 1987, would not advocate a pact with Labour on behalf of the Alliance, however, mainly because of the strength of Labour's left wing.)

Although Steed's (journalistic) article is too brief for him to develop the point, his analysis pays more implicit attention to the findings reported here than does that of Pimlott and others (including, presumably, most of the Labour party). Two aspects of our work are crucial. The first is that whereas Labour is well-placed to take 30–50 seats from the Conservatives with a swing to it of only a few percentage points, it is not well-placed to take many more, and in a large number of seats (as Figure 7.13 makes very clear) it is a long way from being able to mount a potentially successful assault, in parts of the country where Labour support and organisation are now thin. Secondly, and following on from that, not only are those parts of the country the ones where the Alliance has done well in the 1980s but they are also the areas of relative economic prosperity. If that prosperity remains, it is unlikely that Labour will be able to win over many voters – unless there is a radical shift in its policies, and these can be successfully marketed to electors who will be relatively favourably inclined to the government. On the other hand, the Alliance could win some, if it can promote policies that present social justice as a more important feature than the Tories, and can win support for a coalition that would advance on that front. If the prosperity were to be eroded, of course, Labour's chances may improve in those areas, but the willingness of southern voters (especially outside the manual occupational classes) to switch to the Labour party in large numbers would have to remain doubtful. They are more likely to move to the Alliance, and its attractions to them could be enhanced if they saw the pact as meaning that the Alliance was more likely to attain power.

Clearly there are many imponderables, and it is almost certain that the Alliance would gain more from a pact initially, especially if it meant victory in 1991/1992, than would Labour. For Labour, the problem is whether to admit that a pact is the best (perhaps only) path to power in the foreseeable future, and also the realisation that to agree to a pact would undoubtedly require it to shift into the centre-ground and thereby desert some of its long-cherished principles. Were it to do that, it might have difficulty holding on to its traditional votes – though it would be unlikely to lose that many in 1991/1992 to dent its seat-winning capacity seriously in the areas it currently represents, and its performance in office may then secure votes there in the future. For Labour, the pact holds out a possible route to shared power, but many difficulties. The electoral geography of the country at the present time means that, unless there are major shifts in 1991/1992 in the way people vote, there may be no other path.

And the Conservative Response?

What of the Conservative party; will the directions it takes during the third term in any way be influenced by the present geographical situation? One could argue that they need not, that the party has not only won two successive elections with very substantial Parliamentary majorities during a period of major economic and social restructuring but that the results of that restructuring have provided it with a substantial electoral cushion. Its majority is based on the decline of the Labour party in the south and the creation of prosperity there which, if sustained, should both prevent a Labour revival and constrain the advance of the Alliance.

But can the Conservative party sit back on its electoral laurels? The answer is almost certainly 'no', not simply because it wants to win by even bigger landslides in the future but rather because the present situation, and particularly its geography, contains some substantial problems.

For any incumbent government, voter alienation from the political system is a potential threat, because it can be the foundation for challenges to the government's authority and legitimacy outside the confines of normal political discourse. Where the potential for such challenges is spatially segregated – or at least clustered – then the threat increases substantially. It could be argued, therefore, that the growing polarisation in Britain's electoral geography is an indicator of the possibility of such a substantial increase in challenges to the government's legitimacy.

Two indications of such challenges are frequently used. The first is voter turnout, as an indicator of degree of support for the system (Bristow, 1976); the lower the turnout, the greater the level of voter alienation and, potentially, of social unrest. If the geographies of social and economic well-being in Britain had developed to such an extent that substantial portions of the electorate felt alienated from the system, therefore, one would expect lower levels of turnout in the more deprived areas.

Figures 7.27, 7.28 and 7.29 show turnout by constituency at the three elections and provide some evidence of regional variability; Scotland, the West Midlands and much of Inner London have very low turnout rates at each contest, for example. To inquire whether there were significant inter-regional differences, however, analyses of variance were conducted, and Tables 7.6 and 7.7 give both the R^2 values and the average deviations from the national figure for the two sets of regions analysed here. They suggest that the differences were more substantial at the functional regional scale than at the geographical, and that the inter-regional differences were greater at the end of the period than at the start.

Turnout in individual constituencies is usually associated with marginality (Mughan, 1986); the closer the contest, the greater the percentage of the

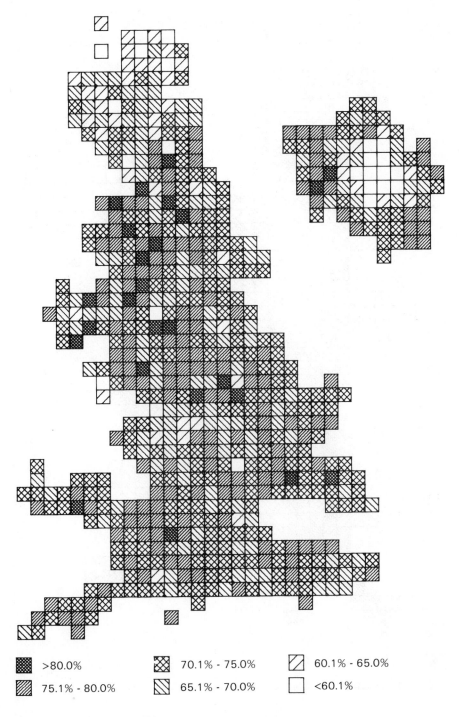

Figure 7.27 Turnout in 1979.

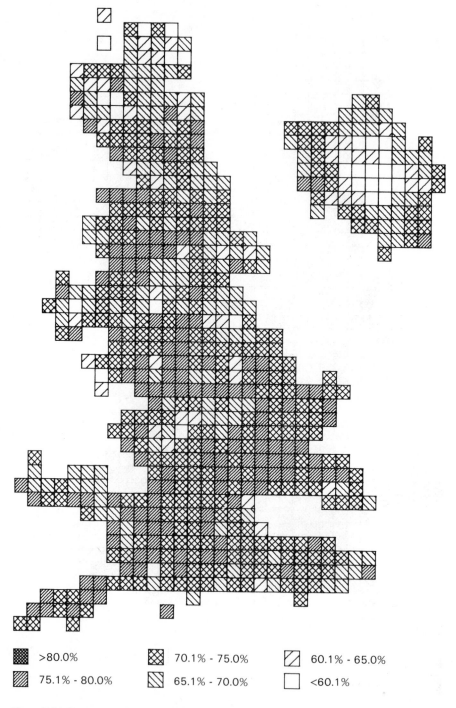

Figure 7.28 Turnout in 1983.

Figure 7.29 Turnout in 1987.

electorate who cast a ballot, partly because they believe that their votes are likely to be important to their parties (where marginality is low, the condition of 'safe seat apathy' is common, with people not bothering to vote because they believe it unnecessary – the party they support is either sure to win or sure to lose) and partly because they are more likely to have been canvassed by one or more of the parties (Johnston, 1987a). To take account of this, the analyses of variance were re-run with marginality held constant (as in a multiple regression; see p. 179) and the average regional deviations were re-computed. This produced the results shown in Tables 7.6 and 7.7, which differ very little from those generated without any consideration of marginality.

Looking first at the geographical regions (Table 7.6) by far the major feature is the fall in turnout in the three Scottish regions and in Rural Wales. In both 1979 and 1983 these four areas recorded average turnout rates above the national figure but in 1987 they were substantially below it, suggesting considerable voter dissatisfaction not just with the Conservative government but with the whole electoral system; Scots and Rural Welsh were losing confidence in the British parliament, it seems. The only other region with substantially lower-than-average turnout was Inner London. This, too, could indicate disaffection, but inner city areas traditionally have relatively low turnouts because of the high mobility of the population. (Interestingly, the other area of low turnout in all three years was the West Midlands Conurbation; along with Inner London, it has the greatest concentration of NCWP households: Figure 5.30.) In general, turnout was well above average in the southern regions, with the exception of London, and closer to the average in the northern regions, suggesting greater voter alienation in the north.

Turning to the functional regions (Table 7.7) an increased polarisation over the period between the relatively deprived regions (in the upper part of the table) and the more prosperous is again clear. In 1987, for example, all of the fifteen regions at the foot of the column, with the exception of Conurban White Collar (including several constituencies with large percentages of students) and Moderately Affluent Scotland had turnout above the national figure, whereas twelve of those at the top recorded percentages below that for Britain as a whole, several of them substantially so. Interestingly, the three recording above-average turnout among the more deprived regions include the Textile Towns and the Intermediate Industrial areas; the latter had relatively low levels of unemployment in 1981.

These findings suggest that the changing geography of economic and social well-being in Britain over the period of the two Conservative governments led to a geography of voter alienation which very much follows the geography of relative deprivation. People in the more depressed areas were less prepared to vote, and thereby indicate some confidence in the electoral system of liberal democracy, than were their contemporaries in the more affluent areas; those in Scotland were particularly affected in this way. Whether this is a widespread and potentially damaging indication of a decline in the state's legitimacy is unclear, but it clearly flags a problem that, as we indicate below, is appreciated by the Conservative party.

Table 7.6 Average Difference from the National Turnout Percentage, by Geographical Region

	Uncorrected			Corrected for Marginality		
	1979	1983	1987	1979	1983	1987
Strathclyde	0.95	0.69	−6.90	1.18	0.93	−5.56
E. Scotland	3.41	1.99	−6.20	3.30	1.78	−6.13
Rural Scotland	1.22	0.94	−15.63	0.85	0.69	−16.39
Rural North	0.44	0.62	2.42	0.50	0.67	2.28
Industrial Northeast	−1.63	−1.59	0.71	−1.55	−1.87	0.76
Merseyside	−0.25	−1.80	1.17	−0.19	−1.67	1.78
Greater Manchester	1.59	−0.54	1.50	1.39	−0.87	0.98
Rest of Northwest	1.64	2.20	3.89	1.45	2.21	3.53
West Yorks.	−0.60	−1.15	1.82	−0.81	−1.63	1.06
South Yorks.	−2.52	−3.90	−1.24	−2.04	−3.71	−0.20
Rural Wales	5.08	6.01	−5.38	4.69	5.63	−6.20
Industrial South Wales	3.42	2.21	2.03	3.87	2.49	3.21
W. Midlands Conurbation	−2.44	−2.02	−1.18	−2.66	−2.27	−1.80
Rest of West Midlands	−0.25	2.34	3.53	−0.36	2.42	3.39
East Midlands	0.93	1.51	3.64	0.76	1.43	3.37
East Anglia	0.19	2.46	3.38	0.02	2.58	3.43
Devon and Cornwall	1.70	3.79	3.19	1.76	3.80	2.64
Wessex	0.64	2.03	4.19	0.74	2.01	3.89
Inner London	−8.97	−11.03	−7.71	−9.21	−11.44	−8.65
Outer London	0.58	−2.02	−0.69	0.55	−1.95	−0.55
Outer Metropolitan	0.25	1.26	2.34	0.50	1.58	2.91
Outer Southeast	−0.89	0.45	2.26	−0.61	0.83	2.58
R^2	0.25	0.38	0.49	0.26	0.40	0.52

The second indicator of declining confidence in the political system and its ability to handle pressing problems is social unrest, which can be manifested in a variety of ways. The most obvious of these is public demonstration of some form, and Britain has had a number of these statements in recent years. Most of them have been in the inner city areas (as Taylor and Johnston, 1984, show). Their origins are complex, and in many instances appear to be linked to bad relationships between the police and members of certain ethnic minorities, but their locations in some of the most deprived parts of Britain suggest the importance of local milieux as predisposing factors.

This polarisation of the country, and its potential political consequences, was recognised by the Conservative government, almost certainly well before the results of the 1987 general election were known. When she returned to Conservative party headquarters on the morning of 12 June, 1987, immediately after victory was ensured, Mrs. Thatcher told party workers that they had a great deal to do in the inner cities. (Her actual words were 'We want them in next time'.) The development of policies to tackle the economic run-down and social deprivation of inner city areas was identified as a major thrust for the

Table 7.7 Average Difference from the National Turnout Percentage, by Functional Region

	Uncorrected			Corrected for Marginality		
	1979	1983	1987	1979	1983	1987
I.C./Immig.	-7.29	-8.58	-6.51	-7.52	-8.88	-6.97
Ind./Immig.	-1.70	-2.43	-0.89	-2.27	-3.20	-1.34
Poorest Immig.	-9.42	-9.36	-9.63	-9.29	-9.13	-9.44
Intermed. Ind.	1.20	1.21	3.24	0.79	0.45	2.81
Old Indust./Mining	1.72	-0.29	1.67	2.23	0.01	2.14
Textile	1.88	1.40	3.24	1.11	0.62	2.63
Poorest Domestic	-2.78	-5.41	-7.15	-1.61	-4.59	-6.29
Conurb. L.A.	-1.97	-3.46	-1.59	-1.98	-3.83	-1.59
Black Co.	-4.61	-2.73	-1.54	-5.10	-3.58	-2.28
Maritime Ind.	-1.38	-1.97	0.32	-1.48	-2.32	0.44
Poor I.C.	-14.53	-14.40	-11.84	-14.05	-14.24	-11.72
Clydeside	-1.33	-4.63	-10.82	-0.87	-4.25	-9.92
Scott. Ind.	2.96	3.43	-7.44	3.21	3.68	-6.78
Scott. Rural	2.67	2.38	-14.09	2.15	2.07	-14.52
High Status I.M.	-4.13	-8.63	-6.79	-4.40	-8.66	-7.12
I.M.	-6.54	-9.35	-6.80	-7.10	-10.04	-7.38
Outer London	1.78	-0.26	1.17	2.16	0.24	1.63
Very High Status	1.95	1.33	2.54	2.89	2.06	2.99
Conurb. W. Collar	0.55	-1.58	-0.15	0.38	-1.74	-0.49
City Service	0.22	-1.16	1.63	-0.37	-1.73	1.01
Resort/Retirement	-0.56	-0.57	1.41	0.05	-0.08	1.55
Recent Growth	-4.97	1.29	2.82	-5.48	1.03	2.52
Stable Ind.	2.19	4.21	4.75	1.80	4.09	4.67
Small Towns	2.19	3.32	3.96	2.01	3.39	3.81
Southern Urban	-0.18	2.48	3.88	0.09	2.94	4.17
Modest Aff.	3.90	4.23	5.32	3.89	4.57	5.38
Met. Ind.	1.27	1.38	2.46	0.62	1.17	2.37
Modest Aff. Scot.	5.50	6.02	-0.10	5.04	5.62	-0.90
Rapid Growth	-1.99	1.32	2.71	-1.66	1.79	3.08
Prosperous/No Ind.	0.40	1.03	2.28	0.90	1.38	2.23
Agricultural	1.50	3.21	0.93	1.60	3.44	0.95
R^2	0.40	0.56	0.53	0.42	0.58	0.54

new government, and many initiatives were conceived in the first weeks of the new Parliament. To a large extent, these continued and crystallised earlier attempts to tackle similar problems. The major economic decline of London's docklands was already being tackled by the London Docklands Development Corporation, for example, an independent body with powers to over-ride local government; a similar Development Corporation was set up in Merseyside after major public disturbances there in 1981; and a series of Enterprise Zones was established to regenerate local economies, again separate from local governments (Anderson, 1983; Hoare, 1985).

These policies suggest that the Conservative government is clearly aware of the potential dangers of the ghettoisation of the unemployed and/or deprived, and the threat that this could be to its legitimacy in parts of Britain at least. Hence it is attempting to win back support in those areas, with policies of regeneration designed to spread the economic optimism that apparently so sustained the party in the 1983 and 1987 general elections. The nature of those policies, with their emphases on private sector development, home ownership and small businesses, suggests that in part at least the government is seeking to produce electoral change by introducing traditional Conservative supporters to areas where the party has been very weak – as, for example, in many of the residential developments in London's Docklands. The goal is to spread the 'enterprise culture' to all parts of Britain, and to win subscribers nationwide to the Conservative ideology of self-help in a private-sector-dominated free market.

At the same time, other government policies are having major indirect influences on the capacity of opposition parties, especially Labour, to sustain an electoral base in constituencies. A major goal of Conservative governments since 1979 has been to break the power of the trade unions – indeed some, such as David Owen, believe that the altered balance of power between employers and unions has been one of the main Tory achievements. By reducing the power of the unions, and discouraging militant attitudes within them, the government has somewhat eroded the role of the trade union movement as a pro-Labour mobilising force. (Though note that in all ballots on political funds, a substantial majority has approved their continuation.) This is well illustrated in the Nottinghamshire coalfield where the split between the National Union of Mineworkers and the Union of Democratic Miners after the 1984–1985 strike led, among other things, to conflict within the Labour party over which trade union should influence Parliamentary candidate selection. And the results in the area reflected that split: Sherwood, with some of the main collieries in the area, was won by the Conservative party in 1983, and Mansfield became an increasingly marginal Labour seat in both 1983 and 1987. As the local power of unions is broken, it seems, Labour's ability to mobilise voters is reduced.

The Conservative policies towards local government also threaten to erode Labour's electoral base, within its heartland as well as in the south. The successive stages of the policy to reduce local government spending by control of the rate levy, and then to replace rates by a community charge (or 'poll tax') initially stimulated much central-local conflict, which came to a head with the unwillingness of several local councils to set a rate in 1986. This conflict provided a mobilising focus for Labour in several areas – such as Merseyside and South Yorkshire -with the party presenting itself as defending local democracy against centralist incursions. But there can be little doubt that the central government has won the conflict in many cases, with Labour local councils having to accept the terms of the financial settlement. The consequence may well be, therefore, that as local government becomes less vocal in 'the fight against Thatcherism', so the ability of the Labour party to mobilise support in its own heartland will decline. The Tories are not letting Labour keep hold of its heartland, therefore: they are invading it, in a variety of ways.

Many policies are targeted at particular areas within the depressed regions, and clearly are therefore directed at the major areas of voter disaffection and anti-Conservative sentiment. As yet, more have been specifically initiated for Scotland and Wales, where the anti-Conservative shift has been very substantial. In part, Scotland and Wales have always been recipients of above-average flows of public money, through their respective government departments (the Welsh Office and the Scottish Office) and in particular the work of the Development Agencies there. That activity clearly has not gained Conservative votes, however, no doubt in part because other policies are seen as clearly directed against those countries, notably Scotland (see p. 89). Thus the government believes that its problem is as much one of public relations as increased investment, in order to regain votes in those peripheral regions.

Government versus Opposition

What we have shown here is that the changing electoral geography of Britain over the 1979–1987 period has produced problems and challenges for the political parties. For Labour, the retreat into the relatively deprived regions of the north creates problems of how to win enough seats to regain power, whereas for the Alliance the inability to build substantial support in many areas, and especially in the north (outside the rural areas), means that it has an insufficiently-prepared launching pad for a major assault on Conservative incumbents. And for the government, while it could sustain itself in power simply by continuing to win in the southern, affluent regions, its loss of support in other areas is not just a blow to its pride but also potentially a threat to the legitimacy of the economic, social and political systems it seeks to defend.

For Labour and Alliance, the issue to be tackled is how to unseat the Conservative government. Were there to be a major and sustained downturn in the economy, this could be possible, although the protection that the current electoral geography gives the government's majority means that it could possibly survive as the largest party in Parliament. Labour and Alliance thus must ponder whether some form of electoral pact is the best way forward. Meanwhile, the Conservative party seeks to maintain its hold of the south by ensuring continued prosperity there and simultaneously to invade the north and regenerate local economies in ways that will win more Tory votes.

If Conservative policies are generally successful, Labour could be the major loser, since its chances of winning many seats in the south are already remote. It may lose relatively few in the north, because of its large majorities in many seats there, but its relative decline could be matched by a resurgence of Alliance support in the south – if the restructured party is successfully launched. The facts of British electoral geography appear to be stacked against Labour at present; it could become the 'class party' of a shrinking, deprived north.

IN CONCLUSION

A changing electoral geography is of substantial interest as a subject for academic analysis. In addition, that changing geography is likely to have substantial implications for the activities of the major actors concerned with attempts to capitalise on, and change, it – the political parties. Thus in this chapter we have explored some of the possible implications of the geography that we have described earlier in the book. We have presented no predictions, because they would be fraught with difficulties and the future is very much an unknown in such a changeable economic and social, let alone political, situation. But political parties must act in terms of their interpretation of the recent past and how the future is unfolding; our discussion here identifies some of the salient issues of that context and their implications for British politics in the immediate future.

——— APPENDIX ———

THE CONSTITUENCIES AND THE REGIONS

This appendix provides a key to the numerous cartograms presented in the book. It is in three parts.

THE CONSTITUENCIES

A key to the location of every constituency is provided in Figure A.1. In that, the numbering system follows the alphabetical listing of constituencies produced by the BBC/ITN (1983) team.

To aid in the identification of constituencies when using the categories, Figure A.2-A.4 locate: (a) the Counties of England and Wales and the regions of Scotland (Figure A.2); (b) the Boroughs of Greater London (Figure A.3); and (c) the main urban places (Figure A.4).

A full listing of the constituencies in alphabetical/numerical order is given below. (The missing numbers — eg 10, 11, 12 — refer to Northern Ireland constituencies.)

1 Aberavon	20 Banbury
2 Aberdeen North	21 Banff and Buchan
3 Aberdeen South	22 Barking
4 Aldershot	23 Barnsley Central
5 Aldridge Brownhills	24 Barnsley East
6 Altrincham and Sale	25 Barnsley West and Peniston
7 Alyn and Deeside	26 Barrow and Furness
8 Amber Valley	27 Basildon
9 Angus East	28 Basingstoke
13 Argyll and Bute	29 Bassetlaw
14 Arundel	30 Bath
15 Ashfield	31 Batley and Spen
16 Ashford	32 Battersea
17 Ashton under Lyne	33 Beaconsfield
18 Aylesbury	34 Beckenham
19 Ayr	35 Bedfordshire mid
	36 Bedfordshire North

37 Bedfordshire South West
42 Berkshire East
43 Berwick upon Tweed
44 Bethnal Green and Stepney
45 Beverley
46 Bexhill and Battle
47 Bexleyheath
48 Billericay
49 Birkenhead
50 Birmingham Edgbaston
51 Birmingham Erdington
52 Birmingham Hall Green
53 Birmingham Hodge Hill
54 Birmingham Ladywood
55 Birmingham Northfield
56 Birmingham Perry Barr
57 Birmingham Selly Oak
58 Birmingham Small Heath
59 Birmingham Sparkbrook
60 Birmingham Yardley
61 Bishop Auckland
62 Blaby
63 Blackburn
64 Blackpool North
65 Blackpool South
66 Blaenau Gwent
67 Blaydon
68 Blyth Valley
69 Bolsover
70 Bolton North East
71 Bolton South East
72 Bolton West
73 Boothferry
74 Bootle
75 Bosworth
76 Bournemouth East
77 Bournemouth West
78 Bow and Poplar
79 Bradford North
80 Bradford South
81 Bradford West
82 Braintree
83 Brecon and Radnor
84 Brent East
85 Brent North
86 Brent South
87 Brentford and Isleworth
88 Brentwood and Ongar
89 Bridgend
90 Bridgwater

91 Bridlington
92 Brigg and Cleethorpes
93 Brighton Kemptown
94 Brighton Pavilion
95 Bristol East
96 Bristol North West
97 Bristol South
98 Bristol West
99 Bromsgrove
100 Broxbourne
101 Broxtowe
102 Buckingham
103 Burnley
104 Burton
105 Bury North
106 Bury South
107 Bury St. Edmunds

108 Caernarfon
109 Caerphilly
110 Caithness and Sutherland
111 Calder Valley
112 Cambridge
113 Cambridgeshire North East
114 Cambridgeshire South East
115 Cambridgeshire South West
116 Cannock and Burntwood
117 Canterbury
118 Cardiff Central
119 Cardiff North
120 Cardiff South and Penarth
121 Cardiff West
122 Carlisle
123 Carmarthen
124 Carrick Cumnock and Doon Valley
125 Carshalton and Wallington
126 Castle Point
127 Ceredigion and Pembroke North
128 Cheadle
129 Chelmsford
130 Chelsea
131 Cheltenham
132 Chertsey and Walton
133 Chesham and Amersham
134 Chester City of
135 Chesterfield
136 Chichester
137 Chingford
138 Chipping Barnet
139 Chislehurst

140 Chorley
141 Christchurch
142 Cirencester and Tewkesbury
143 City of London and Westminster South
144 Clackmannan
145 Clwyd North West
146 Clwyd South West
147 Clydebank and Milngavie
148 Clydesdale
149 Colchester North
150 Colchester South and Maldon
151 Colne Valley
152 Congleton
153 Conwy
154 Copeland
155 Corby
156 Cornwall North
157 Cornwall South East
158 Coventry North East
159 Coventry North West
160 Coventry South East
161 Coventry South West
162 Crawley
163 Crewe and Nantwich
164 Crosby
165 Croydon Central
166 Croydon North East
167 Croydon North West
168 Croydon South
169 Cumbernauld and Kilsyth
170 Cunninghame North
171 Cunninghame South
172 Cynon Valley

173 Dagenham
174 Darlington
175 Dartford
176 Daventry
177 Davyhulme
178 Delyn
179 Denton and Reddish
180 Derby North
181 Derby South
182 Derbyshire North East
183 Derbyshire South
184 Derbyshire West
185 Devizes
186 Devon North
187 Devon West and Torridge

188 Dewsbury
189 Doncaster Central
190 Doncaster North
191 Don Valley
192 Dorset North
193 Dorset South
194 Dorset West
195 Dover
198 Dudley East
199 Dudley West
200 Dulwich
201 Dumbarton
202 Dumfries
203 Dundee East
204 Dundee West
205 Dunfermline East
206 Dunfermline West
207 Durham City of
208 Durham North
209 Durham North West

210 Ealing Acton
211 Ealing North
212 Ealing Southall
213 Easington
214 Eastbourne
215 East Kilbride
216 Eastleigh
217 East Lothian
218 Eastwood
219 Eccles
220 Eddisbury
221 Edinburgh Central
222 Edinburgh East
223 Edinburgh Leith
224 Edinburgh Pentlands
225 Edinburgh South
226 Edinburgh West
227 Edmonton
228 Ellesmere Port and Neston
229 Elmet
230 Eltham
231 Enfield North
232 Enfield Southgate
233 Epping Forest
234 Epsom and Ewell
235 Erewash
236 Erith and Crayford
237 Esher
238 Exeter

239 Falkirk East
240 Falkirk West
241 Falmouth and Camborne
242 Fareham
243 Faversham
244 Feltham and Heston
246 Fife Central
247 Fife North East
248 Finchley
249 Folkestone and Hythe
251 Fulham
252 Fylde

253 Gainsborough and Horncastle
254 Galloway and Upper Nithsdale
255 Gateshead East
256 Gedling
257 Gillingham
258 Glanford and Scunthorpe
259 Glasgow Cathcart
260 Glasgow Central
261 Glasgow Garscadden
262 Glasgow Govan
263 Glasgow Hillhead
264 Glasgow Maryhill
265 Glasgow Pollok
266 Glasgow Provan
267 Glasgow Rutherglen
268 Glasgow Shettleston
269 Glasgow Springburn
270 Gloucester
271 Gloucestershire West
272 Gordon
273 Gosport
274 Gower
275 Grantham
276 Gravesham
277 Great Grimsby
278 Great Yarmouth
279 Greenock and Port Glasgow
280 Greenwich
281 Guildford

282 Hackney North and Stoke Newington
283 Hackney South and Shoreditch
284 Halesowen and Stourbridge
285 Halifax
286 Halton
287 Hamilton
288 Hammersmith

289 Hampshire East
290 Hampshire North West
291 Hampstead and Highgate
292 Harborough
293 Harlow
294 Harrogate
295 Harrow East
296 Harrow West
297 Hartlepool
298 Harwich
299 Hastings and Rye
300 Havant
301 Hayes and Harlington
302 Hazel Grove
303 Hemsworth
304 Hendon North
305 Hendon South
306 Henley
307 Hereford
308 Hertford and Stortford
309 Hertfordshire North
310 Hertfordshire South West
311 Hertfordshire West
312 Hertsmere
313 Hexham
314 Heywood and Middleton
315 High Peak
316 Holborn and St. Pancras
317 Holland with Boston
318 Honiton
319 Hornchurch
320 Hornsey and Wood Green
321 Horsham
322 Houghton and Washington
323 Hove
324 Huddersfield
325 Hull East
326 Hull North
327 Hull West
328 Huntingdon
329 Hyndburn

330 Ilford North
331 Ilford South
332 Inverness Nairn and Lochaber
333 Ipswich
334 Isle of Wight
335 Islington North
336 Islington South and Finsbury
337 Islwyn

338 Jarrow

339 Keighley
340 Kensington
341 Kent mid
342 Kettering
343 Kilmarnock and Loudon
344 Kincardine and Deeside
345 Kingston upon Thames
346 Kingswood
347 Kirkcaldy
348 Knowsley North
349 Knowsley South

351 Lancashire West
352 Lancaster
353 Langbaurgh
354 Leeds Central
355 Leeds East
356 Leeds North East
357 Leeds North West
358 Leeds South and Morley
359 Leeds West
360 Leicester East
361 Leicester South
362 Leicester West
363 Leicestershire North West
364 Leigh
365 Leominster
366 Lewes
367 Lewisham Deptford
368 Lewisham East
369 Lewisham West
370 Leyton
371 Lincoln
372 Lindsey East
373 Linlithgow
374 Littleborough and Saddleworth
375 Liverpool Broadgreen
376 Liverpool Garston
377 Liverpool Mossley Hill
378 Liverpool Riverside
379 Liverpool Walton
380 Liverpool West Derby
381 Livingston
382 Llanelli
384 Loughborough
385 Ludlow
386 Luton North
387 Luton South

388 Macclesfield
389 Maidstone
390 Makerfield
391 Manchester Blackley
392 Manchester Central
393 Manchester Gorton
394 Manchester Withington
395 Manchester Wythenshawe
396 Mansfield
397 Medway
398 Meirionnydd nant Conwy
399 Meriden
400 Merthyr Tydfil and Rhymney
401 Middlesbrough
402 Midlothian
403 Milton Keynes
404 Mitcham and Morden
405 Mole Valley
406 Monklands East
407 Monklands West
408 Monmouth
409 Montgomery
410 Moray
411 Morecambe and Lunesdale
412 Motherwell North
413 Motherwell South

414 Neath
415 Newark
416 Newbury
417 Newcastle under Lyme
418 Newcastle upon Tyne Central
419 Newcastle upon Tyne East
420 Newcastle upon Tyne North
421 New Forest
422 Newham North East
423 Newham North West
424 Newham South
425 Newport East
426 Newport West
428 Norfolk mid
429 Norfolk North
430 Norfolk North West
431 Norfolk South
432 Norfolk South West
433 Normanton
434 Northampton North
435 Northampton South
436 Northavon
437 Norwich North

438 Norwich South
439 Norwood
440 Nottingham East
441 Nottingham North
442 Nottingham South
443 Nuneaton

444 Ogmore
445 Old Bexley and Sidcup
446 Oldham Central and Royton
447 Oldham West
448 Orkney and Shetland
449 Orpington
450 Oxford East
451 Oxford West and Abingdon

452 Paisley North
453 Paisley South
454 Peckham
455 Pembroke
456 Pendle
457 Penrith and the Border
458 Perth and Kinross
459 Peterborough
460 Plymouth Devonport
461 Plymouth Drake
462 Plymouth Sutton
463 Pontefract and Castleford
464 Pontypridd
465 Poole
466 Portsmouth North
467 Portsmouth South
468 Preston
469 Pudsey
470 Putney

471 Ravensbourne
472 Reading East
473 Reading West
474 Redcar
475 Reigate
476 Renfrew West and Inverclyde
477 Rhondda
478 Ribble Valley
479 Richmond and Barnes
480 Richmond (Yorks)
481 Rochdale
482 Rochford
483 Romford
484 Romsey and Waterside

485 Ross Cromarty and Skye
486 Rossendale and Darwen
487 Rotherham
488 Rother Valley
489 Roxburgh and Berwickshire
490 Rugby and Kenilworth
491 Ruislip Northwood
492 Rushcliffe
493 Rutland and Melton
494 Ryedale

495 Saffron Walden
496 St. Albans
497 St. Helens North
498 St. Helens South
499 St. Ives
500 Salford East
501 Salisbury
502 Scarborough
503 Sedgefield
504 Selby
505 Sevenoaks
506 Sheffield Attercliffe
507 Sheffield Brightside
508 Sheffield Central
509 Sheffield Hallam
510 Sheffield Heeley
511 Sheffield Hillsborough
512 Sherwood
513 Shipley
514 Shoreham
515 Shrewsbury and Atcham
516 Shropshire North
517 Skipton and Ripon
518 Slough
519 Solihull
520 Somerton and Frome
521 Southampton Itchen
522 Southampton Test
523 Southend East
524 Southend West
525 South Hams
526 Southport
527 South Ribble
528 South Shields
529 Southwark and Bermondsey
530 Spelthorne
531 Stafford
532 Staffordshire mid
533 Staffordshire Moorlands

534 Staffordshire South
535 Staffordshire South East
536 Stalybridge and Hyde
537 Stamford and Spalding
538 Stevenage
539 Stirling
540 Stockport
541 Stockton North
542 Stockton South
543 Stoke on Trent Central
544 Stoke on Trent North
545 Stoke on Trent South
547 Stratford on Avon
548 Strathkelvin and Bearsden
549 Streatham
550 Stretford
551 Stroud
552 Suffolk Central
553 Suffolk Coastal
554 Suffolk South
555 Sunderland North
556 Sunderland South
557 Surbiton
558 Surrey East
559 Surrey North West
560 Surrey South West
561 Sussex mid
562 Sutton and Cheam
563 Sutton Coldfield
564 Swansea East
565 Swansea West
566 Swindon

567 Tatton
568 Taunton
569 Tayside North
570 Teignbridge
571 Thanet North
572 Thanet South
573 Thurrock
574 Tiverton
575 Tonbridge and Malling
576 Tooting
577 Torbay
578 Torfaen
579 Tottenham
580 Truro
581 Tunbridge Wells
582 Tweedale Ettrick and Lauderdale
583 Twickenham

584 Tyne Bridge
585 Tynemouth

587 Upminster
589 Uxbridge

590 Vale of Glamorgan
591 Vauxhall

592 Wakefield
593 Wallasey
594 Wallsend
595 Walsall North
596 Walsall South
597 Walthamstow
598 Wansbeck
599 Wansdyke
600 Wanstead and Woodford
601 Wantage
602 Warley East
603 Warley West
604 Warrington North
605 Warrington South
606 Warwick and Leamington
607 Warwickshire North
608 Watford
609 Waveney
610 Wealden
611 Wellingborough
612 Wells
613 Welwyn Hatfield
614 Wentworth
615 West Bromwich East
616 West Bromwich West
617 Westbury
618 Western Isles
619 Westminster North
620 Westmorland and Lonsdale
621 Weston Super Mare
622 Wigan
623 Wiltshire North
624 Wimbledon
625 Winchester
626 Windsor and Maidenhead
627 Wirral South
628 Wirral West
629 Witney
630 Woking
631 Wokingham
632 Wolverhampton North East

633 Wolverhampton South East
634 Wolverhampton South West
635 Woodspring
636 Woolwich
637 Worcester
638 Worcestershire mid
639 Worcestershire South
640 Workington
641 Worsley
642 Worthing

643 Wrekin the
644 Wrexham
645 Wycombe
646 Wyre
647 Wyre Forest

648 Yeovil
649 Ynys Mon
650 York

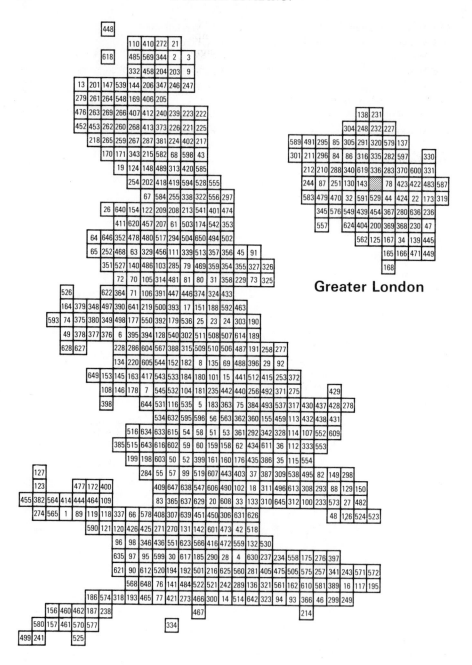

Figure A.1 The location of the 633 constituencies on the cartogram.

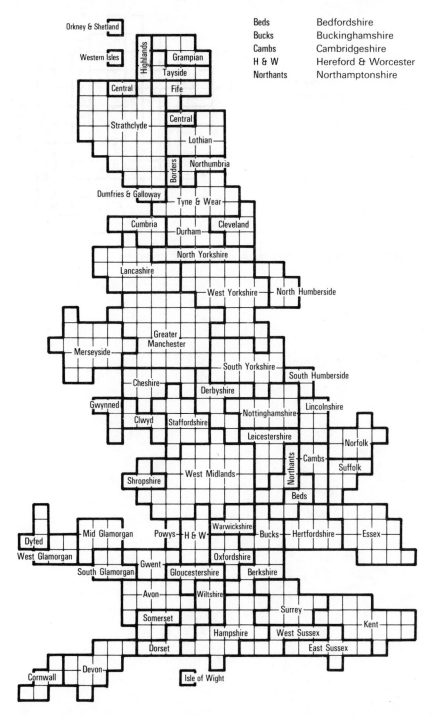

Beds   Bedfordshire
Bucks   Buckinghamshire
Cambs   Cambridgeshire
H & W   Hereford & Worcester
Northants   Northamptonshire

Figure A.2 The county (England and Wales) and regional (Scotland) boundaries on the cartogram.

Grnwch   Greenwich
Hmsth   Hammersmith
Knsngtn   Kensington
Lwshm   Lewisham
Twr Hm   Tower Hamlets
Wmnstr   Westminster

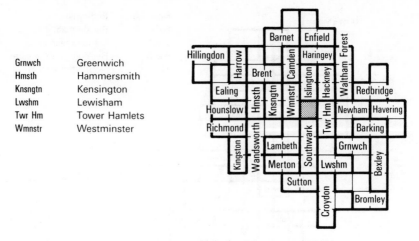

Figure A.3 The boroughs of Greater London on the cartogram.

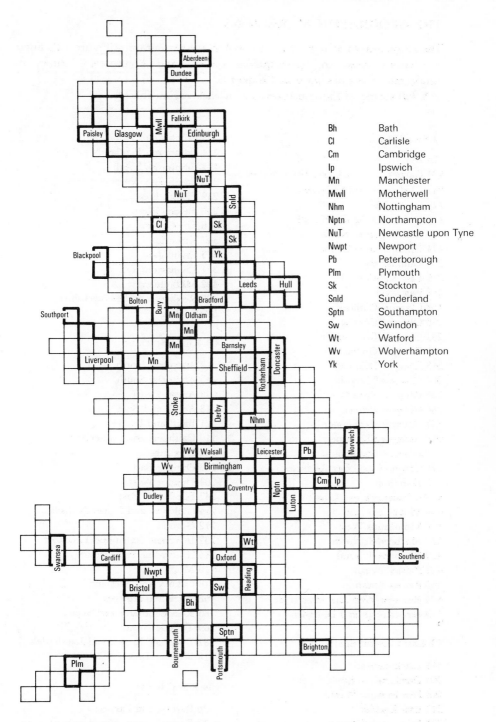

Bh — Bath
Cl — Carlisle
Cm — Cambridge
Ip — Ipswich
Mn — Manchester
Mwll — Motherwell
Nhm — Nottingham
Nptn — Northampton
NuT — Newcastle upon Tyne
Nwpt — Newport
Pb — Peterborough
Plm — Plymouth
Sk — Stockton
Snld — Sunderland
Sptn — Southampton
Sw — Swindon
Wt — Watford
Wv — Wolverhampton
Yk — York

Figure A.4 The main urban places in the cartogram.

THE GEOGRAPHICAL REGIONS

The 22 geographical regions are located in the cartogram in Figure 1.2. Figure A.5 shows them in 'geographical space', and Figure A.6 shows the amalgamated regions used in Chapter 6.

A full listing of the constituencies in each region follows.

01 Strathclyde

  19 Ayr
124 Carrick Cumnock and Doon Valley
147 Clydebank and Milngavie
148 Clydesdale
169 Cumbernauld and Kilsyth
170 Cunninghame North
171 Cunninghame South
201 Dumbarton
215 East Kilbride
218 Eastwood
259 Glasgow Cathcart
260 Glasgow Central
261 Glasgow Garscadden
262 Glasgow Govan
263 Glasgow Hillhead
264 Glasgow Maryhill
265 Glasgow Pollok
266 Glasgow Provan
267 Glasgow Rutherglen
268 Glasgow Shettleston
269 Glasgow Springburn
279 Greenock and Port Glasgow
287 Hamilton
343 Kilmarnock and Loudon
406 Monklands East
407 Monklands West
412 Motherwell North
413 Motherwell South
452 Paisley North
453 Paisley South
476 Renfrew West and Inverclyde
548 Strathkelvin and Bearsden

02 East Central Scotland

144 Clackmannan
205 Dunfermline East
206 Dunfermline West
217 East Lothian
221 Edinburgh Central
222 Edinburgh East

223 Edinburgh Leith
224 Edinburgh Pentlands
225 Edinburgh South
226 Edinburgh West
239 Falkirk East
240 Falkirk West
246 Fife Central
347 Kirkcaldy
373 Linlithgow
381 Livingston
402 Midlothian
489 Roxburgh and Berwickshire
539 Stirling

03 Rural Scotland

  2 Aberdeen North
  3 Aberdeen South
  9 Angus East
 13 Argyll and Bute
 21 Banff and Buchan
110 Caithness and Sutherland
202 Dumfries
203 Dundee East
204 Dundee West
247 Fife North East
254 Galloway and Upper Nithsdale
272 Gordon
332 Inverness Nairn and Lochaber
344 Kincardine and Deeside
410 Moray
448 Orkney and Shetland
458 Perth and Kinross
485 Ross Cromarty and Skye
569 Tayside North
582 Tweedale Ettrick and Lauderdale
618 Western Isles

04 Rural North

 26 Barrow and Furness
 43 Berwick upon Tweed
 45 Beverley

61 Bishop Auckland
73 Boothferry
91 Bridlington
92 Brigg and Cleethorpes
122 Carlisle
154 Copeland
258 Glanford and Scunthorpe
277 Great Grimsby
294 Harrogate
313 Hexham
325 Hull East
326 Hull North
327 Hull West
457 Penrith and the Border
478 Ribble Valley
480 Richmond (Yorks)
494 Ryedale
502 Scarborough
504 Selby
517 Skipton and Ripon
620 Westmorland and Lonsdale
640 Workington
650 York

05 Industrial Northeast

67 Blaydon
68 Blyth Valley
174 Darlington
207 Durham City of
208 Durham North
209 Durham North West
213 Easington
255 Gateshead East
297 Hartlepool
322 Houghton and Washington
338 Jarrow
353 Langbaurgh
401 Middlesbrough
418 Newcastle upon Tyne Central
419 Newcastle upon Tyne East
420 Newcastle upon Tyne North
474 Redcar
503 Sedgefield
528 South Shields
541 Stockton North
542 Stockton South
555 Sunderland North
556 Sunderland South
584 Tyne Bridge

585 Tynemouth
594 Wallsend
598 Wansbeck

06 Merseyside

49 Birkenhead
74 Bootle
164 Crosby
348 Knowsley North
349 Knowsley South
375 Liverpool Broadgreen
376 Liverpool Garston
377 Liverpool Mossley Hill
378 Liverpool Riverside
379 Liverpool Walton
380 Liverpool West Derby
497 St. Helens North
498 St. Helens South
526 Southport
593 Wallasey
627 Wirral South
628 Wirral West

07 Greater Manchester

6 Altrincham and Sale
17 Ashton under Lyne
70 Bolton North East
71 Bolton South East
72 Bolton West
105 Bury North
106 Bury South
128 Cheadle
177 Davyhulme
179 Denton and Reddish
219 Eccles
302 Hazel Grove
314 Heywood and Middleton
374 Littleborough and Saddleworth
391 Manchester Blackley
392 Manchester Central
393 Manchester Gorton
394 Manchester Withington
395 Manchester Wythenshawe
446 Oldham Central and Royton
447 Oldham West
481 Rochdale
500 Salford East
536 Stalybridge and Hyde
540 Stockport

550 Stretford
641 Worsley

08 Rest of Northwest

63 Blackburn
64 Blackpool North
65 Blackpool South
103 Burnley
134 Chester City of
140 Chorley
152 Congleton
163 Crewe and Nantwich
220 Eddisbury
228 Ellesmere Port and Neston
252 Fylde
286 Halton
315 High Peak
329 Hyndburn
351 Lancashire West
352 Lancaster
364 Leigh
388 Macclesfield
390 Makerfield
411 Morecambe and Lunesdale
456 Pendle
468 Preston
486 Rossendale and Darwen
527 South Ribble
567 Tatton
604 Warrington North
605 Warrington South
622 Wigan
646 Wyre

09 West Yorkshire

31 Batley and Spen
79 Bradford North
80 Bradford South
81 Bradford West
111 Calder Valley
151 Colne Valley
188 Dewsbury
229 Elmet
285 Halifax
303 Hemsworth
324 Huddersfield
339 Keighley
354 Leeds Central
355 Leeds East

356 Leeds North East
357 Leeds North West
358 Leeds South and Morley
359 Leeds West
433 Normanton
463 Pontefract and Castleford
469 Pudsey
513 Shipley
592 Wakefield

10 South Yorkshire

23 Barnsley Central
24 Barnsley East
25 Barnsley West and Penistone
189 Doncaster Central
190 Doncaster North
191 Don Valley
487 Rotherham
488 Rother Valley
506 Sheffield Attercliffe
507 Sheffield Brightside
508 Sheffield Central
509 Sheffield Hallam
510 Sheffield Heeley
511 Sheffield Hillsborough
614 Wentworth

11 Rural Wales

7 Alyn and Deeside
83 Brecon and Radnor
108 Caernarfon
123 Carmarthen
127 Ceredigion and Pembroke North
145 Clwyd North West
146 Clwyd South West
153 Conwy
178 Delyn
382 Llanelli
398 Meirionnydd nant Conwy
409 Montgomery
455 Pembroke
644 Wrexham
649 Ynys Mon

12 Industrial South Wales

1 Aberavon
66 Blaenau Gwent
89 Bridgend

109 Caerphilly
118 Cardiff Central
119 Cardiff North
120 Cardiff South and Penarth
121 Cardiff West
172 Cynon Valley
274 Gower
337 Islwyn
400 Merthyr Tydfil and Rhymney
408 Monmouth
414 Neath
425 Newport East
426 Newport West
444 Ogmore
464 Pontypridd
477 Rhondda
564 Swansea East
565 Swansea West
578 Torfaen
590 Vale of Glamorgan

13 West Midlands Conurbation

  5 Aldridge Brownhills
 50 Birmingham Edgbaston
 51 Birmingham Erdington
 52 Birmingham Hall Green
 53 Birmingham Hodge Hill
 54 Birmingham Ladywood
 55 Birmingham Northfield
 56 Birmingham Perry Barr
 57 Birmingham Selly Oak
 58 Birmingham Small Heath
 59 Birmingham Sparkbrook
 60 Birmingham Yardley
158 Coventry North East
159 Coventry North West
160 Coventry South East
161 Coventry South West
198 Dudley East
199 Dudley West
284 Halesowen and Stourbridge
399 Meriden
519 Solihull
563 Sutton Coldfield
595 Walsall North
596 Walsall South
602 Warley East
603 Warley West
607 Warwickshire North

615 West Bromwich East
616 West Bromwich West
632 Wolverhampton North East
633 Wolverhampton South East
634 Wolverhampton South West

14 Rest of West Midlands

 99 Bromsgrove
104 Burton
116 Cannock and Burntwood
307 Hereford
365 Leominster
385 Ludlow
417 Newcastle under Lyme
443 Nuneaton
490 Rugby and Kenilworth
515 Shrewsbury and Atcham
516 Shropshire North
531 Stafford
532 Staffordshire mid
533 Staffordshire Moorlands
534 Staffordshire South
535 Staffordshire South East
543 Stoke on Trent Central
544 Stoke on Trent North
545 Stoke on Trent South
547 Stratford on Avon
606 Warwick and Leamington
637 Worcester
638 Worcestershire mid
639 Worcestershire South
643 Wrekin the
647 Wyre Forest

15 East Midlands

  8 Amber Valley
 15 Ashfield
 29 Bassetlaw
 62 Blaby
 69 Bolsover
 75 Bosworth
101 Broxtowe
135 Chesterfield
155 Corby
176 Daventry
180 Derby North
181 Derby South
182 Derbyshire North East
183 Derbyshire South

184 Derbyshire West
235 Erewash
253 Gainsborough and Horncastle
256 Gedling
275 Grantham
292 Harborough
317 Holland with Boston
342 Kettering
360 Leicester East
361 Leicester South
362 Leicester West
363 Leicestershire North West
371 Lincoln
372 Lindsey East
384 Loughborough
396 Mansfield
415 Newark
434 Northampton North
435 Northampton South
440 Nottingham East
441 Nottingham North
442 Nottingham South
492 Rushcliffe
493 Rutland and Melton
512 Sherwood
537 Stamford and Spalding
611 Wellingborough

16 East Anglia

107 Bury St. Edmunds
112 Cambridge
113 Cambridgeshire North East
114 Cambridgeshire South East
115 Cambridgeshire South West
278 Great Yarmouth
328 Huntingdon
333 Ipswich
428 Norfolk mid
429 Norfolk North
430 Norfolk North West
431 Norfolk South
432 Norfolk South West
437 Norwich North
438 Norwich South
459 Peterborough
552 Suffolk Central
553 Suffolk Coastal
554 Suffolk South
609 Waveney

17 Devon and Cornwall

156 Cornwall North
157 Cornwall South East
186 Devon North
187 Devon West and Torridge
238 Exeter
241 Falmouth and Camborne
318 Honiton
460 Plymouth Devonport
461 Plymouth Drake
462 Plymouth Sutton
499 St. Ives
525 South Hams
570 Teignbridge
574 Tiverton
577 Torbay
580 Truro

18 Wessex

30 Bath
76 Bournemouth East
77 Bournemouth West
90 Bridgwater
95 Bristol East
96 Bristol North West
97 Bristol South
98 Bristol West
131 Cheltenham
141 Christchurch
142 Cirencester and Tewkesbury
185 Devizes
192 Dorset North
193 Dorset South
194 Dorset West
270 Gloucester
271 Gloucestershire West
346 Kingswood
436 Northavon
465 Poole
501 Salisbury
520 Somerton and Frome
551 Stroud
566 Swindon
568 Taunton
599 Wansdyke
612 Wells
617 Westbury
621 Weston Super Mare
623 Wiltshire North

635 Woodspring
648 Yeovil

19 Inner London

 32 Battersea
 44 Bethnal Green and Stepney
 78 Bow and Poplar
130 Chelsea
143 City of London and Westminster
     South
200 Dulwich
230 Eltham
251 Fulham
280 Greenwich
282 Hackney North and Stoke Newington
283 Hackney South and Shoreditch
288 Hammersmith
291 Hampstead and Highgate
316 Holborn and St. Pancras
335 Islington North
336 Islington South and Finsbury
340 Kensington
367 Lewisham Deptford
368 Lewisham East
369 Lewisham West
422 Newham North East
423 Newham North West
424 Newham South
439 Norwood
454 Peckham
470 Putney
529 Southwark and Bermondsey
549 Streatham
576 Tooting
591 Vauxhall
619 Westminster North
636 Woolwich

20 Outer London

 22 Barking
 34 Beckenham
 47 Bexleyheath
 84 Brent East
 85 Brent North
 86 Brent South
 87 Brentford and Isleworth
125 Carshalton and Wallington
137 Chingford
138 Chipping Barnet

139 Chislehurst
165 Croydon Central
166 Croydon North East
167 Croydon North West
168 Croydon South
173 Dagenham
210 Ealing Acton
211 Ealing North
212 Ealing Southall
227 Edmonton
231 Enfield North
232 Enfield Southgate
236 Erith and Crayford
244 Feltham and Heston
248 Finchley
295 Harrow East
296 Harrow West
301 Hayes and Harlington
304 Hendon North
305 Hendon South
319 Hornchurch
320 Hornsey and Wood Green
330 Ilford North
331 Ilford South
345 Kingston upon Thames
370 Leyton
404 Mitcham and Morden
445 Old Bexley and Sidcup
449 Orpington
471 Ravensbourne
479 Richmond and Barnes
483 Romford
491 Ruislip Northwood
557 Surbiton
562 Sutton and Cheam
579 Tottenham
583 Twickenham
587 Upminster
589 Uxbridge
597 Walthamstow
600 Wanstead and Woodford
624 Wimbledon

21 Outer Metropolitan

  4 Aldershot
 18 Aylesbury
 27 Basildon
 33 Beaconsfield
 37 Bedfordshire South West

42 Berkshire East
48 Billericay
88 Brentwood and Ongar
100 Broxbourne
102 Buckingham
126 Castle Point
129 Chelmsford
132 Chertsey and Walton
133 Chesham and Amersham
162 Crawley
175 Dartford
233 Epping Forest
234 Epsom and Ewell
237 Esher
257 Gillingham
276 Gravesham
281 Guildford
293 Harlow
308 Hertford and Stortford
309 Hertfordshire North
310 Hertfordshire South West
311 Hertfordshire West
312 Hertsmere
321 Horsham
341 Kent mid
386 Luton North
387 Luton South
389 Maidstone
397 Medway
405 Mole Valley
416 Newbury
472 Reading East
473 Reading West
475 Reigate
482 Rochford
496 St. Albans
505 Sevenoaks
518 Slough
523 Southend East
524 Southend West
530 Spelthorne
538 Stevenage
558 Surrey East
559 Surrey North West
560 Surrey South West
561 Sussex mid
573 Thurrock
575 Tonbridge and Malling
581 Tunbridge Wells
608 Watford

610 Wealden
613 Welwyn Hatfield
626 Windsor and Maidenhead
630 Woking
631 Wokingham
645 Wycombe

22 Outer Southeast

14 Arundel
16 Ashford
20 Banbury
28 Basingstoke
35 Bedfordshire mid
36 Bedfordshire North
46 Bexhill and Battle
82 Braintree
93 Brighton Kemptown
94 Brighton Pavilion
117 Canterbury
136 Chichester
149 Colchester North
150 Colchester South and Maldon
195 Dover
214 Eastbourne
216 Eastleigh
242 Fareham
243 Faversham
249 Folkestone and Hythe
273 Gosport
289 Hampshire East
290 Hampshire North West
298 Harwich
299 Hastings and Rye
300 Havant
306 Henley
323 Hove
334 Isle of Wight
366 Lewes
403 Milton Keynes
421 New Forest
450 Oxford East
451 Oxford West and Abingdon
466 Portsmouth North
467 Portsmouth South
484 Romsey and Waterside
495 Saffron Walden
514 Shoreham
521 Southampton Itchen
522 Southampton Test

571 Thanet North
572 Thanet South
601 Wantage

625 Winchester
629 Witney
642 Worthing

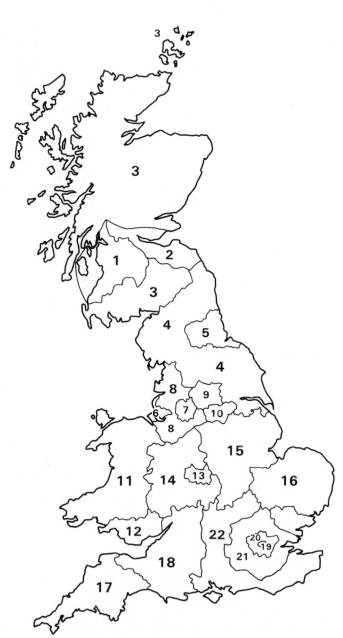

Figure A.5 The 22 geographical regions.

Figure A.6 The seven amalgamated regions.

THE FUNCTIONAL REGIONS

The 31 functional regions are identified by title in Table 1. The following listing is taken from the description of each given by Crewe and Fox (1984, pp. 10–15).

Metropolitan Inner-City Areas with Immigrants.

> Constituencies close to the national average on most variables, although there is a paucity of the highest socio-economic groups and much multi-occupied property. There are large numbers of immigrants, with some 20 per cent of NCWP origin.

Industrial Areas with Immigrants.

> Constituencies with substantial numbers of manufacturing employees and above-average percentages of immigrants. There are few affluent neighbourhoods.

Poorest Immigrant Areas.

> Four constituencies with large immigrant populations living in deprived conditions (high unemployment and overcrowded housing).

Intermediate Industrial Areas.

> Areas of relative economic stability with average unemployment levels. Heterogeneous in their economic base.

Old Industrial and Mining Towns.

> Dominated by manual occupational classes and with few immigrants. Unemployment only just above the national average.

Textile Areas.

> Manufacturing areas with high levels of female employment and of owner-occupied housing. Some immigrant concentration.

Areas with Poorest Domestic Conditions.

> Seven constituencies of low-income people with a lot of unemployment. Housing conditions among the worst in the country, with up to 12 per cent having no inside WC and 9 per cent no bathroom.

Conurbation Local Authority Housing.

> Mainly constituencies with large council estates on the periphery of the major conurbations. Relatively old populations, concentrated in manual occupations and dependent on public transport for commuting. Above-average unemployment.

The Black Country.

> Concentrations of council housing, of immigrants, and of owner-occupied houses in relatively poor condition. Manual occupations dominate, and unemployment high.

Maritime Industrial Areas.

> Large numbers of semiskilled and unskilled manual workers, with large families and low levels of female employment. High unemployment.

Poor Inner-City Housing.
Constituencies with very high percentages of both council tenants and tenants of privately-rented properties; above-average percentages of unskilled manual workers and of unemployment.

Clydeside.
Constituencies with high percentages of council tenants and of large families living in overcrowded conditions; above-average percentages in unskilled and semiskilled manual occupations and unemployed.

Scottish Industrial.
Scottish constituencies with substantial manufacturing bases; high percentage of council tenants and high ratios of people per room.

Scottish Rural.
Distinguished from English rural constituencies by greater densities of room occupation, lower levels of car ownership, and higher percentages of council tenants.

High Status Metropolitan Areas.
Typical inner-city areas with mobile populations, high percentages employed in services, above-average percentages in rented furnished properties and of single-person households. Many professional and managerial workers and few children.

Inner Metropolitan Areas.
As with the previous category in terms of general characteristics but much more council housing and substantial population of immigrants. Mixed socio-economic composition.

Outer London Suburbia.
Affluent suburbs with large percentages in professional and managerial occupations and of owner-occupiers. High levels of car ownership but above-average reliance on public transport for commuting.

Very High-Status Areas.
The highest concentration of professional and managerial occupations and of owner-occupation.

Conurbation White-Collar Areas.
Areas with substantial concentration of single-person households (not pensioners) and of students, with a mixture of owner-occupation and privately-rented homes: service employment rather than manufacturing is the norm.

City Constituencies with Service Employment.
A group of constituencies close to the national average on most variables relating to dwellings, to age structure, and to socio-economic characteristics. Service rather than manufacturing employment dominates.

Resort and Retirement Areas.
High percentage of over-65s and owner-occupied housing.

Areas of Recent Growth and Modern Housing.
New housing occupied by young families, including some of the New Town areas.

Stable Industrial Towns.
Characterised by skilled manual workers in manufacturing industries; low unemployment and above-average proportion of young families.

Small Manufacturing Towns with Rural Hinterlands.
Smaller towns and agricultural areas are incorporated in these constituencies, which have below-average unemployment and above-average owner-occupation.

'Southern' Urban.
Employment in manufacturing above the national average but below-average unemployment and above-average on most of the indicators of relative prosperity; a combination of local manufacturing plus homes for commuters.

Manufacturing Towns with Commuter Hinterlands.
Mixed constituencies comprising both manufacturing industry and residential areas for commuters; above-average percentages of older people, of professional workers, and of owner-occupiers.

Metropolitan Industrial Areas.
Average on many characteristics and with a balance between manufacturing and service industries. Low levels of unemployment, few industrial workers, little housing depreciation, and significant numbers of immigrants: affluent working-class areas.

Modestly Affluent Urban Scotland.
Biased towards service industries and white-collar occupations, but with the high densities of people per room typical of Scotland.

Area of Rapid Growth.
Large percentage of recent immigrants and young families; very low unemployment.

Prosperous Towns with Little Industry.
Little manufacturing present and above-average percentages of both owner-occupiers and professional and managerial workers.

Agricultural Areas.
Agricultural employment on average five times the national figure. High levels of car ownership; little council housing; older population than average.

A full list of the constituencies in each region is given below and Figure 1.3 indicates their locations.

01 Metropolitan inner-city areas with immigrants

86 Brent South
167 Croydon North West
212 Ealing Southall
361 Leicester South
370 Leyton
422 Newham North East
423 Newham North West
579 Tottenham

02 Industrial areas with immigrants

56 Birmingham Perry Barr
63 Blackburn
71 Bolton South East
79 Bradford North
158 Coventry North East
160 Coventry South East
181 Derby South
324 Huddersfield
360 Leicester East
362 Leicester West
387 Luton South
393 Manchester Gorton
468 Preston
518 Slough
550 Stretford
597 Walthamstow
602 Warley East

03 Poorest immigrant areas

54 Birmingham Ladywood
58 Birmingham Small Heath
59 Birmingham Sparkbrook
81 Bradford West

04 Intermediate industrial areas

52 Birmingham Hall Green
67 Blaydon
95 Bristol East
96 Bristol North West
122 Carlisle
135 Chesterfield
159 Coventry North West
174 Darlington
180 Derby North
189 Doncaster Central

191 Don Valley
208 Durham North
209 Durham North West
219 Eccles
333 Ipswich
346 Kingswood
371 Lincoln
417 Newcastle under Lyme
420 Newcastle upon Tyne North
425 Newport East
433 Normanton
437 Norwich North
511 Sheffield Hillsborough
566 Swindon
573 Thurrock
592 Wakefield
598 Wansbeck
604 Warrington North
641 Worsley
644 Wrexham

05 Old industrial and mining towns

1 Aberavon
8 Amber Valley
15 Ashfield
23 Barnsley Central
24 Barnsley East
25 Barnsley West and Penistone
26 Barrow and Furness
29 Bassetlaw
61 Bishop Auckland
66 Blaenau Gwent
69 Bolsover
154 Copeland
155 Corby
179 Denton and Reddish
190 Doncaster North
213 Easington
235 Erewash
303 Hemsworth
337 Islwyn
382 Llanelli
396 Mansfield
414 Neath
444 Ogmore
463 Pontefract and Castleford
498 St. Helens South
503 Sedgefield
543 Stoke on Trent Central

544 Stoke on Trent North
545 Stoke on Trent South
564 Swansea East
578 Torfaen
614 Wentworth
622 Wigan
640 Workington

06 Textile areas

 17 Ashton under Lyne
 31 Batley and Spen
 70 Bolton North East
 80 Bradford South
103 Burnley
111 Calder Valley
151 Colne Valley
188 Dewsbury
285 Halifax
314 Heywood and Middleton
329 Hyndburn
339 Keighley
364 Leigh
446 Oldham Central and Royton
447 Oldham West
456 Pendle
481 Rochdale
486 Rossendale and Darwen
536 Stalybridge and Hyde

07 Areas with poorest domestic
conditions

172 Cynon Valley
327 Hull West
379 Liverpool Walton
400 Merthyr Tydfil and Rhymney
424 Newham South
477 Rhondda
618 Western Isles

08 Conurbation local authority housing

 22 Barking
 51 Birmingham Erdington
 55 Birmingham Northfield
 60 Birmingham Yardley
173 Dagenham
255 Gateshead East
338 Jarrow
355 Leeds East

358 Leeds South and Morley
359 Leeds West
376 Liverpool Garston
380 Liverpool West Derby
391 Manchester Blackley
395 Manchester Wythenshawe
419 Newcastle upon Tyne East
441 Nottingham North
442 Nottingham South
487 Rotherham
506 Sheffield Attercliffe
507 Sheffield Brightside
510 Sheffield Heeley
528 South Shields
555 Sunderland North
556 Sunderland South
594 Wallsend

09 The Black Country

 53 Birmingham Hodge Hill
198 Dudley East
595 Walsall North
596 Walsall South
603 Warley West
615 West Bromwich East
616 West Bromwich West
632 Wolverhampton North East
633 Wolverhampton South East

10 Maritime industrial areas

 49 Birkenhead
 74 Bootle
 97 Bristol South
258 Glanford and Scunthorpe
277 Great Grimsby
286 Halton
297 Hartlepool
325 Hull East
326 Hull North
348 Knowsley North
349 Knowsley South
401 Middlesbrough
460 Plymouth Devonport
474 Redcar
541 Stockton North

11 Poor inner-city areas

 44 Bethnal Green and Stepney

78 Bow and Poplar
283 Hackney South and Shoreditch
354 Leeds Central
378 Liverpool Riverside
392 Manchester Central
440 Nottingham East
454 Peckham
500 Salford East
508 Sheffield Central
529 Southwark and Bermondsey
584 Tyne Bridge

12 'Clydeside'

2 Aberdeen North
203 Dundee East
204 Dundee West
222 Edinburgh East
223 Edinburgh Leith
259 Glasgow Cathcart
260 Glasgow Central
261 Glasgow Garscadden
262 Glasgow Govan
264 Glasgow Maryhill
265 Glasgow Pollok
266 Glasgow Provan
267 Glasgow Rutherglen
268 Glasgow Shettleston
269 Glasgow Springburn
279 Greenock and Port Glasgow
452 Paisley North

13 Scottish industrial constituencies

124 Carrick Cumnock and Doon Valley
144 Clackmannan
147 Clydebank and Milngavie
148 Clydesdale
169 Cumbernauld and Kilsyth
170 Cunninghame North
171 Cunninghame South
201 Dumbarton
205 Dunfermline East
206 Dunfermline West
215 East Kilbride
239 Falkirk East
240 Falkirk West
246 Fife Central
287 Hamilton
343 Kilmarnock and Loudon
347 Kirkcaldy

373 Linlithgow
381 Livingston
402 Midlothian
406 Monklands East
407 Monklands West
412 Motherwell North
413 Motherwell South
453 Paisley South

14 Scottish rural areas

9 Angus East
13 Argyll and Bute
21 Banff and Buchan
110 Caithness and Sutherland
202 Dumfries
217 East Lothian
247 Fife North East
254 Galloway and Upper Nithsdale
332 Inverness Nairn and Lochaber
344 Kincardine and Deeside
410 Moray
448 Orkney and Shetland
458 Perth and Kinross
485 Ross Cromarty and Skye
489 Roxburgh and Berwickshire
569 Tayside North
582 Tweedale Ettrick and Lauderdale

15 High status inner metropolitan areas

98 Bristol West
130 Chelsea
143 City of London and Westminster South
210 Ealing Acton
221 Edinburgh Central
291 Hampstead and Highgate
320 Hornsey and Wood Green
340 Kensington
619 Westminster North

16 Inner metropolitan areas

32 Battersea
84 Brent East
251 Fulham
263 Glasgow Hillhead
282 Hackney North and Stoke Newington
288 Hammersmith

316 Holborn and St. Pancras
335 Islington North
336 Islington South and Finsbury
367 Lewisham Deptford
439 Norwood
549 Streatham
576 Tooting
591 Vauxhall

17 Outer 'London' suburbia

 47 Bexleyheath
 85 Brent North
119 Cardiff North
125 Carshalton and Wallington
137 Chingford
138 Chipping Barnet
139 Chislehurst
226 Edinburgh West
230 Eltham
232 Enfield Southgate
233 Epping Forest
234 Epsom and Ewell
295 Harrow East
296 Harrow West
304 Hendon North
312 Hertsmere
330 Ilford North
356 Leeds North East
445 Old Bexley and Sidcup
449 Orpington
471 Ravensbourne
491 Ruislip Northwood
530 Spelthorne
562 Sutton and Cheam
587 Upminster
600 Wanstead and Woodford

18 Very high status areas

  6 Altrincham and Sale
 33 Beaconsfield
 45 Beverley
 88 Brentwood and Ongar
128 Cheadle
132 Chertsey and Walton
133 Chesham and Amersham
164 Crosby
168 Croydon South
237 Esher
306 Henley

310 Hertfordshire South West
405 Mole Valley
475 Reigate
492 Rushcliffe
496 St. Albans
505 Sevenoaks
519 Solihull
558 Surrey East
559 Surrey North West
560 Surrey South West
561 Sussex mid
563 Sutton Coldfield
626 Windsor and Maidenhead
628 Wirral West
630 Woking
631 Wokingham
635 Woodspring

19 Conurbation white collar areas

  3 Aberdeen South
 34 Beckenham
 50 Birmingham Edgbaston
 87 Brentford and Isleworth
 94 Brighton Pavilion
112 Cambridge
118 Cardiff Central
166 Croydon North East
200 Dulwich
225 Edinburgh South
248 Finchley
305 Hendon South
323 Hove
345 Kingston upon Thames
357 Leeds North West
394 Manchester Withington
418 Newcastle upon Tyne Central
451 Oxford West and Abingdon
461 Plymouth Drake
470 Putney
479 Richmond and Barnes
509 Sheffield Hallam
557 Surbiton
583 Twickenham
624 Wimbledon

20 City constituencies with service employment

 57 Birmingham Selly Oak
 93 Brighton Kemptown

120 Cardiff South and Penarth
121 Cardiff West
134 Chester City of
238 Exeter
280 Greenwich
368 Lewisham East
369 Lewisham West
375 Liverpool Broadgreen
377 Liverpool Mossley Hill
438 Norwich South
450 Oxford East
467 Portsmouth South
472 Reading East
521 Southampton Itchen
522 Southampton Test
523 Southend East
540 Stockport
565 Swansea West
585 Tynemouth
593 Wallasey
636 Woolwich
650 York

21 Resort and retirement areas

 14 Arundel
 46 Bexhill and Battle
 64 Blackpool North
 65 Blackpool South
 76 Bournemouth East
 77 Bournemouth West
141 Christchurch
145 Clwyd North West
214 Eastbourne
249 Folkestone and Hythe
298 Harwich
299 Hastings and Rye
318 Honiton
334 Isle of Wight
366 Lewes
411 Morecambe and Lunesdale
421 New Forest
465 Poole
502 Scarborough
514 Shoreham
524 Southend West
525 South Hams
526 Southport
570 Teignbridge
571 Thanet North

572 Thanet South
577 Torbay
642 Worthing
646 Wyre

22 Areas of recent growth and modern housing

 27 Basildon
 28 Basingstoke
 37 Bedfordshire South West
 68 Blyth Valley
228 Ellesmere Port and Neston
272 Gordon
322 Houghton and Washington
351 Lancashire West
353 Langbaurgh
386 Luton North
399 Meriden
403 Milton Keynes
434 Northampton North
459 Peterborough
535 Staffordshire South East
542 Stockton South
605 Warrington South
638 Worcestershire mid
643 Wrekin the

23 Stable industrial towns

  7 Alyn and Deeside
 75 Bosworth
105 Bury North
109 Caerphilly
116 Cannock and Burntwood
140 Chorley
152 Congleton
182 Derbyshire North East
183 Derbyshire South
199 Dudley West
342 Kettering
363 Leicestershire North West
374 Littleborough and Saddleworth
384 Loughborough
390 Makerfield
397 Medway
443 Nuneaton
464 Pontypridd
488 Rother Valley
497 St. Helens North
527 South Ribble

532 Staffordshire mid
533 Staffordshire Moorlands
607 Warwickshire North
611 Wellingborough
647 Wyre Forest

24 Small towns and rural hinterlands

  16 Ashford
  90 Bridgwater
  92 Brigg and Cleethorpes
 104 Burton
 163 Crewe and Nantwich
 178 Delyn
 184 Derbyshire West
 195 Dover
 241 Falmouth and Camborne
 243 Faversham
 271 Gloucestershire West
 278 Great Yarmouth
 307 Hereford
 315 High Peak
 352 Lancaster
 415 Newark
 493 Rutland and Melton
 504 Selby
 512 Sherwood
 551 Stroud
 554 Suffolk South
 609 Waveney
 617 Westbury
 648 Yeovil
 649 Ynys Mon

25 'Southern' urban constituencies

  35 Bedfordshire mid
  48 Billericay
  62 Blaby
  82 Braintree
 100 Broxbourne
 102 Buckingham
 126 Castle Point
 129 Chelmsford
 149 Colchester North
 150 Colchester South and Maldon
 175 Dartford
 176 Daventry
 216 Eastleigh
 229 Elmet
 242 Fareham

257 Gillingham
308 Hertford and Stortford
341 Kent mid
389 Maidstone
436 Northavon
462 Plymouth Sutton
482 Rochford
484 Romsey and Waterside
534 Staffordshire South
575 Tonbridge and Malling
645 Wycombe

26 Areas of modest affluence with some industry

   5 Aldridge Brownhills
  72 Bolton West
  89 Bridgend
  99 Bromsgrove
 101 Broxtowe
 161 Coventry South West
 220 Eddisbury
 256 Gedling
 274 Gower
 284 Halesowen and Stourbridge
 292 Harborough
 302 Hazel Grove
 309 Hertfordshire North
 388 Macclesfield
 408 Monmouth
 469 Pudsey
 478 Ribble Valley
 490 Rugby and Kenilworth
 513 Shipley
 531 Stafford
 567 Tatton
 599 Wansdyke
 606 Warwick and Leamington
 613 Welwyn Hatfield
 627 Wirral South
 637 Worcester

27 'Metropolitan' industrial areas

  36 Bedfordshire North
 106 Bury South
 162 Crawley
 165 Croydon Central
 177 Davyhulme
 207 Durham City of
 211 Ealing North

227 Edmonton
231 Enfield North
236 Erith and Crayford
244 Feltham and Heston
270 Gloucester
276 Gravesham
293 Harlow
300 Havant
301 Hayes and Harlington
311 Hertfordshire West
319 Hornchurch
331 Ilford South
404 Mitcham and Morden
426 Newport West
435 Northampton South
466 Portsmouth North
473 Reading West
483 Romford
538 Stevenage
589 Uxbridge
608 Watford
634 Wolverhampton South West

28 Modestly affluent urban Scotland

 19 Ayr
218 Eastwood
224 Edinburgh Pentlands
476 Renfrew West and Inverclyde
539 Stirling
548 Strathkelvin and Bearsden

29 Areas of rapid growth

  4 Aldershot
 18 Aylesbury
 20 Banbury
 42 Berkshire East
107 Bury St. Edmunds
115 Cambridgeshire South West
185 Devizes
273 Gosport
289 Hampshire East
290 Hampshire North West
328 Huntingdon
416 Newbury
590 Vale of Glamorgan
601 Wantage
623 Wiltshire North
629 Witney

30 Prosperous towns with little
industry

 30 Bath
117 Canterbury
131 Cheltenham
136 Chichester
153 Conwy
193 Dorset South
252 Fylde
281 Guildford
294 Harrogate
313 Hexham
321 Horsham
501 Salisbury
515 Shrewsbury and Atcham
568 Taunton
581 Tunbridge Wells
610 Wealden
621 Weston Super Mare
625 Winchester

31 Agricultural areas

 43 Berwick upon Tweed
 73 Boothferry
 83 Brecon and Radnor
 91 Bridlington
108 Caernarfon
113 Cambridgeshire North East
114 Cambridgeshire South East
123 Carmarthen
127 Ceredigion and Pembroke North
142 Cirencester and Tewkesbury
146 Clwyd South West
156 Cornwall North
157 Cornwall South East
186 Devon North
187 Devon West and Torridge
192 Dorset North
194 Dorset West
253 Gainsborough and Horncastle
275 Grantham
317 Holland with Boston
365 Leominster
372 Lindsey East
385 Ludlow
398 Meirionnydd nant Conwy
409 Montgomery
428 Norfolk mid
429 Norfolk North

430 Norfolk North West
431 Norfolk South
432 Norfolk South West
455 Pembroke
457 Penrith and the Border
480 Richmond (Yorks)
494 Ryedale
495 Saffron Walden
499 St. Ives
516 Shropshire North
517 Skipton and Ripon

520 Somerton and Frome
537 Stamford and Spalding
547 Stratford on Avon
552 Suffolk Central
553 Suffolk Coastal
574 Tiverton
580 Truro
612 Wells
620 Westmorland and Lonsdale
639 Worcestershire South

___ REFERENCES ___

Abrams, M., Rose, R. and Hinden, R. (1960) *Must Labour Lose?* Penguin, London.

Agnew, J.A. (1984) Place and political behaviour: the geography of Scottish nationalism. *Political Geography Quarterly,* 3, 191–206.

Alford, R.R. (1963) *Party and Society.* Rand McNally, Chicago.

Anderson, J. (1983) Geography as ideology and the politics of crisis: the Enterprise Zones experiment. In J. Anderson, S. Duncan and R. Hudson (editors) *Redundant Spaces in Cities and Regions?* Academic Press, London, 313–350.

Anon (1987) The Alliance: maybe, but what sort? *The Economist.* 304(7513), 20–21.

Archer, J.C. and Taylor, P.J. (1981) *Section and Party.* John Wiley, Chichester.

BBC/ITN (1983) *The BBC/ITN Guide to the New Parliamentary Constituencies.* Parliamentary Research Services, Chichester.

Begg, I. and Moore, B. (1987) The changing economic role of Britain's cities. In V.A. Hausner (editor) *Critical Issues in Urban Economic Development II.* Clarendon Press, Oxford, 44–76.

Bennett, R.J. (1982) *Central Grants to Local Governments.* Cambridge University Press, Cambridge.

Berrington, H. (1983) Decade of dealignment. *Political Studies,* 32, 117–120.

Boddy, M.J. and Fudge, C. editors (1984) *Local Socialism.* Macmillan, London.

Bodman, A.R. (1985) Regional trends in electoral support in Britain, 1950–1983. *The Professional Geographer,* 37, 288–295.

Bogdanor, V. (1983) *Multi-Party Politics and the Constitution.* Cambridge University Press, Cambridge.

Bogdanor, V. (1986) Letter to the editor. *Environment and Planning A,* 18, 1537.

Bogdanor, V. and Butler, D. editors (1983) *Democracy and Elections: Electoral Systems and their Political Consequences.* Cambridge University Press, Cambridge.

Boundary Commission for England 91983) *Third Periodical Report.* Cmnd 8797, HMSO, London.

Boundary Commission for England (1983) *Third Periodical Report.* Cmnd 8797, HMSO, London.

Boundary Commission for Scotland (1983) *Third Periodical Report.* Cmnd. 8794, HMSO, London.

Bristow, H.R. (1984) *A Response to the Government's White Paper 'Streamlining the Cities',* Regional Studies Association, London.

Bristow, S.L. (1976) Partisanship, participation and legitimacy in Britain's EEC referendum. *Journal of Common Market Studies,* 14, 297–310.

Bristow, S.L. (1982) Rates and votes, *Policy and Politics,* 10, 163–180.

Brown, P.J. and Payne, C. (1986) Aggregate data, ecological regression, and voting transitions. *Journal of the American Statistical Association,* 81, 452–460.

Butler, D. (1983) *Governing without a Majority: Dilemmas for Hung Parliaments in Britain.* Collins, London.

Butler, D. and Kavanagh, D. (1984) *The British General Election of 1983.* Macmillan, London.

Butler, D. and Stokes, D. (1969) *Political Change in Britain: The Evolution of Electoral Choice* (first edition). Penguin Books, London.

Butler, D. and Stokes, D. (1974) *Political Change in Britain: The Evolution of Electoral Choice* (second edition). Macmillan, London.

Byrne, D. (1982) Class and the local state: *International Journal of Urban and Regional Research,* 6, 61–82.

Clarke, H.D., Stewart, M.C. and Zuk, G. (1986) Politics, economics and party popularity in Britain, 1979–83. *Electoral Studies,* 5, 123–141.

Cooke, P.N. (1984) Recent theories of political regionalism: a critique and alternative. *International Journal of Urban and Regional Research,* 8, 549–572.

Cooke, P.N. (1987) Britain's new spatial paradigm: technology, locality and society in transition. *Environment and Planning A,* 19, 1289–1301.

Coopers and Lybrand Associates (1983) *Streamlining the Cities: An Analysis of the Government's Case for Reorganising Local Government in the Six Metropolitan Counties. First Report.* Coopers and Lybrand, London.

Coopers and Lybrand Associates (1984) *Streamlining the Cities: An Analysis of the Government's Case for Reorganising Local Government in the Six Metropolitan Counties. Second Report.* Coopers and Lybrand, London.

Cox, K.R. (1969) The voting decision in a spatial context. In C. Board et al. (editors) *Progress in Geography Volume 1.* Edward Arnold, London, 81–117.

Cozens, P. and Swaddle, A. (1987) The British general election of 1987. *Electoral Studies,* 6, 263–266.

Crewe, I. (1973) The politics of "affluent" and "traditional" workers in Britain: an aggregate analysis. *British Journal of Political Science,* 3, 29–52.

Crewe, I. (1982) The Labour party and the electorate. In D. Kavanagh (editor) *The Politics of the Labour Party.* Allen and Unwin, London, 9–49.

Crewe, I. (1985a) How to win a landslide without really trying: why the Conservatives won in 1983. In A. Ranney (editor) *Britain at the Polls 1983.* Duke University Press, New York, 155–196.

Crewe, I. (1985b) Great Britain. In I. Crewe and D. Denver (editors) *Electoral Change in Western Democracies.* Croom Helm, London, 100–149.

Crewe, I. (1986a) On the death and resurrection of class voting: some comments on *How Britain Votes. Political Studies,* 34, 620–638.

Crewe, I. (1986b) Saturation polling, the media and the 1983 election. In I. Crewe and M. Harrop (editors) *Political Communications and the General Election Campaign of 1983.* The University Press, Cambridge, 233–253.

Crewe, I. and Fox, A. (1984) *British Parliamentary Constituencies: A Statistical Compendium.* Faber and Faber, London.

Crewe, I. and Payne, C. (1976) Another game with nature: an ecological regression model of the British two-party vote ratio in 1970. *British Journal of Political Science,* 6, 43–81.

Crewe, I., Sarlvik, B. and Alt, J. (1977) Partisan dealignment in Britain, 1964–1974. *British Journal of Political Science,* 7, 129–190.

Crick, B. (1987) The fundamental condition of Labour. *The Political Quarterly,* 58, 433–440.

Curtice, J. (1986) Political partisanship. In R. Jowell, S. Witherspoon and L. Brock (editors) *British Social Attitudes: The 1986 Report.* Gower, Aldershot, 38–53.

Curtice, J. and Steed, M. 91982) Electoral choice and the production of government. *British Journal of Political Science,* 12, 249–298.

Curtice, J. and Steed, M. (1982) Electoral choice and the production of government. *British Journal of Political Science,* 12, 249–298.

Curtice, J. and Steed, M. (1986) Proportionality and exaggeration in the British electoral system. *Electoral Studies,* 5, 209–228.

Dalton, R.J., Flanagan, S.C. and Beck, P.A. (1984) Introduction. In R.J. Dalton, S.C. Flanagan and P.A. Beck (editors) *Electoral Change in Advanced Industrial Democracies.* Princeton University Press, Princeton.

Damesick, P.J. (1987) Regional economic change since the 1960s. In P.J. Damesick and P.A. Wood (editors) *Regional Problems, Problem Regions, and Public Policy in the United Kingdom.* Clarendon Press, Oxford, 19–41.

Dearlove, J. (1979) *The Reorganisation of British Local Government.* Cambridge University Press, Cambridge.

Denver, D.T. (1987) The British general election of 1987: some preliminary reflections. *Parliamentary Affairs,* 40, 451–457.

Duncan, S.S. and Goodwin, M. (1982) The local state and restructuring social relations: theory and practice, *International Journal of Urban and Regional Research,* 6, 157–186.

Duncan, S.S. and Goodwin, M. (1985) *The Local Government Crisis in Britain, 1979–1984. Part 3: The Final Solution, 1984?* Geography Discussion Paper, New Series no. 15, London School of Economics and Political Science, Houghton Street, London WC2A 2AE.

Dunleavy, P. (1979) The urban basis of political alignment: social class, domestic property ownership and state intervention in consumption processes. *British Journal of Political Science,* 9, 409–443.

Dunleavy, P. (1980a) The political implications of sectoral cleavages and the growth of state employment: Part I , the analysis of production cleavages. *Political Studies,* 28, 364–383.

Dunleavy, P. (1980b) The policital implications of sectoral cleavages and the growth of state employment: Part 2, cleavage structures and political alignment. *Political Studies,* 28, 527–549.

Dunleavy, P. (1987) Class dealignment in Britain revisited. *West European Politics,* 10, 400–419.

Dunleavy, P. and Husbands, C.T. (1985) *British Democracy at the Crossroads. Voting and Party Competition in the 1980s.* George Allen and Unwin, London.

Dunn, R., Forrest, R. and Murie, A. (1987) The geography of council house sales in England - 1979-85. *Urban Studies,* 24, 47–59.

Finer, S.E. editor (1975) *Adversary Politics and Electoral Reform.* Anthony Wigram, London.

Franklin, M.N. (1985) *The Decline of Class Voting in Britain: Changes in the Basis of Electoral Choice 1964–1983.* Clarendon Press, Oxford.

Garrahan, P. (1977) Housing, the class milieu and middle-class conservatism. *British Journal of Political Science,* 7, 125–126.

Gillespie, A.E. and Green, A.E. (1987) The changing geography of producer services employment in Britain. *Regional Studies,* 21, 397–412.

Gudgin, G. and Taylor, P.J. (1979) *Seats, Votes and the Spatial Organisation of Elections.* Pion, London.

Gurr, T.R. and King, D.S. (1987) *The State and the City.* Macmillan, London.

Gyford, J. (1986) *The Politics of Local Socialism.* George Allen and Unwin, London.

Hall, P. (1987) The anatomy of job creation: nations, regions and cities in the 1960s and 1970s. *Regional Studies,* 21, 95–106.

Hamnett, C. (1983) Regional variations in house prices and house price inflation 1979–81. *Area,* 15, 97–109.

Harrison, P. (1983) *Inside the Inner City.* Penguin, London.

Harrop, M. and Miller, W.L. (1987) *Elections and Voters: A Comparative Introduction.* Macmillan, London.

Harvey, D. (1978) The urban process under capitalism. *International Journal of Urban and Regional Research,* 2, 101–132.

Harvey, D. (1985) *The Urbanization of Consciousness.* Basil Blackwell, Oxford.

Heath, A. (1986) Do people have consistent attitudes? In R. Jowell, S. Witherspoon and L. Brook (editors) *British Social Attitudes: The 1986 Report.* Gower, Aldershot, 1–15.

Heath, A., Jowell, R. and Curtice, J. (1985) *How Britain Votes.* Pergamon Press, Oxford.

Heath, A., Jowell, R. and Curtice, J. (1987a) Trendless fluctuation: a reply to Crewe. *Political Studies,* 35, 256–277.

Heath, A., Jowell, R. and Curtice, J. (1987b) Attitudes, values and identities in the British electorate. Paper presented to the Annual Meeting of the American Political Science Association, Chicago, mimeo.

Heath, A. and McDonald, S.-K. (1987) Social change and the future of the left. *The Political Quarterly,* 58, 364–377.

Hechter, M. (1975) *Internal Colonialism.* Routledge and Kegan Paul, London.

Himmelweit, H.T. et al. (1985) *How Voters Decide* (second edition). Open University Press, Milton Keynes.

Hoare, A.G. (1985) Dividing the pork barrel: Britain's enterprise zone experiment. *Political Geography Quarterly,* 4, 29–46.

Home Affairs Committee (1987) *Redistribution of Seats.* H.M.S.O., London.

Husbands, C.T. (1985) Attitudes to local government in London: evidence from opinion surveys and the GLC by-elections of 20th September 1984. *The London Journal,* 11, 59–74.

James, C. (1986) *The Quiet Revolution.* Port Nicholson Press, Wellington.

Johnston, R.J. (1978) *Multivariate Statistical Analysis in Geography.* Longman, London.

Johnston, R.J. (1979) *Political, Electoral and Spatial Systems.* Oxford University Press, Oxford.

Johnston, R.J. (1981) Embourgeoisement and voting in England, 1974. *Area,* 13, 345–351.

Johnston, R.J. (1982) Embourgeoisement, the property-owning democracy and ecological models of voting in England. *Britain Journal of Political Science,* 12, 499–503.

Johnston, R.J. (1983a) Spatial continuity and individual variability. *Electoral Studies,* 2, 53–68.

Johnston, R.J. (1983b) The neighbourhood effect won't go away. *Geoforum,* 14, 161–168.

Johnston, R.J. (1983c) A reapportionment revolution that failed. *Political Geography Quarterly,* 2, 309–318.

Johnston, R.J. (1984) The political geography of electoral geography. In P.J. Taylor and J.W. House (editors) *Political Geography: Recent Trends and Future Directions.* Croom Helm, London, 133–148.

Johnston, R.J. (1985a) *The Geography of English Politics: The 1983 General Election.* Croom Helm, London.

Johnston, R.J. (1985b) People, places and parliaments: a geographical perspective on electoral reform in Great Britain. *The Geographical Journal,* 151, 327–338.

Johnston, R.J. (1986a) Places and votes: the role of location in the creation of political attitudes. *Urban Geography,* 7, 103–116.

Johnston, R.J. (1986b) Putting context into context. *Environment and Planning A,* 18, 1537–1539.

Johnston, R.J. (1986c) The neighbourhood effect revisited: spatial science or political regionalism. *Environment and Planning D: Society and Space,* 4, 41–55.

Johnston, R.J. (1986d) A space for place (or a place for space) in British psephology. *Environment and Planning A,* 19, 599–618.

Johnston, R.J. (1986e) Placing politics. *Political Geography Quarterly,* 5, S63-S78.

Johnston, R.J. (1986f) Constituency redistribution in Britain: recent issues. In B. Grofman and A. Lijphart (editors) *Electoral Laws and their Political Consequences.* Agathon Press, New York, 277–286.

Johnston, R.J. (1987a) *Money and Votes: Constituency Campaign Spending and Election Results.* Croom Helm, London.

Johnston, R.J. (1987b) A note on housing tenure and voting in Britain, 1983. *Housing Studies,* 2, 112–121.

Johnston, R.J. (1987c) The rural milieu and voting in Britain. *Journal of Rural Studies,* 3, 95–103.

Johnston, R.J. (1987d) The geography of the working class and the geography of the Labour vote in England 1983: a prefatory note to a research agenda. *Political Geography Quarterly,* 6, 7–16.

Johnston, R.J. (1987e) What price place? *Political Geography Quarterly,* 6, 51–52.

Johnston, R.J. and Doornkamp, J.C. (1982) Introduction. In R.J. Johnston and J.C. Doornkamp (editors) *The Changing Geography of the United Kingdom.* Methuen, London, 1–12.

Johnston, R.J. and Hay, A.M. (1982) On the parameters of uniform swing in single-member constituency electoral systems. *Environment and Planning A,* 14, 61–74.

Johnston, R.J., Hay, A.M. and Rumley, D. (1983) Entropy-maximizing methods for estimating voting data: a critical test. *Area,* 15, 35–41.

Johnston, R.J., Hay, A.M. and Rumley, D. (1984) On testing for structural effects in electoral geography, using entropy-maximizing methods. *Environment and Planning A,* 16, 233–240.

Johnston, R.J. and Honey, R. (1988) The 1987 general election in New Zealand and the demise of electoral cleavages. *Political Geography Quarterly,* 7,

Johnston, R.J., O'Neill, A.B. and Taylor, P.J. (1987) The geography of party support: comparative studies in electoral stability. In M.J. Holler (editor) *The Logic of Multi-Party Systems,* Nijhoff, Dordrecht, 265–282.

Johnston, R.J. and Pattie, C.J. (1987) Family background, ascribed characteristics, political attitudes and regional variations in voting within England, 1983. *Political Geography Quarterly,* 6, 347–350.

Johnston, R.J. and Pattie, C.J. (1988a) Attitudes and votes at the 1983 general election: explorations of the geography of 'defections'. *Area*, 20,

Johnston, R.J. and Pattie, C.J. (1988b) People, attitudes, milieux and votes. *Transactions, Institute of British Geographers.* NS13,

Johnston, R.J. and Pattie, C.J. (1988c) Are we all Alliance nowadays? Discrimating by discriminant analysis. *Electoral Studies,* 6,

Johnston, R.J. and Rossiter, D.J. (1982) Constituency building, political representation and electoral bias in urban England. In D.T. Herbert and R.J. Johnston (editors) *Geography and the Urban Environment, Volume 5.* John Wiley, Chichester, 113-156.

Johnston, R.J. and Taylor, P.J. (1987) The baby's gone: on regional polarization in British elections. *The Professional Geographer,* 39, 62-64.

Kavanagh, D. (1986) How we vote now. *Electoral Studies,* 5, 19-28.

Keeble, D.E. (1987) Industrial change in the United Kingdom. In W.F. Lever (editor) *Industrial Change in the United Kingdom,* Longman, London, 1-20.

Kellas, J.G. and Madgwick, P. (1982) Territorial ministries: the Scottish and Welsh Offices. In P. Madgwick and R. Rose (editors) *The Territorial Dimension in United Kingdom Politics.* Macmillan, London, 9-23.

King, R. (1979) The middle class revolt and the established parties. In R. King, and N. Nugent (editors) *Respectable Rebels: Middle Class Campaigns in Britain in the 1970s.* Hodder and Stoughton, London.

Kinnear, M. (1981) *The British Voter: An Atlas and Survey since 1885.* Batsford, London.

Lipset, S.M. and Rokkan, S.E. (1967) Cleavage structures, party systems and voter alignments. In S.M. Lipset and S.E. Rokkan (editors) *Party Systems and Voter Alignments.* The Free Press, New York, 3-64.

Lipset, S.M., Trow, M.A. and Coleman, J.S. (1956) *Union Democracy.* The Free Press, Glencoe, Il.

McAllister, I. (1987a) Social context, turnout and the vote: Australian and British comparisons. *Political Geography Quarterly,* 6, 17-30.

McAllister, I. (1987b) Comment on Johnston and Pattie. *Political Geography Quarterly,* 6, 351-354.

McAllister, I. and Rose, R. (1984) *The Nationwide Competition for Votes.* Frances Pinter, London.

Madgwick, P. and Rose, R. editors (1982) *The Territorial Dimension in United Kingdom Politics.* Macmillan, London.

Massey, D. (1984a) *Spatial Divisions of Labour.* Macmillan, London.

Massey, D. (1984b) Introduction: geography matters. In D. Massey and J.Allen (editors) *Geography Matters!* Cambridge University Press, Cambridge, 1-11.

Midwinter, A., Keating, M. and Taylor, P. (1983) 'Excessive and unreasonable': the politics of the Scottish hit list. *Political Studies,* 31, 394-417.

Miller, W.L. (1977) *Electoral Dynamics.* Macmillan, London.

Miller, W.L. (1978) Social class and party choice in England: a new analysis. *British Journal of Political Science,* 8, 257-284.

Miller, W.L. (1981) *The End of British Politics?* Oxford University Press, Oxford.

Miller, W.L. (1984) There was no alternative: the British general election of 1983. *Parliamentary Affairs,* 37, 364-384.

Mitchell, A. (1987) Beyond socialism. *The Political Quarterly,* 58, 389-403.

Moore, B., Rhodes, J., and Tyler, P. (1986) *The Effects of Government Regional Economic Policy.* Department of Trade and Industry, London.

Mughan, A. (1986) *Party and Participation in British Elections.* Frances Pinter, London.

Munro, C. (1986) Legal controls on election broadcasting. In I. Crewe and M. Harrop (editors) *Political Communications and the General Election Campaign of 1983.* The University Press, Cambridge, 294–305.

O'Leary, B. (1987) Why was the GLC abolished? *International Journal of Urban and Regional Research,* 11, 192–217.

Pelling, H. (1969) *Social Geography of British Elections, 1885–1910.* Macmillan, London.

Phillips, A.W. (1958) The relation between unemployment and rate of change of money wage rate in the UK, 1861–1957. *Economica,* 25, 283–299.

Pickvance, C.G. (1986) The basis of local government in Great Britain: an interpretation. In M. Gottdiener, (editor) *Cities in Stress: A New Look at the Urban Crisis. Urban Affairs Annual Review, Vol. 30.* Sage, Beverly Hills, 247–276.

Pimlott, B. (1987a) Is there an alternative to a pact? *The Political Quarterly,* 58, 441–447.

Pimlott, B. (1987b) The importance of Bill Rodgers' departure from the SDP. *New Statesman,* 20 November, 5.

Przeworski, A. and Sprague, J. (1986) *Paper Stones: A History of Electoral Socialism.* University of Chicago Press, Chicago.

Pugh, M. (1985) *The Tories and the People 1880–1935.* Basil Blackwell, Oxford.

Pulzer, P. (1987) The paralysis of the centre-left: a comparative perspective. *The Political Quarterly,* 58, 378–388.

Rasmussen, J. (1973) The impact of constituency structural characteristics on political preferences in Britain. *Comparative Politics,* 5, 123–145.

Robertson, D. (1984) *Class and the British Electorate.* Basil Blackwell, Oxford.

Rodgers, W. (1987) Realignment postponed? *The Political Quarterly,* 58, 404–413.

Rose, R. (1974) Britain: simple abstractions and complex realities. In R. Rose (editor) *Electoral Behavior.* The Free Press, New York, 481–541.

Rose, R. (1982) From simple determinism to interactive models of voting. *Comparative Political Studies,* 15, 145–169.

Rose, R. and McAllister, I. (1986) *Voters Begin to Choose: From Closed Class to Open Elections in Britain.* Sage Publications, London.

Sanders, D., Ward, H. and Marsh, D. (1987) Government popularity and the Falklands War: a reassessment. *British Journal of Political Science,* 17, 281–313.

Sarlvik, B. and Crewe, I. (1983) *Decade of Dealignment.* Cambridge University Press, Cambridge.

Saunders, P. (1984) Rethinking local politics. In M.Boddy and C. Fudge (editors) *Local Socialism?* Macmillan, London, 24–48.

Savage, M. (1987) Understanding political alignments in contemporary Britain: do localities matter? *Political Geography Quarterly,* 6, 53–76.

Scarbrough, E. (1984) *Political Ideology and Voting: An Exploratory Study.* The Clarendon Press, Oxford.

Schattschneider, E.E. (1960) *The Semisovereign People: A Realist's View of Democracy in the United States.* Holt, Rinehart and Winston, New York.

Secretary of State for the Environment (1983) *Streamlining the Cities.* Cmnd 9063, HMSO, London.

SEEDS (1987) *The South-South Divide:* South East Economic Development Strategy, Stevenage.

Sharpe, L.J. (1982) The Labour Party and the geography of inequality: a puzzle. In D. Kavanagh (editor) *The Politics of the Labour Party*. George Allen and Unwin, London, 135–170.

Steed, M. (1986) The core-periphery dimension of British politics. *Political Geography Quarterly*, 5, S91-S103.

Steed, M.(1987) How to nobble the Thatcher vote. *New Statesman*, 27 November, 16.

Taylor, P.J. (1978) Political geography. *Progress in Human Geography*, 2, 153–162.

Taylor, P.J. (1979) The changing geography of representation in Britain. *Area*, 11, 289–294

Taylor, P.J. (1984a) Accumulation, legitimation and the electoral geographies within liberal democracy. In P.J. Taylor and J.W. House (editors) *Political Geography: Recent Advances and Future Directions*. Croom Helm, London, 117–132.

Taylor, P.J. (1984b) The case for proportional tenure: a defence of the British electoral system. In A. Lijphart and B. Grofman (editors) *Choosing an Electoral System*. Praeger, New York.

Taylor, P.J. (1985a) The geography of elections. In M. Pacione (editor) *Progress in Political Geography*. Croom Helm, London, 243–272.

Taylor, P.J. (1985b) *Political Geography: World-Economy, Nation-State and Locality*. Longman, London.

Taylor, P.J. and Johnston, R.J. (1979) *Geography of Elections*. Penguin, London.

Taylor, P.J. and Johnston, R.J. (1984) The geography of the British state. In J.R. Short and A.M. Kirby (editors) *The Human Geography of Contemporary Britain*. Macmillan, London, 23–39.

Thrift, N.J. (1983) On the determination of social action in space and time. *Environment and Planning D: Society and Space*, 1, 23–57.

Thrift, N.J., Leyshon, A. and Daniels, P.W. (1987) The new international financial system: the City of London and the South East of England. Mimeo, Department of Geography, University of Bristol, Bristol.

Todd, J.E. and Dodd, P.A. (1982) *The Electoral Registration Process in the United Kingdom*. OPCS, London.

Townsend, A.R. (1987) Regional policy. In W.F. Lever (editor) *Industrial Change in the United Kingdom*. Longman, London, 223–239.

Waller, R. (1985) *The Atlas of British Politics*. Croom Helm, London.

Waller, R.J. (1987) *The Almanac of British Politics* (third edition). Croom Helm, London.

Warde, A. (1986) Space, class and voting in Britain. In K. Hoggart and E. Kofman (editors) *Politics, Geography and Social Stratification*. Croom Helm, London, 33–61.

Warde, A., Savage, M., Langhurst, B. and Martin, A. (1987) *Class, Consumption and Voting: an Ecological Analysis of Wards and Towns in the 1980 Local Elections*. Lancaster Regionalism Group, Working Paper 23, University of Lancaster.

Webb, P. (1987) Union, party and class in Britain: the changing electoral relationship, 1964–1983. *Politics* 7 (2), 15–21.

Whiteley, P. (1982) The decline of Labour's local party membership and electoral base, 1945–1979. In D. Kavanagh (editor) *The Politics of the Labour Party*. Allen and Unwin, London, 111–134.

Whiteley, P. (1983) *The Labour Party in Crisis*. Methuen, London.

Whiteley, P. (1984) Perceptions of economic performance and voting behavior in the 1983 general election in Britain. *Political Behavior*, 6, 395–410.

Whiteley, P. (1986a) Predicting the Labour vote in 1983: social backgrounds versus objective evaluations. *Political Studies,* 34, 82–98.

Whiteley, P. (1986b) The accuracy and influence of the polls in the 1983 general election. In I. Crewe and M. Harrop (editors) *Political Communications and the General Election Campaign of 1983.* Cambridge University Press, Cambridge, 312–324.

Williams, N.J., Sewel, J.B. and Twine, F.E. (1987) Council house sales and the electorate: voting behaviour and ideological implications. *Housing Studies,* 2, 274–282.

Winn, S. and McAuley, A. (1987) Conflicts in civil defence. *War and Peace. Contemporary Issues in Geography and Education* 2(3), 51–59.

Young, K. and Mason, C. (editors) (1983) *Urban Economic Development.* Macmillan, London.

—— GENERAL INDEX ——

As the book is about general elections in Britain, the political parties are mentioned on just about every page: they are, therefore, excluded from this index.

___ INDEX OF PLACES MENTIONED ___

INDEX OF AUTHORS CITED